MAY 08 — aug. 08 = 1

W9-BUT-884

ARCHITECTURE
A WORLD HISTORY

ARCHITECTURE
A WORLD HISTORY

Daniel Borden, Jerzy Elżanowski,
Cornelia Lawrenz, Daniel Miller, Adele Smith,
and Joni Taylor

Abrams, New York

4

Contents

a Baptistery, Cathedral, and Campanile, page 101

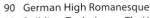

116 Gothic

158 Renaissance

Chartres Cathedral, page 127

Fillippo Brunelleschi: Florence Cathedral, page 170

6

Versailles, page 243

Architecture: A World History

Karl Friedrich Schinkel: Konzerthaus on Gendarmenmarkt, page 309

Charles Garnier: Paris Opéra (Palais Garnier), page 365

8

Daniel Burnham: Flatiron Building (Fuller Building), page 381

Le Corbusier: Notre Dame du Haut, page 415

Sir Norman Foster: Reichstag Dome, page 467

Contents

Pre- and Early History

10,000 BCE–300 CE

Nergal Gate at Nineveh, Assyrian, ca. 700 BCE, Iraq

Pre- and Early

Europe

10,000 BCE
Neolithic period; mud bricks are first used

4800 BCE
Megalithic structures in Brittany

2500 BCE
Bronze Age; Stonehenge

2000 BCE
The Minoans construct large royal palace complexes on Crete

10 000   5000   4000   3000

Middle East

3200 BCE
Sumerians rule Mesopotamia; construction of a proto-ziggurat, the White Temple in Uruk

2100 BCE
Construction of the Ziggurat at Ur

Egypt

3000 BCE
Early Dynastic period; Egyptian state forms; first use of stone as a building material; first pyramid, the Step Pyramid of Djoser, is built

p. 23

History

1600 BCE
The Mycenaeans rule the Mediterranean; royal burial mounds at Mycenae

1200 BCE
Mycenae falls to invaders; start of a 400-year Greek dark age, during which building halts and Greek innovations stall

p. 35

2000	1000	500	300

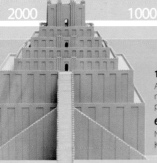

1200 BCE
Assyrian period; King Sennacherib constructs palaces at Nineveh

612 BCE
Neo-Babylonian period; King Nebuchadnezzar II

builds the Ishtar Gate and the Hanging Gardens of Babylon

560 BCE
Persian Achaemenid dynasty; royal palaces and tombs at Persepolis

2575 BCE
Old Kingdom; the Great Pyramids of Giza

2125 BCE
First Intermediate period; Egypt splits in two, with capitals in Memphis and Thebes

1550 BCE
New Kingdom; construction of large temple complexes near Thebes and royal tombs in the Valley of the Dead; reigns of Pharaohs Hatshepsut and Ramses II

332 BCE
Greco-Roman period; Ptolomaic pharaohs build temples in an early Egyptian style; cross-influences with Roman architecture mean that innovations and styles are shared between the two

Pre- and Early History

The study of ancient architecture is more than a history of old ruins. Ancient buildings are fossils that map the progress of cultures. Farming was the key factor that transformed nomadic hunter-gatherers into Neolithic settled peoples. This revolution began in about 6000 BCE in the Middle East and, by 2000 BCE, had spread to Africa, Europe, and Asia. The Mesoamericans began farming around 1500 BCE. Permanent structures were constructed and basic building techniques developed. New specialized professions emerged, such as priests and craftsmen. Metal tools developed and building materials such as timber, mud brick, and stone were soon mastered. Over centuries, new social institutions were invented and took physical form as buildings.

■ **Round House**, reconstruction, Sumerian, ca. 2900–2460 BCE

■ **Bronze Age Round House**, reconstruction, ca. 1800–1500 BCE, Egyptian Museum, Cairo

Poulnabrone Dolmen Tomb, 3200–2900 BCE, County Clare, Ireland

Tomb of the Persian King Cyrus, ca. 530 BCE, Pasargadai, Iran

Houses and Tombs

Russian archaeologists have unearthed a 14,000-year-old dwelling constructed of animal skins stretched over a frame of mammoth bones. The cone-shaped house had a hole at the top to let out smoke. Later Neolithic houses filled the same basic needs for hearth and home. While the function and layout of houses were similar across cultures, building materials varied. In Mesopotamia and Egypt, mud brick was used. Europeans built wooden longhouses with thatched roofs. Later, dwellings grew in size to shelter both people and farm animals.

Early humans buried their dead close to their homes, and abandoned houses were sometimes used as tombs. Heavy stones were placed over the bodies to protect them. Later, whole tomb structures were built using massive stone slabs called megaliths. As beliefs in an afterlife developed, royal tombs like the Egyptian pyramids grew to monumental proportions.

Towns and Fortresses

Advances in farming led to cooperation between clans and the construction of the first real towns. Çatalhöyük was an early village built in Anatolia, Turkey, between 6500 and 5700 BCE. The boxy mud-brick houses were built side by side, without streets, like pueblos. Residents gained access to their dwellings through the roofs.

As communities grew, they competed with one another for resources, and warfare made the fortification of cities a necessity. The first settlement at Jericho in Israel, from about 8000 BCE, was a large collection of round huts surrounded by a stone wall, in some places 26 feet (8 meters) thick. The Mediterranean Mycenaean Empire developed through warfare, and its capital, Mycenae, was on a defendable hilltop. The gates of Mycenae and Babylon later became ceremonial monuments decorated with reliefs.

■ **Reconstruction of Mycenae**, ca. 2000 BCE, Greece
■ **Relief from the Palace of Assurnasirpal II**, ca. 850 BCE, Nimrud, Iraq

■ Relief from the Tripylon Hall, a. 450 BCF, Persepolis, Iran

■ Pieter Bruegel he Elder: The Tower of Babel, 563

Palaces and Temples

A ruling class of kings and priests were granted the power to lead communities and make laws; soon, palaces and temples were built. For the first time, buildings were used for public spectacle. The earliest known monarch, Egypt's king Narmer, took power around 3100 BCF. Palaces were a display of communal power and pride. They were built in prominent locations and decorated with precious materials and art. The Persian capital Persepolis was a collection of grand halls designed as theatrical settings for the ceremonies of imperial power.

Early religions looked to the heavens to explain the mysteries of life. Stonehenge was used to predict the movement of the stars, and a temple dedicated to a mother goddess was built at Hagar Qim in Turkey around 3000 BCE. The ziggurats of Mesopotamia were stepped pyramids designed to lift mortals closer to the heavens.

Prehistoric Architecture

10,000–1500 BCE

■ Single family houses, barns, and communal dwellings were built ■ Early buildings were made from natural materials such as timber, clay, and mud bricks ■ Massive stone slabs were used to mark graves and important sites
■ *left:* **The Menhirs of Carnac**, ca. 3300 BCE, Carnac, Brittany

10,000 BCE Neolithic culture appears on the east coast of the Mediterranean; grains are cultivated and mud bricks are used

8000 BCE Neolithic culture spreads to Syria and Iraq

7000–5500 BCE Communities appear in southern and central Europe

3500 BCE Neolithic cultures in the Tigris and Euphrates river valleys develop into Bronze Age urban civilizations, and the Sumerian civilization emerges as a prominent culture

1800–1500 BCE Bronze Age technologies arrive in Europe, improving construction techniques

Other Works

Çatalhöyük, ca. 7500 BCE, Anatolia, Turkey

Mehrgarh, ca. 7000–3200 BCE, Buluchistan, Pakistan

Skara Brae, ca. 3100–2500 BCE, Orkney, UK

Around 10,000 BCE, people began farming and creating the first architecture in their settled communities. In Turkey and the Middle East, early buildings and towns were constructed from mud bricks, while Neolithic Europeans used timber framing and made walls of woven sticks covered with clay. The first buildings were primarily for the practical uses of shelter and storing food. However, early humans also created monuments, including graves and other ceremonial structures. Stone circles and menhirs, or upright rows of megalith stones, were erected. Several of these architectural feats, such as the menhirs of Carnac, still stand. The tallest stone at Carnac stands 60 feet (18 meters) high. Though the purpose of these monuments is uncertain, they show humankind's early desire to manipulate nature on a large scale and to leave behind lasting markers of their existence.

■ **Stonehenge**, ca. 3100–2200 BCE, Wiltshire, UK

Stonehenge is an example of megalithic construction that began as a series of circular ditches ca. 3100 BCE. The 12-foot- (4-meter-) high stones were erected 1,100 years later, a re-

markable engineering feat. The stones are oriented to precisely mark the location of the sun on the summer solstice, showing a sophisticated knowledge of astronomy. Little is known of the builders, but some believe the site to have been a place of worship.

■ **Reed-Thatched Houses**, reconstruction, ca. 1800–1500 BCE, Roeschitz, Austria

Because only stone structures have survived, we see Neolithic people as preoccupied with monuments and death. Less durable dwellings, such as these, are known only from their foundations, which contained holes for their timber structure. These round houses are typical of the Aunjetitz culture in Germany and Austria. Dug partly into the ground, they had walls of wood mesh covered with clay and thatched roofs. Large rectangular buildings, called longhouses, sheltered whole communities. One end of a longhouse was used for grain storage, the middle for sleeping and eating, and the area near the door for work.

■ **Cueva de Menga Grave at Antequera**, ca. 3000–2000 BCE, Spain

A dolmen is a type of Neolithic tomb built from upright stones and capped by a horizontal roof slab. Cueva de Menga is the largest dolmen in Europe, built using 32 megaliths, the largest of which weighs 180 tons. As was typical, after the burial chamber was completed, the whole structure was buried under an artificial hill. When it was discovered and opened in the 19th century, the skeletons of several hundred people were found inside.

Ancient Egypt

ca. 3100–ca. 2040 BCE

■ Egypt emerged as a great civilization ■ Cities of the dead were built for the ruling class ■ Imhotep, history's first known architect, designed the first pyramid at Saqqara ■ Stone replaced mud brick as a building material ■ *left:* **Walls of Grave Compound**, Djoser Complex, ca. 2609–2590, Saqqara

■ **ca. 3100–2700 BCE** The Egyptian state is founded and early hieroglyphic writing appears

ca. 2950–2700 BCE Early Dynastic Period, during which the capital city of Memphis is created, and the first pyramid, the Step Pyramid at Saqqara, is constructed

ca. 2660–2160 BCE Old Kingdom; the Great Pyramids are built at Dahshur and Giza

ca. 2160–2040 BCE The First Intermediate Period of Egypt, during which Egypt is split into two states, ruled from Memphis in the north and from Thebes in the south

■ **Heb-sed Court in the Djoser Complex**, ca. 2630 BCE, Saqqara

The pyramid complex includes the Heb-sed Court for religious ceremonies and a miniature city for the dead to inhabit. The architect Imhotep used stone with great creativity. Columns were carved to resemble bundles of papyrus reeds, and the stone ceilings were fashioned to look like wood logs.

By 3100 BCE, the Egyptians had developed the hallmarks of a great civilization—a written language, religion, and a dynastic ruling class. The capital city Memphis was one of several busy centers along the Nile River. Buildings were constructed of sun-dried mud bricks and timber. Early pharaohs were buried in mastabas, one-story brick boxes with a burial chamber below. Few mastabas are still in existence.

The practice of burying the dead of the ruling class in mastabas changed around 2630 BCE with the erection of the Step Pyramid for the pharaoh Djoser. Not only did the architect Imhotep build Egypt's first large-scale pyramid, he also introduced the use of stone as a building material. It worked so well that he was later declared a god. The pyramid is the centerpiece of a large complex of tombs, altars, and courtyards protected by a deep trench and a 30-foot- (10-meter-) high wall built of stone bricks (pictured above).

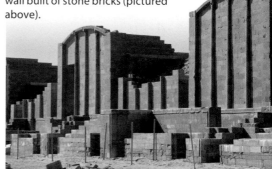

Other Important Works

Abydos Necropolis, ca. 3000–2000 BCE, Abydos	Red Pyramid of Snefru from the Dashur Necropolis, 2605 BCE, Dahshur
Sloped Pyramid of Snefru, 2551 BCE, Dahshur	Pyramid of Teti, ca. 2323 BCE, Saqqara
Pyramid of Unas, ca. 2345 BCE, Saqqara	Mastaba of Idu, ca. 2145 BCE, Giza

▇ Grave of Mereruka, ca. 2300 BCE, Saqqara

The souls of the pharoahs were expected to reside with the gods, while the souls of nobles would live for eternity in their tombs. The tombs of nobles were filled with material goods and food offerings for use in the afterlife. Mereruka, a nobleman who lived 300 years after Djoser, was entombed in one of the largest and finest mastabas at the Saqqara necropolis. A life-size statue of Mereruka is in a niche overlooking one of the 32 chambers, all of which are decorated with wall paintings showing scenes of his family and daily life in the Old Kingdom.

▇ Imhotep: Step Pyramid of Djoser, ca. 2630 BCE, Saqqara

Imhotep's design for this building evolved throughout its construction. First, a traditional one-story mastaba was built over a burial chamber. Unsatisfied, Imhotep added one mastaba on top of another until the structure became the six-tiered pyramid we see today. A casing of white limestone covered the structure, though only a few traces of it remain.

The Great Pyramids

About 75 years after the construction of the Step Pyramid of Djoser, Djoser's grandson, Khufu—son of Snefru—began his own pyramid. Learning from the mistakes of Snefru's pyramids, the architects devised ingenious techniques to build Khufu's Great Pyramid on a truly monumental scale. At 480 feet (146 meters) high, the pyramid was the world's tallest building until Lincoln Cathedral was completed in 1300. Along with the two later pyramids next to it, the Great Pyramid remains one of humankind's greatest achievements.

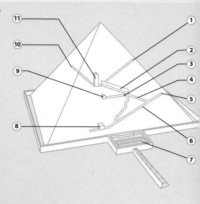

The Great Pyramid of Khufu has two air shafts and two main chambers. Near the center of the pyramid lies the main room—the King's Chamber—and the Queen's Chamber lies just beneath.

The masonry inside the Great Pyramid is so fine that a knife tip cannot be inserted between the stones. The Grand Gallery, shown above, leads to the King's Chamber. Thought to be the pharaoh's burial room, today it holds only an empty sarcophagus.

The Great Pyramid of Khufu is made of about 2,400,000 blocks, each weighing an average of 2.5 tons. The rough interior blocks were quarried nearby, but the granite for the interior King's Chamber came from about 500 miles (800 km) away.

Pre- and Early History 10,000–300 BCE

Legend:
1 Air Shafts
2 Grand Gallery
3 Horizontal Passage
4 Ascending Passage
5 Entrance
6 Descending Passage
7 Mortuary Temple
8 Subterranean Chamber
9 Queen's Chamber
10 Air Shafts
11 King's Chamber

Great Pyramids, 26th century BCE, Giza

Many mysteries surround the pyramids, especially their construction. How were 2 million blocks of stone quarried, dressed, and moved into place? Theories include the use of long, straight ramps leading to the top of the structure, or a ramp winding up the outside of the pyramids. Some scientists believe an internal ramp was used to build them, and that it still lies inside. The

estimated number of workers needed ranges from 30,000 to 300,000 men working for 20 years. The Pyramid of Menkaure (foreground), son of Khufu, is about half as tall as his father's. The three main pyramids were surrounded by a necropolis of the tombs of nobles, including the small pyramids for Menkaure's queens. The scale of the project is staggering, but perhaps equally impressive are the leaps made in technical skill—builders, who started working with stone only 75 years earlier, were able to master masonry on such a large scale.

Middle and Late Egypt

ca. 2040 BCE–ca. 300 CE

■ Thebes became the new capital of Egypt ■ Pharaohs built massive temple complexes ■ The Valley of the Kings necropolis was created ■ Post-and-lintel construction was used ■ Greek and Roman cultures influenced design
■ *left*: **Ramses II**, ca. 1400 BCE, Luxor

ca. 2040 BCE Thebes becomes Egypt's capital

1550–1070 BCE Egypt's New Kingdom; royal burials in the Valley of the Kings

332–30 BCE Greek Ptolemaic pharaohs build new temples

30 BCE Rome conquers Egypt

ca. 300 CE Christianity replaces Egyptian religions, and temples are abandoned

Around 2040 BCE, 1,000 years after the Great Pyramid at Giza had been built, the Egyptian capital was moved south to Thebes on the upper Nile River. A new necropolis, or city of the dead, was created across the Nile in the Theban Hills on the west bank of the river. For nearly 500 years the area known as the Valley of the Kings, was the location of the tombs of the pharaohs and powerful nobles. A new town, Deir el-Medina, had to be built nearby to house the hundreds of workers needed for the massive building projects.

The pharaohs also had massive temple complexes built along the east bank of the Nile River using sandstone and granite from nearby quarries. The temples were 🔊

■ **Senemut: Hatshepsut's Mortuary Temple**, ca. 1460 BCE, Deir el-Bahri

Hatshepsut was one of the most successful female pharaohs, ruling Egypt for 22 years. Her royal

adviser, Senemut, designed her funerary temple as a series of colonnaded terraces set against the surrounding high cliffs. Located near the Valley of the Kings, the terraced temple was

decorated with statues of Hatshepsut and landscaped with trees and scented herbs. A courtyard on the second terrace leads to the sanctuary, cut deep into the cliff.

Other Works

Mortuary Temple of Amenhotep III, dismantled, ca. 1350 BCE, from the necropolis at Thebes, Luxor

Temple at Abu Simbel by Ramses II, 1265 BCE

Mortuary Temple of Ramses II (Ramesseum), 13th century BCE, from the necropolis at Thebes, Luxor

Tomb of Nefertiti, 13th century BCE, from the necropolis at Thebes, Luxor

Pre- and Early History 10,000–300 BCE

■ **Temple of Amon**, 1530–323 BCE, Karnak

The temples at Karnak were the most revered in
Egypt. Thirty generations of pharaohs built additions, each trying to outdo their predecessors. The
great forecourt of the Amon temple was added in
about 850 BCE. The column capitals represent
papyrus buds. Further along the main axis is the
great hypostyle hall with 134 towering columns.
The complex covers almost half a square mile
(one square km) and also contains many smaller
temples and a total of ten pylons.

■ **Temple of Horus**, 237–57 BCE, Edfu

The Edfu site is the best preserved Egyptian
temple complex. Built in the Greek Ptolemaic period, its plan includes the traditional entry pylons, a courtyard, and two hypostyle halls laid out
on an axis. Eighteen massive sandstone columns
fill the first hypostyle hall, whose ceiling is carved
to represent the sky. After the Romans forbade
the worship of non-Christian gods, the temple
was abandoned. For centuries it lay buried under
the sands—only the tops of its 98-foot- (30-
meter-) high pylons were visible.

Middle and Late Egypt

surrounded by high walls and accessible only to priests and nobles. Interiors were typically laid out on a single processional axis oriented along the path of the sun. Towering pylons marked the entrance. Carved and painted with images of the pharaoh triumphant in battle, the pylons were like billboards advertising the pharaoh's divine power. Visitors passed through an open courtyard, ringed by stone columns made to resemble mammoth papyrus or lotus flowers, to a hypostyle hall, a roofed forest of columns separating the material world from the sacred. Light and space were reduced with each step in the procession until the visitor reached the main sanctuary, which had low ceilings and was shrouded in darkness.

■ **Temple of Isis at Philae**, 500 BCE–164 CE

The temple complex is located on an island in the Nile River. Visitors pass through two pylon gateways, a courtyard, and a hypostyle hall before reaching the main temple, built by Pharaoh Ptolemy XI. In the 1970s, a new dam threatened to flood the temple, so the entire complex was relocated.

■ **Trajan's Pavilion**, ca. 164 CE, Philae

The Philae complex includes buildings exhibiting Greek and Roman influences. The entry pavilion to the island is composed of 14 columns with floral capitals that blend Egyptian lotus blossoms with the Greek Corinthian style. The interior walls are carved with reliefs showing the Roman Emperor Trajan offering gifts to the Egyptian gods Isis and Osiris.

Pre- and Early History 10,000–300 BCE

Amenhotep III: Temple at Luxor, Hypostyle Hall,
a. 1370 BCE, Thebes

Pharaoh Amenhotep III built this temple on the east bank of

Ramses II: Temple at Luxor, Pylon Entrance,
a. 1250 BCE, Thebes

One hundred years after the temple was built, Pharaoh Ramses II added these entrance pylons, carved with scenes from his military victories against the Hittites. Two seated figures of Ramses II flank the entry, and a red granite obelisk stands in front. Originally there were two obelisks, but the twin is now at Place de la Concorde, Paris.

the Nile to stage the annual festival of Opet. A colonnade leads to a courtyard, with reliefs depicting the coronation of the pharaoh by the gods. The hall

has double rows of columns, decorated with papyrus bud capitals. Beyond are the sacred chambers, which were later converted to a Roman temple.

Middle and Late Egypt

Mesopotamia and Persia

ca. 3200–330 BCE

■ Sumerians built cities and stepped ziggurats in present-day Iraq ■ Mud brick was widely used ■ Assyrians adopted Sumerian styles ■ King Nebuchadnezzar II rebuilt Babylon ■ King Darius founded Persepolis
■ *left*: **Winged Bull Gateway**, 721–705 BCE, found in Khorsabad, Iraq

■ **ca. 3200 BCE** The proto-ziggurat White Temple is built in the Sumerian city of Uruk

2112–2095 BCE Sumerian ruler Ur-Nammu builds the ziggurat at Ur

705–681 BCE King Sennacherib constructs palaces at the Assyrian capital Nineveh

605–562 BCE King Nebuchadnezzar II builds the Ishtar Gate and the Hanging Gardens of Babylon

559–330 BCE Persian Achaemenid dynasty; Persepolis and royal tombs are built

■ **Ziggurat at Ur**, Sumerian, ca. 2113–2096 BCE, Iraq

The ziggurat at Ur is the best preserved of the ancient ziggurats. The stepped pyramid has a core of mud brick finished with an outer casing of fired brick. Its walls have flat buttresses and slope in slightly with the ziggurat's elevation, to exaggerate height. Three converging ramps lead to the first platform, and a central stairway continues to the top, where a small temple to the city's patron god Nanna once stood.

While the Egyptians were building cities on the Nile, another urban civilization developed in the region between the Tigris and Euphrates rivers, in present-day Iraq. In this area, known as Mesopotamia, the Sumerian culture thrived. They developed agriculture and invented a written language, which they etched into clay tablets. Their cities were mainly composed of mud-brick buildings. Wet clay was pounded into wood molds and left to dry in the sun. Later, the Sumerians began firing bricks in ovens, resulting in harder and more durable building materials. Pigmented glazes were added to the bricks to create brilliant colors.

The cities of Mesopotamia were dominated by stepped pyramids called ziggurats. Unlike Egyptian pyramids, ziggurats were not built as tombs, but rather as man-made mountains that reached to heaven. The Sumerian gods were associated with the large distant mountains to the east, and the ziggurats were

Ishtar Gate, Babylonian, ca. 600 BCE, Iraq

The Ishtar Gate was the largest and most beautiful of eight entrances into the ancient city of Babylon. After devastating invasions, King Nebuchadnezzar II ordered the gate's construction as part of a fortified wall to protect the city. The gate was finished with bricks glazed with a deep blue color and decorated with relief images of dragons and young bulls. The arched central opening resembles later Roman triumphal arches. A 1-mile- (1.6-km-) long processional way led from the gate to the city's main temple. It was lined with tall blue-glazed brick walls with reliefs of 120 lions. Each year, statues of the gods were paraded through the Ishtar Gate and down the processional way during the New Year's celebration. Nebuchadnezzar II carried out other ambitious building projects throughout Babylon. His own palace complex included the famous Hanging Gardens of Babylon, named as one of the Seven Wonders of the Ancient World.

Etemenanki Ziggurat at Babylon, Babylonian, 605–562 BCE, Iraq

Believed to be the inspiration for the biblical Tower of Babel, the ziggurat was part of a religious complex located in the city center. The tower had seven tiers, with a temple to the god Marduk on top. An earlier ziggurat nearby was already 1,000 years old when invaders destroyed it in 689 BCE. King Nebuchadnezzar II rebuilt the tower as part of his reconstruction of Babylon. Excavations show it had a square base plan and three stairs. The Greek historian Herodotos described the ziggurat as multi-colored, suggesting it was finished with glazed brick. Alexander the Great conquered Babylon and ordered the ziggurat's destruction in 323 BCE.

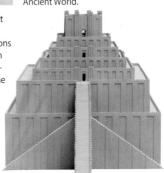

fashioned to resemble these mountains, bringing the people both physically and symbolically closer to the gods. A small temple on top of the ziggurat was intended as a home for the city's patron god.

Sumerian religious beliefs and architectural styles were adopted by other peoples in the region. When King Hammurabi founded the holy city of Babylon, he built a great ziggurat there. The Assyrians did the same at Khorsabad and Nineveh. They also adopted the Sumerian system of priest-kings and built grand palaces to house them. When the Persians conquered Mesopotamia in 539 BCE, they built the royal city of Persepolis, in present-day Iran. The city was inspired by the influential architecture of great cities like Babylon and Nineveh.

Other Works

White Temple at Uruk, ca. 3200–3000 BCE, Iraq

Ziggurat at Sialk, 2900 BCE, Iran

Ziggurat of Agargouf, ca. 1500 BCE, Iraq

Assyrian City of Ashur, 1400–900 BCE, Iraq

Choqa Zanbil Ziggurat, 1250 BCE Susa, Iran

Palace of Ashur-Nasir-Pal II at Nimrud, 879 BCE, Kalhu, Iraq

Tomb of Cyrus the Great, ca. 530 BCE, Pasargadae, Iran

Achaemenid Tombs, begun 486 BCE, Naqsh-e Rustam, Iran

■ **Reconstruction of Nineveh**, Assyrian, ca. 705–681 BCE, near Mosul, Iraq

Nineveh had a brief but glorious reign as capital of Assyria. Beginning in 705 BCE, King Sennacherib rebuilt the city. He broadened streets and built gardens that were watered by the world's first aqueduct system. His own 138,000-square-foot (12,820-square-meter) palace had glazed brick paneling and monumental bronze sculptures .

■ **Nergal Gate at Nineveh**, Assyrian, ca. 700 BCE, Iraq

King Sennacherib built a 7.5-mile- (12-km-) long brick wall that wrapped around Nineveh. Fifteen towering gates led into the city, each named after an Assyrian god. The Nergal Gate was flanked by stone sculpture of human-headed winged bulls and may have served as a ceremonial entrance. Despite the fortifications, Nineveh was invaded and destroyed in 612 BCE.

Rock-Carved Tomb of Artaxerxes II, Persian, 358–353 BCE, Persepolis, Iran

Persepolis was the home of the Achaemenid dynasty, whose empire reached to Mesopotamia and Egypt. Unlike Mesopotamians, who lived in the low plains to the west, the Persians were surrounded by mountains and had access to large amounts of stone. Like the Egyptians, they were skilled stone cutters. The royal residence at Persepolis was itself built on a terrace carved into the side of Mount Rahmat, and the palace buildings included stone columns and stairs carved with relief sculptures. The tombs of three Achaemenid kings are carved into the cliffs above Persepolis. The tomb of Artaxerxes II is based on the nearby grave of Persepolis's founder King Darius. The rock face is sculpted to resemble a building facade. The beam and columns framing the opening are believed to depict the entrance to the palace at Persepolis. Inside was a small chamber with the king's stone sarcophagus.

Palace of Darius, Persian, 518–486 BCE, Persepolis, Iran

The Persian king Darius was inspired by Mesopotamian palaces when he founded the royal city of Persepolis. His own palace had thick walls and massive granite doorways carved with relief sculptures. The ceilings were of ebony and teak. Next to the palace was the *Apadana*, a vast ceremonial hall rising 82 feet (25 meters) high. Only 13 of its 72 stone columns remain.

Megaliths

The word *megalith* means "large stone." The first megalithic structures, tombs, and rows of standing stones, called "menhirs," were built near the coasts of Brittany and Portugal around 4800 BCE. Even by today's standards, the stones were colossal. The largest menhir in Brittany was originally 65 feet (20 meters) tall and weighed 350 tons. No one is certain how these monuments were built, but their sheer size has made them invulnerable to the passage of time.

🔲 **Hagar Qim Temple**, ca. 3600–2500 BCE, Malta

One advantage of megalithic construction is durability. The temple at Hagar Qim has remained intact for as long as 5,000 years. The complex contains six oval-shaped rooms. The outside walls are composed of naturally formed slabs, the largest weighing 20 tons. The entrance portals are carved blocks that form a *trilithon*—two uprights supporting a lintel across the top. The blocks are notched to fit tightly together.

🔲 **T-shaped Megalith**, ca. 1500–800 BCE, Torralba de Salort, Minorca, Spain

The Talayot culture erected T-shaped megaliths on the island of Minorca. Scholars believe that the top stones were raised by lifting one end and then the other to build a timber frame beneath.

◧ **Reconstruction of an Ancient Crane**

Moving large stones required knowledge of the lever and the use of counterweights. Archaeologists believe that methods of megalithic construction were spread by seafaring people, and these techniques may have first been used for building and sailing ships. Sailors learned to use timber construction and strong ropes to master the powerful forces of wind and sea. These same tools were later used to construct simple cranes.

Unfinished Egyptian Obelisk, 2686–2134 BCE, Aswan

The Egyptians were masters of cutting and transporting enormous blocks of stone. The Lateran Obelisk, now in Rome, was carved from a single block of red granite 105 feet (32 meters) high, and weighs over 400 tons. A tomb painting shows that workers moved stone blocks on sledges over wet ground. No metal tools have been found, so it is still debated how the Egyptians cut their stone. However, in order to quarry granite they must at least have evolved iron tools—more than 1,000 years before the Iron Age is conventionally understood to have begun.

Megaliths

Minoan and Mycenaean

ca. 2700–ca. 1200 BCE

■ The Minoans were the first civilization in Europe ■ Palace complexes were built on Crete ■ The Mycenaeans on mainland Greece dominated the Mediterranean ■ Fortified cities and *tholos* were built ■ Both cultures inspired Greek culture ■ *left:* **Treasury at Atreus**, ca. 1250 BCE, Mycenae, Greece

■ **ca. 2700–1600 BCE** The Minoans' trading routes bring new building techniques from the Egyptians, Syrians, and Persians

ca. 2000 BCE The Minoans build their first royal palace

ca. 1600–1200 BCE Fortified cities are built in newly occupied lands

ca. 1525–1300 BCE Tholos are constructed at Mycenae for rulers

ca. 1370 BCE An earthquake destroys the palace at Knossos, marking the end of Minoan culture

ca. 1200 BCE Mycenae falls to invaders, resulting in a 400-year Greek dark age

The first European civilization was created by the prosperous sea-trading culture of the Minoans. The Minoans built sprawling palaces on the Mediterranean island of Crete and communicated with other Mediterranean and Near Eastern cultures, learning building techniques from them. Their buildings were created from a mixture of mediums such as mud brick, stone, and plaster.

The Mycenaeans, on the Greek mainland, were warriors, and their king, Agamemnon, led the Greeks in the Trojan War. They built compact cities with heavy, fortified walls throughout the lands that they conquered. These cities suited their warring lifestyles. As well as fortified cities, domed tombs buried in hills, or *tholos* were built for their rulers. Centuries of both clashes and exchange between the two cultures later led to the architectural styles found in ancient Greece.

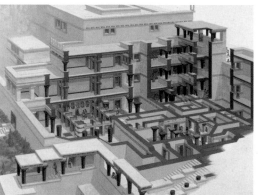

■ **Palace of Knossos**, reconstruction, Minoan, ca. 1700–1400 BCE, Phaistos, Crete

The Palace of Knossos was a sprawling complex of 1,300 rooms linked by staircases, light wells, and courtyards. Parts of the building were five stories high, and its plan was so complex that it is believed to be the inspiration for the myth of the labyrinth. Earthquakes eventually caused the building to collapse and, consequently, the end of Minoan culture.

Ancient Mediterranean Architecture

Palace of Knossos, Minoan,
a. 1700–1400 BCE, Phaistos, Crete

The palace walls were decorated with frescoes depicting
sports and religious ceremonies.
Minoan columns were possibly
inspired by Egyptian designs.
Rather than stone, the Minoans
used trunks of cypress trees
turned upside down so that the
wider trunk was at the top and
the bottom tapered inward.
Mounted on a simple stone
base, the tree trunks were
painted red and topped with a
round, pillow-shaped capital.

Lion Gate, Mycenaean,
ca. 1250 BCE, Mycenae, Greece

The Mycenaeans ruled much of
the Mediterranean world. Their
capital, Mycenae, was located
at a remote hilltop fortress surrounded by a massive wall. The
stones that comprised the wall
were so huge that they were
called cyclopean, because it
was thought that only the
mythical one-eyed giants could
have lifted them. The monu-

mental Lion Gate was the main
entrance to the city. The heavy
framing slabs recall Neolithic
megaliths, but the triangular
stone above the opening is a
structural innovation because it
redirects the weight of the
above stones to the sides and
allows for the 10-foot- (3-meter-)
wide opening. The carved relief
of lions, now missing their
metal heads, was meant to protect the city and its royal house.

Minoan and Mycenaean

Antiquity and Early Christianity

600 BCE–600 CE

Tholos Temple of Athena Pronaia, 380–360 BCE, Delphi

Antiquity and

38

Greece

776 BCE
First Olympic Games signal rebirth of Greek culture

700 BCE
Archaic period; early wooden temples use the Classical orders

600 BCE
Stone replaces wood construction in Greek temples

450 BCE
High Classical period; Athens rules the Mediterranean; Greek architecture spreads to Italy, Africa, and Asia Minor

432 BCE
The Acropolis and Parthenon in Athens

p. 47

600	400	200	100

Rome

750 BCE
Rome is founded

500 BCE
Formation of the Roman Republic; beginning of the construction of temples based on

earlier Etruscan models from central Italy and some Greek models

146 BCE
Rome conquers Greece and adopts Hellenistic styles of architecture

27 BCE
Roman Empire; Roman Forum is built; wide use of concrete and the Corinthian order

p. 55

Early Christianity

Early Christianity

50 CE
Christians are persecuted and meet in secret churches

310 CE
Emperor Constantine converts to Christianity and builds first basilica churches

330 CE
Constantinople is founded as the Christian capital of Roman Empire

333 CE
Construction of the Old St. Peter's Basilica in Rome

p. 65

150 BCE
Greco-Roman period; the Stoa of Attalus is built

| 100 | 200 | 400 | 600 |

79 CE
Mt. Vesuvius buries Pompeii

82 CE
Construction of the Colosseum

125 CE
Construction of the Pantheon

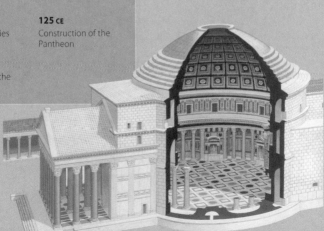

p. 60

Architecture and Ideals

In 40 BCE, the Roman architect Vitruvius wrote that buildings should have three attributes: *firmitas*, *utilitas*, and *venustas*—"strength," "utility," and "beauty." The Romans inherited these architectural principles from the Greeks, whose monuments embodied these ideals. Greek architects developed a system of ideal building proportions that was inspired by nature. Known as the Classical orders, they were later adopted by the Romans.

   Greek culture reached its zenith during the 5th century BCE. Athens had become a democracy, Socrates's and Plato's schools of philosophy flourished, and the Athenian leader Pericles began construction of the Acropolis. Architecture played an important role at the *agora*, the civic center of the city, which housed the *bouleuterion*, the governmental building where democracy was invented and first flourished.

■ **Philipp von Foltz: Pericles Orating on the Pnyx**, 1852

■ **Zeus Altar**, 180 BCE, from Pergamon, Turkey. Pergamon Museum, Berlin

Roman Crane,
reconstruction,
a. 30 BCE

Stabian Baths,
a. 62 CE, Pompeii

Building Technology

The achievements of the ancient Egyptians set the standard for Greek architects. The Great Pyramid of Giza was over 2,000 years old when the Greek historian Herodotus saw it in around 440 BCE. Inspired by the Egyptians, Greek sculptors learned to carve stone into naturalistic human forms. Around 600 BCE, architects used the same techniques to transform their fragile wooden temples into durable stone monuments.

Egyptians and Greeks used simple post-and-lintel construction, which requires many columns to support short horizontal beams above. The Romans developed the arch as a means of spanning greater distances in their bridges and aqueducts. Concrete was a major breakthrough that enabled fluid forms like the barrel vault and dome. Enormous Roman baths and the domed Pantheon and Hagia Sophia are proud successors to the monuments of ancient Egypt.

Power and Spectacle

In Greece, theaters taught morality, and sporting events were part of religious festivals. Julius Caesar enlarged the Circus Maximus so that 250,000 Romans could watch chariot races, and Roman emperors used entertainment as a tool to control the masses. The brutal punishment of criminals in the Colosseum

instilled fear in the people. Roman imperial ambitions pushed architecture to scale new heights. Nero's Domus Aurea, and the vaults of the Basilica of Maxentius dwarfed the Roman Forum. Military victories were marked by public spectacles that included temporary arches, which were later developed into permanent monuments to imperial power.

■ **Chariot Race in the Circus Maximus,** reconstruction, Rome

■ **Relief from the Arch of Marcus Aurelius,** ca. 182 CE, Rome

Buddhist Stupa,
begun 271 CE,
Anuradhapur,
Sri Lanka

Hagia Sophia,
532–537 CE,
Istanbul

Temples and Churches

The Greek temple was literally a house for the gods. The Parthenon in Athens housed a giant statue of the city's goddess Athena, and only priests and selected elites could go inside. Roman temples were even more exclusive. Based on earlier Etruscan temples, they were more enclosed than Greek models, and set on a high base. Early Jewish temples were seen as a private dwelling places for God, though in spiritual form. Rituals occurred outside. In Asia, Buddhist stupas were solid mounds used as a focus for private meditation, while in Mesoamerica the Mayans built their temples on top of pyramids, closer to heaven.

The rituals of Christianity required a new building type that invited the public inside. Early basilicas were modest descendents of early Christian house churches, but the dramatic interior of Hagia Sophia in Istanbul was inspired by the Roman ideal of creating an architectural spectacle.

Introduction

Classical Orders

The Classical orders are systems for designing buildings based on proportions between the individual parts. The ancient Greeks developed the orders in their early wooden temples. They used a basic structural system—the post-and-lintel, or vertical columns supporting horizontal beams. The Classical orders gave their buildings an aesthetic sophistication by ensuring consistency and visual harmony between buildings, regardless of size or materials used.

There are three orders: the Doric, Ionic, and Corinthian. Each has a unique set of rules defining its use. In theory, historians can use the orders like architectural DNA to reconstruct a temple from a single column or piece of entablature. The orders were later adopted by the Romans, who added elements such as arches and vaulting. Forgotten for centuries during the Dark Ages, the orders were rediscovered during the Renaissance. Since then, architects have used them to design buildings that have a sense of timelessness and elegance.

■ **Corinthian Temple of Diana**, ca. 200 CE Evora, Portugal

Each order has a unique column design. Doric columns, from the Greek mainland, are broad with capitals composed of a round, pillowlike echinus and a flat, square bottom slab called an abacus. The thinner Ionic columns' curling volute capitals originate from the Greek colonies in Asia Minor, while the Corinthian capital, a variation on the Ionic, has carved acanthus leaves.

Column Proportions of the Three Orders

Beginning with Palladio in the 1st century BCE, architects have studied Greek and Roman buildings to establish the ideal proportions for the three orders. Columns are distinguished by the ratio between their base diameter and height—for a Doric column, it is about 1:6, for an Ionic column, 1:9. The slight tapering of the columns at the top is called entasis, and the area above the columns is known as the entablature. Buildings created in the Doric order have a frieze with alternating triglyphs and metopes creating rectangular areas of high and low depth. Triglyphs are styled after elements of earlier wooden construction and are fashioned after the ends of wood beams. The triangular pediment below the roof line was sometimes filled with sculptures, as at the Parthenon.

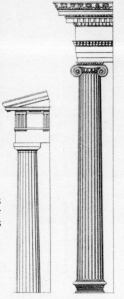
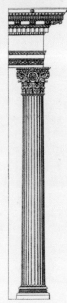

Classical Orders

Greek Architecture

ca. 600–146 BCE

- A new Greek culture emerged after a dark age ■ The Greeks devised a system of building proportions known as the Classical orders ■ Great stone buildings were constructed ■ Greece's architecture was exported to its colonies
- *left:* **Stoa of Attalus**, reconstruction, 159–138 BCE, Athens

ca. 600 BCE The Greeks begin using stone for their public buildings

ca. 480–323 BCE Athens is the capital of a massive empire; Greek temples and theaters are built in colonies throughout the Mediterranean

449–432 BCE The Acropolis is constructed at Athens

146 BCE The Romans conquer Greece and adopt Greek architectural styles

For centuries after the fall of the Mycenaeans, Greece languished in a cultural dark age. When a new Greek culture emerged, it included a strict system of architectural proportion known as the Classical orders (p. 44). The earliest Greek structures, built of mud brick and timber, have long since disappeared. Around 600 BCE, the wooden Temple of Hera at Olympia was rebuilt, piece by piece, with more durable and fireproof stone. Soon, Greek architects had mastered the art of building with marble and limestone. The Classical orders, now translated into stone, came to define a timeless and universal standard of architectural beauty. Although ancient Greece conjures ⊂

Other Works

Temple of Hera, ca. 600 BCE, Olympia

Temples at Paestum, 550–200 BCE

Temples at Agrigento, ca. 500–400 BCE

Theater at Delphi, ca. 400 BCE

Temple of Apollo, ca. 330 BCE, Delphi

Theater at Epidauros, ca. 330 BCE

Temple of Apollo, 310 BCE, Didyma

■ **Stoa of Attalus**, reconstruction, 159–138 BCE, Athens

A *stoa* is an open, colonnaded building or a covered pedes-trian street lined with shops or offices, found near the market in most Greek cities. This *stoa*, two stories high and 377 feet (115 meters) long, is decorated with marble Doric and Ionic columns. Twenty-one rooms line the back of the building. Reconstructed in the 1950s, the building is now a museum.

Temple of Hephaistos, 449 BCE, Athens

Though less famous than its neighbor the Parthenon, this is the best-preserved ancient Greek temple in the world. All of the structure's Doric columns and pediments are intact, and even most of the original roof remains. Unfortunately, the friezes and other decorations have been lost to looters over the centuries. The temple was converted into the Christian Church of St. George in the 7th century CE. This saved the exterior, but the ancient interior was removed and replaced by the structures of a Christian church.

Lysicrates Monument, 335 BCE, Athens

Lysicrates was a wealthy Athenian who sponsored a dramatic chorus in the annual theater competition. The chorus won first prize. This small building, which commemorates the triumph, originally served as the base for the bronze prize itself. Many such monuments lined the street leading to the nearby Theater of Dionysus, but only this one has survived. It is notable as one of the first uses of the Corinthian order in Greek architecture.

Greek Architecture

images of stone monuments, most Greeks lived in modest structures with mud-brick walls and timber columns and roofs. Greek houses were usually one story with several small rooms around an open courtyard that served as a dining and living room. Each city had a *palaestra*, or gymnasium, and a *bouleuterion*, a meeting place for the town council. Women shopped at the *agora*, an outdoor market, and filled their vases with water at a public fountain house. Temples were off-limits to most people, and ceremonies were performed outdoors—usually at an altar in front of the building.

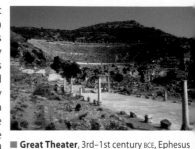

■ **Great Theater**, 3rd–1st century BCE, Ephesus

The Greeks saw drama as the highest form of culture, and every town had a theater. Tiers of stone seats were set into a hillside, and a small building, called a *skene,* served as the stage set. The theater at Ephesus, a wealthy port city, held 25,000 spectators.

■ **Athenian Treasury House**, reconstruction, 510 BCE, Delphi

The city of Delphi was sacred and neutral to all Greeks, even when warring among themselves. Each Greek city-state built a treasury house to hold offerings to please Apollo and to thank the Oracle for her advice. The looting of these buildings was a key event in the downfall of Greece. The Athenian Treasury, a small Doric temple, has been reconstructed using mostly original material.

Tholos Temple of Athena Pronaia, 380–360 BCE, Delphi

Delphi was the home of the oracle of Delphi, a revered woman who made predictions of the future. The earliest shrines at Delphi, predating the oracle, were dedicated to the Earth Goddess. Athena replaced the Earth Goddess in the Olympian pantheon, but the veneration of feminine wisdom and spiritual consciousness continued. This finely detailed round shrine, or *tholos*, was at the center of the sanctuary of Athena Pronaia. The leaf-adorned capitals of its columns are representations of the sacred forest groves of the old Earth Goddess religion. The round form, a break from the rigid right angles of earlier temple plans, appears inspired by this feminine milieu and anticipates the curved forms in Roman architecture.

■ **Satyrus and Pythius: Mausoleum at Halicarnassus**, ca. 353 BCE, near Bodrum

Mausolus was a Persian governor who spent lavishly to rebuild his capital, Halicarnassus. After his death, his wife spared no expense on his tomb. Greek architects designed a 148-foot (45-meter) marble edifice overlooking the city. Four sculptors, one for each side, embellished the tomb with sculptures. The building was so impressive that it was named one of the Seven Wonders of the Ancient World. After earthquakes toppled the upper portion, its stones were used to build a nearby castle.

Greek Architecture

The Acropolis

ca. 550–404 BCE

- The Acropolis was a sacred hilltop in Athens dedicated to the goddess Athena
- Early temples were destroyed by the Persians ■ The sculptor Phidias oversaw their reconstruction ■ The completed buildings were a triumph of Greek architecture
- *left:* **Mnesicles: The Erechtheion**, 421–405 BCE, Athens

ca. 550 BCE First temple dedicated to Athena is built on the Acropolis

480 BCE Persians attack Athens and destroy the temples on the Acropolis

461–429 BCE Pericles rules Athens during its golden age of peace and prosperity; he begins the rebuilding of the Acropolis and puts the sculptor Phidias in charge

438 BCE The Parthenon temple and its cult statue of Athena are dedicated

432 BCE Completion of Parthenon sculptures

404 BCE Athens is conquered by the Spartans during the Peloponnesian War and construction on the Acropolis ends

The collection of buildings on the Acropolis represent the high point of ancient Greek architecture. The flat-topped h overlooking Athens was the site of a Bronze Age fortress an later housed temples to the goddess Athena. Early archa temples to the protectors of the city stood on this site, but 480 BCE, after a devastating war with the Persians, the Acro olis lay in ruins. As Athens entered its golden age, the rul Pericles commissioned the sculptor Phidias to oversee th reconstruction of the Acropolis. Phidias skillfully laid o the structures on the Acropolis to create spatial harmor and heighten visual drama. Each structure was placed to r late spatially to one another and the landscape. Most of th buildings were built to Doric proportions, though some en ploy Ionic elements. The Acropolis is more of a high city tha a temple complex and was added to throughout the Hell nistic and Roman periods.

■ **The Propylaea**, 437–404 BCE, Athens

The Propylaea was a gate that surrounded the Acropolis. Today, the ruined

marble columns of the Propylae still serve as the entrance to the temples of the Acropolis. Built under Pericles, the Propylaea w not meant to serve as a fortifica tion, but rather as a demarcatio of where the holy area of the Acropolis began. The gate was fashioned out of white marble, accented with gray marble or limestone and reinforced with iron. Construction of the Propy laea was never fully completed, due to the outbreak of the Pelo ponnesian War between Athens and Sparta.

■ **Callicrates: Temple of Athena Nike**, 427 BCE, Athens

Though small, the Temple of Athena Nike sat in a prominent location overlooking the grand stairway to the Acropolis. The tiny site forced Callicrates to design a small structure only 11 feet (3.4 meters) high. The temple has tetrastyle, or four-columned, porticoes on both the front and back. The ratio of the columns' diameter to height is 1:7, slightly squatter than the typical Ionic ideal of 1:9, but the columns are capped with Ionic capitals. The 16.5-square-foot (5-square-meter) interior held a wooden cult statue of Athena Nike, the goddess of victory. The entablature was decorated with relief sculptures. The friezes depicted victories of the Greek military.

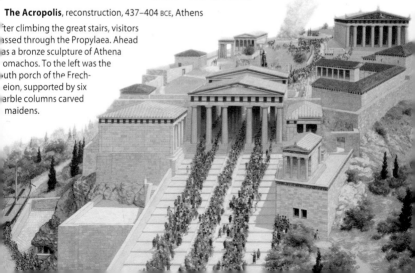

The Acropolis, reconstruction, 437–404 BCE, Athens

ter climbing the great stairs, visitors ssed through the Propylaea. Ahead as a bronze sculpture of Athena omachos. To the left was the uth porch of the Frech- eion, supported by six arble columns carved maidens.

The Parthenon

The Parthenon is the largest temple on the Acropolis and is revered as an ideal examp of the Doric order. The temple was dedicated to the goddess Athena and housed monumental statue titled Athena Parthenos (Athena the Virgin), hence the nam Parthenon. Following the destruction of an earlier temple in 480 BCE, the Greek ruler Pe icles assigned Ictinus and Callicrates to oversee the reconstruction. They designed peripteral temple with the proportions of the Doric order. Later the Parthenon was con verted into a church dedicated to Parthenos Maria (the Virgin Mary). In 1687, Athen was attacked, and the Parthenon was used as a munitions storehouse. A mortar ignite the gunpowder within and destroyed the building. Archaec ogists are working to rebuild the ancier temple.

Sculptural decoration was an integral part of Greek temples. The triangular pediments on the Parthenon's east and west facades contained statues showing scenes from the life of Athena. The smaller, square metope panels below were carved with mythical battle scenes. Originally, the sculptures were painted in bright colors, which have long since faded. In 1801, Lord Elgin carried most of the marble sculptures to London and they are now in the British Museum.

The large room within the Parthenon held the statue of Athena. The artist Phidias sculpted Athena's skin from ivory and used gold fabric for her clothes. There were no windows and light came only from torches or through the open entrance. A pool of water in the floor reflected shimmering light up onto the statue.

The plan of the Parthenon is rectangular and built in proportion to the Doric ratio of 9:4. The 48 marble columns were over 33 feet (10 meters) high. They supported a roof composed of wooden trusses and covered by tiles made of thin sheets of overlapping marble called *imbrices* and *tegulae*. A double colonnade of Doric columns supported a paneled wood ceiling. Within the Parthenon was a large interior room that housed the cult statue of Athena. Behind the statue was a smaller square room that contained the treasury of the Athenian League and contained votive offerings to the goddess. Both the treasury and the hall of Athena had entrance porches.

Ictinus and Callicrates with Phidias: The Parthenon, 447–422 BCE, Athens

The architects of the Parthenon used subtle optical effects to heighten the temple's proportions. The stylobate, or base, curves up slightly so that it is higher in the middle on all four sides. The columns all lean in slightly, exaggerating the height of the building. The columns themselves are wider at the base, with a curved upward taper, or entasis, and corner columns are slightly thicker and closer to their neighbors. Visitors to the Parthenon first saw it at a three-quarters angle, with a full view of the west pediment and the north colonnade. As they moved closer, details of the sculptures became clearer. Upon reaching the entrance, they caught a glimpse of the statue of Athena through the colonnade.

Early Roman Architecture

ca. 600 BCE–100 CE

■ Early Romans embraced Greek culture ■ Classical orders were used ■ The Romans adopted Etruscan innovations like structural arches ■ Military victories expanded Rome's influence ■ Temples and aqueducts were built in new territories ■ *left:* **Roman Maison Carrée**, 19–16 BCE, Nîmes

ca. 600–300 BCE The Etruscans build temples and tombs in central Italy

ca. 550 BCE Greek Doric temples at Paestum, Italy

ca. 300 BCE The Romans absorb Etruscan culture and architecture

ca. 30 BCE Vitruvius writes his influential *The Ten Books of Architecture*

ca. 50 BCE–100 CE Roman buildings are built in far-flung provincial cities

Other Works

Temple of Alatri, ca. 600–300 BCE, reconstructed at the Villa Giulia, Rome

Cloaca Maxima, ca. 600–200 BCE, Rome

Temple of Jupiter Capitolinus, ca. 200 BCE, Rome

Temple of Augustus and Livia, ca. 25 BCE, Vienna

■ **Casa Sannitica**, reconstruction, ca. 200 BCE, Herculaneum

Like Pompeii, Herculaneum was an Italian town buried in the eruption of Mt. Vesuvius in 79 CE. This

Roman architects owed a large debt to the Greeks. The dressed their buildings in the Classical orders and decc rated them with copies of Greek statues. Many distinctl Roman features, such as the arch, were developed by th Etruscans, who had lived in Italy centuries before. Thes two cultures combined to produce the Roman style. Th Roman Maison Carrée in Nîmes uses the Greek style bu is based on Etruscan models. Greek temples sat close t the ground, with steps and columns wrapped all aroun This building is on a high podium. Stairs, only in the fron lead to a porch of Corinthian columns.

house, one of the oldest in the town, was based on Etruscan models. The large atrium was the center of the home. A loggia, decorated with Ionic columns, wrapped around the second floor, with bedrooms and offices opening onto it. The atrium roof sloped inward and opened in the center, allowing sunlight and rainwater to enter. Richly decorated with stucco and frescoes, the house likely belonged to a prosperous businessman.

Aqueduct, ca. 100 CE, Segovia

The Romans learned hydraulics from the Etruscans, who had built early sewers to drain Rome's swamps. Using the science of arch building, the Romans were able to engineer monumental aqueducts. This example, built of unmortared granite blocks, towers 92 feet (28 meters) above the streets of Segovia and still carries water 19 miles (30 km) from a spring.

■ **Thermopolium**, ca. 100 CE, Ostia Antica

Restaurants like this served hot food as well as spiced wine from clay jars set in the marble counter. The Romans pioneered the use of concrete to create curved forms. Here, the walls and arches are concrete, poured into a brick veneer that served as a framework and molded the concrete to look like bricks. The mosaics that adorn the building's floors were a Greek innovation.

Early Roman Architecture

The Colosseum

When Emperor Vespasian came to power in 69 CE, Rome was in a state of chaos. In order to appease the masses, he announced the construction of an enormous public amphitheater. His sons Titus and Domitian succeeded him as emperor, creating the Flavian dynasty and giving the building its official name, the Flavian Amphitheater. When the amphitheater opened in 80 CE, the historian Dio Cassius wrote that Rome celebrated with 100 days of games during which 9,000 animals were killed. For centuries, the Colosseum witnessed staged battles between man and beast and man against man, and was even flooded for mock naval battles. Built to seat 50,000 spectators, its efficient system of tiered seating and spacious passageways remains a model for stadium design to the present day. Later damaged by fire and earthquakes, the Colosseum was abandoned, and its walls were used as a marble quarry. In 1749 Pope Benedict XIV called for its preservation as a shrine to the early Christians martyred there. Today the Colosseum is a vivid monument to the aspirations and decadence of imperial Rome.

The oval shape of the Colosseum's arena floor prevented combatants from backing into corners. Two years after it opened, Emperor Domitian ordered the construction of a network of tunnels below the floor where gladiators and animals could be held. Trap doors allowed cages or scenery to be lifted from below. Tunnels connected to aqueducts were used to flood the stage for naval battles, while pipes to the city sewer could later drain it.

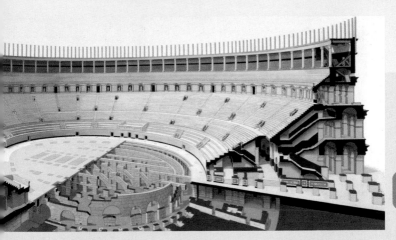

ne Colosseum's three-tiered cade resembles the design of oman aqueducts. The arcades e faced by three-quarter col- umns and entablatures—Doric on the first story; Ionic, second; and Corinthian, third. An attic story has Corinthian pilasters and square windows. At the top, brackets carried the masts from which the *valerium*, a can- opy for shade, was suspended.

■ **The Colosseum**, 72–80 CE, Rome

The Colosseum was built on a drained lake bed in Em- peror Nero's once lavish gardens. A 131-foot (40- meter) statue of Nero stood near the site, and it was this "colossus" that gave the amphitheater its popular name. Over centuries, the bronze statue was remolded to resemble new rulers and in the end melted down, but the name still endures.

Roman Urban Planning

55 BCE–ca. 300 CE

■ City planning ideas were adopted from the Greeks ■ Grid plans were used first for military camps, then for colonial cities ■ Military expansion carried Roman city planning to Europe, Africa, and the Middle East
■ *left:* **City of Ostia**, ca. 100 CE, near Rome

55 BCE Julius Caesar conquers Gaul and invades Britain; his military camps develop into towns

64 CE A fire destroys large areas of Rome; Emperor Nero imposes sweeping changes in the city plan

79 CE Eruption of Mt. Vesuvius buries the cities of Pompeii and Herculaneum

ca. 100–300 CE Provincial cities like Timgad are designed with a rectilinear grid plan based on the designs of Roman military camps

ca. 300 CE Following invasions, a 24-foot- (8-meter-) high brick wall is built around Rome

■ **Palace of Diocletian**, reconstruction, ca. 300 CE, Split

Diocletian built this luxurious palace on the Adriatic Sea after he was forced to retire as emperor in 305 CE. Like a small city, it was divided into four sectors by two main streets, the *cardo* and *decumanus*. Today the remains of the palace have been absorbed into the old town area in Split.

At its height, Rome was a metropolis of nearly a million people. However, the city that had grown organically over centuries was a maze of narrow streets, most just wide enough for a single cart. After a fire in 64 CE, Nero proposed an orderly rebuilding of the city, but had little success. As their empire spread, the Romans seized the opportunity to create new cities from scratch. They designed grid plans based on their military camps, with two wide axis streets, a north-south axis called the *cardo* and an east-west axis known as the *decumanus*. The town center was located at the intersection of the two roads. Like Greek cities, they had a market, temples, and theaters, though the Romans added public baths. A fortified wall often surrounded the city. Houses were usually simple, mud-brick boxes, but prosperous cities like Ostia, a port city near Rome, had brick apartment blocks rising five stories high.

Antiquity and Early Christianity 600 BCE–600 CE

Caesarea Maritima, reconstruction, 25–13 BCE, Israel

Herod the Great was named ruler of Judea in 37 BCE. He spent lavishly to rebuild a small port town into his capital, which he named to please his patron Augustus Caesar. Caesarea was soon the largest port in the eastern Mediterranean and a major site in biblical history as the home of the Roman prefect Pontius Pilate. Its residents enjoyed a spacious plan of gridded streets, a theater, hippodrome, and public baths. An aqueduct brought water from springs. Herod added a temple to Augustus and built his own palace on a promontory in the ocean. Today, much of the city lies underwater.

Other Works
City of Emerita Augusta, ca. 25 CE, now Merida, Spain
City of Camulodunum, ca. 49 CE, now Colchester, UK
Ruined City of Herculaneum, 79 CE, Italy
City of Timgad, ca. 100 CE, Algeria

■ **Typical Housing Block**, reconstruction, ca. 79 CE, Pompeii

Pompeii was buried under volcanic ash after the eruption of Mt. Vesuvius in 79 CE. Archaeologists who uncovered the ruins found a snapshot of Roman urban life. Houses were tightly packed together, and spaces along the streets were rented as stores or workshops. Rather than having windows to the outside, rooms were arranged around interior courtyards or roofed atria, which had openings to let in sunlight and rainwater. Rear courtyards were gardened family sanctuaries.

Roman Urban Planning

Roman Empire

44 BCE–312 CE

■ The Roman Empire's expansion brought new wealth to Rome ■ Emperors built monuments to glorify themselves and please the people ■ Concrete allowed for new architectural forms such as vaults, arches, and domes ■ *left*: **Interior of the Pantheon**, ca. 125 CE, Rome

■ **44 BCE** Murder of Julius Caesar

27 BCE–14 CE Reign of Augustus Caesar

64 CE Great Fire of Rome destroys much of the city

64–68 CE Emperor Nero builds his Domus Aurea

82 CE Colosseum completed

ca. 120 CE Emperor Hadrian builds his villa in Tivoli

ca. 125 CE Pantheon built

216 CE Baths of Caracalla completed

312 CE Constantine becomes emperor and converts to Christianity

■ **Pantheon**, ca. 125 CE, Rome

Originally a temple dedicated to the seven Roman gods, the Pantheon is a daring early example of concrete construction. The interior space is based on a perfect sphere, and its coffered ceiling is still the largest nonreinforced concrete dome in the world. In the center of the dome, an oculus allows a beam of light to shine in. Now a Christian church, the Pantheon is the best preserved building of its era.

The Roman Republic ended with the murder of Julius Caesar and the naming of his adopted son Augustus Caesar as Rome's first emperor. During his 41-year reign, Augustus spent lavishly to improve the capital city of his empire, claiming to have turned a city built of brick into a city of marble. He encouraged the use of Greek architectural styles, and during his reign the Corinthian order became the standard for Roman public buildings. Over the next 300 years, succeeding emperors followed Augustus' example by building monuments to please the gods and impress the Roman people. The city's central forum was a favored and prominent location for monuments, including grand temples and triumphal arches. Roman architects developed innovations to expand on the Classical vocabulary inherited from the Greeks. They combined

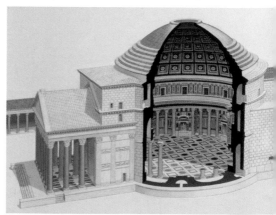

Antiquity and Early Christianity 600 BCE–600 CE

Daily Life on the Forum Romanum at the Beginning of the 3rd Century, color print

The main forum in Rome was the pulsing heart of the city and center of the empire. Long basilicas defined the sides of its rectangular plan. Over time, as temples and monuments were added, the space took on visual drama and variety.

Other Works

Mausoleum of Augustus, 28 BCE, Rome

Domus Aurea, by Severus and Celer, 64–68 CE, Rome

Hadrian's Villa, ca. 120 CE, Tivoli

Mausoleum of Hadrian, 135 CE, Rome

Arch of Severus, 205 CE, Rome

■ **Roman Forum**, 1st century BCE–3rd century CE

As the empire collapsed, Rome's buildings fell into ruin. Gold and bronze were stripped off, columns were carted away for reuse, and marble was burned for cement. By the 8th century, the former heart of the empire had become a cow pasture. Excavation of the temples and buildings continues today.

Roman Empire

arches with Greek styles in projects such as the Colosseum. Colonial expansion carried Roman architecture to the far reaches of the empire. Temples, amphitheaters, and public baths served the citizens of Roman cities in Europe, Africa, and Asia Minor. Arched bridges and aqueducts improved trade and sanitation. The invention of concrete in the 1st century BCE freed Roman architects from the limitations of post-and-lintel construction. They created daring new forms like the great dome of the Pantheon and the vast vaulted spaces of public baths. However, these ambitious monuments often pushed Roman engineering skills past their limits. Ultimately, many of the buildings, like the empire, collapsed.

■ **Baths of Caracalla**, reconstruction, 212–216 CE, Rome

Roman public baths required large interior spaces free of support columns. At the bath sponsored by the emperor Caracalla, a sequence of pools—from hot to warm to cold—was housed in spaces with appropriately fluid forms. These spaces pushed the limit of the Romans' skills with concrete. The largest room, the vaulted tepidarium, measured 82 x 164 feet (25 x 50 meters), with a ceiling height of 125 fe (38 meters). A complex system of piping and coal-fired heate lay beneath the baths. The complex could hold 16,000 people and included a gymnasium, shops, and two libraries.

■ **Vitruoya: Library of Celsus**, ca. 110–135 CE, Ephesus

The library at Ephesus has a monumentality that belies its small size. It was built to honor Celsus Polemeanus, a governor whose tomb lies beneath it.

Marble steps lead to the unusual facade with two levels of columned bays capped by alternating triangular and curved pediments. To emphasize the main entry, the base curves up toward the middle, and the

Corinthian columns of the center bay have larger capitals Inside, 12,000 scrolls were stor in specially designed niches in wall separated from the exterio walls by cavities, which provide protection from moisture.

■ Basilica of Maxentius, 308–312 CE, Rome

The Basilica was the largest building in the Roman Forum. The three remaining barrel vaults that composed the north aisle were only a third of the building. A central nave ran down the middle, with a matching vaulted aisle on the south. Basilicas were meeting places for lawyers and politicians. Earlier versions had simple flat roofs. The brick-faced concrete arches and vaults show the influence of public baths.

Arch of Titus, ca. 81 CE, Rome

The Arch of Titus, in the Roman Forum, is the oldest surviving Roman triumphal arch. Such arches were first built during the Roman Republic as temporary structures to celebrate military victories.

During the empire, permanent arches were built of marble with fine detailing, often using the Corinthian order. A total of 36 arches were built in Rome, though only 5 remain. The Arch of Titus was built after the young emperor's death to commemorate his defeat of an uprising in Judea in 70 CE. A relief sculpture inside the arch shows the emperor carrying spoils from the destroyed temple in Jerusalem. The arch was originally capped by a bronze chariot and horses.

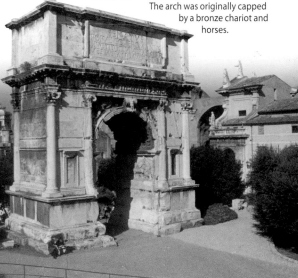

63

Antiquity

Roman Empire

Early Christian Architecture

ca. 230–450

■ Early Christians congregated in houses rather than in churches ■ Emperor Constantine had churches built throughout the empire ■ The Roman basilica was used as the model for early churches

■ *left:* **Palace Basilica of Constantine**, 310, Trier

ca. 230 Persecuted Christians worship secretly in homes serving as churches

312 Emperor Constantine legalizes the practice of Christianity and builds the first basilica churches, modeled after the basilica of his own palace

325 St. Peter's Church in Rome is built, with a transept giving the building a T-shaped plan, inspiring later cross-shaped churches

325–450 Conversion to Christianity increases, and basilica churches are built throughout the Roman Empire

Other Works

Christian House Church, ca. 232, Dura-Europos

St. Peter's Basilica, ca. 324–335, Rome

Church of the Holy Sepulcher, ca. 335, Jerusalem

St. Paolo Fuori le Mura, 386–395, Rome

St. Maria Maggiore, ca. 432–440, Rome

When Constantine became Roman emperor, Christianity was a small cult whose persecuted followers were forced to meet in secret. Constantine's decision to embrace Christianity after a religious vision changed the course of architectural history. Unlike pagan worship, Christianity needed a large interior space. As a model, Constantine chose a Roman basilica that was part of his palace. The basilica, a roofed meeting hall, served many purposes including throne room. By replacing his throne in the apse with an altar, Constantine transformed the basilica into the first Christian church. He went on to found many churches, including the first St. Peter's in Rome.

■ **Palace Basilica of Constantine**, 310, Trier

When Emperor Constantine built his provincial palace in Trier, this building was his throne room. It is the largest surviving single-room Roman structure. Most earlier basilicas were entered through a door on one long side, but the entrance of Constantine's basilica was situated at one end. Visitors walked the long axis to his throne at the other end. This axis later evolved into the nave of churches.

■ Mausoleum of St. Costanza, ca. 360, Rome

Built as a tomb for Constantine's daughters Costanza and Helena, this round brick building was later turned into a church and named after Costanza. Twelve pairs of marble Corinthian columns support a central dome, illuminated by clerestory windows. The building's circular plan, ambulatory, and dome inspired centrally planned Byzantine churches. Domes were also incorporated into basilica churches, such as in the Church of the Holy Sepulcher in Jerusalem.

Basilica Church of St. Sabina all'Aventino, 2–432, Rome

ilt in the basilica form, St. bina all'Aventino is unusually light, thanks to the large clerestory windows along the length of the building. The church's wooden front doors are original and contain some of the ear- liest depictions of Christ. The Corinthian columns may have come from the Temple of Juno Regina, which stood on the nearby Aventine Hill.

Byzantine Architecture

330–554

■ Constantinople (now Istanbul) was founded ■ Ravenna became the western capital of the Roman Empire ■ New structural techniques were used for Hagia Sophia ■ Buildings were decorated with mosaics
■ *left:* **Church of St. Vitale**, ceiling vaults, 527–548, Ravenna, Italy

■ **330** Byzantium becomes the capital of the Roman Empire

395 The Roman Empire is divided into western and eastern empires

402 The capital of the western empire is moved to Ravenna, a small but easily defended Italian city near the Adriatic Sea

532–37 Eastern Emperor Justinian builds the church of Hagia Sophia in Constantinople

554 Rome is reduced to a camp of about 30,000 people, while Constantinople has about 1 million people

The city of Rome was weak and militarily vulnerab when Emperor Constantine dedicated his "New Rome" the Greek city of Byzantium, later called Constantinop Soon after, the Roman Empire was split in two, with se arate capital cities for each half—Constantinople in th east and the Italian city of Ravenna in the west. Amon the structures from this period, Hagia Sophia in Istanb is exceptional both for its scale and the technical darin of its construction. The monuments of Ravenna, a though smaller, are nevertheless renowned for their flu space and stunning mosaic decoration. Unlike earli Roman floor mosaics made with stone, Byzantine m saics were made from glass, either in brilliant colors layered with gold leaf. The ceiling vaults of the octa onal Church of St. Vitale in Ravenna appear to dissolv replaced by angels, animals, and holy apostles floating a sea of heavenly light.

■ **Mausoleum of Galla Placidia**, 425–430, Ravenna, Italy

This small tomb for the daugh of Emperor Theodosius I, built the form of a Greek cross, is th earliest and best preserved of Ravenna's mosaic monument The vaulted ceilings and cupo are covered with glass and go leaf tiles depicting a beardless Jesus Christ and his 12 apostle as well as fanciful geometric motifs. The windows are pane of translucent stone.

Anthemios and Isidoros: Hagia Sophia, interior, [5]32–537, Istanbul

[Af]ter mobs destroyed the [ca]thedral of Constantinople in [53]2, Emperor Justinian vowed [to] rebuild on a monumental [sc]ale. He gave his architects the [dif]ficult task of placing a round [do]me on a square-planned [ch]urch. Their daring solution [wa]s to use concave triangular [se]ctions of masonry, called pen[de]ntives, that carry the dome's [we]ight to corner piers. The [rib]bed dome rises 184 feet (56 [m]eters) and seemingly floats [ov]er a row of small windows. [Em]bellished with multicolored [ma]rble and gold mosaics, the [bu]ilding is both a culmination [of] Roman architectural ambi[tio]ns and an inspiration for later [bu]ildings. Orthodox churches [to]day use the central plan and [do]me, and Islamic shrines, like [th]e Sultan Ahmed Mosque, are [mo]deled after it.

■ **Anthemios and Isidoros: Hagia Sophia**, exterior, 532–537, Istanbul

Perhaps due to its daring design or shortcuts taken in its construction, the dome of Hagia Sophia collapsed after an earthquake in 563 and was replaced with the current version. Later, the support walls were rebuilt and heavily reinforced. Crusaders sacked the city in 1204, leaving the building badly damaged. In 1453, it was converted to a mosque, and Christian mosaics were plastered over. Now a museum, the building has been restored.

Byzantine Architecture

Pre-Mughal Architecture

3300 BCE–ca. 500 CE

■ The city of Harappa flourished in the Indus River valley ■ Invasions brought new
technology, architectural styles, and religion ■ Hinduism, Jainism, and Buddhism in
spired cave temples and stupa mounds ■ Buddhism spread styles throughout Asia.
■ *left:* **Cave Temples at Ajanta**, 450–500 CE

■ **ca. 3300–1300 BCE** The Harappan cities flourish in the Indus River valley

500 BCE Invasion by the Persians brings the techniques for stonework and sculpture

268–231 BCE Reign of Emporer Ashoka, a Buddhist convert who builds stupas and other shrines

ca. 100–800 CE The style of stone-carved temples develops

ca. 500 CE The largest Buddhist university in the world is built at Nalanda

■ **Great Stupa at Sanchi**, 200 BCE–200 CE, near Bhopal in Madhya Pradesh State

A stupa is a brick and plaster hemisphere, usually containing a relic or marking an important site. The earliest existing example of a Buddhist stupa, the Sanchi stupa was dedicated by Emperor Ashoka. The simple mound was embellished with gates facing the four directions. Though carved from stone, the walls are fashioned after wood.

While ancient Mesopotamia and Egypt flourished, a small
civilization took root in the fertile Indus River valley. Citi
such as Harappa and Mohenjo-Daro in western India an
Pakistan had sophisticated urban planning, and ameniti
such as public sewers. Centuries of invasions, first by th
Aryans, and later by the Persians and Greeks, resulted in a
eclectic Indian culture that drew styles, innovations, and in
spiration from other advanced cultures. When the Gree
retreated in 322 BCE, the Indian leader Chandragup
Maurya reconquered lands and founded the Mauryan d
nasty. His grandson, Ashoka, embraced Buddhism, leadin
to the creation of monuments and temples. With th
spread of Buddhism throughout much of Asia, early Indi
architectural styles shaped the continent.

Antiquity and Early Christianity

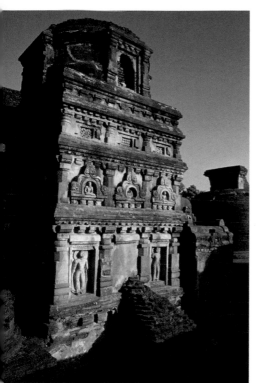

■ **Corner Tower of the Stupa of Sariputra**, ca. 500 CE, Nalanda, Bihar State

Nalanda was home to one of the world's earliest and largest universities—a center of Buddhist study containing monasteries, temples, and a library. The tower sits next to a stupa marking the remains of Sariputra, one of Buddha's disciples. Masterfully sculpted, it was later the source of a utilitarian, structural design for free-standing buildings.

■ **Rock-Carved Temple at Ellora**, ca. 350–700 CE, Maharashtra State

India has a long tradition of temples carved into the sides of stone cliffs. The complex at Ellora includes hundreds of shrines built by followers of the three faiths—Hinduism, Buddhism, and Jainism. The rooms, decorated with rows of elaborate columns and reliefs, served as large meeting halls for monks and visiting pilgrims. Architectural styles differ depending on the religious use.

Other Important Works	
ncient City of arappa, . 3300–1600 BCE, ınjab, Pakistan	Buddhist Cave Temples and Carvings at Karli, ca.100 BCE, Karli, Maharashtra State
ncient City of ohenjo-Daro, . 2600–1700 BCE, kkur, Pakistan	Stupa at Amravati, ca. 100 BCE, Amravati, Maharashtra State
ncient City of ataliputra, one remains from . 273 BCE, near Patna, har State	Stupa at Nagarjunakonda, ca. 200–300 CE, Nagarjunakonda, Andhra Pradesh State

Pre-Mughal Architecture

Early Buddhist Architecture

ca. 520 BCE–594 CE

■ Emperor Ashoka built commemorative columns and stupas ■ Monastic complexes flourished in Sri Lanka and Nepal ■ Stupas evolved into decorative towers ■ Buddhism and Buddhist architecture spread via the Silk Road
■ *left:* **Dhamekh Stupa**, 500 CE, Sarnak, India

ca. 520 BCE Buddhism is founded by Siddhartha Gautama

ca. 250 BCE Indian emperor Ashoka converts to Buddhism

68 CE Emperor Ming builds the first Buddhist temple in China

ca. 150 CE Indian ruler Kanishka builds a stupa, inspiring later pagodas

594 CE Empress Suiko embraces Buddhism in Japan

For more than 200 years after its conception, Buddhism was merely a small denomination within Hinduism. This changed when the Indian emperor Ashoka embraced the Buddhist philosophy of pacifism and converted to the religion. He marked important sites in the life of the founder Siddhartha Gautama by erecting stone columns and building stupas—simple brick or stone mounds. His campaign to spread Buddhism throughout Asia enjoyed great success and led to the proliferation of Buddhist architecture. The Sri Lankan king also converted and built many stupas and Buddhist monasteries. Over centuries, the domelike stupas grew upward into towering structures. As the religion spread east along the Silk Road, these masonry towers evolved into the delicate wooden temples and towering pagodas of China and Japan.

■ **Swayambunath Stupa**, ca. 500 CE, Kathmandu, Nepal

Nepal, the Buddha's birthplace, was one of the first countries to adopt Buddhism. Early Buddhist stupas were simple, dome-shaped mounds. Though a stupa might contain a relic, pilgrims do not enter it but rather walk around it while praying. The stupa is a diagram of the cosmos: the dome represents heaven sheltering the world, and the spire of golden disks, here sitting on a cube painted with the eyes of Buddha, symbolizes a succession of higher heavens leading to the ultimate paradise. These decorative towers, or *chatri*, evolved into the layered, multiroofed pagoda form, first in Nepal and later in the Far East.

Pagoda at the Kofuku-ji Temple, ca. 600 CE, Nara, Japan

Pilgrims from China and Japan traveled on the Silk Road to India, where they visited holy Buddhist sites. Upon their return, inspired by the towering masonry stupas that they had seen there, they erected the tall and slender wooden pagodas that are typical of Japanese and Chinese Buddhist architecture. The five-tier pagoda at the Kofuku-ji Temple in Nara is one of the oldest wooden buildings in the world. Structurally, the tower resembles five boxes stacked one atop the other. The heavy overhanging roof eaves give the building stability, serving as balancing counterweights at each level. The three-ton spire atop the structure holds the uppermost levels in place and centralizes the building's weight. Originally built at Kyoto, the pagoda has interlocking posts and beams that were dismantled when the entire 164-foot-tall (50-meter-tall) structure was reassembled in Nara when it was made the imperial capital in 710 CE. Each level of the pagoda contains a small crystal tower and the ground floor has four statues of the Buddha.

Other Important Works	
Maya Devi Temple and Gardens, ca. 300 BCE, Lumbini, Nepal	Dambulla Cave Temple and Monastery, ca. 100–300 CE, Sri Lanka
Stone Columns Built by Emperor Ashoka, ca. 245 BCE, India and Nepal	Kanishka's Stupa, ca. 150 CE, Peshawar, Pakistan
White Horse Temple, 68 CE, Luoyang, Henan Province, China	Rock-Carved Temples at Ajanta, 450–500 CE, Maharashtra State, India

■ **Stupas**, begun 161 BCE, Holy City of Anuradhapura, Sri Lanka

In the 2nd century BCE, Anuradhapura was a center of Buddhist worship. Monasteries and stupas covered an area of over 25 miles (40 km). The five elements of the stupa form can be clearly seen: a square base, a hemispherical dome, a conical spire, a crescent moon, and a circular disc. Together, these represent the crowned Buddha on his throne.

Early Buddhist Architecture

Early Chinese Architecture

220 BCE–700 CE

■ Neolithic Chinese built villages and tombs ■ China was unified, and construction of the Great Wall began ■ Classic Chinese architectural styles developed under the Han dynasty ■ The arrival of Buddhism inspired early temples ■ The pagoda form appeared ■ Buddhist shrines were carved into cliffs

220 BCE Emperor Qin Shi Huang first unifies China under the Qin dynasty; his mausoleum complex in Xian covers 1.3 square miles (2 square km)

206 BCE–220 CE During the Han dynasty many classic Chinese building styles first appear

ca. 100–700 CE Buddhist Chinese-style pagodas and temples are built throughout the unified empire

For centuries, China's vast area was populated by remo[te] tribes, some nomadic and others living in farming villag[es] surrounded by stamped-earth walls. In 220 BCE, China wa[s] unified, and parts of the Great Wall were constructed t[o] protect the country's borders.

Under the Han dynasty, the classic style of Chinese a[r]chitecture developed. Palaces and temples were laid o[ut] symmetrically. A grid of round columns supported a larg[e] horizontal roof with upturned eaves. Light, nonstructur[al] walls served as screens against the elements. The India[n] stupa form was combined with the Chinese *lou*, a mult[i]story watchtower, to create Buddhist pagodas.

Antiquity and Early Christianity

Pagoda, 669 CE, at Xingjiao Buddhist Temple, Shaanxi Province

A combination of the layered Indian stupa tower and Chinese watchtowers, the first Chinese pagodas were built of wood and square in plan. Later pagodas were octagonal or round. This early brick pagoda marking the burial site of Xuanzang, a pilgrim who brought Buddhist scriptures back from India, has distinctly Chinese features such as projecting roof eaves.

Other Works

Qin Shi Huang Mausoleum, 207 BCE, Xian, Shaanxi Province

Mogao Caves, begun ca. 400 CE, Dunhuang, Gansu Province

Longmen Caves, begun ca. 500 CE, Henan Province

Songyue Temple Pagoda, 520 CE, Dengfeng, Henan Province

Four Gates Pagoda, 611 CE, Licheng, Shandong Province

Great Wall of China, 500 BCE–1600 CE

The world's longest man-made structure, the Great Wall began as a series of rammed-earth fortifications. Successive emperors marked changing borders by extending the wall using stone and brick. The present wall dates from the 15th century. In 1449 CE, the Mongols in the north defeated the Ming dynasty, who had rebuilt the wall to protect their capital, Beijing.

■ **Pavilion at Old Dragon Head (Lao Long Tou)**, ca. 220–210 BCE, near Shanhaiguan

Situated at the starting point of the Great Wall, the Old Dragon Head was built under Emperor Qin and renovated in the 15th century. Multilevel buildings first appeared in China under the earlier Han dynasty, and Emperor Qin, whose massive building campaigns also include the Terracotta Warriors, spread the upturned eaves and steep roofed style throughout China.

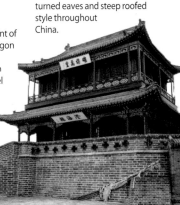

Early Chinese Architecture

Mesoamerican Architecture

1200 BCE–900 CE

■ The Olmec developed written language, a calendar, and built the first cities in Mesoamerica ■ Pyramids, symbols of power and religious devotion, dominated cities ■ Built without using advanced technologies
■ *left:* **Pyramid of the Sun**, ca. 100 CE, Teotihuacán, Mexico

■ **1200–400 BCE** The Olmec thrive on the Mexican Gulf Coast

ca. 100 BCE The Mayan city of Teotihuacán is founded not far from present-day Mexico City; Mesoamerica enters its classic period

ca. 600 CE An unknown event destroys the civilization at Teotihuacán

900 CE Classic period of Mayan culture ends; most cities are abandoned, but cities in the Yucatán, including Chichen Itza, continue to thrive

■ **Palenque**, ca. 600 CE, Chiapas, Mexico

High in the mountains of central Mexico, Palenque has some of the finest surviving Mayan architectural and sculptural examples. This palace, with its unusual four-story tower, has distinctive steeply pitched roofs. Broad openings in the stone walls give the buildings a feeling of lightness and airiness. The site includes temples and an aqueduct, which redirected a nearby river to flow under the main plaza.

Antiquity and Early Christianity

Pre-Columbian cultures in Mesoamerica developed simil[ar] architectural styles through cultural exchanges. Similariti[es] between the cultures include iconographic decoration[,] pyramid construction, and city layouts that were heavi[ly] influenced by the cardinal directions. Despite lacking tec[h]nologies such as metal tools and pulley systems, Mesoame[r]icans constructed limestone post-and-lintel structures an[d] used stepped arches that without keystones. The first civ[i]lization in the Americas, the Olmec, built cities along th[e] fertile Mexican Gulf Coast, but disappeared around 400 BC[E.] About 500 years later, nearby Teotihuacán grew into th[e] largest city in the Americas, with power comparable to tha[t] of Rome. Laid out on a neat grid, the city housed 150,00[0] people, and had markets, baths, and ball courts.

■ Pyramid of the Sun,
ca. 100 CE, Teotihuacán, Mexico

The Pyramid of the Sun served as an archetype for later temples. The pyramid marked one end of the main axis of the city. A twin structure, the Pyramid of the Moon, was erected at the opposite end. This style of stepped, flat-topped pyramid, known as *talud-tablero*, was adopted by other civilizations in the area.

■ Temple of the Mask,
ca. 700 CE, Tikal, Guatemala

The Mayan city of Tikal grew to a population of 100,000 and covered 23 square miles (60 square km). Its large temple complex contains many limestone pyramids, some as high as 230 feet (70 meters). The pyramids contained tombs for the Mayan rulers and were topped by temples. Evidence shows they were finished with brightly painted plaster, and some even had stucco masks adorning the walls.

Other Important Works

Olmec City of La Venta, ca. 900–400 BCE, Tabasco State, Mexico

Mayan City of El Mirador, ca. 500 BCE–ca. 100 CE, El Petén, Guatemala

Mayan City of Uaxactun, ca. 500 BCE–ca. 400 CE, Petén, Guatemala

Great Pyramid of Cholula, ca. 200 BCE–1200 CE, Puebla State, Mexico

Totonac City of El Tajín, ca. 100–1300 CE, Vera Cruz, Mexico

Mayan City of Altun Ha, ca. 200–900 CE, Belize District, Belize

Mayan City of Copán, ca. 400–800 CE, Honduras

Mayan City of Calakmul, ca. 400–800 CE, Campeche, Mexico

Mayan City of Uxmal, ca. 700–1100 CE, Yucatán State, Mexico

Early Architecture in the Americas

Romanesque

790–1140

Benedictine Abbey Church of Maria Laach,
begun 1093, near Andernach

Romanesque

790–1030
Carolingian and Early Romanesque in Germany

The spread of Christianity requires new architectural styles; in Germany, building techniques develop according to functional needs in monasteries and churches

p. 84

800	850	900

800–1140
Late Romanesque in Spain and Italy

Romanesque architecture develops in churches along pilgrimage routes; thick-wall construction fortifies civic buildings and castles; in Spain the style is influenced by Moorish architectural styles

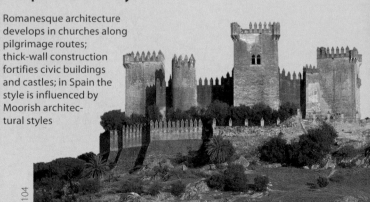

p. 104

Around the World:
Asia and
the Americas

While the spread of Buddhism in the Far East spreads the pagoda form, Muslim architects begin developing mosque architecture in the Middle East; in South America religious fervor leads to the building of massive pyramids

1000   1050   1100

1000–1140
High Romanesque
in France and
the UK

The monastery of Cluny in France is one of the most influential buildings; the Norman invasion spreads the style to the UK

p. 99

Origins of Medieval Architecture

Around the time of Charlemagne, the main centers of power in the Middle Ages were Constantinople, Baghdad, Cordoba, and Aachen. These political spheres also defined areas of cultural and religious influence. The capital of the Byzantine Empire, Constantinople, was the bastion of Christianity in the East, while Rome and Aachen became the foci in the West. Baghdad and Cordoba were the hubs of the Islamic world. Architecturally these regions were separate, but there was an exchange of information and skilled laborers. Constantinople traded with Italian city-states and with the caliphate in Cordoba, which meant that Byzantine craftsmen produced mosaics for monasteries in Italy and mosques in Spain. Meanwhile, Italy enjoyed the protection of the Carolingian Empire, and surviving Roman buildings served as models for Carolingian architecture.

■ **Great Mosque** entrance, begun 785, Cordoba, Spain

■ **Gatehouse of the Lorsch Monastery**, detail, ca. 792–805, Rhineland, Germany

St. Cyriakus, westwork, ~983, Genrode, Germany

St. Pantaleon, interior of westwork, ca. 966–980, Cologne, Germany

From Carolingian to Romanesque

The evolution of the church from Carolingian times to the mature Romanesque of Speyer or Cluny reflected the changing needs of the church and state. Contrary to the mosque, which had very few architectural needs and could be enlarged at will, the church was planned from the start as a finite building, and major changes involved total reconstruction. New functional requirements resulted in a recombination of parts, generating new plans. The aisled basilica, known from Roman times, was revived, as well as the centrally planned church. The Palatine Chapel was based on St. Vitale in Ravenna, and the Abbey Church of Fulda on Old St. Peter's in Rome. Complex Christian liturgy combined with specific political symbolism required appropriate architectural responses. Consequently, the westwork, transept, apse, or crypt was rethought by each generation of builders.

Introduction

Elements of Architecture

Certain elements, like the westwork, were Carolingian inventions, but the apse existed in pre-Christian times, and the transept had already appeared in the 4th century. These architectural elements often combined practical and symbolic needs. For example, the westwork consisted of a narthex and chapel, where the monarch participated in services. For this reason, it was symbolic of secular power within the church. The semicircular apse was used in secular buildings of ancient Rome and later in early Christian churches. It subsequently evolved into a convenient way to house altars and relics at the periphery of the church without disrupting their role as a focal point within the space they occupied. The ambulatory that used to circle the crypt underground was moved up and integrated with the aisles to provide a path for masses of pilgrims to visit holy relics.

■ **Speyer Cathedral**, 1030–1106 Germany

■ **Paray-le-Monial** choir with radiating chapels, 1090–1 France

Romanesque 790–1140

Fontevraud Abbey, cloister, th century, ance

Rochester stle, keep, 12th ntury, Kent, UK

Medieval Institutions

The cathedral, the monastery, and the castle developed as distinct building types representing the religious and administrative centers of power in medieval Europe. Each type evolved more or less separately under different geopolitical circumstances. The cathedral derived from the early Christian basilica and thrived in urban centers. The monastery flourished during the Carolingian era as a hub of rural administration. Finally, the castle evolved later as a response to the unstable political climate of the 10th and 11th centuries. These three basic building types persisted and evolved throughout the Middle Ages. Small forts turned into elaborate citadels that formed complex systems of defense. Humble monastic institutions grew into influential abbeys. Cathedrals were consistently enlarged and upgraded, symbolic of the power of both bishops and kings.

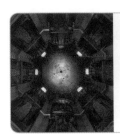

Carolingian Renaissance

800–ca. 871

■ Carolingian monarch Charlemagne promoted architecture based on early Christian models ■ In size, organization, and detail, buildings reflected canonical Roman works ■ The basilica was reintroduced as an architectural form
■ *left:* **Odo of Metz: Palatine Chapel**, octagonal dome, ca. 790–ca. 800, Aachen

■ **800** Charlemagne crowned Holy Roman Emperor in St. Peter's, Rome; the Palatine Chapel is dedicated

814 Charlemagne dies

820 Plan for an ideal monastery drawn at St. Gall, establishing a model for medieval monasteries

843 Charlemagne's empire is divided

ca. 871 Fall of the Carolingian Empire

Other Works

Monastery of Centula (now Saint-Riquier), ca. 800, near Amiens, France

St. Salvator, 804–875, Werden near Essen, Germany

Church of Germigny-des-Prés, 806, near Saint-Benoît-sur-Loire, France

Abbey Church of Fulda, 821, Germany

Church of Saint-Germain, 841–859, Auxerre, France

■ **Gatehouse of the Lorsch Monastery**, ca. 792–805, Lorsch, Germany

This gatehouse stood at

Romanesque 790–1140

In a strategic effort to develop an empire with a culture to rival that of Rome, Charlemagne spread culture to maintain cohesion throughout the Holy Roman Empire. The Benedictine monasteries that he set up were often the only source of social structure in an otherwise dispersed population. By promoting Latin as the official secular and religious language he was able to preserve the Classical texts in circulation. Overtly, not much remains of his architectural legacy. Yet many of the Romanesque and Gothic churches and monasteries functioning today were built on the foundations of Carolingian architecture.

the entrance to the Lorsch Monastery. Scholars debate over the use of its first-floor hall, but morphologically the building is clearly linked to a *westwork*. The elements of a westwork—the arched entrance, the upper hall, and the two stair towers—are recombined here in a creative evocation of the Roman triumphal arch.

Odo of Metz: Palatine Chapel, 800,
chen, Germany

e Palatine Chapel is all that is left of a palatial
mplex built by Charlemagne and based on the
teran in Rome. Charlemagne was clear about
s intentions of inheriting the legacy of the
man Empire and used architecture to assert
at claim. Strongly based on the church of St.
ale in Ravenna, but with a distinctly Carolin-
an simplicity, the chapel is a centralized domed
ilding with arcades that join to an ambulatory
d a double-height gallery.

Church of St. Vitus, westwork, 873–885,
nedictine Abbey at Corvey, Germany

e disposition of programmatic elements in the
estwork gave Carolingian church facades a spe-
c character. The westwork was both function-
y and symbolically the gateway to the church.
at Lorsch, a triple arcade opens onto a low
ulted vestibule flanked by staircases that lead
a double-height chapel space above. The twin-
wered facade of the westwork became a stan-
rd for most Romanesque and Gothic churches
western Europe.

Carolingian Renaissance

Monasteries

The political reality of medieval Europe was complex. There were no cohesiv states and, most importantly, no fixed capitals. Emperors and their courts move from place to place, relying on monasteries to conduct day-to-day administrativ tasks. Although the overarching authorities were the emperor and the pope, i reality it was the local duke, bishop, or abbot who governed. In such a pluralisti geopolitical climate the monastery wa an oasis of organized and compara tively safe life. With their schools, bath and hostels, monasteries catered bot to the local population and to the in creasingly numerous pilgrims.

At Fontenay Abbey in Burgundy, France, the two centers of monastic life were the church and cloister. The upper floor provided residences, and the ambulatory on the ground floor enclosed a garden with a central well. As a Cistercian monastery, the order rejected the increasingly economically and politically driven practices of Cluny in search of a simple life based on work and prayer. They built dams, mills, and factories within their abbeys, and their architecture was appropriately utilitarian. Somewhat akin to modern Functionalism, walls were plain, vaults were of stone, and decoration was minimal.

ideal monastery was nned under Charle- gne. The objective of the sign was to organize and arate the various users of onastery. At its center

La Grande Chartreuse, unded 1084, near enoble, France

unded in the 11th cen- y, the abbey was there- er repeatedly destroyed

were the monks in the church and cloister; to the north, the school and houses for the abbot and visitors; and to the south, the barns and workers' lodgings.

and rebuilt. Its present form dates from the 1600s, but follows the original Carthu- sian guidelines, showing the lasting impact of medieval monastic architecture.

Ottonian Cathedrals

936–ca. 1030

■ Under Otto I the reinstated Holy Roman Empire built the earliest Romanesque churches ■ Ottonian cathedrals refined Carolingian styles ■ The Carolingian westwork was revived and expanded
■ *left*: **Capital at St. Michael**, begun 1010, Hildesheim, Germany

■ **936–973** Reign of Otto I

1000 Structural bay system emerges at St. Gertrude in Nivelles

1001 Systematization of the cathedral plan and section along square modules at St. Michael in Hildesheim

1015 First bronze doors since Roman times, cast for St. Michael, Hildesheim

ca. 1030 Romanesque style matures

After the relative stability of the early 9th century and th renaissance of Classical architecture in western Europ under the auspices of the Carolingian Empire, the ne stable period began with the reign of Otto I in 936. Li Charlemagne, the Ottonian emperors understood that strong church was an important element in maintainir political control over their large territories. The late 9 century brought the Vikings, Magyars, and Arabs, ar with them, the destruction of monasteries and churche There were massive rebuilding campaigns to repair th empire that were carried out on a larger scale than eve before. New roads and bridges leadir between rebuilt monasteries mea that pilgrims could travel to holy des nations. Larger groups meant larg churches, and the evolutionary proce of the Carolingian basilica continued

■ **St. Cyriakus**, 961–983, Gernrode, Germany

Understanding the early Romanesque interior i the key to following the development of ecclesiastical architecture in Europe. Some elements were borrowed directly from Roman or Byzanti precedents, others were adopted from Carolingian churches, and some were Romanesque reterpretations. At St. Cyriakus, tribune galleries run above the side aisles, completely changing the proportions of the nave wall. Instead of the frieze that traditionally separated the ground-floor arcading from the clerestory above, a second level of smaller, tightly spaced arcades was introduced. The nave achieves further dynamis through alternating square piers and columns.

St. Pantaleon, westwork, 966–980, Cologne, Germany

tonian churches strove to stematize spatial relationps. Carolingian architecture ovided strong regional precents, with the westwork resuring as a display of military d imperial power within the urch. Cathedrals began to ve two fully developed apsed ds, complete with transepts d towers, making it more agmatic to enter the church ng the side aisles. The basic ments of the basilica—nave, e aisles, transept, choir, and se—were articulated as sepae volumes. Towers were cted over the increasingly portant transept crossing, in dition to the ones often nking the east and west ends. Pantaleon is one of the few viving examples of an Otton westwork. The church es not have an apse, so inad an arched entrance is still sent below the chapel, ere the traveling monarch uld worship and rest.

St. Michael, south elevation, gun 1010, Hildesheim, many

it. Michael, the elements of a basilica are extruded to form distinct solids. The church looks as if it were constructed from large blocks. The power of Ottonian architecture lies precisely in its geometric clarity. These majestic buildings must have inspired confidence.

Other Important Works	
Abbey Church of Gernrode, 959–963, Germany	St. Gertrude, begun 1000, Nivelles, Belgium
Mainz Cathedral, begun 978, Germany	St. Bartholomew, 1017, Paderborn, Germany
Essen Cathedral, late 10th century, Germany	Limburg an der Haardt, 1025, Germany

German High Romanesque

ca. 1030–ca. 1190

■ High Romanesque evolved from Ottonian architecture ■ Romanesque construction was heavy, with thick walls and monumental piers supporting tall naves ■ Many Romanesque churches were modified or reconstructed ■ *left*: **Speyer Cathedral**, interior, ca. 1030–1106

■ **ca. 1030** High Romanesque is established in Germany with the building of Speyer Cathedral

ca. 1050 Romanesque churches begin to be built along pilgrimage routes throughout Germany

1063–78 The Cloister of Our Dear Lady in Magdeburg is rebuilt to include three naves running down a cruciform layout

ca. 1190 After Saint-Denis is built in Paris in 1140, Gothic styles begin to spread throughout Europe, finally replacing Romanesque as the dominant style in Germany 50 years later

Although the particular stylistic direction a church too depended on the political power that was behind its con mission as well as regional influences and tradition German Romanesque remained surprisingly uniform. T volumes seen in Ottonian churches and the basic spat organization remained the same. Plans became increa ingly rigorous, but it was the evolution of the nave w that took precedence. With Speyer Cathedral, Germa developed a mature Romanesque style that would la for centuries, even while other parts of Europe had a ready adopted Gothic styles. At Speyer the nave wall i fused to remain flat. The arcade grew taller, the main pie became larger and supported a layered wall of bli arches, pilasters, and shafts. In a later building phase, t original timber roof was replaced with a stone vault vided into bays. The nave wall was remodeled to refle the new structural logic.

■ **Speyer Cathedral**, aerial view, ca. 1030–1106

Medieval churches were built a specific geopolitical contex Along with the monastery, th cathedral was one of the two centers of life in the Holy Roman Empire. As the seat of bishop, it was a source of rea administrative power for the gion. The market square facir the west end of Speyer was t secular manifestation of that power, and it stood, with the cathedral, in the heart of the c

Benedictine Abbey Church Maria Laach, begun 1093, Andernach

...ly 1,000 years old, Maria ...ch is still a functioning Bene...ne monastery. Six heavy ...rs rise from the surround-

Mainz Cathedral, early 11th ...ury

...thick Romanesque exterior ...ainz Cathedral is more var-...han that of Maria Laach. ...galleries supporting the ...s in the apse and crossing ...r expose the depth of the ...ive walls. The cathedral is ...posed of red sandstone ...has been added to succes-...y in Gothic and Baroque ...signs.

ing fields. In pairs they mark, terminate, or reinforce the horizontal elements of the church—the nave and transepts. Octagonal, square, or round in plan, they seem to channel the comfortable inertia

of the late Romanesque. The walls are thick and opaque, and the interior is devoid of sophisticated layering. Only the blind arcading and thin shafts artfully subdivide the exterior surfaces of Maria Laach.

Other Works

Hersfeld Abbey, begun 1038, Bad Hersfeld

St. Maria im Kapitol, begun ca. 1040, Cologne

Trier Cathedral, primarily 11th and 12th centuries

Worms Cathedral, ca. 1120–1181

Church of the Apostles, begun 1190, Cologne

German High Romanesque

The Vault

The size, durability, and aesthetics of roof and ceiling designs occupied architects even in the earliest days of building. To create a monumental space, the roof had to span large distances. While this was achievable in wood, stone was is durable and less prone to fire. Greeks spans were limited by narrowly spaced columns, but the Romans wanted to build large, unobstructed spaces and so used vaults on an unprecedented scale. A timber roof works in tension, because the vertical loads are distributed along the beams, but stone has limited tensile capabilities and works best in compression. The arch answers this problem by working only in compression, and the simplest barrel vault is basically an extruded, or repeated, arch.

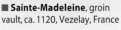

■ **Sainte-Madeleine**, groin vault, ca. 1120, Vezelay, France

The groin vault is the result of the intersection of two barrel vaults of equal diameter at right angles to each other. The points of intersection form paraboloids that are known as groins.

Groin vaults are useful when two volumes—such as the nave and transept of a church—need to be joined. They can also be used as individual components of a system of repeating structural bays, replacing the cumbersome barrel vault. In contrast to the barrel vault, the groin vault allows some of the gravitational pull to be transferred directly to point supports or piers, rather than over the entire length of the wall.

■ **Saint-Guilhem-le-Déser Abbey**, barrel vault, 1050–7 Languedoc-Roussillon, Fran

The barrel vault is the simple and oldest form of vault. By horizontally extending the a wider areas were able to be covered than would have be with post-and-lintel construction. This early innovation w problematic in that the weig of the barreled ceiling put t much stress on the side wall pushing them outward.

rak des Chevaliers, ribbed dripartite vault, begun 4, near Homs, Syria

quadripartite ribbed vault e last, and most important e of the vault's evolution. n this innovation, more in- te designs—such as sixpar- net, star, fan, cell, and palm ting—would later become sible. The quadrapartite t is a variation on the groin t, but with two pointed el vaults intersecting in- stead of two semicircular ones. However, the *rib* in the vault is the key to understanding skeletal construction, a spe- cialty of the Gothic period. The groin vault is more effective at transferring the weight of the ceiling to point supports, but loads the transverse wall and produces massive outward thrust. The ribs function like structural funnels, gathering the load from the vault and transferring it directly to point supports, essentially elimi- nating the need for a contin- uous expanses of thick walls. The point supports create a shape that produces less of an outward push, allowing piers to be thinner and the buttresses smaller. During the construc- tion of a vaulted area, the ribs were used as scaffolding for the building of the *webbing*—the area that creates the vaulted ceiling, filling in the space be- tween ribs.

The Vault

Cluniac Pilgrimage Churches

910–1130

■ Cluny contributed to the development of Romanesque in France ■ The needs of pilgrims resulted in innovations ■ Jerusalem, Rome, and Santiag de Compostela were the three main Christian pilgrimage sites
■ *left*: **Abbey Church of Saint-Philibert**, interior, begun ca. 1008, Tournus

■ **910** The Cluny Abbey is founded by the Duke of Aquitaine

927 Cluny I is dedicated

ca. 955–981 Construction of Cluny II replaces the Carolingian church

ca. 1010 Cluny II is vaulted

ca. 1014 First radiating chapels are built at Saint-Martin in Tours

ca. 1088 Construction starts on Cluny III, the final phase of the Cluny Abbey Church

1130 Cluny III completed

■ **Abbey Church of Saint-Philibert**, apse with radiating chapels, begun ca. 960–1120, Tournus, France

A key link between Carolingian architecture and mature French Romanesque, the deep *westwork* gives onto an airy nave. There, ingenious vaulting consists of five transverse vaults that act as buttresses allowing for large clerestory windows. The choir has some of the earliest radiating chapels.

Romanesque 790–1140

The development of the Cluny Abbey Church is a micocosm of the development of French Romanesque architecture. France was far less unified than the neighbor German empire, and invasions from the Vikings and Ma yars, along with internal strife, slowed French architectural progress. In the north, Normandy developed its o dignified style, partly through Cluniac reform. The Benedictine abbey at Cluny had become one of the most powerful landowners and administrators in Europe. Contra to tradition, which gave each monastery self-governan the Cluniac abbots commanded almost 1,500 Benedictine monasteries. The main Benadictine abbey was founded in 910 and grew sizably in both land owners and political influence over three consecutive stages. T 11th century also saw a rise in the popularity of

■ **Saint-Sernin**, choir and crossing tower, 1080–1120, Toulouse, France

Whereas at Saint-Philibert th radiating chapels are rectangular additions projecting outwardly from the ambulatory Saint-Sernin compact semicircular niches complement th layout. The exterior wall is surprisingly well articulated, putting Saint-Sernin in the mature stage of French Romanesque The tower stresses the importance of the crossing, the dimensions of which are echoed throughout the entire plan.

Cluniac Pilgrimage Churches

pilgrimages; therefore, churches along main pilgrimage routes were upgraded. Cluny encouraged pilgrimages, but may initially have been resistant to some of the early architectural innovations that came from them. By amassing high-quality relics, independent churches and monasteries competed to attract the most visitors, giving towns both income and prestige. Some of the innovations in plan, like radiating chapels, which were developed separately in pilgrimage churches, were later adopted at Cluny III.

■ **Cluny III**, ca. 1088–1130, Cluny, France

Much of the third phase of the abbey church at Cluny was destroyed during the French Revolution, but the surviving fragments still convey its sheer immensity. Parallel to the Norman efforts, the church was a direct step toward the soaring styles of Gothic architecture. It incorporated elements developed in the pilgrimage churches and combined them with an unprecedented geometrical rigor, clarity of detail, and structural sophistication. Pointed arches and external buttresses were used to relieve lateral thrust, allowing for greater nave height. Stone shafts rose next to Classical fluted pilasters, texturing the tall arcade.

Monastic Architecture

96

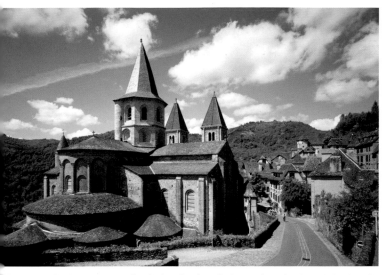

Abbey Church of Sainte-Foy, view from the northeast, 1050–1120, Conques, France

On the evolutionary scale of French Romanesque, Sainte-Foy falls between Saint-Philibert and Saint-Sernin. At Sainte-Foy the westwork was exchanged for a lighter screen facade, which allowed for direct access to the nave. The transept and choir were integrated, creating a more unified space, and the radiating chapels merged smoothly with the exterior walls. The ambulatory extended the line of the aisles, while auxiliary chapels capped the transepts at their eastern ends—a typically Burgundian trait. The continuous route through the side aisles and around the ambulatory meant that pilgrims could get to the relics displayed in the radiating chapels without disturbing on-going services. This type of plan developed in almost all the pilgrimage churches in France along the routes to Santiago de Compostela. The staggered roofs of the choir, ambulatory, and chapels of Sainte-Foy mirror the landscape.

■ **Cluny III**, ca. 1088–1130; engraving ca. 1890, Cluny, France

Built for the abbots' complex requirements, Cluny boasted a huge narthex, two transepts, six towers, five aisles, and many projecting chapels. In size alone, the transepts rivaled the entirety of the largest churches of the time.

Cluniac Pilgrimage Churches

England and the Normans

911–1140

■ In the 10th and 11th centuries Normans embarked on a massive buildin
campaign to ensure the permanence of their colonization efforts
■ Norman architecture was strong, simple, progressive, and versatile
■ *left*: **Abbey Church of Notre-Dame**, nave, ca. 1017–55, Bernay, France

■ **911** The Norman state is
officially established in
nothern France
1066 The Norman Con-
quest of England
1093 First documented rib
vaults at choir aisles of
Durham Cathedral
ca. 1120 Wooden vaults at
Saint-Étienne, Caen, re-
placed with rib vaults
1128–33 Nave at Durham
follows with rib vaulting
1140 Gothic architecture
is popularized with the
building of Saint-Denis

English Romanesque is somewhat unique because it w
imposed on England by the Normans. In France, Norm
architecture was making great headway compared
German Imperial Romanesque. Its forms were light
without sacrificing their monumentality—traits that h
Normandy moving boldly in the direction of the soari
styles of Gothic. Paradoxically this all ended with t
Norman Conquest of England in 1066. After this, the f
ther evolution of Norman architecture happened wit
an Anglo-Saxon context. This new Anglo-Norman arc
tecture diverged from the styles of its French predec
sors, but evolved to dramatically influence Euro
through the Gothic period.

■ **Ely Cathedral**, begun
ca. 1080, England

Ely Cathedral features a rema
ably consistent and well-
proportioned nave wall but
not have stone vaulting desp
contemporary vaulting inno
tions. Heavier than its predecessor Saint-Étienne at Caen
Ely achieves a uniformity of e
pression that can be seen as
ther rigid or refreshing in the
context of the ornamented
Durham or Gloucester cathe
drals. In contrast, its exterior
evation is an early example c
the English tendency toward
ornament, which later becam
a trait of the Decorated style

Abbey Church of Notre-Dame, 1037–67, Jumièges, France

Jumièges was largely destroyed, but apart from Mont-Saint-Michel it is a rare surviving example of early Norman architecture. Scholars point out the Greek proportions of the main elevation, which derives its form from the Carolingian westwork. The nave was very tall, with an enormous tower over the crossing—an element later introduced in almost every English cathedral.

■ **Durham Cathedral**, begun 1093, England

Durham Cathedral is a pivotal structure for Anglo-Norman and European architecture. Apart from its unprecedented size, the building gave rise to an aesthetic that influenced English Romanesque and Gothic architecture. On an international scale, Durham is known for the first documented use of ribbed vaulting. This should not be confused with the later advent of Gothic skeleton structures; rather, Durham was a key step toward articulating the nave wall and the vault as one continuous surface that embraces the worshippers. Similar achievements were made at Speyer Cathedral or in the pilgrimage churches of France by using simple transverse arches carrying a barrel or groin vault. The ribbed vault is not only structurally more efficient than barrel vaulting, but allows for a more complex reading of space. At Durham Cathedral, further complexity is achieved by returning to the alternating pier system of early Romanesque, introducing great variation in the treatment of the piers and cylinders.

England and the Normans

Northern Italy

1016–ca. 1174

■ Northern Italian Romanesque was less conservative than the southern style and was often colorful ■ Lombardy and Germany exchanged ideas and craftsmen ■ Tuscany was heavily influenced by Classical traditions ■ *left*: **St. Ambrogio**, atrium, begun ca. 1080, Milan

■ **1016** A military victory of Pisan and Genoese fleets over the Saracens (Arabs) at Sardinia spurs massive building campaign throughout Pisa

ca. 1040 Diaphram arches are introduced at St. Maria Maggiore in the Lombard town of Lomello

1063 Pisan fleet captures Palermo; the Islamic-inspired dome of Pisa Cathedral is begun

1076 The Countess Matilda begins a stable rule of Tuscany

ca. 1117 Rib vaulting is installed at St. Ambrogio in Milan—an early occurrence of the innovative vaulting technique in Europe

1118 Pisa Cathedral is consecrated

ca. 1174 The tower at Pisa begins leaning after the first phases of construction; architects compensate by building taller stories on the leaning side, thereby worsening the problem

■ **St. Miniato al Monte**, early 12th century, Florence

At once referential and light, the facade of St.

The Romanesque architecture of Lombardy and Tusca is completely unique, due partly to the fact that the gions had a great deal of political autonomy. Unencu bered by imperial dictum, the wealthy towns of northe Italy began a long process of self-governance that eve tually led to harsh conflict between the city-states. Lo bardy developed an ambitious architectural program, built mainly in brick and, therefore, in monochrome, w limited amounts of detail. Tuscan marble allowed cit like Pisa and Florence to develop stunning polychro surfaces with a level of detail unparalleled in Romanes architecture from any other region.

Miniato al Monte foretells the elegance of its interior. The Classical references are clear—the temple front, with its pediment and abstract pilasters. This is playfully set atop a much larger horizontal base. The facade's blind arcade like a lining lifted from the cur apse inside and unraveled ove the elevation.

Baptistery of St. Giovanni, 59–1128, Florence

Miniato al Monte and the btistery of St. Giovanni both ve elements of their interiors tured on their exteriors. The eriors give such sophisti- ed clues to the structure and ailing of their respective in- ors that one can imagine ning the building inside out. e rhythm of the blind arcades t enliven the eight exterior ls of the baptistery is echoed de by beautiful pilasters and umns supporting a con- uous entablature. Arcading s the clerestory windows l supports the segmented ne. A golden mosaic covers entire surface of the dome's rior, shimmering in the light from the lantern above. lantern crowns the eight- ed roof's exterior, accentu- g the divisions.

Pisa Baptistery, Cathedral, Campanile, begun 1153, 3, and 1174

distinct and powerful build-

ings at Pisa form a sophisticated urban ensemble. The baptistery is the cathedral dome, just re-formed. Its base flows from

one building to another, as does the delicate arcaded screen that climbs the leaning campanile, or bell tower.

Other Works

St. Maria Maggiore, ca. 1040, Lomello

Modena Cathedral, begun 1099

St. Michele, ca. 1100–60, Pavia

Piacenza Cathedral, 1122–58

St. Zeno Maggiore, after 1123, Verona

St. Michele, begun 1143, Lucca

Lucca Cathedral and Cam- panile, 11th century onward; facade 13th century

Islam & Christianity in Spain

711–1492

■ The Muslim rulers of southern Spain descended from the Umayyad dynasty in Damascus ■ Architectural forms were derived from early Syrian models ■ A local architectural culture developed that influenced both the Muslims and Christians in Spain

- **711** Muslim armies conquer Spain
- **961–976** Great Mosque of Cordoba extended
- **1236** Cordoba falls to Christian armies
- **1238** Alhambra Citadel in Granada begun as the seat of the Nasrid dynasty
- **1333** Conversion of the Alhambra from a citadel into a palace begins
- **1492** Spanish armies take Granada, ending Muslim rule in Spain

Political struggles over Spain between Christians and Muslims led to a diverse architectural style on the Iberian Peninsula. After the fall of Cordoba in 1236, its Great Mosque was converted into a church. The magnificent 10th century sanctuary was left intact, even after the construction of a 16th-century cathedral at the center of the hypostyle prayer hall, a building with columns supporting a flat roof. From this position, the cathedral rose from the never-ending rows of arches, its buttresses hooking into the columnar grid. The earlier mosque had been so massive that an entire cathedral could go unnoticed within its walls. The moment of transition between the seemingly infinite horizontality of the mosque and the vertical pull of the cathedral is at once jarring and sublime—perhaps a metaphor for the ambivalent relationship that defined Islam and Christianity in Spain. The followers of the Ca

■ **Great Mosque**, begun 785, Cordoba

The first of its kind in Europe, the Great Mosque at Cordoba served for centuries as a model for Moorish architecture throughout the Iberian Peninsula. The mosque that stands today is a result of many building campaigns under both Islamic and Christian rule. The original mosque was much smaller than it is now, with only 10 rows of arcades reaching the *kibla,* the wall orienting worshippers toward Mecca in the south. Caliph al-Hakam II extended the Great Mosque in the mid-10th century, adding not only further rows of arcades, but also ornamental domes with complex patterns of intersecting ribs.

Great Mosque, interior, begun 785, Cordoba

…en how complex the interior feels, the Great
…sque is astonishingly simple in plan. A contin-
…s wall defines the regular quadrangle. The
…: third of the building is devoted to an exterior
…rt, and the remaining part is an expansive
…postyle hall used for prayer. Two tiers of arches
…y the roof, the lower set supported by an-
…ue stone columns and capitals. The poly-
…ome effect comes from using a combination
…tone and brick wedges.

Cathedral of Santiago de Compostela,
tico de la Gloria, 1168–88

…rims from all over Europe met near the Pyre-
…s Mountains and traveled to Santiago de
…mpostela, the purported resting place of the
…stle St. James. The Romanesque portals of the
…edral have been incorporated into the later
…oque facade, a reminder of the medieval ori-
…s of the pilgrimage.

Islam & Christianity in Spain

Umayyad dynasty of Syria, who conquered the Iberian Peninsula in the early 8th century, immediately adapted the architectural practices of the ruling Visigoths, who themselves had in turn been exposed to the architectural legacy of the Roman Empire. Romanesque architecture developed in northern Spain in parallel, as more territory was captured by the Christian houses of Aragon and Castile. One of the most notable examples of Spanish Romanesque architecture is Santiago de Compostela Cathedral, which was one of the primary Christian pilgrimage sites in Europe.

■ Castle of Almodóvar del Río, 8th–14th century, reconstructed 20th century, near Cordoba

Apart from the mosque, the palace-citadel was one of the main building types of Islamic Spain. Having conquered the Iberian Peninsula, Arab armies built a line of fortresses along the border with Christian northern Spain. Other strongholds were built in the south, atop old Roman fortifications. After the decline of the caliphate of Cordoba in the 11th century, southern Spain fractured into several smaller Muslim states, each new emirate building its own capital and palace-citadel.

**Alhambra, Court of
Myrtles**, 14th century,
Granada

By the time the Alhambra was
built, Moorish architecture had
half a millennium to evolve.

Like many late styles, its forms
were ripe and elegant, but also
somehow poignant. The Al-
hambra is a collection of pavilions arranged around large
courts with prominent water

features. Every effort is made to
reduce structural solidity. Arcades float atop reflective pools
as water runs in narrow canals
into rooms filled with mesmer-
izing ornamentation.

Islam & Christianity in Spain

Norwegian Stave Churches

1016–ca. 1250

■ Traditional wood frame construction lined with boards, roofed with shir
gles, and treated with tar ■ Approximately 1,300 stave churches have bee
indexed; of those, 28 survive in Norway
■ *left*: **Urnes Stave Church**, detail, 11th–12th century, Sogn og Fjordane

1016–30 The spread of Christianity in Norway is enforced during the reign of King Olaf II

1031 King Olaf II is canonized, prompting the construction of shrines

ca. 1050 Stave churches begin to appear throughout Norway

ca. 1130 Urnes, one of the oldest surviving stave churches, is constructed atop the foundations of an even older church

1150–1250 Most existing stave churches are built

ca. 1250 The construction of stave churches begins to be phased out

Other Works

Heddaln Stave Church, 12th and 13th centuries, Notodden, Telemark

Hopperstad Stave Church, ca. 1150, Vik, Sogn og Fjordane

Kaupanger Stave Church, ca. 1150–1200, Sogndal, Sogn og Fjordane

Gol Stave Church, 13th century, reconstructed, Olso Folk Museum

During the Middle Ages wood was the most popular a often the only building material used in northern Europ Scandinavia was dotted with wooden forts, houses, ar later, churches. In Norway alone more than 1,000 wood churches were built over the course of three centuri Although this tradition has all but disappeared, rema ably, 30 original stave churches have survived. These ha been used to reconstruct other churches. In these simp buildings, the Romanesque use of stone was artfully e pressed in wood. Stave churches were built entirely wood, either dovetailed or pegged and wedged, b never nailed. Columns, capitals, arches, and portals we carved to mimic Romanesque details. These were oft combined with both figurative and abstract motifs fr Norse mythology.

■ **Borgund Stave Church**, interior, ca. 1150–1200, Lærd Sogn og Fjordane

The existing stave churches Norway are not stylistically h mogeneous. They vary great in plan, structure, and size. Borgund is a large stave chu with a complex plan and section. Freestanding colum braced to carry the tall roof, support the central portion the rectangular nave. A narrc ambulatory encircles the nav echoed by an exterior porch Three gables and an apse project from the main volum

orgund Stave Church,
150–1200, Lærdal,
n og Fjordane

term *stave* comes from the
se word *stavr*, referring to
large wooden posts that
ned the structural basis for
churches. The system of
ed posts set on founda-
al stones created a stable
flexible frame around which
church could be con-
cted. At Borgund, the 12 in-
r posts support the tallest
ion of the roof, which then
ends almost to the ground
three separate slopes.
ng to the weather, there are
arge windows, only peep-
s in a portion of the nave
, analogous to the
story of Romanesque
ches. The apse roof follows
general profile of the nave
choir but then separates
the main volume and proj-
into an amusing turret.
n a single window over the
porch brought dim light
the building, but candle-
services were common.

■ **Urnes Stave Church,**
ca. 1130, Luster, Sogn og
Fjordane

Of the 28 stave churches surviving in Norway, UNESCO chose
Urnes to represent this building
typology as a World Heritage
Site. One of the oldest surviving
churches, it was built using decorative elements from a previous 11th-century structure. Its
carvings are exquisite, uniting
Christian symbolism with sinuous abstractions of dragons
and lizards.

Norwegian Stave Churches

Secular Architecture

1066–1142

■ Castles in the UK and Ireland developed in the late 9th century as a respon[se]
to Viking invasions ■ Earth and wood castles were rebuilt in stone under th[e]
Normans ■ Permission to build a castle was granted by the king
■ *left*: **White Tower, Tower of London**, interior, ca. 1077–97, London

Anglo-Saxon England had efficient fortifications befo[re]
the Norman Conquest of 1066, but very few stone str[uc]-
tures were built. William the Conqueror changed this [sit]-
uation entirely in the second half of the 11th century. [His]
first major accomplishment was the construction of t[he]
Tower of London, at the edge of the city, overlooking t[he]
Thames and surrounding countryside. The tower w[as]
both a royal residence and a key fortress, influencing [ar]-
chitectural styles for fortifications throughout Engla[nd].
With the launch of the first Crusade in 1095, military arc[hi]-
tecture was particularly important. Contact with the E[ast]
meant the introduction [of]
new technological inn[o]-
vations that could be [...]
be brought back for u[se]
in European wars and [put]
to the test abroad.

■ **White Tower, Tower of London**, ca. 1077–97

The White Tower is the keep[, a]
residence, built within the fo[rti]-
fied complex of the Tower o[f]
London. The keep is rectang[ular]
in plan, with stair towers at
three corners and the fourth [oc]-
cupied by a semicircular pro[jec]-
tion that contains the chape[l].
The upper floor includes two
large halls and the royal cha[pel],
all surrounded by a gallery
running along the perimete[r]
walls.

Other Important Works

Qal'at Salah El-Din (Fortress of Saladin), 10th–12th century, near Haffeh, Syria	Castle Keep, begun ca. 1080, Newcastle-upon-Tyne, UK
Colchester Castle, 1069–1100, Essex, UK	Rochester Castle, begun ca. 1080, Kent, UK
Richmond Castle, 1071–86, Yorkshire, UK	Hedlingham Castle, ca. 1140, Essex, UK

■ **Dover Castle**, keep, begun ca. 1180, Kent, UK

The windows at the White Tower were enlarged in the 18th century, making it appear more hospitable to a 21st-century visitor. Yet it is the ominous solidity of Dover that communicates the real purpose of the fortified residence: defensibility. During the Romanesque period, the main defensive positions were on the roof instead of at the slits or loops that came into use later.

Krak des Chevaliers, begun 1142, near Homs, Syria

Krak des Chevaliers was an advanced piece of military technology. A set of fortified walls with rounded projections formed a complex polygon. Inside, a wide buffer zone gave way to a massive inner structure, with layered walls that provided several lines of defense. The castle was an important military outpost from which Crusaders could control the Syrian coast.

Secular Architecture

East Asian Religious Architecture

960–1185

■ Buddhism, Confucianism, and Shinto played key roles in the architectu of East Asia ■ Building materials included brick, wood, and terra cotta

■ **960** The Song dynasty begins in China

1000 Pure Land Buddhism begins to spread in Japan

1127 Southern Song dynasty is established after the collapse of the northern realms

1044 During a thunderstorm, lightning strikes and burns down the wooden predecessor of the Iron Pagoda

1103 The *New Yingzhao Fashi*, an updated manual of architecture and construction, is completed and disseminated

1185 The relative stability of the Heian period ends in Japan

■ **Longhua Si Temple**, pagoda, 977, Shanghai

The pagoda at Longhua Si Temple was rebuilt several times. Reconstructions were faithful to the original and the pagoda remains a good example of the architecture of the Northern Song dynasty. Octagonal in plan, its seven stories decrease proportionally in size. Each layer was fitted with a separate roof.

Romanesque

In contrast to the disarray of medieval western Euro China was an organized and well-administered state t expressed itself through sophisticated literature, art, architecture. Construction throughout the empire came standardized, and, by 1103, the Song dynasty created a manual of architecture and construction survey of current architectural practices with sam plans, detail drawings, cost estimates, and lists of st

dard materials and th dimensions. Meanwh Pure Land Buddhism came a guiding influe in 11th-century Jap The practice had de oped in India during 2nd century. At the r gion's core lay the c cept of the "pure lar which, if visualized pr erly, would become or place of rebirth. S visualizations were ba on mandalas, and ser as meditation devi Art and architecture w also designed to se meditative purposes, the form of the tem became the object meditation.

**hoenix Hall at
do-in**, 1053, Kyoto

hall is an example
design based on
dea of a Pure Land
alization. As an
ct of meditation, it
approached from
ack so as not to
pt the view from
ake.

■ Iron Pagoda, 1049,
Kaifeng, China

The logic of this pagoda
and of Greek temples
are similar, in that
original wood struc-
tures were replaced
with durable materials,
in this case glazed brick,
while maintaining the
original form.

Other Important Works

r Hill Pagoda,
yan Monastery,
 Suzhou,
gsu Province,
a

Harmonies Pagoda,
un 970,
uilt 1156–65,
gzhou, Zhejiang
nce, China

Liaodi Pagoda at
Kaiyuan Monatery,
1055, Ding County,
Hebei Province, China

Sanju-sangen-do, 1164,
Kyoto, Japan

Itsukushima Shrine,
rebuilt 1168, Itsuku-
shima Island, Japan

East Asian Religious Architecture

Great Mosques of Early Islam

632–892

■ Early mosques were generally quadrangular in format, with an emphas
on horizontality ■ Arcaded galleries surrounded an open court ■ Mosqu
served as places of prayer, schools, community centers, and courts of law
■ *left*: **Dome of the Rock**, interior, ca. 685–691, Jerusalem

● **632** Mohammed dies

634–637 Damascus and Jerusalem fall to Muslim armies

660–750 Reign of the Umayyad caliphs, with power centralized in Damascus

710 Umayyad palace Qasr Kharaneh built in Jordan

711 Muslim invasion of Spain begins

762–767 The city of Baghdad is founded, as a circular enclosure with a palace, mosque, and four symmetrically placed gates

ca. 750 Roman monumental forms are fully incorporated into Islamic architecture

836 Samarra is laid out as the new capital of the Abbasid caliphate

847–861 Samarra is enlarged under the reign of Abbasid caliph al-Mutawakkil; Abu-Dulaf Mosque constructed

892 Abbasid caliphate is reestablished in Baghdad; the old capital Samarra is soon abandoned

■ **Dome of the Rock**, ca. 685–691, Jerusalem

Islamic architecture was usually situated in densely packed Middle Eastern cit-

From its very inception, Islamic architecture was sop
ticated. Architects working in the conquered anci
cities of Damascus and Jerusalem had thousands of ye
of architectural history to adapt to the new needs
mosques. This was done with remarkable speed and e
adapting the Roman monumental forms of basilica
baths to their own programmatic religious needs. Us
the Classical language of the column, arch, vault, or do
Muslim architects worked with confidence and ene
creating completely new morphologies for the mosc
the palace, and the market.

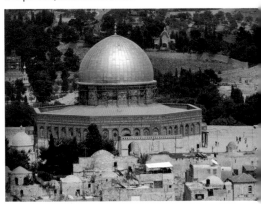

ies. In contrast, the Dome of the Rock testifies to the power of Islam over the city, as it was constructed in solitary splendor. Like the Palatine Chapel a century

later, this strict octagonal buil
borrowed from the influentia
Vitale in Ravenna. A golden d
protects the rock housed with
sacred to both Muslims and J

Romanesque

...eat Mosque, 709–715,
...ascus

...amascus, as in most
...r mosques, the main
...e is a democratic open
...Apart from a shrine

...u-Dulaf Mosque,
...861, never com-
...d, Samarra, Iraq

...ity of Samarra was
...lished as the cap-
...f the powerful Ab-
...l caliphate in
...Within 30 years
...apital was
...ed back to
...dad and the
...was left to de-
... Nevertheless,
...onuments,
...d-
...wo
...rk-

particular to Damascus, the
only other focal point is the
mihrab, protruding from
the main quadrangle of
the mosque and indi-
cating the direction of

mosques, the old
Caliphate Palace, and
several other buildings,
have survived as relics.
The entire Samarra ar-
chaeological area
has been designated
as a World Heritage
Site, partly in
response to the
substantial dam-
age sustained
during the
American-led oc-
cupation
of Iraq
since
2003.

prayer, toward the holy city of
Mecca. In the uniform space an
ultimate sense of direction is
given by the rows of people
praying toward their geo-
graphic spiritual center.

Other Works

Mosque of 'Amr ibn al-'As,
begun 641, Cairo

Great Mosque of Isfahan,
begun 772, Iran

The Caliphate Palace (Qasr al-
Khalifa), 836–837, Samarra, Iraq

The Great Mosque and its
Spiral Minaret, 849–852,
Samarra, Iraq

Great Mosque of Qairawan,
9th–13th century, Tunisia

Mosque of Three Doors, 866,
Qairawan, Tunisia

Mosque of Ahmad ibn Tulun,
876–879, Cairo

Great Mosques of Early Islam

Ancient Pueblos

ca. 1000–ca. 1300

■ The Anasazi inhabited large parts of southwestern North America ■ They were the ancestors of modern-day Pueblo peoples ■ Many cliff dwellings a stone pueblos were discovered in the late 19th century and later excavated ■ *left*: **Cliff Palace**, ca. 1200–ca. 1300, Mesa Verde National Park, Colorado

■ **ca. 1000** Stone begins to be used, along with the traditional mediums of wood and mud, as a construction material

ca. 1130–80 The Pueblo Bonito is abandoned

1276–99 The Great Drought takes place in what is today the southwestern United States

ca. 1300 The Anasazi people abandon their communities

The main social space for the Pueblo peoples was *kiva*—a round, subterranean room that served spirit political, and familial purposes similar to the function a chapel or parish church in Europe. The Anasazi live large communities of up to 1,000 people, divided into milial units. The life of each family revolved around kiva, so that several round kivas would be intersper with tight rows of rooms used for living, storage, a sometimes even burial. The entire pueblo could be co pared in scope to the large communal European abb of the same era.

Other Works

Tuzigoot, occupied from ca. 1000, Verde River valley, Arizona

White House, 1066–1275, Canyon de Chelly National Monument, Chinle, Arizona

Montezuma Castle, ca. 110C Verde River valley, Arizona

Aztec Ruins National Monu ment, 1111–15 and mid-13t² century, Aztec, New Mexico

Great Kiva at Casa Rinuand **(Corner House)**, ca. 1150, Chaco Canyon National Park, New Mexico

■ **Cliff Palace**,
ca.1200–ca. 1300, Mesa Verde National Park, Colorado

Around 1150 the Anasazi, who

Romanesque

traditionally lived in pit houses on the mesa, began to move to sheltering cliff dwellings. They retained the circular forms of

the pits, turning them into and adding multilevel hous that hugged the natural co tours of the cliffs.

Pueblo Bonito, dwellings, 920–ca. 1180, Chaco Canyon National Park, New Mexico

The tallest structures at Pueblo Bonito were at the back of the structure, along the protective north-facing windowless curve.

Pueblo Bonito, 920–1180, Chaco Canyon National Park, New Mexico

Pueblo Bonito was a semicircular, five-story megastructure gathering a village with hundreds of inhabitants into one building. In plan it looked somewhat like a cell, with a membrane, nucleus, and free-floating elements. In section it resembled a Roman theater, stepping down to a central plaza. Its straight edge was capped off by a layer of rooms.

As in many surrounding communities, dwellings faced south, stepping down so that the roof of one was the terrace of the next. At Pueblo Bonito, there were about 30 family kivas and two central community kivas. These were backed by layers of rooms that had different uses depending on the availability of light. Roads leading to neighboring settlements and resource areas have been discovered.

Gothic

1140–1520

Rouen Cathedral, detail of the west facade, late 15th century

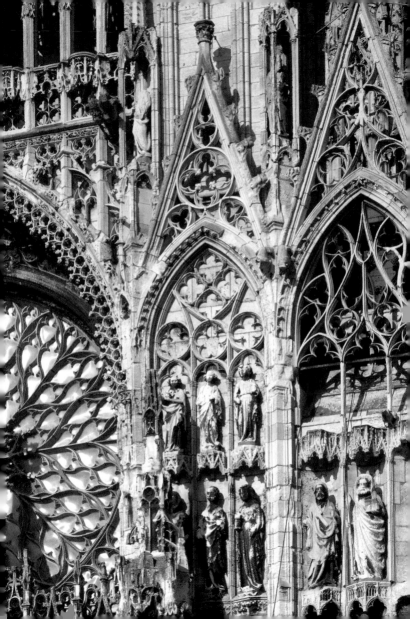

Gothic

1140–1500
Gothic in France

The construction of the choir of Saint-Denis, near Paris, creates an "architecture of light" using skeletal frames that compartmentalize buildings and increase the possibilities of height and ornamentation

p. 129

1220–1520
Rayonnant and Flamboyant Gothic

In France and England structural elements such as vaulting and ribs become increasingly intricate and ornate

| 1100 | 1150 | 1200 | 1250 | 1300 |

p. 141

1174–1517
Gothic in the UK

Gothic styles spread from France to the UK, where Flamboyant, or Decorated, and Perpendicular styles create new forms of tracery and vaulting

p. 133

1220–1520
Mediterranean Gothic

Italian Gothic architecture features polychrome surfaces and geometric forms; in Spain and Portugal, Flamboyant Gothic mixes with highly ornate local styles such as the Manueline style

Around the World:
Southeast Asia and Africa

As European cathedrals grew taller, cultures in Southeast Asia were building massive temple complexes that also reached to the heavens, while in Ethiopia, churches were hollowed out of the earth

00	1450	1500	1550	1600

230–1520
othic in Central nd Northern urope

rman, Austrian, Polish, d Bohemian architects opt French Gothic les, building wider uctures of brick

p. 155

p. 148

Gothic Architecture

The emergence of Gothic architecture can be traced to a region surrounding Paris called the Île-de-France. The revolutionary architectural movement did not develop suddenly in isolation; instead, many of the elements that define Gothic architecture were initially borrowed from other cultures or invented to solve structural problems encountered by Romanesque masons. Around 1050, masons began to replace wooden roofs with stone vaults. This posed immense structural problems but inspired a conceptual shift toward spatial unity. The first mature Romanesque nave of Speyer Cathedral emphasized verticality to a much greater degree than ever before. This was accomplished by dramatically changing the composition of the nave wall from a solid plane pierced with openings to a series of vertical piers providing support to the structurally audacious stone vaults.

■ **Speyer Cathedral**, side aisle, 1003–1106, Germany

■ **Durham Cathedral**, vaults after 1128, UK

Lincoln Cathedral, blind arcade St. Hugh's choir, 1230, UK

Wells Cathedral, chapter house, early 14th century, UK

The Rebirth of Geometry

Gothic architecture is partly indebted to a revival of mathematics and science. The principal mathematical operation behind early Romanesque work was addition. Romanesque forms were arranged in groups, and they remained distinctly separate. Innovative elements, like the pointed arch or the ribbed vault could not fulfill their structural potential until the envelope of solid masonry had disappeared. With the rediscovery of Euclidian geometry in the early 12th century, architects stopped relying solely on addition. Building was still based on intuition to a large degree, but proficiency in geometry allowed for accuracy in drawing and, consequently, construction. Division, intersection, rotation, and superposition were operations that could now be performed, both in plan and section, to achieve unprecedented levels of volumetric complexity.

Introduction

A Synthetic Approach

A talent for synthesis put Gothic architects in a completely new stylistic and ideological category. The elements of Gothic—pointed arches, ribbed vaults, flying buttresses, and tripartite facades—were united in one seminal building: the Abbey Church of Saint-Denis, near Paris. Many of these elements had been developed earlier in both French and English churches. For example, the first ribbed vaults were most likely installed in the choir at Durham Cathedral around 1090, followed by the nave of Saint-Étienne at Caen in the 1120s. Pointed arches were used for centuries in Islamic architecture before being adopted on a grand scale at Cluny starting in 1088. Cluny also boasted large buttresses that reached over the side aisles, in anticipation of the Gothic flying buttress. The twin-towered facade, so central to the 21st-century idea of Gothic, started out as the Carolingian

■ **Saint-Étienne**
nave, begun 106
Caen, France

■ **Saint-Étienne**
facade, begun
1068, Caen, Fran

aint-Denis,
–1281, near

llard de Hon-
urt: Laon
edral Tower
, ca. 1230,
ce

westwork. It was later refined in early Norman churches like Jumièrges and in the revolutionary west facade of Saint-Étienne in Caen. The church of Saint-Étienne was important for many other reasons. Its nave wall, although Romanesque in detail, hinted at Gothic openness and transparency. It was one of the first buildings in France to employ the ribbed vault, albeit one of the last Norman works completed before the talented Norman architects left for England with the court of William I. The center of the Gothic movement shifted to Île-de-France and the urban centers of Laon, Chartres, and Paris. At Laon Cathedral, heavy masonry walls still support and anchor the building, but its imaginative towers are examples of how geometry was used to attain fluid and dramatic effects. In plan, the towers were based on two sets of rotated squares—a technique later used to develop complex piers on a diagonal orientation.

Introduction

Mysticism and Reason

By the 1200s the Crusades had become a source of money and knowledge. Economic prosperity, combined with a rediscovery of Classical texts, meant that philosophy was free to develop. The term *Scholasticism* describes a range of medieval philosophical schools of thought that flourished concurrently with the birth of Gothic architecture. In essence, the Scholastics endeavoured to reconcile faith with reason. Compared to Romanesque architecture, which was additive in nature, Gothic masons attempted to represent the totality of heaven on earth in a single design. The concept that there was one ideal cathedral—a synthesis of all available technical and theological knowledge—led to a remarkable consistency in early French Gothic work. Scholasticism, with its hierarchical arrangement of information, provided a system by which cathedral design could be standardized.

■ **Amiens Cathedral**, nave, begun 1220, France

■ **Chartres Cathedral**, nave, after 1194, France

Gothic 1140–1520

For example, the west facade of Notre Dame in Paris was arranged along a grid of squares, circles, and rectangles elegantly classified according to their place in a prescribed architectural hierarchy. Other facades, such as those at the cathedrals in Chartres or Reims, were either more robust or more organic, but all conformed to a certain geometrical rigor. From the Scholastic perspective, the Gothic insistence on structural legibility was completely consistent with the notion that faith and reason could coexist in a clear and transparent way. This synthesis of opposing ideals was the core of the Gothic obsession with overriding the basic static properties of materials. The urge to sculpt stone so as to deny its material presence has rightly been termed *dematerialization*, in an effort to explain the mystical effect of Gothic architecture. The light that filtered through the fantastic stained glass windows of Chartres was the final ingredient in this process.

Introduction

The Birth of Gothic

1140–1281

■ Religious fervor sparked the construction of many churches ■ Light w
used as an element of design ■ Skeletal structures replaced load-bearing
walls ■ Architectural elements such as the pointed arch, the flying buttress, the rose window, and the triple portal were first used together

■ **1140–44** West facade
and ambulatory of Saint-
Denis is built

ca. 1144 Abbot Suger describes the construction
of Saint-Denis

ca. 1160 Laon and Paris
cathedrals begun

1194–1220 Chartres
Cathedral is rebuilt in the
Gothic style after fire

ca. 1200–50 West facade
of Notre Dame de Paris is
built

1231–81 Construction of
nave and choir at Saint-
Denis

Other Works

Abbey Church of
Saint-Étienne, vaults, late
11th century, Caen

Durham Cathedral,
choir-aisle vaults, later
choir, and nave vaults,
1093–1133

Nave of Sens Cathedral,
begun ca. 1130

Notre Dame de Paris,
begun ca. 1160

Nave of Noyon Cathe-
dral, begun ca. 1170

Soissons Cathedral,
south transept, begun
ca. 1180

The building that marks the beginning of the Gothic
is the Abbey Church of Saint-Denis, near Paris. It was b
under the direction of Abbot Suger, one of the most in
ential political figures of the time. Suger, describing
construction of Saint-Denis, wrote of a new light that v
to pervade his church, one that would aid the religious
perience. Following the Neoplatonic emphasis on God
light, Suger argued that the contemplation of phys
beauty would lead to enlightenment. It was the wil
turn light into an element of architecture that logic
led to the replacement of solid walls with skeletal str
tures and windows. Through a strict geometrical
tionale, the architecture of light came to influence bu
ing techniques for centuries.

■ **Abbey Church of Saint-
Denis**, 1140–1281, near Par

Saint-Denis was the first
building to use and unify al
the architectural elements t
define Gothic as a style. Poir
arches, column clusters, an
cross-rib vaulting had been
seen before, but it was not
the building of Saint-Denis t
these elements came togeth
in a coherent whole. The res
was a skeletal enclosure bas
on freestanding columns ra
than solid walls. In the amb
tory, stone ribs support bric
vaults—a technique that al
lowed for minimal scaffoldi
during construction.

Chartres Cathedral, after 1194

At Chartres, the focus was on interior rather than exterior clarity. The cathedral's external beauty lies in how clearly the layers of construction throughout different campaigns can be seen. Begun during the early Gothic period, the western facade is a fusion of a late Romanesque base with an early Gothic facade and a late Gothic spire. Chartres was structurally revolutionary for its time. When it was built, the cathedral's vaults were the highest in Europe, and were supported by flying buttresses. At 118 feet (36 meters) tall, the nave is an uninterrupted volume framed by clustered columns and remarkable fenestration. The cathedral retains almost all its medieval stained glass, filling the interior with splashes of colored light.

Laon Cathedral, interior and facade, begun ca. 1160

Though Laon retains round arches and heavy walls of Romanesque architecture, the deep recess of the portals and windows create a characteristically Gothic play of light and shadow. The playful facade lacks the rigor and structural unity of Paris or Amiens, but its monumental nature made it a prototype for other Gothic churches. The triple portal, the rose window, and the open gallery are basic elements of a Gothic facade. The nave's divisions and systems clearly borrow from Romanesque designs, with the exception of one important innovation: the new triforium passage, a low arcade below the clerestory, which added extra light to the nave. This element was retained in later Gothic churches, replacing the earlier tribune gallery as the separation between the arcade and the expanded clerestory above.

Notre Dame de Pari.

Notre Dame de Paris is neither the tallest nor the most extravagant of Gothic cathedrals but has a monumental dignity and clarity of plan that has made it an architectural icon. Later modified, the first plan of Notre Dame was strikingly compact. A long nave with a semicircular apse was embraced by a double ambulatory that continued alongside the nave, forming the side aisles. The transept projected only slightly beyond the exterior walls, but did not interrupt the rhythm of the aisles. Although the simplification of form and absolute emphasis on verticality of later churches is still muted at Notre Dame, its satisfying proporti and well-integrated ornament unify the space. The scholastic movement in

enced the strict compartmentalizat of early Gothic works, but also int duced contrast into architecture– Notre Dame, slender shafts fall unin rupted down the height of the t nave wall, but stop abruptly, balanc on massive capitals.

🔲 **Notre Dame**, chevet with buttressing, 1163–1230, Paris

The flying buttresses at Notre Dame were amor the first of their kind and were modified during construction phase that enlarged the clerestory windows. Architects sacrificed exterior clarity fc terior light, obscuring the exterior walls, and making them less tangible and more mysteriou

◀ **Notre Dame**, nave, after 1178, Paris

Full of contrast, Notre Dame has thin, transpare nave walls, essential to the sublime light of Got buildings, resting on monumental piers. The co plex problem of creating an illusion of weightle ness both inside and out is solved through the of light—the interior is dematerialized with ligh and the exterior with the complexity of shadow

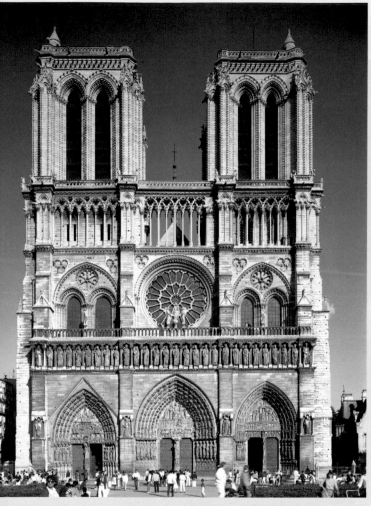

...tre Dame, facade,
...–50, Paris

...acade of Notre Dame is
...ing but vertical. It does
not appear to rise fluidly from
the soil, like Reims. Instead it is
an orderly and comprehensible
image based on primary geometrical figures: the square,
the circle, and the triangle, arranged on a grid throughout
its elevation.

Notre Dame de Paris

High Gothic in France

ca. 1195–1284

■ Pilgrimages to churches increased, and larger churches were built to house the masses ■ Development of a coherent Gothic architectural language ■ Architects strove to create the tallest possible structures ■ *left:* **Reims Cathedral**, west portal, 14th century, Reims

■ **ca. 1195–ca. 1215** Construction of Bourges Cathedral
1211–90 Construction of Reims Cathedral (construction of the facade lasts through to the 15th century)
1220–35 Construction of Amiens Cathedral
1225–72 Construction of Beauvais Cathedral
1284 Vaults at Beauvais Cathedral collapse

During the High Gothic period in France, cathed[rals] evolved in several ways: plans became increasingly rig[or]ous, sculptures were integrated into the facades, and motifs in clerestories and rose windows alike flowed m[ore] freely with each generation. But it was the drive to re[ach] ever higher that influenced all aspects of 13th-century [ar]chitecture. Architects knew that the illusion of vertica[lity] was as important as height itself. Everything became ta[ller] and more fragile looking. In Amiens, colonnettes re[ach] uninterrupted from the floor all the way to the [key]stones of the vaults, pulling the eye up w[ith] dramatic force. In contrast, the windows [were] delicate and fragile, accentuating the w[alls'] lack of weight-bearing ability and crea[ted] room for stained glass windows. The cli[max] of the period's obsession with great hei[ght] came to an abrupt end with the collaps[e of] the vaults at Beauvais Cathedral, ushe[red] in a new era of smaller buildings an[d] focus on detail.

■ **Amiens Cathedral**, west facade, begun 122[0,] Amiens

As a synthesis of the elemental character of Lao[n,] the geometric rigidity of Paris, and the sculptu[ral] unity of Reims, Amiens represents the apex of [High] Gothic technical and decorative achievement. Soaring in the facade, the central rose window [sits] atop a gallery filled with statues of kings, while [or]ganic decorations wriggle their way up the but[t]resses. Inside, the nave climbs to an astoundin[g] 138 feet (42 meters), containing the largest int[ernal] volume of any complete cathedral in France.

Bourges Cathedral, interior
view of choir, begun ca. 1195,
choir completed ca. 1215,
Bourges

Most cathedrals are typically divided into choir and nave by a transept. The lack of a transept at Bourges blurs this distinction and led to a system of inner and outer aisles. These aisles run along the entire perimeter of the building and vary in height, so that the church obtains a curious pyramidal profile. While losing the quality of having a singular volume like other churches, the multiple vault heights create a fantastic spatial complexity. On the exterior, the buttresses gracefully mimic the three roof slopes.

■ **Bourges Cathedral**, exterior view of choir,
ca. 1215, Bourges

After the introduction of a double ambulatory encircling the choir with inner and outer passageways (notably at Saint-Denis), this area grew in complexity and was given the French term *chevet* to describe the ensemble that comprised the apse, ambulatory, and radiating chapels. At Bourges, the plan of the eastern end is more compact than its contemporaries, featuring chapels tucked neatly in between the buttresses. The tall chapel roofs and the three different ceiling levels are also visible on the interior.

Other Important Works	
Coutances Cathedral, 1208–74	Auxerre Cathedral, completed ca. 1234
Reims Cathedral, begun 1211	Choir of Amiens Cathedral, ca. 1236
Chevet of Le Mans Cathedral, 1217–34	Clermont-Ferrand Cathedral, ca. 1248–1355
Choir of the Beauvais Cathedral, begun ca. 1225	Limoges Cathedral, 1273–1327

Rayonnant and Flamboyant Gothic in France

1220–1500

■ Architects concentrated on details and ornamentation ■ Windows becar larger, with more glass ■ Interiors were brighter and felt more spacious

1220 Reims architect Jean Le Loup first links the triforium and clerestory

1226–70 Louis IX reigns in France

ca. 1230 First mature Rayonnant works appear at Troyes and Saint-Denis

1231–81 Abbot Suger's choir at Saint-Denis is linked to a west narthex with a new nave and transepts

1246 Sainte-Chapelle is begun in Paris

1254 Louis IX returns from the Seventh Crusade

1337–1453 Hundred Years' War between England and France

1500 Many early Gothic buildings are finished in late Gothic styles

In the Rayonnant style the early and High Gothic obs sion with height was replaced with a systematic refi ment of detail. Smaller churches and chapels were b anew, while many existing buildings were moderniz enlarged, or simply finished in the new style. The Ab Church of Saint-Denis was almost totally rebuilt, w Chartres Cathedral and Notre Dame de Paris recei elaborate new transept facades. Rayonnant-style bu ings were no longer demonstrations of religious fe but were concerned with more secular exploration architectural language. After over 300 years, the limit Gothic architecture were finally reached in the 16th-c tury French late Gothic style known as Flamboy. named after the extravagant flame-shaped tracery t filled the last Gothic windows, portals, and facades. elaborate stone tracery of Flamboyant Gothic archi ture is usually fashioned after the same S-curved line is found in much Gothic art.

■ **Rouen Cathedral**, detail the west facade, late 15th century

The Flamboyant style was c cerned with surface treatm rather than the structural o spatial problems that had mostly been solved during High Gothic period. By virt being added to existing bu ings, Flamboyant ornamen tion was often only an appl of overlapping layers of tra

■ Troyes Cathedral, crossing,
ca. 1230

Less concerned with height,
13th-century architects focused
on refining the nave wall. By replacing columns with groups of
colonnettes and running them
up the entire height of the wall,
they achieved progressively
more unified interior elevations. Vertical elements, like the
clerestory tracery, elegantly
dropped down to pick up the
arches of the triforium below,
uniting the levels.

133

Late Gothic in France

inte-Chapelle, vaults in
pper hall, 1246–48, Paris

Court style betrayed a
ving secular influence on
ch ecclesiastical architec-
Louis IX was eager to build
ine asserting his power

over the young French nation.
The pivotal objects legitimizing
that power were precious relics
often brought back from the
Crusades. Many scholars point
to the jewel-like quality of
Sainte-Chapelle as a response

to the intricate metal reli-
quaries made to carry these objects of medieval worship.
Above the parish church, the
private upper hall was simplified to one entirely glazed
space.

Rayonnant and Flamboyant Gothic in France

Gothic Cathedrals

Medieval masons understood that forces in a building could be expressed as directional loads, or vectors. The structural feats in the construction of Gothic cathedrals were a creative way of separating vertical and lateral loads by redistributing spaces. Working with the same design and construction methods used for centuries, cathedral architects introduced innovations that were pivotal to the development of Gothic planning. By modifying the system of vaulting and using flying buttresses, architects gained an unprecedented freedom in plan. This created the Gothic aesthetic as well as the structural support needed for the new heights of cathedrals.

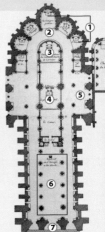

■ **Reims Cathedral**, plan, 1211–1311

Legend:

1 Radiating chapels
2 Ambulatory
3 Choir
4 Crossing
5 Transept
6 Nave
7 Narthex

a Transverse rib
b Flying buttress
c Clerestory
d Triforium
e Buttress
f Main arcade
g Aisle

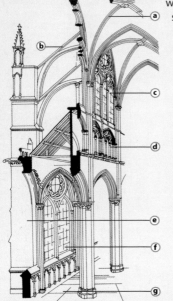

Gothic 1140–1520

The four-part ribbed vault, flying buttress, and the use dead weight for stability revolutionized medieval construction. Gothic churches were based on sets of flexible structural bays instead of the monolithic barrel vault. Using adjustable ribs, masons could vary the proportions of each bay without affecting its height. The geometry of the pointed arch produced small lateral loads and transferred the vertical ones directly down to the supporting columns. Any residual lateral forces were removed through flying buttresses connected to weighty pillars outside.

eims Cathedral, main
e looking west, mid-13th
ury

nave wall of a High Gothic

cathedral is composed of the
following elements in ascending order: the arcade linking the
nave with its aisles, the trifo-

rium that takes up the blind
space of the aisle roof, and
finally the clerestory window
reaching up to the nave vault.

Gothic Cathedrals

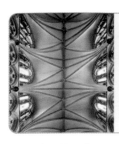

Early Gothic in the UK

1174–1280

■ At first influenced by France, English Gothic later evolved along independen[t] lines ■ Interior and exterior ornamentation was playful and creative ■ Contra[s]ting colors and materials created an illusion of depth in the designs
■ *left*: **Lincoln Cathedral**, St. Hugo choir vaults, after 1174

1174 Great Fire at Canterbury destroys the Norman choir; architects from the UK and France are invited to inspect the damage and propose new solutions

1178 Master mason at Canterbury William of Sens is injured and is replaced by William the Englishman

1192 Geoffrey de Noiers begins rebuilding Lincoln Cathedral

1230 West facade of Lincoln Cathedral completed

1245 Work begins on Westminster Abbey

1280 Angel Choir at Lincoln Cathedral is completed as the prototype for the Decorated style

Other Works

Roche Abbey, ca.1172, Yorkshire

Wells Cathedral, nave and transept, begun 1185

Salisbury Cathedral, 1220–60

Peterborough Cathedral, west front, 1237

Hereford Cathedral, north transept, ca.1260

The desire to preserve Norman heritage in buildings, rath[er] than replacing it altogether by foreign styles, determin[ed] the evolution of Gothic architecture in England. Engl[ish] churches were planned using an additive system, in c[on]trast to the compact and unified plans of their French co[un]terparts. As consecutive elements were added, volum[es] and elevations became longer and taller. The feature[s of] English Gothic—the separation of parts and lengthening [of] buildings—are attributed to the practice [of] increasing size through additi[on] done over several building ca[m]paigns. Later, Salisbury Cat[he]dral was constructed in [a] single campaign, but it [re]tains the basic f[ea]tures that h[ave] come to def[ine] English Gothi[c.]

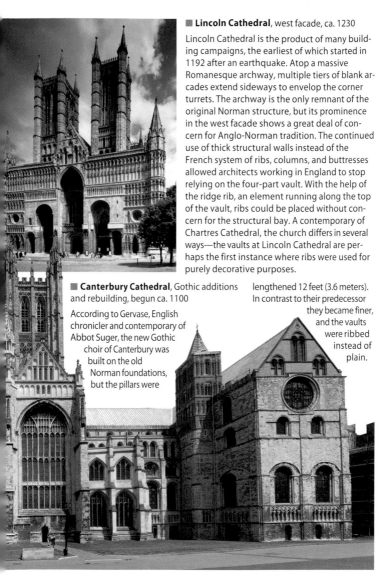

■ Lincoln Cathedral, west facade, ca. 1230

Lincoln Cathedral is the product of many building campaigns, the earliest of which started in 1192 after an earthquake. Atop a massive Romanesque archway, multiple tiers of blank arcades extend sideways to envelop the corner turrets. The archway is the only remnant of the original Norman structure, but its prominence in the west facade shows a great deal of concern for Anglo-Norman tradition. The continued use of thick structural walls instead of the French system of ribs, columns, and buttresses allowed architects working in England to stop relying on the four-part vault. With the help of the ridge rib, an element running along the top of the vault, ribs could be placed without concern for the structural bay. A contemporary of Chartres Cathedral, the church differs in several ways—the vaults at Lincoln Cathedral are perhaps the first instance where ribs were used for purely decorative purposes.

■ Canterbury Cathedral, Gothic additions and rebuilding, begun ca. 1100

According to Gervase, English chronicler and contemporary of Abbot Suger, the new Gothic choir of Canterbury was built on the old Norman foundations, but the pillars were lengthened 12 feet (3.6 meters). In contrast to their predecessor they became finer, and the vaults were ribbed instead of plain.

Westminster Abbey

Henry III commissioned the rebuilding of Westminster Abbey in the Anglo-French Gothic style. Preoccupied with geometry, Gothic buildings that were built by French architects had plans based on regular grids, with an emphasis on height. The English Gothic method instead presupposed long volumes that were subdivided into various programmatic elements. Westminster Abbey combined French height and sleek proportions with English length, resulting in a truly monumental space. Unlike in France, where royal functions were distributed between different buildings at Reims, Saint-Denis, and Paris, Westminster Abbey was at once England's coronation church, mausoleum, and national shrine. As part of a complex of buildings of which only Westminster Hall survives, it was the most important church in England, as well as the center of governance.

■ **Westminster Abbey**, beg⟨
1245, London

Designed in direct reference t⟨
French counterparts, Westmir⟨
ster Abbey included features
often absent from other Englis⟨
cathedrals. A thin nave wall re⟨
quiring flying buttresses, an un⟨
obscured clerestory, and a che⟨
with radiating chapels were a⟨
borrowed from contemporary
French models. Yet the Englis⟨
combined traditional and exp⟨
mental styles to distinguish W⟨
minster Abbey from its French
prototypes. The prominent
transepts, subdivisions of spa⟨
and great length, typical even
pre-Gothic plans, were combi⟨
with an abundance of color a⟨
variation in details that guar-
antied a distinctly English flav⟨

◀ **Westminster Abbey**, Lac⟨
Chapel, fan vaulting, 1503–1⟨

The lady chapel was often
added to the east ends of E⟨
lish cathedrals in honor of t⟨
Virgin Mary. Although the
foundation stone was laid i⟨
1220, this chapel was repla⟨
in the early 16th century. T⟨
ceiling is an exquisite exam⟨
of fan vaulting, paralleled c⟨
by King's College Chapel at
Cambridge. The vaults' sto⟨
decoration conceals the str⟨
tural ribs beneath lavish
hanging fan cones.

Westminster Abbey

Late Gothic in the UK

1280–1517

■ The crossing tower, the Lady chapel, and the chapter house are elements
cathedral design particular to the UK ■ The tierceron vault, lierne vault, and
fan vault are consecutive elements in the evolution of vaulting techniques
■ *left:* **Wells Cathedral**, strainer arches reinforcing the crossing piers, ca. 133

1280 Exeter Cathedral
begun
1285 Work in the
Decorated style begins
on Wells Cathedral
1292 St. Stephen's Chapel
begun at Westminster
1310 Extra ribs are added
to the vaults at Exeter
ca. 1330 Elaborate vaults
in Wells choir create uniform surface; structural
bays eliminated
1331–37 First signs of
Perpendicular style at
Gloucester Cathedral
1441 King's College,
Cambridge, founded
1517 Protestant Reformation begins

While chronologically loosely parallel to the Rayonnant a
Flamboyant styles, the Decorated and Perpendicular sty
were strikingly different from the French manner. The
ditive logic of English cathedrals meant that each elem
along the sequence of spaces from the narthex throu
the main nave, the transept, the choir, and finally the L
chapel could be designed separately. The variety was
tonishing, but two particular schools of thought emerg
in the early 14th century. Of the two, the Perpendicu
lasted longer, persisting in various forms well into the 1
century; however, it was the freedom of the Decora
style that returned to the European continent to influe
late Gothic, espe-
cially in
Bohemia.

■ **King's College Chapel**, 1446–1515,
Cambridge

Unlike the Flamboyant style, which was
primarily a system of two-dimensional
patterning, the Perpendicular style was
responsible for a number of astounding
spatial effects. An example of the mature Perpendicular style is the King's
College Chapel at Cambridge, founded
in 1441, but not completed until 1515
under Henry VIII. A freestanding structure reminiscent of Sainte-Chapelle in
Paris, it is over 250 years younger and,
as such, balances at the historical brink
of the Reformation, rather than resting
at the center of medieval faith.

xeter Cathedral, west
de, begun 1280

mparison to the monu-
tal elevations of Paris or
ens, with their grids of
gnizable French Gothic
ents such as the double
ers or the rose window,
er's west facade offers a
cally different and more
ful interpretation of
ieval spirituality. At one
brightly painted, it ap-
s like a horizontal screen, as
statuary were just tem-
rily suspended.

■ **Gloucester Cathedral**, cloister, 1331–57

A highly complex building throughout, several
elements of Gloucester Cathedral are pivotal
works in the evolution of the Perpendicular style.
Its choir is one the first mature expressions of the
Perpendicular in its sharp, rectilinear wall tracery,
while the more humble cloister is cited as the
first fan vault in the UK.

Other Important Works	
York Minster, nave, begun ca. 1280	Bristol Cathedral, choir, Lady chapel, ca. 1330
Ely Cathedral, choir, tower, Lady chapel, 1321–49	Wells Cathedral, chapter house, choir and crossing, early 14th century
Lichfield Cathedral, Lady chapel, ca. 1330	

**hn Wastell: King's Col-
Chapel**, fan vaulting,
–15, Cambridge

nost original creations of
erpendicular style are the
aults that enclose late
ic chapels throughout the
ohn Wastell redesigned
an vaults at King's College
the lierne, or connected,
s proposed earlier.

Late Gothic in the UK

Late Gothic in Germany

ca. 1230–ca. 1520

■ First Gothic buildings in Germany combined ribbed vaults and pointed
arches with Romanesque exteriors ■ Germany developed its own Gothic
style by combining French and English elements with local practices
■ *left:* **Strasbourg Cathedral**, west facade, begun 1277

ca. 1230 Rayonnant style established in France

ca. 1235 First mature Gothic buildings begun in Marburg and Trier

1248 Construction of Cologne Cathedral begins

ca. 1290 Decorated style takes hold in England

1322 Choir at Cologne is finished; at 141 feet (43 meters) high it rivals Beauvais Cathedral

ca. 1390–ca. 1420 Influential German architects from the Parler School work on facades and towers at Ulm, Strasbourg, and Freiburg

ca. 1520 Artists and architects bring Renaissance styles back to Germany from Italy

■ **Cologne Cathedral**, choir vaults, 1248–1322

Cologne Cathedral was designed in 1248, but was not consecrated until 1322. At the time, only its towering choir was in place. The long process allowed architects to incorporate ambitious elements of Amiens and Beauvais such as the unusually high arcade and small triforium.

Strongly rooted in the Romanesque tradition, Germany adopted Gothic architecture much later than France and England. Because of this, it is hard to speak of anything but late Gothic in Germany. The style can be divided in two parallel trends: The first was derived from the French tradition and resulted in cathedrals such as Cologne, Strasbourg, and Ulm, which borrow greatly from the French style. The second took the churches of mendicant orders as models, combining them with elements of the English Decorated style to produce wonderful interiors. Strasbourg and Cologne were faithful Rayonnant copies, with the exception of the innovative tracery on the west facades and the openwork towers that gave German Gothic facades a uniquely narrow appearance.

■ Hans von Burghausen: St. Martin's Church, nave, ca. 1387–ca. 1500, Landshut

The parish church's interior is at once simple and mysterious. This was achieved through the manipulation of the building's proportions and the way light enters the space. The columns are so slender that they seem to hang in tension. The ribs' geometry makes the eye shift from column to column in an attempt to understand the structure.

■ Cologne Cathedral, facade and west towers under construction, begun 1248

One of the tallest churches in the world, the construction of Cologne Cathedral lasted well beyond the Middle Ages. As part of a national Gothic Revival project the towers were finished using the original plan in the 19th century.

Other Works

burg Cathedral, tower and
ir, 1275–1513

Cathedral, west facade
tower, begun 1377, com-
ed 1881–90

alkirche, by Hans von
ghausen, 1407–61, Landshut

uenkirche, by Joerg Gang-
er, 1468–88, Munich

rch of St. Lorenz, choir, by
rad Heinzelmann, later
rad Roriczer, 1477,
emberg

rch of St. Anne, 1499–1522,
aberg

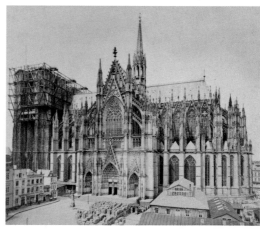

Late Gothic in Germany

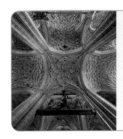

Bohemian and Polish Gothic

1333–ca. 1500

■ Gothic in central and eastern Europe evolved late ■ Master masons combined French cathedral designs with the English Decorated style ■ Tendency toward irregular or mannered design ■ Influenced by the Parler family
■ *left:* **St. Mary's Church**, vaults over the crossing, 1342–1502, Gdansk, Pola[nd]

1333–70 Reign of Polish king Casimir III; prosperity creates a building boom

1344 St. Vitus Cathedral designed by French architect Matthias of Arras

1347–51 Black Plague sweeps across Europe

1348 Charles University is founded in Prague

1352 Holy Roman Emperor Charles IV employs Peter Parler to continue work on St. Vitus Cathedral

ca. 1500 Italian Renaissance styles begin to gain popularity

Other Works

Charles Bridge, by Peter Parler, begun 1357, Prague

All Saints Chapel, by Peter Parler, 1370, Prague

Malbork Castle, begun 1380s, Malbork, Poland

Church of St. Barbara, by Peter and John Parler, begun 1388, Kutna Hora

Church of the Holy Cross, by Heinrich and Peter Parler, 1410, Schwäbisch-Gmünd, Germany

Late Gothic architecture in central and eastern Eur[ope] was as diverse as the political influences and border [re]gions of the area. In 1346 Charles IV made Prague the c[ap]ital of the Holy Roman Empire, commissioning a n[ew] stone cathedral from the French architect Matthia[s of] Arras. Unlike in France, important Gothic building[s in] northern and eastern Europe were often built of br[ick,] creating a style known as "Backstein Gothic." The s[hift] from stone to brick architecture was influenced by [the] unavailability of stone, economic considerations, and [the] local building culture. Internationally influenced, [the] imaginative treatment of the interiors, especially [the] vaulting, can be attributed to Bohemian master mas[ons] familiar with the English Decorated style.

■ **Peter Parler: St. Vitus Cathedral**, clerestory wind[ow] after 1356, Prague

At St. Vitus Cathedral, Fren[ch] Gothic combines with the c[re]ativity of the Parler family. [The] family of master masons w[as in]fluential in central Europe [dur]ing the 14th century. Peter Parler completed the cathe[dral] in Prague after the death o[f his] predecessor. His changes t[o the] plan and details of the Fren[ch] design brought a troubled [air] to the interior. The sacristy vaults are adorned with str[ange] hanging ribs, and angled r[ibs] create an uneasy rhythm in [the] clerestory windows.

Benedikt Ried: Vladislav Hall, Prague Castle, 1493–1502, Prague

Benedikt Ried was responsible for the largest secular hall in medieval Europe. Uninhibited by the height and compositional rules of ecclesiastical interiors, at Prague Castle Ried was able to create a space that grows from the floor as it envelops from above. At the brink of the Renaissance, his organic references in the vault ribs were a remarkable abstraction of nature into stone, creating an awkward beauty from personal imagination.

■ **St. Mary's Church**, 1342–1502, Gdansk, Poland

St. Mary's is a huge, fortresslike hall church towering over the Hanseatic city of Gdansk in northern Poland. Unlike churches in southern Poland built of a combination of brick and stone, St. Mary's is constructed entirely of brick. The immense flat exterior walls are made possible by buttresses projecting inside, which are hidden by side chapels. Complex patterned vaults rest on molded pillars.

Bohemian and Polish Gothic

Fortified Cities

Carcassonne and Mont-Saint-Michel
1204–1448

■ Present-day Mont-Saint-Michel and Carcassonne are the result of major restoration work ■ Restorations focused on Gothic and Picturesque qualit■ ■ *left*: **Crossing Tower**, begun 11th century, Mont-Saint-Michel, France

■ **1204** New monastic buildings are built at Mont-Saint-Michel with exquisite Gothic vaulting

1226 External defensive walls are built around Carcassonne

1262 The residents of Carcassonne are expelled by the king after a revolt

1270 The old chancel of Carcassonne Cathedral is demolished to make room for a new Gothic chancel, completed in the 1320s

1448 The choir at Mont-Saint-Michel is begun in the Flamboyant style to replace the destroyed Romanesque choir

The origins of fortified cites and towns are as varie■ the places themselves. Some were ancient forts like ■ cassonne, occupied and rebuilt by consecutive invac■ Others, such as the castles on the Loire, were villages■ monasteries whose inhabitants built fortifications du■ the violent 9th and 10th centuries. Still others were c■ missioned by dukes or kings and built in one campaig■ military outposts. Mont-Saint-Michel is a combinatio■ all three, but due to its unique situation on an out■ accessible by foot only at low tide, it does not fit any ■ category completely. Carcassonne, on the other han■ the definitive example of the ancient fortified cit■ spontaneous network of narrow winding streets lea■ up to a central castle or church. During the 19th cen■ Eugène Viollet-le-Duc (p. 348) renovated Carcasso■ restoring the city's Gothic elements.

■ **Fortified City of Carca■ sonne**, primarily 13th and centuries, France

Carcassonne is one the old■ fortifications in France. Loc■ on the site of a prehistoric fort, Romans later built sto■ fortifications there during ■ 1st century BCE. Later, Visig■ Arabs, and Franks all occup■ and added to the fortress. ■ existing castle, church, anc■ walls date back to the 12th■ 13th centuries, when the t■ acquired its picturesque m■ dieval look.

Gothic Fortifications

Mont-Saint-Michel, Tour a Liberté, 11th–16th ...ury, France

...entire history of medieval ...lo-Norman and later French ...itecture is revealed on one ...y outcrop named Mont-...t-Michel. Begun as a Bene-...ne abbey and Norman ...ary outpost during the ... century, it sits in a shallow ...off the coast of Normandy.

Tied to France, but reaching out to England, its architecture reflects the remarkable tension that existed between the two countries. At Mont-Saint-Michel opposites were reconciled. The bold fortifications spoke of the invincibility of its medieval builders. Yet the same people prayed to God with humility, from fragile chapels balanced over cold waters.

■ **Mont-Saint-Michel**, view from the east, 11th–16th century, France

The nave and transept of the abbey church cross at the peak of the mountain, where a tower both conquers and ennobles the summit of the island. The Romanesque nave was sophisticated for its time, with a lightness that anticipated Gothic additions. The nave terminates with a sublime Flamboyant-style choir almost as tall as the tower itself. Its spiky pinnacles seem to grow out of the mountain island.

Iberian Gothic

ca. 1220–1522

■ Mediterranean cities developed their own style, following the simple mendicant hall churches ■ The more extravagant Isabelline and Manueline styles derived from the Flamboyant, but included Islamic and marine-inspired element
■ *left:* **St. Maria de Vitória Monastery**, cloisters, begun 1387, Batalha, Portug

Influenced by both French and German architecture, I
rian Gothic was greatly influenced by Bourges Cathedr
spaciousness and density. Although it borrowed fr
other countries, the southern manifestation of the Got
style was nevertheless unique. The structures are clear a
strong, usually wider and shorter than their French co
terparts. The highly ornamented Manueline style evol
in Portugal. In a climate where light is abundant, the ch
concern is to provide shelter from the sun rather than in
it inside. Filtered light was used to bring out structural
tails and the depths of the intricate interior spaces.

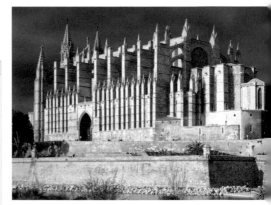

■ **Palma de Mallorca Cathedral**,
begun 1306

Built on the site of an earlier
mosque, the Palma Cathedral has
closely spaced buttresses that absorb the weight of the buildin
and allow the interior column
be thin and very tall. The centr
mass of the church is hidden a
its many spires and buttresses

eville Cathedral, begun
2

cathedral at Seville is im-
se and complex. Its vast
aisled Gothic plan is sur-
ded by later additions of

**urch of St. Maria de
ria**, begun 1386, Batalha,
ugal

church of St. Maria de Vi-
was named for the victory
talha that, in practical
s, gave Portugal its inde-
lence. The new state was
r to show its cultural
gth by building a church
would rival the great
edrals of northern Europe.
ing oddly out of place in
bright Portuguese sun, the
ow and delicate motifs of
nglish Perpendicular can
en on the eclectic facade.

sacristies and chapels, all
stuffed with Baroque altars,
sculptures, and woodwork. The
effect conveys the wealth and
power of the Spanish crown
and its newly formed American

colonies. More refined than
Palma de Mallorca, its delicate
pillars soar to meet stunning
star-shaped vaults, borrowed
from the English Decorated
style.

Iberian Gothic

Late Gothic in Northern Italy

1209–1420

■ Gothic architecture made little impact in Italy ■ Gothic elements were used as two-dimensional motifs in screen facades ■ Contrasting colors of marble resulted in striking polychrome walls

■ *left:* **Milan Cathedral**, pinnacles, after 1387

■ **1209** St. Francis of Assisi founds the Franciscan monastic order

1308–21 Dante Alighieri writes *The Divine Comedy*

1348 Outbreak of the Black Plague stops enlargement of Siena Cathedral

1386 Construction of the Milan Cathedral in the Rayonnant style begins

1387–1401 Scholarly debates take place over the construction of Milan Cathedral

1420 Renaissance styles are incorporated into Florence Cathedral

Gothic architectural styles arrived late in Italy, and huma ist Renaissance thought began early, resulting in Got architectural styles being only an inflection upon the p dominantly Classical tradition. Even key buildings st as the cathedrals of Florence or Siena were transitio moments between the established Italian Romanesc and new Renaissance ideas. With the founding of ine pendent city-states in the 13th and 14th centuries, t absolutist role of the church was greatly diminish Italian cathedrals were often funded by the city or its garchy and built by civic consensus. The very nature of t process prohibited powerful individuals such as Abb Suger from materializing unified ideas of God and ligh vertical masterpieces of faith and political ego. Itali Gothic styles were often highly ornate and colorful.

■ **Milan Cathedral**, facade begun 1386, completed earl 19th century

Milan Cathedral was poised be the masterpiece of Italia Gothic architecture. Archite and scientists from Italy, Fra and Germany were invited t discuss and contribute to th proposed plans of 1387. Cor sensus was hard to reach, as architects defended their ov building cultures and styles being superior methods. Th Neo-Gothic facade was com pleted only in the early 19th century.

ena Cathedral,
13th century

Siena Cathedral is intensely
mented. The facade has
e marble bands dominat-
over thinner green inlays.
le, the proportions are al-
d, and equal value is given
hite and green marble,
cing an aesthetic that re-
ancient Egypt. Leading
ts worked on further sculp-
ornamentation.

Other Works

Maria Novella, begun 1246,
ence

rancesco, 1250, Bologna

Croce, by Arnolfo di Cambio,
un 1294, Florence

rancesco, Gothic rebuild-
begun 1320, Siena

eto Cathedral, by Lorenzo
ani, 1330

◀ **Milan Cathedral**,
nave, begun 1386

The effect inside Milan
Cathedral is mystical.
Shadows are cast on
the heavy pillars that
march down the cathe-
dral's five wide aisles.
Unusual hexagonal
column capitals with
large statues top the
continuous row of
pillars.

■ **Basilica of St.
Francesco d'Assisi**,
1228–53, Assisi

A simple Latin cross in
plan, the monastery
contains upper and
lower pilgrimage
churches. Splendid
frescoes cover the
interior.

Late Gothic in Northern Italy

Italian Civic Architecture

1183–ca. 1500

■ New secular architecture was constructed in Italy in response to politic changes ■ Civic buildings were accompanied by the construction of churches and bourgeois residences

■ *left:* **Doge's Palace**, detail of the arcade, 1424, Venice

1183 Peace of Constance gives northern Italian states semi-independence

1215 Construction begins on Siena Cathedral

1347–48 The Black Plague in Italy

1352 Capella di Piazza begun at the base of the municipal tower in Siena, in commemoration of the deliverance from the Black Plague

1386 Milan Cathedral begun

ca. 1440 Piazza St. Marco established as a public square in Venice

1453–ca. 1500 Constantinople falls, and spoils are brought to Venice; Venice takes control of the Mediterranean economy

Italian city-states, such as Milan, Venice, Florence, Siena, began to gain power toward the end of the 1 century and commissioned consciously planned c buildings to establish their power. They were perhaps first examples of deliberate urban planning at the pu level since ancient Rome. Many factors led to this ren sance of urban life, but the most important was the political process that emerged in northern Italy with new millennium. The struggle for power between pope and the German emperors left room for developing Italian bourgeoisie of artisans, guild m bers, and merchants to join with local aristocracy in cr ing powerful city-states with considerable independe By passing tax reforms and creating civil infrastructure the form of police forces and law courts, they ensured litical and economic stability as well as public safet factors crucial to the development of prosperous c and, indeed, public architecture.

■ **Doge's Palace**, 1424, Venice

One of the three main build that define the famous Piazz St. Marco, the Doge's Palace the Venetian Gothic arch, wh heavily influenced by Byzant and Arab styles. The column pointed Gothic arches creat horizontal planes on the building's facade, and their tracery adds wild ornament to the otherwise stoic facad

◀ **Piazza del Campo with Palazzo Pubblico**, 1298–1348, Siena

Established in 1287 by municipal ordinances, the Campo in Siena was an organized act of urban planning in late medieval Italy. In a successful attempt to unite partisan factions, the Campo was built on unclaimed sloping land between the three rivaling sectors. The complex process of preparing and leveling the site for a new city center was the result of a sophisticated administrative process rather than of organic growth. In a gesture of reverence, palaces faced the fan-shaped piazza and the dominant Palazzo Pubblico, the equivalent of a town hall. The basic programmatic elements of the palazzo included an ornate meeting room with large windows on the upper floor overlooking the piazza, an arcade on the ground floor for elite merchants, and a balcony for speeches.

Other Works

wn Halls at Brescia and
odena, late 12th century

lazzo del Popolo, 1213–67,
di

lazzo del Broletto, 1215,
no

azzo del Capitano, begun
1293, Todi

azzo Vecchio, 1299–1310,
rence

■ **Doge's Palace**, southwest corner, 1424, Venice

Venice's architectural response to its watery location was to build light structures. The unstable soil conditions translated into an aesthetic of latticed arcades that seem to float over the city's canals.

▲ **Piazza del Campo**, established 1287, Siena

Situated in front of the city hall, the square slopes gently toward it like an amphitheater. The rooflines of the houses of wealthy Sienese families line the piazza, symbolically standing shorter than the city hall.

Italian Civic Architecture

Southeast Asia

Angkor Wat and Bagan
ca. 1090–ca. 1430

■ The Bagan kings and the Khmer of Cambodia were contemporaries ■ Ove 2,000 religious structures were built in Bagan

■ *left:* **Angkor Wat**, detail, early 12th century, near Siem Reap, Cambodia

■ **ca. 1090** King Kyanzittha begins construction of numerous temples based on the Shwezigon Pagoda

1113–50 Reign of Suryavarman II; Angkor Wat built in the capital city of the Khmer Kingdom

1177 Angkor reconquered after being attacked by the Chams

1181 King Jayavarman VII converts to Buddhism and builds Angkor Thom over the ruins of the old capital

1287 Bagan is sacked by the Mongols

ca.1430 Khmer abandon Angkor Thom after the kingdom is sacked by the Thai

The Khmer and Bagan kingdoms occupied large are roughly equivalent to present-day Cambodia a Myanmar (Burma). Although the sites are now accessi to tourists, political turmoil has made it difficult to co duct archaeological research and comprehensive resto tion programs. As a result, much remains to be disc ered about the relationships between architecture a local religious practices. At Angkor Wat, geometry play a major role in defining the layout of the main temple voted to Vishnu. According to Hindu beliefs, the squ was the ultimate celestial form. Multiplying, dividing, perimposing, and layering the square was the answer constructing the perfect building. At Arimaddanapu which was the capital of the kingdom of Bagan (a known as Pagan), the stupa, a form of burial mound, v reinterpreted to produce complex domed shrines Buddha, and temples were built by the wealthy.

■ **Angkor Wat**, early 12th century, near Siem Reap, Cambodia

The largest of many Hindu temples built in the ancient Khmer capital, Angkor Wat is a layered rectangular compound surrounded by a wide moat. Rich with detail and highly symbolic, it is meant to evoke both a mandala rising from the primordial ocean and Vishnu's mountain abode.

Gothic

Shwezigon Pagoda, 11th century, near Bagan, Myanmar

The Shwezigon Pagoda was the archetype for later pagodas in the region. Gilt in gold leaf, the temple is not entered by worshippers, but is rumored to hold relics of the Buddha.

Ancient City of Bagan, 12th–13th centuries, Myanmar

Made of bricks from the dusty soil on which they stand, thousands of domed structures dot the plains of Bagan. The stupas, pagodas, and temples are built in many different architectural styles.

Rock Churches of Lalibela

ca. 1185–1270

■ Rock-hewn and cave churches existed in Akum, Tigray, and Lalibela in Ethiopia ■ The Lalibela monoliths were entirely isolated from the surrounding rock ■ The churches have been use since the 13th century

■ *left:* **Bet Ghiorgis (St. George's Church)**, early 13th century

ca. 1185 King Gebre Mesqel Lalibela ascends to the Ethiopian throne

1187 Jerusalem is recaptured by Muslims; King Gebre Mesqel Lalibela orders the carving of several rock-cut churches in Lalibela to create a new Jerusalem

ca. 1229 King Gebre Mesqel Lalibela dies; Bet Ghiorgis (St. George's Church) may have been commissioned as a memorial church; legend states that St. George oversaw the construction

1270 End of the Zagwe dynasty, which had ruled this area of Ethiopia since the 9th century

The rock-hewn churches at the Ethiopian town of Lalib rank among the most interesting interpretations of ar tectural tectonics and of the very nature of building. 12 churches cannot really be classified as buildings, fo build means to assemble something larger from sma elements. Instead, these churches are enormous carvi hewn out of solid red volcanic rock, presumably v hammer and chisel. Although laborious, the proces making the churches was straightforward. H trenches were dug around the corners of the monoli which were then carved inside and out to mimic corni pilasters, columns, and lintels—elements that usually structural roles in buildings, but that here are purely namental. Despite their sculptural qualities, structural bility must have been an issue in creating the churc since the hollowed monoliths cause stress to the through compression and, more importantly, tensio

Gothic

■ **Bet Mariam**, 12th–13th centuries

The Rock Churches of Lalib are part of a system of tunn passages, crypts, and water tures. Bet Mariam (the Chur of Mariam) sits in the midd a large court carved directl of the volcanic rock terrane connected by a narrow pas to Madhane Alam, the larg the churches, which bears a striking resemblance to a G temple, with its sloping roc and peristyle.

■ Bet Amanuel, 12th century

The churches at Lalibela are extremely varied in style. Built in three major groups—a northern, western, and eastern group—they seem to draw on Classical, Byzantine, and Islamic architecture while also incorporating several traditional Ethiopian aspects into their designs. Bet Amanuel is part of the eastern group. Its symmetric and Classical facade dividers mimic an actually built structure. The church is thought to have possibly been a royal chamber.

Other Works
Bet Medhani Alem, 12th–13th centuries
Bet Mascal, 12th–13th centuries
Bet Denagel, 12th–13th centuries
Bet Golgotha Mikael and King Lalibela's Tomb, 12th–13th centuries
Bet Mercoreos, 12th–13th centuries

⬛ Ghiorgis (St. George's ⬛h), early 13th century

⬛iorgis was the last church ⬛built at Lalibela and is ⬛ted to St. George, the ⬛al saint of Ethiopia. Fash⬛ on a cruciform plan re⬛ing a Latin cross, the ⬛ is in an 82-square-foot ⬛uare-meter) pit that is ⬛d via a tunnel. The ⬛ was carved atop a three-⬛base and, as with tradi-⬛ Ethiopian churches, has ⬛west-facing doors.

Rock Churches of Lalibela

Renaissance

1420–1620

Andrea Palladio: Villa Capra (La Rotunda), 1566–91, Vicenza

Renaissance

p. 205

1519–1598
Renaissance on the Iberian Peninsula

Gothic styles remained strong in Spain and Portugal, which were greatly influenced by the Moorish tradition. During the late Renaissance the Desornamentado style developed

Around the World:
India and East Asia

In India, architects of the Mughal empire were greatly influenced by Islamic and Persian styles. Meanwhile, in East Asia, terraced temples, palaces, and fortresses were built with swooping eaves

1550   1600   1620

00–1620
naissance in ntral and stern Europe

an architects were ught to Germany, tria, Poland, and emia by wealthy pa-s in order to mod-ze central and eastern opean residences

opo Strada
erto Luchese
er von Bentheim
rg Ridinger
s Holl

Pedro Machuca
Juan Bautista de Toledo
Juan de Herrera

p. 217

p. 211

Renaissance

The rediscovery of architectural styles and theories from Roman antiquity was the catalyst that set off the Renaissance. The first depictions of ancient architecture emerged in Rome at the beginning of the 15th century, when a single copy of Roman architect and engineer Vitruvius's *Ten Books Concerning Architecture* was discovered.

One of the first Renaissance architects, Filippo Brunelleschi of Florence, had started studying the architecture of antiquity before the discovery of Vitruvius's text. Brunelleschi was fascinated by the idea that ideal building proportions could be ascertained from mathematical and geometrical principles. He and other Renaissance architects studied the proportions of Classical buildings, making humans the measure by which all things were gauged. Renaissance architecture thus became the replication of natural

■ **St. Lorenzo** **Old Sacrisity**, 1419–1428, Florence

■ **Palazzo Du** courtyard, ca. Urbino

Capitoline Hill, Rome

forms. The experience of the individual, and scientific observation, took precedence and became known as humanism, and a new form of literature, the architectural treatise, developed alongside the philosophical change. Treatises usually contained lessons about the rules of proportion, column orientation, types of buildings, and structural elements.

Secular buildings such as large city palaces, were built throughout Florence, Verona, Vicenza, Venice, and Rome. Fashioned after the villa of the Roman emperor Hadrian in Tivoli, new clients sought to build large countryside estates. Architects such as Andrea Palladio, Giulio Romano, and Raphael were commissioned to construct ornate countryside homes. In terms of religious architecture, Brunelleschi, Bramante, and Michelangelo used centralized floor plans, and cathedrals were typically crowned with an enormous dome above the crossing.

Introduction

St. Maria de
Consolazione,
begun 1508, To
Italy

Clear geometric decorative forms were characteristic of the early Italian Renaissance (1420–1500). These
elements began to play an important role during the
High Renaissance (1500–1530). Sculptural columns,
pilasters, and cornices dominated architecture.
Round double windows, popular during the early
Renaissance, were abandoned in favor of horizontal
designs featuring windows with pediments. Architects experimented with geometry and sought new
forms of architectural harmony.

Italian architects of the late Renaissance
(1530–1620) aggrandized the styles of antiquity.
Columns of the "giant order," spanning two floors,
were popular, and statues were arranged in small
niches. Ornamentation from late antiquity such as
garlands, rams' heads, masks, and vines became fashionable. These went against the late Renaissance emphasis on straight, solid forms, and Mannerism, an
anti-Classical style, developed in response.

Renaissance 1420–1620

. Maria dei
acoli, 1481–89,
ce

ancellery,
il, 1534–37,
ge

Germany, France, Northern and Eastern Europe

Renaissance styles first began to appear in German architecture about 100 years after their spread throughout Italy. Until that time, German architects merely copied designs from pattern books and treatises, rarely actually traveling to Rome to study the buildings of their contemporaries or those of antiquity. Because of this, early Renaissance designs from northern Italy were mixed with German Gothic styles. The Fuggers, a wealthy German banking family, financed the construction of the first Renaissance buildings in southern Germany. The style gained popularity and spread to Austria and eastern Europe via the Hapsburg family, who brought Italian architects, and consequently Renaissance architecture, to the Holy Roman Empire.

In central and eastern Europe, Polish and Bohemian princes commissioned Italian architects to build Renaissance castles and churches. Rounded arches, the

Classical orders, and geometric floor plans slowly replaced Gothic designs. Polish Renaissance architecture was also heavily influenced by the style of architects from the Netherlands.

As in Germany, Poland, and Bohemia, France favored Gothic architecture for quite some time and adopted Renaissance designs slowly. The French maintained a high level of ornamentation, as was popular in Gothic architeture, managing to appropriate sculptural designs to the new style. France became the forerunner for European castle construction during the Renaissance. Castles, or *châteaux,* such as Chambord and Fontainebleau, with their ornate designs and extensive gardens, were greatly influential throughout Germany, the Netherlands, and Bohemia. French decorative motifs were often appropriated in other European designs and mixed with both Dutch and Italian designs.

Renaissance 1420–1620

wer of
m, 1515–21,
ɔn

**Giralda
Tower)**, 1568,
e

Residences in England, Spain, and Portugal

Architecture in England and on the Iberian Peninsula developed its own style, far removed from the designs of Italian Renaissance architects. As in Germany, the Renaissance had a delayed and sporadic effect. Gothic styles in Spain and Portugal retained their status as a symbol of the power and might of the Catholic tradition, and the recapture of Spanish territory from the Moors sparked new interest in Gothic forms in order to glorify the church's power. Local traditions were seldom blended with styles from antiquity. New directions of architecture included the sparse, minimalistic Desornamentado style.

In England, the Renaissance wasn't popularized until the reign of Queen Elizabeth I. Known as Elizabethan architecture, Italian styles were incorporated into Gothic designs. Architects mixed geometric floor plans with medieval fortified styles, creating a distinctly English style of architecture.

Introduction

Filippo Brunelleschi

1377, Florence—1446, Florence

■ Leading builder of domes in Florence ■ His technical prowess and knowledge of the architecture of antiquity gained him great prestige ■ Developed a system by which he could measure the dimensions of a room exactly, thereby becoming a pioneer of freestyle perspective

1377 Born in Florence

1392–98 Trains as a goldsmith

1402 Participates in a contest for the two bronze doors of the Florentine Baptistery, but his design loses to Ghiberti's

1402–04 Travels for his studies to Rome, probably with Donatello

1415 Creates his first linear perspective drawing, greatly influencing both art and architecture

1417 Designs a cupola for the Florence Cathedral

1446 Dies in Florence

Other Works

Palazzo di Parte Guelfa, 1421–22, Florence

Sagrestia Vecchia (the Old Sacristy) of St. Lorenzo, 1421–40, Florence

Barbadori Chapel at St. Felicità, 1423–25, Florence

Palazzo Busini, before 1427, Florence

St. Maria degli Angeli, 1434–37, Florence

St. Spirito, 1434–82, Florence

Filippo Brunelleschi is one of the key figures of Renaissance architecture. Although his early works were very much related to Gothic designs, he later developed an individual architectural style that combined elements from Tuscan Romanesque and Gothic—such as massive pillars, lancet arches, and medieval ornamentation—with a formal style from antiquity—columns, elegant pillars, and geometric forms and proportions. Brunelleschi established fixed mathematical and technical principles in his designs. He was able to make a clear break with the styles of Gothic architecture with the design and construction of the massive dome of the Florence Cathedral (p. 170). Brunelleschi was also an innovator of perspective drawing and construction techniques.

■ **Pazzi Chapel, St. Croce**, 1429– Florence

This small chapel one of the first centrally planned constructions of the Renaissance. The arcaded facade's middle cupola mirrors the shape of main interior space. The inner chamber was originally planned as a burial chapel for the family of the benefactor Andrea de' Pazzi.

spedale degli Innocenti, 1424–45, Florence

elleschi's design of the Ospedale degli Inno-
i, an orphanage, included a nine-part *loggia*,
llery, that is arcaded with composite arches
mix the Classical orders. In contrast to Gothic
es, half-circle arches are used, spanning a
r space and creating a more geometric fa-
. As with many of his other buildings,
elleschi was concerned with mathematic
geometric precision in the design.

silica of St. Lorenzo, 1420–69, Florence

elleschi linked elements of local building
tion with elements of the architecture of an-
y. The evenly arranged windows allow a
istent amount of light into all the sections of
e, which was an innovation from medieval
tecture. The combination of gray sandstone
tures and white plasterwork is one of
elleschi's trademarks.

Filippo Brunelleschi

The Dome of Florenc

In 1294 the citizens of Florence decided to build a new cathedral. As one of the richest Renaissance city-states, Florence was able to afford a building of phenomenal size. Filippo Brunelleschi's (p. 168) bold dome, designed after most construction had finished, was a groundbreaking achievement in engineering. The design relied on the law of physics that two correlating, inclined structures will mutually support one another. Brunelleschi positioned bricks in an overlapping ring arrangement, using a fast-drying mortar to join them in a herringbone pattern. He was therefore able to abandon traditional methods of scaffolding.

Composed of two shells, the inner shell supports the wei of the outer shell. This syste was first developed in antiq Ten marble columns, intertwined within the structure, also help support the dome

■ **Filippo Brunelleschi: Dome of Florence Cathedral**, 1420–36

The Florence Cathedral is a monument to a city's self-confidence. Following decades of architectural standstill, the citizens of Florence decided in 1357 to push ahead with the construction of the massive cathedral. Brunelleschi won the

design competition in 1418 with his piecemeal herringbone-patterned dome. Almost immediately builders faced the problem of constructing the building's curvature, because an architect had never before, not even during antiquity, been able to erect a circular room that could span a 138-foot (42-meter) diameter.

The enormous height of the dome was increased throug the construction of an octagonal foundation. Large rour windows illuminate the dor

Cathedral

...ome reflects the Floren-...opography, influenced by ...ommunal spirit of the city, ...alized around and united ...e church. Brunelleschi's dome stood at the forefront of modern cathedral design. At 502 feet (153 meters) in length, and 125 feet (38 meters) in width, the cathedral is the fourth-largest Christian cathedral in the world, following St. Peter's Basilica in Rome, St. Paul's Cathedral in London, and the Milan Cathedral.

The Dome of Florence Cathedral

Leon Battista Alberti

1404, Genoa–1472, Rome

■ The most influential architectural theoretician and humanist of the ea[rly]
Renaissance ■ Reacted to the Roman architect Vitruvius ■ Considered t[o]
have discovered central perspective, which was later used in architecture
■ His churches and palaces inspired numerous subsequent architects

■ **1404** Born in Genoa

1429 The Alberti family returns to Florence after over
50 years of exile, and Leon
Battista is exposed to the
Florentine tradition

1436 Publication of *De Pic-
tura*, in which Alberti
claims that painting should
be the fundamental basis
for architecture

1450 Publication of his
most influential work *De Re
Aedificatoria*, in which he
outlines building ideals

1450 Construction of the
unfinished Tempio Malat-
estiano in Rimini, in which
he tries to exhibit the standards outlined in *De Re
Aedificatoria*

1472 Dies in Rome

Alberti, a comprehensively educated humanist and m[an]
of letters, was one of the most eminent architects of [the]
early Italian Renaissance and is celebrated to this da[y as]
one of the founders of modern architectural theory. In [his]
treatise *Ten Books of Architecture*, he defined the laws [of]
ideal architecture. According to Alberti, ideal architect[ure]
was based on the harmonious interplay of structural fo[rm,]
function, and decorative design. His architecture [was]
therefore greatly inspired by the constructions, theo[reti-]
cians, and building practices of antiquity. As one of [the]
first Renaissance architects, Alberti experimented fur[ther]
with Classical orderings of columns and mathemat[ical]
proportions. For the facades of his churches and pal[aces]
he preferred to use elements from antiquity, such [as]
columns and the form of the triumphal arch, as his mo[tif.]
Alberti's work subsequently influenced Neoclassicists [and]
the architects of the Baroque era.

■ **Tempio Malatestiano**,
1450–68, Rimini

Alberti's first assignment w[as]
the reconfiguration of a Go[thic]
church into a mausoleum f[or]
Sigismondo Malatesta, the [lord]
of Rimini. For the church's f[a-]
cade, Alberti employed the
motif of the Roman triump[hal]
arch. The wide middle entr[ance]
arch leads into the interior
nave, and the side arches o[rigi-]
nally acted as niched chape[ls]
for the sarcophagi of the ow[ner]
and his loved ones.

, Maria Novella, 1458–71,
nce

rti clad the multicolored
le facade of the Domin-
church with a pattern of
etric forms. Using the
ince to the Roman Pan-

theon as the prototype, ordered columns, pilasters, and a
deep portal niche were added
to the design. The volutes,
which span the gap from the
ground floor to the narrower
upper floor, were originally

ornamental elements from antiquity, and were adapted by
Alberti to serve a new function.
These scrollshaped elements
would later be greatly nfluential
for the facades of the Baroque
period.

■ **Palazzo Rucellai**, 1446–51,
Florence

Alberti's design incorporated
pilaster orderings for the first
time. Modeled after the Colosseum, there were Doric
columns on the ground floor,
then Ionic, and Corinthian on
the top floor. Alberti altered the
style by raising the pilasters
from the masonry slightly, emphasizing the verticality of the
facade. The palace's clarity and
austerity was a novelty later im-
itated throughout Rome.

Leon Battista Alberti

Ideal Urban Planning

1450–1593

■ The styles of antiquity inspired Renaissance urban planning ■ Earlier
cities were reorganized ■ Utopian plans for ideal states were popular ye
seldom realized ■ Rich citizens patroned massive building campaigns t
reshaped Renaissance Europe

■ **Piazza Ducale**,
1492–94, Vigevano

Vigevano was rebuilt between 1492 and 1494. The town received its new piazza under the order of Ludovico il Moro, a

Other Works

Rome's Water Supply Infrastructure, redesigned by Leon Battista Alberti, ca. 1450

Central Plan of Florence, by Giorgio Vasari, ca. 1555

Mannheim Gridded Layout, 1606, Germany

Cities were the central stages of power during the Re
sance. The technical and artistic developments of the
aissance were adopted in the construction and plan
of new cities, as architects sought to create a better w
Strong building laws were passed, which were uphe
architect guilds. Palaces constructed by the new n
classes took over city landscapes, replacing small w
shops and market stalls. Streets and alleyways bec
centrally organized according to rules of perspective,
cathedrals, castles, palaces, and town halls were mc
into the center of the city. The discovery of gunpov
drove builders to fortify their new cities with trenches
bastions in order to create more easily defendable c
Consequently Renaissance cities often resembled mi
mountains in terms of their size.

member Sforza dynasty of Milan.
Thought to have been designed
by Bramante, the piazza is surrounded on all three sides by
facades that are all uniformly designed and aligned. The houses of
wealthy citizens were found here.
Residential areas were

located on the upper floor, w
businesses were at street lev
The elongated space is nearl
the ideal proportions of 1 : 2,
the city's main street gives o
the square through an arcade
unites the entire area.

erro della Francesca:
l City, ca. 1470, Galleria
onale delle Marche, Urbino

echnique of using linear
pective, attributed to the
n artist and architect Fil-
Brunelleschi, revolution-

ized both art and architecture
during the Renaissance.
Through this innovation architects were able to envisage
projects in an orderly fashion
and create more accurate drafts
and studies. This 15th-century
painting of the Renaissance

ideal—a city constructed in
accordance with the rules of
perspective—is harmonious
and balanced. Because Renaissance architects looked back to
antiquity as the age of reason
and order, they adopted similar
styles in their own ideals.

■ **Bernardo Rossellino: Palazzo**
Piccolomini, 1459, Pienza

Pope Pius II rebuilt his hometown of
Pienza in 1459, including the construction of Palazzo Piccolomini on the
town square. Nearby the palace he also
erected a cathedral, an episcopal
palace, and a town hall, framing the
trapezoidal piazza. The cathedral stood
in the center, around which all building
axes were oriented. Rossellino modeled his designs for the Palazzo
Piccolomini on Leon Battista
Alberti's Palazzo Rucelai
in Florence.

Donato Bramante

1444, Fermignano–1514, Rome

■ Leading architect of the Italian High Renaissance ■ Made Rome the leading architectural center of its time ■ Judiciously combined local archi tecture forms with new ideals ■ Revolutionized church design by aban doning the old longitudinal style in favor of a circular design

1444 Born in Fermignano, near Urbino

1468 Begins training as an architectural painter

1479–82 Works at the court of Ludovico Sforzas in Milan as an architect

1482–99 Active as an ar- chitect in Milan

1499 Flees to Rome due to the invading French army

1503 Offers his services to the pope in Rome

1514 Dies in Rome

No one changed architecture in Rome in such a short riod of time more than the initiator of the Italian High F aissance, Bramante. Within only a decade he create new, revolutionary style of architecture. After an inte study of ancient Roman ruins, he developed a new ch design that was centrally planned, and which wc come to epitomize the new style of architecture. mante combined squares, circles, octagons, and cro throughout his floor plans in order to express the id of mathematical and geometrical equilibrium. He als corporated elements of ancient pagan temples within designs for Christian churches, thereby causing his ar tectural style to embody the arti aesthetic, and humanistic goals of age. The formal principles of his w would serve as a model for the fol ing generation, and his style would tinue to be replicated outside of Ro well into the 17th and 18th centuri

■ **St. Maria delle Grazie**, 1492–98, Milan

The churches Bramante constructed in Milan were situated within the local architectural t tions. Geometric forms and fragmented, eve distributed ornaments are mixed with the m traditional elements of the Lombardic Gothi style. Horizontal zones supersede one anothe within a decorative band located around the tire east wing of the Dominican church of St Maria delle Grazie. The eastern building serv the tomb of the Moro dynasty. Bramante ch ancient tombs to serve as his personal inspir behind the design of the central dome.

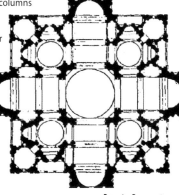

Other Works by Bramante

St. Maria Presso St. Satiro, 1478–82, Milan

St. Maria in Abbiategrasso, facade, 1497, Milan

Cloister of St. Ambrogio, detail, 1498, Milan

St. Maria della Pace, cloister, 1504, Rome

Cortile del Belvedere, begun 1505, Vatican

Palazzo Tribunali, draft, 1508, Rome

St. Maria del Popolo, chorus, 1509, Rome

Palazzo Caprini, ca. 1510, Rome

■ **St. Peter's**, initial draft, 1505–06, Rome

Bramante also designed St. Peter's Basilica in Rome. Pope Julius II condemned Bramante's plans and they were abandoned, but the four arches that had already been built nonetheless determined the later form and size of the finished cathedral.

Pietro in Montorio, Rome

ante created an entirely ype of memorial church his design. The church s freely upon a tiered plat- nd is surrounded by a r colonnade of Doric col- which reveal the Roman nce found in many Re- nce churches. Indeed, an- Rome can be viewed as odel and ideal of Renais- architecture. The central this church pays tribute orebears, but without a copy of antiquity. The ns are constructed ac- cording to mathematical principles; the spaced intervals between them equating to four times the width of the columns themselves, whereas the space between the columns on the interior wall equates to the width of two columns. The ornamental bands found on the columns are an interpretation of ancient traditions, which Bramante repeated on the sanctuary's interior and on the outside of the structure itself.

Donato Bramante

Guiliano da Sangallo

Giuliano Giamberti
ca. 1443, Florence—1516, Florence

■ Worked during the transition to the High Renaissance period ■ Drafter o
many famous Florentine buildings ■ Worked for the popes in Rome ■ Arc
tect of St. Peter's Basilica for a short time ■ Also a sculptor and engineer

■ **ca. 1443** Born Giuliano
Giamberti, son of a stone
cutter and carpenter in
Florence
1463 Travels to Rome to
study ancient architecture
1465 First documented
evidence of his detailed
sketchbooks
After 1470 Sets up a workshop in Florence with his
brother Antonio da
Sangallo
1514 Takes over the construction of St. Peter's Basilica with Raphael in Rome
for a short time
1516 Dies in Florence

Giuliano da Sangallo was the most important inter
diary link between the architectural styles of the e
Renaissance and the later High Renaissance period
completed many sketchbooks during his intensive st
of ancient Roman architecture, and these sketches
greatly impacted both his mature style and the des
of later architects. Sangallo's churches, palaces,
drafts demonstrate his remarkable affinity for the art
elements of the early Renaissance period. The harm
ously proportioned room sequences and facades tha
created united both regional and Roman elements
most famous design, St. Maria delle Carceri in Prato,
an outstanding impact on the development of H
Renaissance church architecture as well as the ens
Baroque period.

...lazzo Gondi, 1490–94,
...nce

...e palace of the Florentine
...ent Giovanni Gondi, San-
...produced an elegant de-
...hat left the heavy, solid
...es of the early Renais-
...far behind. The promi-
...e of the brickwork recedes
...h of the three equally
...stories. The round-arch
...ws on the ground floor
...rrounded by blocks that
...r the curve of the
...ay, creating a star shape.
...urtyard's vaulted arcade
...ly ornamented.

Other Works by Sangallo

Palazzo Pazzi-Quaratesi, 1478,
Florence

Villa Poggio a Caiano, draft,
1485, Florence

St. Spirito, sacristy, 1488–92,
Florence

St. Maria Maddalena de Pazzi,
cloister, 1492, Florence

Palazzo della Rovere, 1496,
Savona

Cappella Gondi in St. Maria
Novella, marble decorations,
1503, Florence

■ **St. Maria delle Carceri**,
1485–1506, Prato

Sangallo completed the earliest
known example of a cross-
shaped building plan of the Renaissance in the tiny pilgrim
church of St. Maria delle Carceri.
He constructed a domed room
atop the cross-shaped floor
plan. The geometrically
structured composition of the
rooms is also reflected on the
building's exterior. A systematic
design of dark sandstone atop
white walls emphasizes the
geometrical proportions of the
two-story facades.

Guiliano da Sangallo

Michelangelo Buonarroti

1475, Caprese—1564, Rome

■ Master and most engaging artist of the Italian High Renaissance ■ Drafte
architecture for the Medici patrician family in Rome and Florence ■ St. Pete
Basilica in Rome was the high point of his architectural career ■ His ingeni
constructions anticipated elements of Mannerism and the Baroque style

1475 Born in Caprese, Tuscany

1488 Began his education as a painter under Domenico Ghirlandaio

1494 Flees to Bologna

1496–99 First extended visit to Rome

1505 Employed in Rome to build Pope Julius's tomb

1529 Named official military engineer of Florence

1546 Overtakes the construction of St. Peter's Basilica

1564 Dies in Rome

■ **Biblioteca Laurenziana**, 1524–71, Florence

Michelangelo created a magnificent library to house the valuable book collection of the Medici Pope Clemens VII. Three sets of stairs—the middle staircase for nobles, the side pair for the servants— make up the elegant entryway. Michelangelo inventively played with round, angular, and oval forms within the structure, and inserted a curved staircase and an interior area decorated like a theater.

As an architect, Michelangelo was a revolutionary ge
whose work epitomizes the greatest attributes of Ren
sance architecture. Michelangelo pursued new direct
not only in his paintings and sculptures, but also in hi
chitectural designs. He extracted the more Classical
ments of the Renaissance, such as columns, pillars,
methods of wall decoration, from their original con
thereby creating an entirely novel understanding of a
tectural style and its composition. Suddenly the arran
ment of the inner and outer rooms became interchan
able, as columns disappeared from the walls to stan
scarcely noticeable niches. In this manner an adapt
and invigorating form of architecture developed, w
was to be the forerunner of European Baroque.

Other Works

nb of Pope Julius, begun
5, Rome

azzo Farnese, redesign,
4, Rome

Lorenzo, draft of facade,
8, Florence

orenzo, new sacristy,
un 1520, Florence

azzo Senatorio, draft,
0–52, Rome

ate St. Trinita, draft, 1557,
ence

ta Pia, 1561–65, Rome

**Maria degli Angeli e dei
iri**, 1563–66, Rome

Church of St. Maria degli
li in Rome was con-
ted in the center of the
s of Diocletian. Michelan-
incorporated the ancient
uins and the arches of the
arium into a cross-shaped
h. The assembly hall was
st 328 feet (100 meters)
and formed the central
Michelangelo thereby not
eferenced old forms but
erpreted ancient ideals in
rchitectural designs.

🏛 **St. Peter's**, dome, 1546–64,
Rome

After he took over the building
of the new St. Peter's, Michelangelo returned to the original
building plans from Bramante
and made possible the construction of the largest dome in
Europe. Michelangelo stream-
lined the entire floor plan, rejecting the outlines added by
his predecessor Antonio da Sangallo. Instead, Michelangelo
concentrated the order of the

rooms solely upon the design of
the enormous central dome.
The four supporting columns
were strengthened, and the
foundations can be seen
through a window in the floor.
The entire construction was
based upon an outer supporting shell and an inner shell supported by sixteen pairs of ribs.
The foreshortened perspective
of the four-sided panels in the
ceiling add to the optical illusion of endless height.

Michelangelo Buonarroti

St. Peter's Basilica

At the beginning of the Renaissance, St. Peter's Basilica was still the anci basilica that Constantine I built. Within a few decades, however, one of the mic iest and largest cathedrals in the world was built. In 1455, the initial plans for expansion of the church's foundations were prepared, and before long they

veloped into a gigantic new construction project. Many famous architects worked on the over 200-year-long development and planning of the cathedral, including Bramante (p. 176), Raphael (p. 184), Michelangelo (p. 180), and Bernini (p. 230). Each architect contributed innovative ideas and drafts of ever-increasing size and magnificence. Early drafts featured a centralized floor plan with four arms of equal length. From 1605 to 1621, under the direction of Carlo Maderno, St. Peter's Basilica acquired its present form. From the standard design of a church with a cross-shaped floor plan grew an enormous central nave with lateral rows of columns.

Michelangelo conceived the powerful, 433- (132-meter-) tall dome over the putative gra St. Peter the Apostle. A gigantic window drum soars above the round floor plan, which the arch of the dome sits. After death of Michelangelo in 1564, the rection of the dome's building wa passed on to Giacomo della Porta

The floor plan of St. Peter's Basili spans an area of about 50,000 squa feet (4,645 square meters), large enou for 60,000 people. The layout changed a Greek cross to a Latin cross as the floor evolved with each successive architect w took on the project.

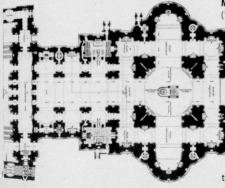

Renaissance 1420–1620

Peter's Basilica, facade after the drafts of
 Maderno, and Michelangelo's dome,
 –12, Rome

 Maderno was only able to construct the
 de after great difficulty. The nave of the
 ch was exceptionally wide, and the in-
 ent Pope Paul V required that there
 structural link between the vestibule
and the papal bureau. There was also an
aesthetic problem: the facade should practically
remain in the background, so as not to obstruct
the view of Michelangelo's magnificent dome.
To solve these problems, a two-story cross
structure was built using the Corinthian
order. Second-floor windows provide a
platform for papal speeches.

APOST·PAVLVS·V·BVRGHESIVS·ROMANVS·PONT·MAX·AN·MDCXII·PONT·VII

St. Peter's Basilica

Raphael

Raffaello Santi
1483, Urbino—1520, Rome

■ Created groundbreaking designs in villa architecture ■ Copied the sty_
of late antiquity and absorbed them into his palace facades ■ Anticipate_
architectural characteristics of Mannerism

■ **1483** Born, most likely in Urbino
1504 Moves to Florence and begins his career as a painter
1508 Travels to Rome in the service of Pope Julius II
1513 Creates many influential architectural drafts
1515 Becomes the foreman in the construction of St. Peter's Basilica
1518 Present at the start of the building of the Villa Madama in Rome
1520 Dies in Rome

Not only was Raphael a talented artist, but he was als_ accomplished architect. As an architect, he was emplo_ above all as a designer. Only a few of his drafts were e_ built, but those that were realized were notable m_ stones in the history of Renaissance architecture. His c_ ception of the Villa Madama in Rome became legend_ Planned as a residence for official state visitors of _ pope, the Villa Madama replicated descriptions of anc_ villas. His visionary draft envisioned terraces, founta_ thermal springs, a theater, and a collection of anc_ relics. For the first time since antiquity, the surround_ gardens were included in the architectural designs_ lowing the architect to create a full experience. Rapha_ contemporaries, Donato Brama_ (p. 176) in particular, also orien_ themselves toward ancient archi_ ture. It was his works, however, _ remained unparalleled in terms of _ closely the buildings replicated _ styles of Roman antiquity.

■ **St. Maria del Popolo**, Chigi Chapel, 1513_ Rome

Raphael understood his works as a complete_ sion. He united sculpture, painting, and mos_ with the tomb of the Chigi family. The pyram_ shaped graves were an invention by Raphae_ signed as a metaphor of death. Four pillars c_ the weight of a windowed dome, allowing th_ city of Rome to be seen through the window_ The small mausoleum appears much larger a_ mightier than it actually is.

Other Works by Raphael

Palazzo Jacopo da Brescia, draft, 1514, Rome

St. Eligio degli Orefici, draft, 1514, Rome

St. Peter's Basilica, draft, 1514, Rome

Palazzo Alberini, draft, 1515, Rome

Palazzo Vidoni-Caffarelli, facade draft, 1515, Rome

Palazzo Branconio d'Aquila, 1518, Rome

Palazzo Pandolfini, facade, 1517, Florence

The Palazzo Pandolfini is a rare exception in which High Renaissance architecture found a place in Florence. Roman design is found within the prominent window frames enclosed by small columns on the upper floor, and in the enormous sculptures organized according to ancient patterns. Only the entrance, made of rectangular stone blocks, originates from Florentine tradition.

lla Madama, balcony, n 1518, Rome

main entrance of the Villa ama lies directly across the Vatican, behind which ds a complex of buildings ned for visitors of state. igantic complex includes quarters for the guests, a , and marketplaces.

ael was given the task of ng a design that followed tyles of ancient villas. To nplish this he studied the n of the imposing Hadrian n Tivoli. He designed a m of decoration for the ny on the main floor that oyed ancient themes and

paintings from the Roman Empire in a completely original and novel way.

Raphael

Jacopo Sansovino

Jacopo d'Antonio Tatti
1486, Florence—1570, Venice

■ The most prominent architect in Venice during the Renaissance ■ Responsible for Venice's main square, the Piazza St. Marco ■ Decorated the facades of Venice with styles drawn from antiquity

■ **1486** Born Jacopo d'Antonio Tatti in Florence

1502 Begins studying with Andrea Sansovino, whose name he adopts

1505 Travels to Rome, where he studies sculpture and meets Bramante and Raphael

1518–28 Works in Rome as a sculptor and restorer

1528 Begins working in Venice, where he is commissioned for large building campaigns

1529 Appointment to state architect of Venice

1545/46 Is sentenced to prison, due to the collapse of some parts of the Libreria Vecchia

1570 Dies in Venice

Other Works

Scuola Grande della Misericordia, 1532, Venice

St. Francesco della Vigna, interior, 1534–54, Venice

La Zecca (the Mint), 1537–54, Venice

Procuratie Vecchie, 1538, Venice

Villa Garzoni, 1547–50, Ponte Cassale

Sansovino's designs helped to shape Renaissance Ver and the city as it is today. His designs of palaces, churc and public buildings for the Venetian government verted back to the styles of antiquity, which he combi with elements from local building traditions. He was first architect to change the typically flat Venetian faca to highly decorative ones. With the use of columns, gaged columns, statues on roofs, and opulent decorat Sansovino created a vivid richness that had not b known in Venice before.

■ **Biblioteca Marciana**, 1536–88, Venice

This library forms the western side of the Piazza St. Marco. The archi- tectural sculpture on the upp floor and enclosed mezzanine lighten the heavy architectur style of the 21-bay arcade.

...ggetta di St. Marco,
...-40, Venice

...iazza of St. Marco not only
...rwent a change in design
...so a reorganization of its

...lazzo Cornaro della Ca' Grande,
...-61, Venice

...ovino was the family architect for the
...hy Venetian banking family the
...ros. Like many wealthy families during
...enaissance, the Cornaros commissioned
...uilding of a palace. The palace was built
...ding to the archetype of Roman city
...es from antiquity. The ground floor is
...of *ashlars*, or unfinished blocks of stone,
...he main entrance opens onto Venice's
...d Canal. Above that are paired Ionic
...ns and, on the uppermost floor, paired
...thian columns. The paired columns on
...cade add a thickness to the overall fa-
...hiding the unusual height of the top
... behind the three-tiered facade. Because
...size, the palace bears the additional
... *Ca' Grande*, Italian for "large house."

functions. Sansovino built the Loggetta di St. Marco at the foot of the bell tower, or *campanile*, across from St. Marco's Cathedral. The campanile collapsed in 1902, destroying the Loggetta, but it was rebuilt exactly. The building is richly endowed with designs that recall the styles of antiquity.

Jacopo Sansovino

Vincenzo Scamozzi

1548, Vincenza–1616, Venice

■ Active architect in northern Italy and important architectural theorist c the late Renaissance ■ Finished many of Andrea Palladio's designs ■ Hi work was closely oriented on Palladian-style architecture, but was origina in its usage of early Baroque forms

● **1548** Born the son of Gian Domenico Scamozzi, a carpenter and architect, in Vicenza

1570 Studies under his father

1572 Establishes himself in Venice

1578–80 Travels to Rome and Naples

1599 Travels to Prague, Germany, and Paris

1604 Travels to Salzburg

1615 Publishes his architectural treatise *L'Idea della Architettura Universale*

1616 Dies in Venice

■ **Villa Pisani (La Rocca)**, 1576, near Lonigo

Scamozzi's inspiration for the Villa Pisani was Palladio's earlier Villa Rotonda. The rooms are grouped around a cross-shaped hall, forming a quadratic floor plan. The uniaxial symmetry of the rooms and the compact blocks of the outer walls are typical characteristics of Scamozzi's style. Natural stone, directly hewn from the site, was used to build the structure.

Renaissance 1420–1620

Vincenzo Scamozzi was one of the greatest architect theorists of his time. His earliest designs of pala churches, and villas were strongly influenced by the s of Andrea Palladio (p. 192). However, he later develo his own distinctive style after several study t throughout Europe. His designs were based in his te nical and scientific knowledge, and he worked to a disproportionate employment of columns and other c orations. Scamozzi's facades and floor plans were o designed in accordance with geometric and mathen ical principles, one of the few rules he borrowed from tiquity. His style was important for the developmer Mannerist architecture—a late Renaissance rejectio pure Classicism that favored different, often radically ferent, treatments of forms from antiquity.

...urch of St. Giorgio Maggiore,
...leted 1610, Venice

...y years after Palladio's death in 1580,
...ozzi completed the facade of the church of
...orgio Maggiore in Venice. Scamozzi's work
...likely deviated from the original designs,
...ng a more Classical scheme that has been
...y influential for architects of generations
...ow.

Other Important Works by Scamozzi	
Palazzo Godi, 1569, Vicenza	Villa Molin, 1597, Padua
Palazzo Trissino, 1577, Vicenza	Villa Duodo, 1605–16, Monselice
St. Nicolò da Tolentino, 1591–1602, Venice	Palazzo Contarini degli Scrigni, 1609–16, Venice

...ocuratie Nuove, 1582–99,
...e

...ps Scamozzi's most fa-
...contribution to the city of
...e, the Procuratie Nuove is
...ed at the southern end of
...azza St. Marco. Of the
...facades that surround the
...e, the Procuratie Nuove is
...ost Classical. After
...ozzi's death, work on the
...or was altered under
...esco Smeraldi. The
...ng was completed by
...ozzi's student Baldassare
...nena.

Vincenzo Scamozzi

Giulio Romano

Giulio di Pietro Gianuzzi, also Giulio Pippi
ca. 1499, Rome—1546, Mantua

■ Main representative of Italian Mannerism ■ Distorted perspectives an
consciously abnormal uses of structural decoration ■ A painter and an
architect ■ Learned his craft from Raphael in Rome

ca. 1499 Born Giulio di
Pietro Gianuzzi in Rome

1515 Studies with Raphael

1520 Takes over Raphael's
studio in Rome, co-
managing it with Giovanni
Penni after Raphael's
death

1524 Summoned to
Mantua by the patron
Federico Gonzaga

1525–34 Designs and
paints the frescoes in the
Palazzo del Te

1546 Dies in Mantua before he is able to take on
his position as the over-
seer of the construction of
St. Peter's

In1524, patron of the arts Federico Gonzaga took Gi
Romano, who had already been celebrated as a paint
Rome, to Mantua in northern Italy. He put his talents a
architect to the test, achieving great renown with
works. Romano broke from traditional principles of R
aissance architecture, building more colorful and pla
structures. The pictorial layout of his palaces and v
wasn't the only aspect of his work to play with optic
lusions, as his constructions were also arranged li
stage design. There are surprising elements through
the design that disrupt the usual harmony of proport
and ratios. The varied facades, distorted perspectives,
deliberate use of irregular decorations from antiq
make Romano's architectural style an inventive, ex
rating, and a highly individual variant of Mannerism.

■ **Villa Lante**, 1520–24, R

The Villa Lante was origina
conceived by Raphael, but
pleted by Romano followi
death. Like his mentor, Ron
innovatively used new elements that were unusual f
architecture of the High Re
sance. Romano varied the
dian geometric layout by c
bling up Classical arch
sequences. Emphasis on th
edges of the building, cus-
tomary in architecture, is n
present and the remaining
dows are arbitrarily disper
on the facade.

Palazzo del Te, 1525–34, Mantua

Palazzo del Te is a summer pleasure palace—accordingly, Romano handled the elements of composition in a jaunty manner. The facade uses Palladian motifs, which were common at the time, but instead of using a raised central arch, Romano employed a series of equivalent arches. He also varied proportions of motifs from the High Renaissance in the wall. The shifted proportions of the external structure—unequal niches, simulated masonry, irregular friezes—are several of his design innovations.

Other Important Works by Romano

Palazzo Maccarani di (Palazzo Brazzà), 1522–24, Rome	St. Benedetto, restoration of the cloister, 1540–44, Polirone
Palazzo Cicciaporto-, 1521–22, Rome	Palazzo Ducale, 1544, Mantua

■ Casa Romano, 1540, Mantua

The facade's lines are accentuated by the use of artificial masonry and extravagant details. The windows are crowned by shallow pediments and are set in arches accentuated by fan shaped masonry motifs. A small statue of Mercury stands in a niche over the central door, emphasizing the main entrance.

Giulio Romano

Andrea Palladio

Andrea di Piero della Gondola
1508, Padua–1580, Vicenza

■ The most significant Renaissance architect and theorist ■ Initiated ne
rules of villa architecture ■ Revolutionized Venetian church facades usi
temple motifs from antiquity ■ Influenced architects throughout the w

1508 Born in Padua

1521 Begins an apprenticeship in Vicenza to become a mason and sculptor

1538 Becomes acquainted with the humanists in northern Italy, via Count Giangiorgio Trissino

1541 Undertakes the first of four trips to Rome

1570 Publication of the architectural treatise *The Four Books of Architecture*

1580 Dies in Vicenza

Proportion, symmetry, and the allusion to elements o
tiquity are the distinguishing hallmarks of Andrea
ladio's architectural style. His designs have clear f
plans and characteristically symmetrical facades wit
lars, pilasters, porticoes, pediments, and mezzanines.
ladio adopted proportion and symmetry from his anc
Roman predecessors, traveling several times to Rom
order to study ancient Roman styles. His greatly infl
tial reinterpretation and publication of the proport
and symmetry of Roman architecture, use of two-stor
cades, hierarchically ordered columns, and sculp
floors were functionally appropriated to the nee
people during the Renaissance.

Other Works by Palladi
Villa Pisani, 1544, Bagnolo
Villa Barbaro, 1554, Maser
Casa Antonini, 1556, Udine
St. Pietro di Castello, 1558, Venice
St. Giorgio Maggiore, 1562, Venice
St. Francesco della Vigna, 15 Venice
Villa Cagollo, 1565, Vicenza

■ **Villa Poiana**,
ca. 1545–50 Poiana
Maggiore, Vicenza

The villa's facade demonstrates the chief motifs of

Palladian architecture. Five small windows comprise the mezzanine level, and the facade's central and flanking parts are symmetrically proportioned, united by the pedi-

ment. Due to the patron's fa
history, which had a long mi
tradition, Palladio refrained f
using elaborate decorations
to make the villa appear fort

192

Late Renaissance in Italy

la Capra (La Rotonda),
-91, Vicenza

principal example of
villa architecture, the villa's

la Cornaro, 1552–54,
bino Dese, Treviso

illa's two-story columned
ace, lined with Ionic and
thian columns, gives the
grandiose appearance
visible from the street.
ecorative interior merges
quarters and work areas
gh the duplication of the
floor and the open unity
en the side wings and en-
. The main floor was de-
d to look like an ancient
atrium—a style popular
he oldest members of the
racy.

corridors lead from all four
columned halls to the central tur-
reted room. Palladio combined
orderly square, circular, and cubic

forms within his plan and followed the format of ancient temples, opening the building to
the surrounding landscape.

Andrea Palladio

Michele Sanmicheli

1484, Verona–1559, Verona

■ The most famous pupil of Bramante in Rome ■ Influenced the appear ance of Verona ■ His incomparable style consisted of strong, organized, and richly decorated forms of the late Renaissance period
■ *left:* **Palazzo Bevilacqua**, piano nobile, 1534, Verona

■ **1484** Born the son of an architect in Verona
1500 Studies in Rome under Donato Bramante and the Sangallo family
1510–24 Employed as the church architect in Orvieto
1526 Receives commissions to build fortifications in Rome and Piacenza
1528 Becomes the builder of the republic of Venice and designs fortifications for the city
1559 Dies in Verona

Michele Sanmicheli built fortifications in the servic the republic of Venice for Verona, Bergamo, and the of Venice itself, strengthening their protective func through the addition of elegant city gates. Roman umphal archways, gables, small figural sculptu weaponry, and friezes featuring ancient motifs testi the militarism of these strongholds, which count am the most commanding works of representational a tecture. Sanmicheli developed a similar style within palace designs. Characteristics of his architecture inc rustic brickwork on the ground floor, triumphal arc around large windows, and striking sculptural detail

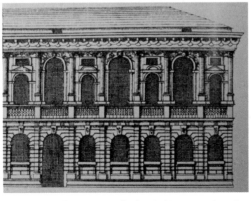

Other Works by Sanmich

Petrucci Chapel in St. Domen 1516–24, Orvieto

Villa Soranza, 1520, Padua

Palazzo Canossa, 1530–37, Verona

Fortifications, 1540, Crete

Porta St. Zeno, 1542, Verona

Fortifications, 1543, Zadar, Croatia

Palazzo Pompei, 1551, Veron

Porta Palio, 1557, Verona

Madonna di Campagna, 155 Verona

■ **Palazzo Bevilacqua**, 1534, Verona

Sanmicheli expanded upon traditional elements

of palace architecture, using ashlars—dressed masonry—on the lower floor and sculpturally diverse columns to divide the fa-

cade into unique niches. Late Roman antiquity was the sou of inspiration for the rich dec tion throughout the castle.

lazzo Grimani, 1540–62, Venice

cheli effortlessly modified his architecture
t it incorporated the city's rich traditions.
d after the traditional palaces along the
e Grande, the Palazzo Grimani has asym-
cal rooms of varying heights that are clev-
d elegantly hidden behind the harmonic
facade of the building, thereby allowing
commonly large ground floor to have
unevenly arched entrances. The grooved
ns and pillars are one of the only unified el-
s to appear within all floors. The discrete,
ndicular shadowing effect is the chief at-
e of the Palazzo Grimani, which also has the
terior balcony in the history of Venetian
design.

■ **Porta Nuova**, 1535–40, Verona

Sanmicheli's design for the Porta Nuova gate in
Verona is distinguished by its strong use of the
Doric order and sculptural masonry.

Michele Sanmicheli

Baldassare Peruzzi

1481, Ancaiano—1536, Rome

■ One of the most important Italian architects of the late Renaissance
■ His style anticipated traits of Mannerism ■ Documented Roman archi
tectural forms in sketchbooks ■ Also active as an interior designer and v
one of the most famous theater set designers in Rome

1481 Baptized in Ancaiano, near Siena

1503 Becomes a colleague and student of Bramante and Raphael

1520–27 Head of construction of St. Peter's Basilica in Rome

1529 Architect of the dome and fortress of Siena

1530 Becomes a member of the Vitruvian Academy

1530s Works as a painter and architect in Rome

1536 Dies in Rome

Baldassare Peruzzi was one of the greatest archit
during the Renaissance, even though only a few of
works were ever actually built. His architectural style
regarded by his contemporaries as elegant and dem
He created his ornate and magnificently decorated d
without resorting to the romanticized Renaissance mo
Peruzzi preferred to use static and linear forms to cr
powerful contrasts of individual architectural for
Supporting elements . such as columns, pillars,
window frames were often incorporated into, rather t
separated from, the smooth surfaces of the walls. Abs
tion and sophistication characterize Peruzzi's uni
style.

196

Late Renaissance in Italy

Renaissance 1420–1620

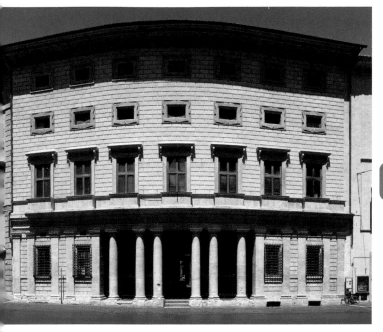

lla Farnesina, 1508–11,

wo-story facade of the
Farnesina summer resi-
e expresses a subtle new
n that appears to separate
uilding's levels with the
and cornice. In reality, the
ture consists of one tightly
borated facade. The base
nposed of two Classical
which are constructed
a smaller ratio than was
non for palace facades at
me. The angular columns
nely cut windows
ize the facade without
ig use of sculpture or a
mic pattern.

■ **Palazzo Massimo alle
Colonne**, 1532–36, Rome

The Palazzo Massimo alle
Colonne demonstrates Peruzzi's
unique talent of designing a
lightly curved facade and novel
columned entrance. To accredit
the rich heritage of the Massimo
family, whose roots traced back
to antiquity, Peruzzi incorporated Classical elements into the
facade. The columns at the
entrance are constructed following the format of Classical
temples, whereas the convex
facade of the building follows
the design of the ancient Mar-
cellus Theater. Peruzzi created
an integrated facade arrange-

ment without resorting to the
traditional practice of separating all of the building's levels
with cornices.

Other Works by Peruzzi

Villa Volte Alte, 1505, Siena

La Sagra, alterations, 1515,
Carpi

Villa Farnese, *rocca* foundations, with Antonio da Sangallo,
1530, Capraola

Villa Farnesina, frescoes and interior designs, after 1530, Rome

St. Onofrio and St. Maria della
Pace, chorus decoration, after
1530, Rome

Baldassare Peruzzi

French Châteaux

1494–1620

■ Ecclesiastic architecture retained late Gothic styles for a long time ■ Fren[ch]
royalty was particularly well disposed toward new ideas ■ Châteaux becam[e]
models for noble residences throughout Europe ■ Developments included
the *corps de logis* and intricate lighting effects in galleries

■ **1494** The French invasion of Italy reveals the Italian Renaissance to France

1515–47 Reign of François I, under whose patronage many Italian architects come to France

ca. 1520 Châteaux of the Loire River valley are built by France's wealthy elite

1531 Formation of the first School of Fontainebleau and the popularization of Italian interior décor

1535 Pierre Lescot begins work on the Louvre

1547–59 Italian Catherine de' Medici is married to the French king Henry II

1620 Marie de' Medici popularizes Baroque styles

■ **Château Chambord**, staircase, 1526–37, Loire Valley

The double-helix staircase runs openly through the center of the château's floors. Two parallel shafts allow for undisturbed movement from top to bottom. The staircase stands out as the center point of the castle, and is surrounded by the long windows of the central towers.

Gothic styles remained popular for a long time in Fran[ce]
The Italian Renaissance style was first adopted into Fre[nch]
châteaux in the Loire River valley and, by 1530, was [a]
popular style for all noble houses. New constructi[on]
rarely featured extensive ornamentation, but were st[ruc]-
turally intricate, like their Gothic predecessors, and th[ere]-
fore intricate looking. Floor plans departed slowly f[rom]
the divided layouts of Gothic architecture, but gradu[ally]
a uniquely French style developed. Châteaux consis[ted]
of a complex of buildings centered around a squa[re]-
shaped inner courtyard, enclosed on all sides. The co[rps]
de logis, or central main building, contained living q[uar]-
ters and was usually flanked by a striking staircase [and]
decorative secondary rooms. In contrast to secular bu[ild]-
ings, French churches of the Renaissance era kept tru[e to]
their Gothic roots, as their arched style developed [into]
the Flamboyant style. Renaissance architecture

âteau Chambord,
–37, Loire Valley

Château Chambord's roof is
orised of over 300 towers,
es, and chimneys, creating
nning example of French

âteau Chambord, floor

ite its multifaceted facades
elaborate roofing, the floor
of Château Chambord is
mely symmetrical. Four
corridors extend in a cross
ation from the central
orate staircase on each
into living space. Living
es are also found within
ound towers located at the
ing's corners and at the
ratic core of the build-
-the corps de logis—in a
ar style to a medieval
e.

château architecture. The
densely concentrated ornamentation, including sculpted
leaves and lilies, is reminiscent
of Gothic ornamentation.
French Renaissance designs

often included four round
corner towers with conical
roofs, gabled dormer windows
that break through the plane of
the roof, and simple rectangular crossbar windows.

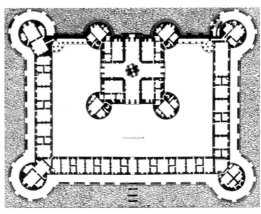

French Châteaux

reached its height in France under King François I (1494–1547). The successful compromise between French building traditions and Roman architecture is evident within the changes made in his Loire River châteaux of Amboise and Blois. An even arrangement of small columns, rectangular windows, high roofs, and numerous towers creates an elegant and symmetrical aesthetic. Decorative elements included monograms, salamanders, and framed reliefs featuring motifs from ancient mythology. Many châteaux, such as the Château Chenonceau, were bordered by geometrically planned Italian-style gardens that helped foster a unity between the architecture and the surrounding landscape. The chief court architects of the independent French style were Pierre Lescot, Philibert de l'Orme, and Jean Bullant. Their drafts are distinctive for their manifold experimentation with the styles of antiquity and elements of the Italian Renaissance. Monumental architectural elements became part of French designs with the adoption of triumphal arches and wide column arrangements.

■ **Château Fontainebleau**, 1527–50, Fontainebleau

Until the construction of the Louvre, the Château Fontainebleau was the only residence of François I, and was decorated accordingly. The large gallery that united the castle with the older monastery buildings later became a milestone in the history of French architecture. Also, the painting gallery and ballroom were unprecedented, as both styles of room were, until this time, unknown in both France and Italy.

rre Lescot: Southwest
of Cour Carrée at the
re, 1546–51, Paris

ecture of the French Re-
nce changed dramatically
the second half of the
entury, and Paris was at
nter of this development.
rticality of Gothic styles
placed by horizontally
rted structures. French
ects appropriated the
styles, creating a dis-
unique French style.
precision, antique pro-

portion, and geometrical order-
liness was united with French
decorations. The southwest
wing of the Louvre was built by
the royal court architect Pierre
Lescot, who mixed Italian
architectural styles such as organized pillars, columns, and
powerful cornices with the
playful sculptural decoration
that was popular during the
Gothic period in France. Italian
designs appear again in the
Classically styled round arches
found on the first floor, and in

the alternating semicircular and
triangular-shaped pediments
above the windows, which
reach all the way to the ceiling
on the main floor. Other than
the Classical ordering of the
window pediments, French
ornamental details, such as
sculpted leaves and armor, are
found throughout the facade.
Jean Goujon, a French sculptor
who had learned his trade in
Italy, created the facade decorations with outstanding quality
and precision.

French Châteaux

Germany and Austria

ca. 1500–1618

■ Renaissance styles spread slowly throughout the divided Holy Roman Empire, and German architecture remained Gothic for a long time ■ Renaissance styles spread to Austria from the first German Renaissance city, Augsburg ■ Few churches were constructed after the Reformation

■ **ca. 1500** Under Emperor Maximilian I, southern Germany becomes a major economic power; the Fuggers commission Renaissance buildings

ca. 1525 The Reformation and the Peasants' War give Germans more power and influence

1540 Castles are used as permanent residences, and new commissions for tombs, stables, and armories come with the growth of princely states

1555–1618 Peace of Augsburg; monasteries are abandoned; cities assume responsibility for the needy; increase in the number of hospitals built

■ **Jacopo Strada: Hall of Antiquities at Residenz**, ca. 1569–71, Munich

Jacopo Strada, an architect from Mantua, designed this hall of antiquities to house the sculptural collection of Prince Albrecht V. Strada copied the style of the Grand Gallery of the Château Fontainebleau, near Paris, using a windowed walkway to present and highlight the artwork.

Gothic styles remained strong in Germany, and the Renaissance did not spread to north of the Alps for quite some time. A German banking family, the Fuggers, had close ties to Italian businesses and brought Renaissance architects to Germany. By 1500, the Italian-influenced secular and religious constructions in Augsburg anticipated later stylistic shifts in architecture. In contrast to the French, only a few German architects actually studied in Italy, and the majority continued to copy the styles they knew from Italian and French books that were brought to Germany. Between 1550 and 1620 architects of the Weser River valley, between Kassel and Bremen, developed a unique style, influenced by the Dutch. In northern Germany, conservative territorial princes remained true to their traditional building styles. In contrast, the princes in the south had more contact with Italians and adopted Renaissance styles more readily. Still, it was only in

**Georg Ridinger: Johannis-
burg Castle**, 1605–14,
Aschaffenburg

Constructed of red sandstone,
the Johannisburg Castle is one
of the first large-scale German
castles to use a quadratic floor
plan, which was previously reserved only for very small castles or luxury palaces. The
repetition of the facade's windows and wide cornices is
punctuated by the four massive
corner towers and central
gable. The corner towers add a
vertical element to the design.

**trance of the Ottohein-
Wing at Heidelberg**
e, 1556–59, Heidelberg

of the first Renaissance
s in Germany, the Heidel-
Castle's Ottoheinrichs
has an uncommonly rich
e. Influenced by both
and Italian architecture,
ndows are united in tight
etry, similar to contempo-
alian palaces. The four
s are lavishly decorated,
6 statues in small niches
led after designs from an-
/. Sculpted by Dutch
or Alexandeer Colins,
ater built for the Haps-
, the statues are located
en columns and sturdy
es decorated with Italian
is. Also, the stone delin-
s of the facade's floors
rved with figures. Dutch
nce can be found in the
l floral motifs and the
scheme of the virtues
anets, following designs
Flemish architect Cor-
loris.

1584, with the construction of St. Michael's Cathedral in Munich, that Italian Renaissance styles made a significant presence in the Holy Roman Empire. Southern German principalities began to surpass other smaller states in terms of power and might, and an important symbol of prestige was the adoption of the Italian Renaissance styles. Because of this, the style became important in the north. Emperor Maximilian I (1459–1519) and Ferdinand I (1503–1564) brought architects from all over Europe to their court in Vienna. However, in Austria, the Renaissance manifested itself with greater ease in literature and other art forms. Once the style was adopted, though, it remained popular for quite a long time.

■ Alberto Luchese: Ambras Castle, inner courtyard, ca. 1576, Innsbruck

The castle of the archduke Ferdinand II consists of many different building complexes, including a ballroom and a giant Renaissance-style garden. The Italian architect Alberto Luchese designed the palace with four stories and four wings on a square-shaped floor plan. The quadratic inner courtyard is decorated with elaborate frescoes featuring motifs that were commonly found in the decoration of contemporary Italian palaces. The ground floor is painted to resemble brickwork, and the windows and doors are fashioned out of shiny frames. Tiny painted round arches between the windows depict figures from the Bible alongside imagery from Greek and Roman mythology.

■ Elias Holl: Town Hall, 1614–20, Augsburg

The symmetrical and auste cade of the town hall is fra by two monumental tower The gabled central area en sizes the building's height. oval, rectangular, and trian gular window pediments a the volutes on the upperm tier are modeled on Italian palace architecture. The fa fronts an equally large inte

Other Works

Fugger Chapel at St. Anne's Cathedral, 1509–12, Augsburg

The Fuggerei, by Thomas Krebs, 1516–23, Augsburg

Hartenfels Castle, by Konrad Krebs, 1533–36, Torgau

Swiss Court of the Hofbur Imperial Palace, 1552, Vienna

Castle Eggenberg, ca. 1625, Graz

■ **Lüder von Bentheim: Town Hall**, 1595–1612, Bremen

With the erection of grand municipal buildings, northern German cities sought to assert their importance in the Holy Roman Empire. The town hall in Bremen follows models of other northern German town halls. The town hall in Leiden, for example, has a similar arcade hiding a small gangway tucked in behind it. Also, the prominent central gable protrudes slightly, following the examples of the town halls of Leiden and Antwerp.

e Italian Room at the shut Residence, ca. 1536, shut

visiting Italy, the Bavarian duke Ludwig X commissioned a residence in the Italian style. Most of the drafts for its construction and decoration followed the designs of the Italian architect Giulio Romano. The vaulted room was decorated using Italian craftsmanship.

Renaissance in Germany and Austria

Northern Renaissance

ca. 1500–ca. 1630

■ The northern bourgeoisie preferred Gothic gabled houses, and late Goth and traditional styles continued to dominate ■ City residences were occu by governors because regional princes of the north spent their time traveli ■ Architecture in the north developed more slowly than other artistic form

■ **ca. 1500** Belgium and the Netherlands are at the forefront of European trade, prompting wealthy merchants to build estates

1543 The Rossum family constructs residences in Renaissance styles in Amheim, Vaasen, and Zaltbommel

1572–80 After winning independence from Spain, the Netherlands develops its own styles of architecture; cities, guilds, and individuals fund new town halls and banks

ca. 1630 Baroque styles emerge

Other Works

Palace of Margaret of Austria, by Rombout II Keldermans, begun 1507, Mechelen

Palace of the Prince Bishops of Liège, 1526–38

Salm Inn, 1534, Mechelen

Oude Kerk, tower, by Joost Jabsz Bilhamer, 1566, Amsterdam

Leiden Town Hall, facade, ca. 1597–1600

The Renaissance began in northern Europe about years later than in Italy. Gothic elements such as gaze balconies, gates, and delicately decorated facade: mained common in the north until that point. An i vidual variety of architecture developed in Belgium the Netherlands that was different than the architec found in Renaissance Italy. The designs of small mic class homes with tall sliding gates and simple floor p changed little with the passage of time. Belgian Dutch architects typically utilized elements from ar uity only as decoration. Thus, northern European arch ture remained largely the same until the early century—when the first architectural texts relatin Roman architectural styles appeared and Italian st were sporadically adopted in the north.

■ **Lieven de Key: Vleesh (Butchery)**, tower design, 1602–04, Haarlem

Lieven de Key was one of t most famous architects in Netherlands during the Re sance. In the Vleeshal, his signs blend popular north styles, such as the gabled with Italian Renaissance in ences, such as polychrome facades like those found in Siena and Florence, and po friezes. Quoining, or the w accentuated corner stones shows the adaptation of p ular French styles.

...nelis Floris de Vriendt:
...Hall, 1561–64, Antwerp

...own hall was one of the
...uildings to mimic the hori-
...outlines found in Italian
...s. The Flemish architect

Cornelis Floris de Vriendt, who
had traveled to Rome, drafted
the town hall in the Renaissance style. A ground floor arcade placed atop square bases
is indicative of Italian influence.

However, northern architectural features, such as the separate
tower portion of the facade and
a highly ornamented entrance-
way, remained, and were combined with the new styles.

...Civil Registry, 1534–37,
...e

...ade of the Old Civil Reg-
...lites elements of
...ity with late Gothic
...creating a striking Ren-
...ce facade. The symmet-
...ignment, Classically or-
...columns, and sculptural
...s on the roof indicate
...n influences. Divided
...rs along the building's
...and the gabled roofs
...size the remnants of late
...and French styles that
...emained popular in
...and Belgian architecture.

Northern Renaissance

Renaissance in the UK

1540–1605

■ The Renaissance had only marginal influence in the UK ■ Large cour
estates were built in the style of French châteaux, with limited influence
from Italian architecture ■ Italian Renaissance architecture and the infl
ence of Palladio first gained hold through the work of Inigo Jones

1540 Hampton Court Palace is completed

1558–1603 Under Elizabeth I, the landed gentry begin to build large estates and castles in both the cities and countryside

1600 Queen Elizabeth I finances elaborate palaces, often favoring buildings built on foundations shaped in the form of the letters *E* or *H*

1605 The English architect Inigo Jones becomes acquainted with the work of Palladio; as the architect of the Royal Court, his designs followed the style of Palladio and Roman antiquity, thereby establishing Palladianism in the UK

■ **Hampton Court Palace**, 1540, near London

Lord Chancellor and Archbishop Thomas Wolsey commissioned this 500-room estate. The popularity of Gothic styles is notable in the ornately decorated parapets and steeples. Two embedded portrait busts of ancient rulers, located within the main entrance, indicate the influence of Italian styles in the UK.

British architecture was bound to Gothic styles unti
reign of Queen Elizabeth I. As during the Gothic pe
Tudor-style buildings were ornamented with floral
geometrically constructed designs on the walls, wind
and parapets. Nobles newly appointed during the T
family's reign (1485–1603) tended to build asymmet
residences made of brick. Arched windows mad
pressed and lead-lined windows, uneven rooftops
towers, decorative corner stones, and ornate chim
are other notable characteristics of Tudor styles. Only
the onset of the 17th century did British architec
begin to fully adopt the styles of other societies, inclu
the French, Dutch, and Italians. Later architects su
Inigo Jones and Sir Christopher Wren (p. 292) devel
a style known as Palladian architecture, which aligne
self closely with the style of the Italian architect An
Palladio (p. 192).

**liam Cecil: Burghley
e, 1565–87, Stamford**

rgest Elizabethan estate,
rghley House is symmet-
laid out and consists of
ings. The roofs were dec-
d with Gothic elements
s towers, lanterns, arches,
lumns. It is only in the in-

terior where the influence of
French and Italian Renaissance
styles is noticeable—the clock
tower, northwest staircase, and
decorations of the private
chapel, with an altarpiece by
the Italian artist Paolo
Veronese, are indicative of continental Ren-aissance styles.

Other Works
Longleat House, by Robert Smythson, 1567–80, Warminster
Hardwick Hall, by Robert Smythson, 1587–99, Chesterfield

■ **Robert Smythson:
Wollaton Hall**, 1580–88,
Nottingham

Wollaton Hall was built according to a symmetrical design centered around a mighty
central tower. The light-colored
facades, made of sandstone, are
typical of the Elizabethan style.
Pediments and towers obscure
the flat roofs. The large, osten-
tatiously decorated hall in the
center of the estate, however,
follows the style of French
châteaux.

Renaissance in the UK

Iberian Renaissance

1519–1598

■ Gothic architecture remained the preferred building style longer in Sp
and Portugal ■ Elements of Moorish architecture were revived ■ The
Italian Renaissance had relatively little influence ■ In the late Renaissan
intricate ornamentation styles were replaced by simpler, stronger forms

● **1519** King Charles V avoids Moorish styles during his reign; instead, Italian architectural models are preferred

1556–98 During Spanish absolutism under King Philip II, the unadorned Desornamentado style dominates

1567 Juan de Herrera, Spain's most important Renaissance architect, takes over the building of el Escorial after the death of Juan Bautista de Toledo

1598 The Plateresque style evolves into Baroque

Renaissance architecture of the Iberian Peninsula w
mix of various styles. Early Renaissance architecture c
bined Moorish and Gothic styles. It was only with
onset of the 16th century that an original style called
eresque emerged. The word comes from the silversi
trade and characterizes the rich, ornate, filigree dec
tive elements of Spanish and Portuguese architect
Sumptuously modeled medallions, animal heads
cutcheons, and small finials decorate the often sin
monumental buildings. Another direction in architect
the Desornamentado style, developed concurrently
the Plateresque style. Demure yet ornately adorned c
positions are representative of this latter, unique for
Spanish architecture.

Other Works

Tower of Belém, 1515–21, Lis
Portugal

Granada Cathedral, ca. 1523,
Spain

Alcázar of Toledo, 1537, Spai

La Giralda (Bell Tower), 1568
Seville, Spain

Castle Aranjuez, facade, 157
Aranjuez, Spain

São Vicente de Fora, begun
Lisbon, Portugal

■ **El Escorial**, 1561–81, near Madrid

The largest castle in Spain was a monastery, church, library, palace, and tomb for Spanish kings and was situated in the geographic center of Spain. The gray granite composition was constructed in a realistic, ch
style and is considered the c
example of Desornamentad
architecture.

Renaissance 1420–1620

lace of Charles V,
–68, Granada

palace of Charles V,
ted in the Alhambra of Gra-
, was intended to be a
ument for the Reconquista,
e seven-and-a-half-century-
process by which Catholics
med the Iberian Peninsula

from the Moors. For this reason,
any Moorish influences were
avoided in the design. Elements
from antiquity, repopularized
by the Italian Renaissance, became the chief architectural
features. The large center tower
in the middle of the square-
shaped palace was unique to

Spanish Renaissance architecture. The two-level circular interior is reminiscent of ancient
villas, and the floor plan of
Hadrian's Villa in Tivoli. The
palace contained an arena for
bullfights, modeled on the
Colosseum, in which the audience sat in the upper gallery.

■ **Jerónimos Monastery**,
16th century, Lisbon

Jerónimos Monastery is fashioned in the Manueline style.
King Manuel I, influenced by
discoveries overseas, commissioned buildings decorated
with nautical imagery. The style
bridges the Portuguese Gothic
and Renaissance styles. Typical
sculptural motifs include
crucifixes, royal emblems, and
columns featuring depictions of
aquatic plants, anchors, knots,
and shells.

Iberian Renaissance

Eastern Europe

1458–1618

- Cultural exchange arose between the courts of Italy and eastern Europ
- Slavic princes had cities built in a pure Italian style ■ East European Re
aissance grew under the Jagillonian royal dynasty ■ Matthias Corvinus,
king of Hungary in the 15th century, was an important patron of the arts

● **1458–90** Hungary's king, Matthias Corvinus, commissions buildings in the Italian Renaissance style

1518 King Sigismund I marries Bona Sforza, who brings Italian architects and artists to the Polish-Bohemian court

1526 The Hapsburgs inherit the kingdoms of Bohemia and Hungary; art and architecture flourishes at all the Hapsburg courts

1541 The Ottoman army invades eastern Europe and destroys many Renaissance buildings, particularly in Budapest

1618 The Thirty Years' War begins

Other Works

Vladislav Hall in Hradschin, by Benedikt Ried, 1493–1502, Prague

Bakócz Chapel, begun 1507, Esztergom, Hungary

Villa Hvezda, 1555–58, near Prague

Large Ball Court in Royal Gardens, by Boniface Wolmut, 1567–69, Prague

Armory, 1593–1612, Gdansk, Poland

In eastern Europe local princes and kings commissio
castles, palace chapels, and churches. Educated and w
travelled, they were aware of the developments of
Italian Renaissance and the architectural theories of an
uity and comissioned work from Italian architects. Ita
arches, slender pilasters, the Classical orders, and fl
plans overtook local building traditions. Imperial conr
tions with western Europe brought further influer
from Germany, the Netherlands, and France.

■ **Francesco Fiorentino: Wawel Royal Castle**, 1504–48, Kraków

The five-cornered inner courtyard of the Polish royal palace marks a high point of European Renaissance architecture. A multiple-story courtyard surrounded by columned arcades was built using Italian noble castles and the Roman Vatican Palace as a m
The head architect, Francesco Fiorentino, came from Floren
At around the same time, the Sigismund Chapel in the cho
Kraków's Wawel Cathedral w
built in full Italian style.

■ **Giovanni Battista di Quadro: Poznan Town Hall**, 1536–60

After a fire in 1536, a new facade in the Italian style was erected in front of the remains of the Poznan Town Hall. The citizens of Poznan hired Giovanni Battista di Quadro, a Polish-Italian Renaissance architect, to build the project. He applied the basic form of the northern Italian loggia, such as those that are found at Piazza St. Marco in Venice and at Andrea Palladio's Palazzo della Ragione in Vincenza—a porticoed colonnade, open only on one side—to the Polish town hall. Three consecutive loggias, surrounded by archways, decorate the monumental facade. The top story forms a slightly setback, windowless half-story, renowned for its unusual height—because of this, the town hall is known as the "Polish attic." This attic level is highly ornamented with images of kings, a clock, and doors from which two mechanical goats come out to battle at noon.

lvedere (Royal Summer ce), 1538–63, Prague

the building of the ure castle of Ferdinand I, elvedere was built as part e complex, in the model of nmer residence. The build- in the center of flower ens. Elegant rows of arch- open onto the gardens the ground floor, in a style r to the architecture of lleschi's Spedale degli In- ti hospital in Florence.

Eastern Europe

Mughal Empire

1530–1707

- Architecture of the Mughal period combined Hindu and Islamic buildin styles ▪ The tolerant mind-set of the Mughal emperor led to architectura diversity ▪ Technical building innovations from Persia were adopted ▪ Luxury and wealth were displayed through decorative splendor

1530 Humayun becomes Great Mughal of India and invites Persian artists to his palace; three-sided vaulted niches, called *iwan*, become characteristic elements of almost all Mughal architecture

1540 Under Sher Shah, local building styles become more prominent

1556 During Akbar's reign, the court workshops in Agra, Delhi, and Fatehpur Sikri are centers of activity for artists and architects

1638 Shah Jahan moves the capital from Agra to Delhi

1707 End of the reign of Aurangzeh, the last Great Mughal to commission large-scale architectural works

The influence of Islamic and Persian architecture beca even stronger in India under the sovereignty of the f Mughal rulers. The Persian-Islamic-influenced culture these foreign rulers first started to combine itself with ments of Indian architecture after 1526. Mosques, ton and palaces of the early Mughal period merged Hindu chitectural tradition with Islamic ornamentation and novations. Elements of Islamic architecture, such as pointed arch, the onion-shaped dome, minarets, and saic decorations started to supersede the plentiful nu bers of intricately detailed figures of older Hindu temp Technological advances accompanied the new style architecture, and it became possible to build even la structures, such as the construction of high-wa domes, throughout India. The usage of Indian red sa stone inlaid with white marble and semiprecious sto imparted a distinctively Indian colorfulness to Mu architecture.

▪ Panch Mahal Palace in Fatehpur Sikri, 1569–74

Following the model of Islamic urban planning, multi-level palaces,

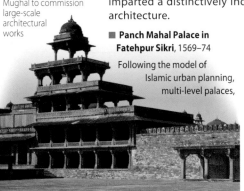

gardens, a marketplace, a wat works and innumerable roofe streets, staircases, and terrace were assembled into one com in the city of Fatehpur Sikri. Th five-story palace of Panch Ma situated directly in the middle the entire ensemble. The pala bears witness to the two oppo sing styles of architecture in I during this period—the figur architecture of Hinduism and geometric style of Islam.

ausoleum of Sher Shah, 540, Sasaram

nausoleum is located on f a two-tiered quadratic te in the center of an artifi- ea. The octagonal floor

plan, the dome and its lotus- shaped tip, inner arcade, and corner pavilions on the defense wall are all characteristic of In- dian tombs constructed in the Mughal Empire.

■ **Mausoleum of Humayun,** 1564–72, Delhi

The monument mixes Persian elements, like the double- shelled dome and layered décor, with Indian red sandstone.

Mughal Empire

East Asian Architecture

1368–1580

■ The Ming dynasty in China was an epoch of great palaces, grave chambe
and exquisite private gardens ■ Monumental, boxlike forms replaced the
delicate architecture of the Song style ■ Large stone fortifications were bu
in Japan ■ The Buddhist tea ceremony demanded new architectural form

■ **Hall of Prayer for Good Harvests, Temple of Heaven and Earth**, 1420, reconstructed 1889, Beijing

The goal of royal architecture during the Ming dynasty was to make humans feel small when gazing up toward the enormous buildings surrounded by immense open space, creating humility before the royal house. The size and heights of the buildings demonstrated their significance within the temple complex. The Hall of

Renaissance

China's temples and palaces served as the sem
example for all of East Asian architecture. Many temp
were constructed as multitudinous rows of great halls
rolling roofs located upon terrace foundations. The c
plex circuit of buildings was designed around a rec
gular floor plan in which all buildings were oriented al
a central north-south axis. Traditional wood construc
was gradually replaced by massive structures in wh
almost an entire city was housed, from bridges to un
ground tombs. Meanwhile, Japanese castles feature
minimal style—an aesthetic contrast to the decora
splendor of the Ming dynasty in China. Integrated
ments of Japanese design such as artificial gardens m
reference to natural landscapes.

Prayer is an example of a triple-gabled circular building. The round dome symbolizes the heav-ens and was supported by int columns that symbolized the sons and months of the year.

...meji Castle, ca. 1333–46,
...t 1580, Japan

...troduction of European
...ms led to an entirely new
...of architecture in Japan—
...rtified city. In Himeji the

castle uses beauty and function
in concert. Multileveled super-
structures were raised above
massive stone foundations to
provide a protective distance.
The castle complex, from the

late Monoyama period, is a typical example of a Japanese fortress with walls, embrasures, and
towers atop a high foundation.
There are 82 buildings in the
entire fortified city.

Other Works
Silver Pavilion of Jisho-ji, 1482, Kyoto, Japan
Wat Xieng Thong, ca. 1559, Louang Phabang, Laos
Candra Kasem Palace, 1577, Ayutthaya, Thailand
Teahouse in Saihoji Temple, ca. 1600, Kyoto, Japan

**...angdeokgung Royal
...e**, 1405–12, Seoul

...gdeokgung was the only
...e that architecturally fol-
...the Korean style of the Yi

dynasty. Following the Chinese
model, the administrative
center, living quarters, and the
secret garden consisting of canals, ponds, bridges, and pavi-

lions are all harmonically arranged. In contrast to the
ostentatious and complex Ming
designs, the Korean palaces
were brightly colored.

East Asian Architecture

Baroque

Baroque

p. 242

220

p. 235

p. 249

p. 267

1650–1770
Iberian Baroque

Baroque architecture is popular in Spain and Portugal and is exported to the colonies in the Americas

João Frederico Ludovice
Niccolo Nasoni
Eufrasio López de Rojas

1700   1750   1800

15–1790
coco

)co architecture and
·ior decoration is
·boyantly decorative

·nn Lukas von
·ebrandt
·po Juvarra
·nn Michael Fischer
·çois de Cuvilliés
·cesco Bartolomeo
·relli p. 270
·ppe de La Guêpière

Around the World:
Islamic, Ottoman, Japanese, and Latin American Architecture

Islamic and Ottoman architecture develops intricate domes; Japanese architecture develops the Shoin and Sukiya styles; Latin American churches adopt Baroque styles

p. 277

Baroque and Rococo

The term *baroque* comes from the Portugese word *barocco*, which means "an irregular pearl." The term was aptly applied to the dynamic architectural style that was about spectacle, drama, and color and spread from Italy throughout Europe in the 16th, 17th, and 18th centuries. Facades were designed with curving walls and floor plans were composed of inter-locking ovals. Columns and pilasters were paired and the distance between them varied, becoming smaller as they approached the center of facades, as though they were speeding up. These dynamic lines and sur-faces combined art and architecture into one entity, creating playful illusions of light, color, and texture. Baroque churches included frescoes, trompe l'oeil, ornamentation, domes, and decorated chapels. Inte-riors were elaborately detailed, and exteriors were a powerful clash of concave and convex surfaces.

■ **Baldassar◼ Longhena: S Maria della Salute**, 1631- Venice

■ **Gian Lore◼ Bernini: Baldachino Peter's Basil◼** 1624–33, Vat

Baroque 1550–1790

Baroque began in Italy, where, as part of the Counter-Reformation, the Catholic Church sought to attract the masses away from Protestantism. In order to do this, churches became more ostentatious than ever. The innovative designs of the two great rivals, Gian Lorenzo Bernini and Francesco Borromini, were not only the start of a worldwide architectural style, but also a ploy to attract the public. Pope Urban VIII and Pope Innocent X commissioned many churches and papal residences, such as the colossal buildings of the Vatican in Rome, that pay tribute to the power of the Baroque plan.

Although the style began as an important part of the struggle for religious superiority, Baroque palaces, civic buildings, town squares, and sculptures emerged throughout Italy. From Italy it spread to the rest of Europe, and each country developed its own local interpretation of Baroque architecture.

Introduction

Baroque France

In France, the Baroque style was predominantly used to glorify the absolutism of King Louis XIV. Despite its development in ecclesiastical architecture in Italy, the power of the French monarchy and the wealthy elite developed Baroque designs in secular châteaux. Estates and palaces were designed down to the smallest details. Elaborate gardens, fountains, and interior decorations were incorporated into the designs of architects, who worked closely with interior designers and landscapers.

Baroque châteaux were typically designed on a three-part plan. The *corps de logis*, the centermost section, was framed by two wings. The building was approached by a *cour d'honneur*, a large courtyard, surrounded on three sides by the corps de logis and the two wings. Grandiose interiors, such as marble staircases and mirror halls, displayed the wealth of the royal courts. In Paris, *hôtels particuliers*, urban private residences, were built for the new middle class.

■ **Francois Mansart: Châ Berny**,1623-2 Val-de-Marne

Central European Baroque Styles

Baroque architecture spread to southern Germany, Austria, and Bohemia, from northern Italy. Both religious architecture and the residences of the royal Hapsburg and Schönborn families took on elaborate Baroque forms. The style was widely used by the ruling elite to associate themselves with foreign cultures and to assert their worldliness. Wealthy families brought Italian architects to their courts, while others commissioned local architects who had studied in Italy. Catholic southern Germany followed suit with the Vatican's theory that architecture could be used as a tool to spur the masses to religious devotion. Following the 30 Years' War, Baroque spread to Bohemia. Elaborate churches that were heavily influenced by northern Italy were built in a style known as Bohemian Baroque. As in Italy, churches used oval floor plans.

■ Alonso Ca
Granada Cat
dral, 1667

Baroque Throughout the World

In the UK, Baroque architecture was slowly adopted. Rather than being influenced by the architecture of Italy, where the style originated, Baroque was brought to the UK from France by Sir Christopher Wren. Wren's style was less flamboyant than that found in Italy or Germany, and buildings were designed on more Classical plans.

On the Iberian Peninsula, Spanish and Portuguese architects combined Baroque dynamism with Gothic traditions. The Churrigueresque style, a variation of Baroque, was exported to Spanish-ruled southern Flanders and across the Atlantic to the colonies in the Americas. As Christianity spread, so too did the building style as intricately carved facades were combined with local craftsmanship and materials.

While Baroque spread, other developments were occurring in the East. The Islamic architecture of the powerful Ottoman empire was characterized by the innovative and profuse treatment of domes.

d Quirin and
as Damian
: St. Johann
muk, 1750,
:h

tthäus
l Pöppel-
:
jer,1722,
en

Rococo and the Peak of Flamboyant Architecture

Rococo architecture developed in the 18th century, taking the illusions and decoration of the Baroque period to a new extreme. The style enjoyed great popularity with the ruling elite throughout much of Europe. In France, King Louis XV favored the more delicate curves of Rococo designs. The term *rococo* comes from the French *roccaille*, meaning "stonework." The name most likely developed as a descriptive term for the shell-like stucco work that adorned late Baroque interiors. In central and eastern Europe, ornate Baroque architecture incorporated pastel colors and theatrical stucco ornamentation into the designs of facades and interiors. Rococo architecture often appears more delicate than its Baroque predecessors because of its frivolous and profuse use of color and gold on cupid, shell, and flower motifs. It fell out of favor in the late 18th century and was replaced by a return to rational geometric organization in Neoclassical architecture.

Introduction

Giacomo Barozzi da Vignola

1507, Vignola—1573, Rome

■ Writer, engraver, and architect ■ Worked with Michelangelo ■ Was p
architect to Pope Julius III and the Farnese family ■ His round dome wa
influential for church designs throughout the world
■ *left:* **Detail of the Villa Giulia**, 1550–53, Rome

- **1507** Born in Vignola
- **1536** Works as a painter in the Vatican
- **1541–43** Stays at Fontainebleau
- **1550** Appointed architect to Pope Julius III
- **1550–53** Villa Giulia
- **1559–73** Villa Caprarola
- **1562** Publishes influential *Rules of the Five Orders*
- **1564** Continues work on the two domes at St. Peter's
- **1568** Begins Il Gesu
- **1573** Dies in Rome

Giacomo Barozzi da Vignola was an influential Italia
chitect born in the city from which he took his name
spired by Vitruvius, he visited Rome to draw and s
Classical buildings. During this period he also spent
at Fontainebleau near Paris. He was a perspective the
and his treatise *Rules of the Five Orders of Architec*
which explained Classical building proportions, is o
the most important pieces in the canon of architec
theory. His churches and villas traversed the styles o
late Renaissance, Mannerism, and Baroque, and hi
sure homes housed Pope Julius III and the Farnese fa
Il Gesu is the mother church of the Jesuits and se
standard for ecclesiastical architecture.

■ **Il Gesu**, 1568, Rome

The Church of the Holy Name of Jesus (Il Ge
was designed on the request of Pope Farne
the new order of the Jesuits. The church wa
model for future churches worldwide, comb
the shape of the Latin cross with the oval d
style of the Renaissance. Visitors enter the l
nave directly. The side chapels—which are
arated from the nave—and lack of aisles dir
the visitors' attention to the altar.

Other Important Works

Achille Bochil, 1545–55, Bologna	St. Peter's Domes 1564, Vatican
Villa Farnese, 1559–73, Caprarola	Villa Lante, 1566, Bagnaia
Palazzo Borghese, 1560–1613, Rome	St. Francis of Assi Church, 1569–16 Assisi

a Giulia, 1550–53, Rome

ned as a retreat for Pope Julius III, the villa
n urban front entrance and a rural rear
ce accessed from the Tiber River. The
e front facade is divided into two levels.
ntrance is decorated with three rustic arch-
dered by Doric columns on each side. The
the building consists of loggias, or
d galleries, and a sunken *nymphaeum*, or
in area, with elaborate gardens.

Andrea della Via Flaminia, 1551–54,

nall church lies near to Villa Giulia and is
up of an oblong base and an oval dome,
e for its time. It is constructed from the gray
of Florence and is mostly unadorned, ex-
r the flat Corinthian columns with shell-
d niches above the doors. Two antique
ornices divide the dome and temple roof.

Giacomo Barozzi da Vignola

Baroque in Italy

Gian Lorenzo Bernini

1598, Naples–1680, Rome

■ Sculptor, painter, and architect of Italian Baroque ■ Lived and worked
in Rome ■ Used tricks of light and color to create illusions ■ Buildings
corporated concave and convex surfaces to create a sense of movement
■ Built grand palazzi, public squares, and fountains ■ Rivaled by Borror

● **1598** Born in Naples

ca. 1608 Moves to Rome

1623 Election of his supporter, Pope Urban VIII

1624–33 Works on the renovation of St. Bibiana's facade and the Baldachino in St. Peter's

1629 Architect of St. Peter's in the Vatican

1644–55 Builds Cornaro Chapel with the *Ecstasy of St. Theresa*

1655–67 Pontification of Alexander VII

1665 Travels to France, but the Louvre commission is given to Perrault

1680 Dies in Rome

Other Works by Bernini

St. Peter's Baldachino, 1624, Vatican

Cornaro Chapel, St. Maria della Vittoria, 1645–52, Rome

Palazzo di Montecitorio, 1650, Rome

Castengandolfo Church, 1658–61, Rome

Arricia Church, 1662–64, Rome

Scala Regia, 1663–66, Vatican

Louvre Plans, 1664–66, Paris

Gian Lorenzo Bernini was a talented sculptor, pai
poet, and architect of the Baroque age. His art expres
the emotive ideals of the Catholic Counter-Reformat
and he was a religious follower of the Jesuit order. Ber
worked for Popes Urban VIII and Alexander VII buil
churches and creating statues. The Baldachino canop
St. Peter's was elaborate, sculptural, and daring—ble
ing architecture with sculpture. Tricks of light and sh
ows were often used to highlight his statues, such as
remarkable *Ecstasy of St. Theresa*. He built secular b
ings such as palazzi and fountains that became mo
throughout Europe. Talented at creating illusion thro
painting, Bernini used sculptural surfaces to co
movement and drama in his architecture. He was a
of the other great Baroque architect, Borromini (p. 2

■ St. Andrea al Quirinale
1658–71, Rome

In St. Andrea al Quirinale, s
ture and architecture are
unified in what Bernini con
ered his perfect work. The
Jesuit church is oval in plan
with the altar and entrance
the shorter axis. At the entrance, large Corinthian pi
ters frame a semicircular p
tico, supported by Ionic
columns. Two concave wa
frame the forecourt, creati
dynamism in the facade. In
concealed light sources ar
placed above the altars.

■ Palazzo Barberini, 1628–32, Rome

Following the death of Carlo Maderno, Bernini worked with his rival, the young Borromini, on the Palazzo Barberini, the residential villa for Pope Urban VIII. The central two-story hall has symmetrical wings thrusting out around it, and the raised gardens are in the style of ancient Rome. There are two staircases, each designed by one of the rivals. A loggia with three tiers of arch-topped windows gives the illusion of depth. In the center of the plaza is another creation by Bernini, the Fountain del Tritone.

Peter's Square, 1656–67, an

ni wanted to give visitors npression of being em- d by the arms of the h. The approach is all theater and drama and can hold thousands of people. Rather than following the traditional, centrally planned and balanced layout of the Renaissance, Bernini created an elliptical area consisting of two half-ovals of freestanding Doric columns, four deep. The straight colonnades that lead from the oval forecourt to St. Peter's widen slightly as they approach the cathedral, creating a distorted sense of perspective and aggrandizing the church.

Gian Lorenzo Bernini

Francesco Borromini

1599, Bissone—1667, Rome

- Fascinated by geometry and Galileo ■ Began his career by assisting Carlo Maderno ■ Used interlocking oval and triangular floor plans in the designs of his churches ■ Extravagant, individual style and technique ■ Played with decorative features on domes ■ Lifelong rival of Bernini

1599 Born at Lake Lugano in Bissone, Switzerland

1619 Goes to Rome, where he works with his relative Carlo Maderno

1629–32 Works with Bernini on St. Peter's and Palazzo Berberini, which contributes to his lifelong jealousy

1634 First independent commission at St. Carlo, which exhibits his unique style

1642 Begins Palazzo di Propaganda, which indicates Gothic influences

1644–55 Reign of Pope Innocent X, who was favorable to Borromini

1655 Innocent X dies; Borromini loses commissions

1667 Commits suicide and is buried in his last project, St. Giovanni dei Fiorentini

Francesco Borromini was born at Lake Lugano in Switzerland and was the son of a mason. He moved to Rome at the age of 15 and initially worked with his relative Carlo Maderno on St. Peter's Basilica. After Maderno's death, he worked with Bernini (p. 230), but they developed a famously fierce rivalry that persisted throughout Borromini's life. His architecture was derived from idiosyncratic methods and imaginative planning, and his buildings came to represent the extravagant and dramatic mood of the Baroque. His unconventional genius can be seen in his use of complex spatial compositions, where he used a system of interlocking triangles and ovals to create a sense of movement where surfaces were clearly stated. Both the interiors and the exteriors of his many projects for Pope Innocent X combine geometric rationality with imaginative dramatics. With the death of the Pope, he lost many if his commissions and fell out of favor.

St. Ivo was built for the university, and so many of the elements, such as the spire and layout, symbolize wisdom. Built at the end of the courtyard, the concave facade merges with the surrounding buildings but reflects the extra complexity of drum and dome. The church's layout is based on two triangles that form a hexagonal center and six-pointed star, and the dome combines rational geometry with Baroque dynamism.

■ **Palazzo Sapienza and St. Ivo alla Sapienza**, dome and facade, 1640–60, Rome

Other Works by Borromini

Cappella del St. Sacramento, 1627, Rome

Palazzo Spada, 1632, Rome

Oratory of St. Phillip Neri, 1637, Rome

Maria dei Sette Dolori, 1642–48, Rome

Palazzo Pamphili, 1645–50, Rome

St. Giovani in Laterano, 1646–49, Rome

Villa Falconieri, 1648, Frascati

▼ St. Carlo alle Quattro Fontane, 1634–68, Rome

The corner church is an early example of Borromini's extravagant style. The floor plan is based on interlocking ovals, with walls that seem to snake around the alter and chapels. The concave-convex facade undulates, despite the four straight columns on each floor. Niches and statues are integrated into surfaces, and the dome is coffered with designs of stars and crosses.

Agnese in Agone, 1653,

nese in Agone was built mmemorate St. Agatha. mini worked on the h after the death of Giro- Rainaldi, changing the points and incorporating of the Pamphili Palace. still a circle, the ground akes the form of a Greek as the deep chapels pro-

duce a long axis parallel to the facade. This precedes the popular oval dome that came to signify the Baroque style. The concave facade supports a high drum, and the dome is framed by two towers that are of northern Italian influence. It is one of the more restrained of Borromini's designs. As with several of his other works, Borromini lost the commission when Innocent X died.

Francesco Borromini

Pietro Berrettini da Cortona

1596, Cortona–1669, Rome

■ Painter, illustrator, draftsman, and architect ■ Formed the trio of leading
Baroque architects with Borromini and Bernini ■ Received papal and arist[o]-
cratic commissions from Pope Urban VIII and the Barberini family ■ Used
trompe l'oeil in his paintings and architecture ■ Director of the Painters' G[uild]

● **1596** Born in Cortona

ca. 1610 Studies in Florence under Andrea
Commodi

1612 Travels to Rome and
joins the studio of Baccio
Ciarpi

1618 Creates anatomical
plates that are published
100 years after his death
and inspire later artists

1626 Designs for the
Sachetti brothers

1633 Pope Urban VIII
commissions the Palazzo
Barberini frescoes

1634 Director of Academy
of St. Luke

1656–57 Construction of
St. Maria della Pace

1658–62 Construction of
St. Maria in Via Lata

1669 Dies in Rome

Other Works

SS. Ambrogio e Carlo,
1612–19, Rome

Villa Pigneto, 1626–36,
Castel Fusano

Chapel of the
Immaculate Conception,
1633, Damasco

Pitti Palace, 1637,
Florence

Designs for the Louvre,
1664, Paris

Pietro Berrettini da Cortona was born in Cortona in[to a]
family of artists, including his uncle and instructor Fili[ppo]
Berrettini. He studied in Florence, where his painting s[kill]
came to the attention of the Sachettis and conseque[ntly]
Pope Urban VIII, who gave him large fresco commissi[ons]
including work at the Palazzo Barberini. In Rome, [his]
reputation as a master painter and architect grew. [His]
churches and aristocratic houses were striking exam[ples]
of the High Baroque style, and his eye for detail is evic[ent]
in his creations in both paint and stone. His interiors[, fa]-
cades, and frescoes incorporated illusionism, or tron[pe]
l'oeil, tricking the eye by playing with dynamic surfa[ces]
and realistic imagery. As director of the Painters' Guil[d of]
St. Luke, he instructed talented artisans. He is burie[d in]
San Martino in a crypt that he designed.

■ **St. Maria in Via Lata**,
1658–62, Rome

The two-level church was
renovated by Cortona for A[lex]-
ander VII and is influenced [by]
Pamphili in Piazza Navona. [The]
busy street in front of the
church becomes a spectacl[e]
and the structure is reminis[cent]
of a Roman viewing pavilio[n.]
Large loggias and Corinthi[an]
columns are repeated on b[oth]
levels. On the upper level, [a]
large arch breaks the entab[la]-
ture and is framed in a triar[n]-
gular pediment. It was to b[e a]
hippodrome of the festive

. Maria della Pace, facade,
–57, Rome

na's redesign of the facade
e church shows how elabo-
movement can be created
ne. By its very shape, this
ch both incorporates and
ds out from the surround-
buildings, which were
olished and rebuilt to em-
ize the church, bending
nd its piazza and enclosing
ace. Most striking is the
d convex portico that
es forward, unifying the
ch and forecourt. The first
is modeled after an an-
temple, with full Tuscan
nns. In contrast, the second
has Corinthian columns
oncave and convex sur-
. Real and false windows
he interweaving of motifs
o the building's dynamism.
na transformed the piazza
n urban stage.

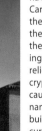

■ SS. Luca e Martina, 1635–64, Rome

With the design of the SS. Luca e Martina, Cortona's fame reached its apex. Commissioned by
Cardinal Francesco Barberini, he designed both
the interior and the exterior of the buiding for
the Academia di San Luca. The church stands on
the edge of the ruins of the Roman Forum. During the construction of the building, St. Martina's
relics were discovered in the foundations of the
crypt. This helped to ensure papal funding. Because of the discovery, the church retains the
names of both St. Luca and St. Martina. The
building's layout forms a Greek cross with
curved ends, and the double-columned framed
facade consists of Cortona's signature convex
and concave surfaces. The upper interior level,
where the arms join in a ribbed central cupola, is
of a white stucco, while the crypt is colorful and
ornate.

Pietro Berrettini da Cortona

François Mansart

1598, Paris—1666, Paris

■ Father of French Classicism ■ Detailed planner ■ The widely used man⋯
roof is named after him ■ Experimented with the layouts of chapels and c⋯
ches ■ Rarely worked for the monarchy but rather for wealthy private clie⋯
■ *left:* **Dome of Château de Blois**, 1635–38, Loire Valley

■ **1598** Born in Paris

1635 Builds first private residence in Paris, the Hôtel de la Vrillière, which sets the standard for French *hôtels*

1646 Great-nephew Jules Hardouin Mansart born; later follows in his great-uncle's footsteps and uses his ideas

1660–61 Remodels Hôtel Carnavalet

1660s Designs for the Louvre are submitted, but not executed

1665 Prepares designs for a huge domed mausoleum for the Bourbons at Saint-Denis

1666 Dies in Paris

Other Works by Mansart

Château de Berny,
1623–27, Val-de-Marne

Hôtel d'Aumont, 1630,
Paris

Hôtel de la Vrillière,
1635, Paris

Maisons Lafitte,
1642–51, Paris

Hôtel Guénégaud-du-
Plessis,1648–60, Paris

Hôtel de Guénégaud-
des-Brosses, 1651–55,
Paris

François Mansart was the son of a carpenter, trained ⋯ sculptor, and was influenced by Salomon de Brosse ⋯ Jacques Androuet du Cerceau. He built townhouses ⋯ châteaux for his bourgeois clients and set the standard ⋯ the Parisian *hôtel*, adding elegance to French Classic ⋯ The mansard roof—a steeply sloped roof with a short ⋯ peak—is named after him, although he did not inver ⋯ He experimented with centrally planned churches ⋯ kidney-shaped layouts and opened crossings. His reno⋯ tions blended the old with the new. Temperament⋯ character, he was known to tear down his own build⋯ and restart.

■ **Château de Blois**, 1635–38,
Loire Valley

Mansart's Orléans wing of the Château de Blois was built for the king's brother but never com-

pleted. All that remains of his creation is the central block, which contains three floors w⋯ Doric, Ionic, and Corinthian columns, and a colonnade.

âteau de Balleroy, 1626, Normandy

hâteau de Balleroy is one of the earliest of
art's private commissions, yet his severe
cal forms can already be seen. The main
ng is monumental in size and detail, and
ain courtyard, or *cour d'honneur*, is framed
o side pavilions. The interior's cantilevered
ase was an engineering feat for its time. As
as to be a permanent residence and not
country retreat, Mansart incorporated the
t of the village into his design, an early form
n planning.

l de Grâce Church, 1645, Paris

al de Grâce Church was commissioned by
of Austria on the occasion of the late and
ngly miraculous birth of her son. The
h has a centralized dome combined with a
ayed out on a Latin cross. The nave has no
but side chapels, and the corner chapels
ked to the main space. Mansart did this by
g diagonal links through the crossing piers
er to connect the chapels with the center.
cade is in an Italian style.

François Mansart

Jules Hardouin Mansart

1646, Paris—1708, Marly

■ Great-nephew of François Mansart and developed his ideas about space and light ■ Official architect to Louis XIV ■ Was chief architect at Versailles after Louis Le Vau ■ His buildings symbolized the power of the monarchy ■ Was adaptable to the tastes of his clients

■ **1646** Born in Paris

1675 Appointed the royal architect to Louis XIV

1678 In charge of the extensions at Versailles, continuing from Le Vau

1685 Appointed to the position of premier architect for the king

1699 Appointed superintendant of buildings

1690s Works on the interior decoration at Versailles, Trianon, and Marly

1698 Designs Place Vendôme

1708 Dies in Marly, near Paris

Other Works

Pavillion de Manse, 1659–89, Auvergne

Château de Saint-Germain-en-Laye, 1663–82, near Paris

Château de Dampierre-en-Yvelines, 1675–83, Dampierre-en-Yvelines

Place des Victories, 1684–86, Paris

Pont Royal, 1685–89, Paris

Château de Meudon, 1695, Meudon

Place Vendôme, 1698, Paris

Jules Hardouin Mansart inherited the legacy, name, architectural plans of his great-uncle François Mar (p. 236). He studied with Libéral Bruant and worked in French Baroque style. As director general of the Maiso. Roi, he oversaw the construction of the royal palaces town planning projects. Following Louis Le V (p. 240) initial extensions, he built grandiose facades at sailles to suit the monarchy's taste for power and pres Adaptable, he could also build with elegant simplicity dome at Les Invalides is one of the largest in the world

■ **Grand Trianon**, 1687–88, Versailles

At the Grand Trianon, an elegant open colonnade known as a peristyle connects the royal apartments. The windows reach down

to ground level, becoming th first "French windows." These dows opened the structure into the garden. Hardouin M sart also designed the founta linking the interior and exter

âteau de Marly, 1679–1686, Marly-le-Roi

arly Château was designed to be a
t for Louis XIV away from the pressures
rt life. Hardouin Mansart built a
palace to house the king and his
, but it soon grew to include
ate gardens, cascades, and 12
te pavilions for guests. The
au had frescoes painted by
s Le Brun, a decorative
rade, and over 200 sta-
hat depicted ancient
and goddesses. A
ticated hydraulic
n supplied water to
rden fountains.

■ **Dome of Les Invalides**,1679–91, Paris

Hardoin Mansart worked with Libéral Bruant
at the veterans' hospital and continued the
project after Bruant's death. Les Invalides's
large ribbed dome dominates the building's structure. He raised the columned
drum area of the dome by adding an
extra attic level above the
cornice, creating one of the
greatest examples of
Baroque architecture.
Within, the dome
dominates the
interior as the cen-
terpiece of the
chapel.

Jules Hardouin Mansart

Louis Le Vau

1612, Paris–1670, Paris

■ Leading Baroque architect in France ■ Influenced by Italian architecture and based his work on Baroque styles ■ Worked with Charles Le Brun on d[...] ration and André Le Nôtre on gardens ■ Contemporary of François Mansa[...] ■ Utilized space in innovative ways ■ One of the chief architects at Versai[...]

■ **1612** Born in Paris

1634 Designs first building, the Hôtel de Bautru, for Michel Villedo

1654 Designs new wings and colonnade of the Louvre

1654 Appointed first architect to the king

1657–61 Works on Vaux-le-Vicomte

1661 Commissioned to rebuild the Galerie d'Apollon in the Louvre

1669 Transforms Versailles from a hunting lodge into a great palace

1670 Dies in Paris

■ **Hôtel Lambert**, 1642–44, Paris

In one of the elegant hôtels designed for the Île Saint-Louis, Le Vau used untraditional ideas and imaginative planning for the small, irregular site. Planned around a central courtyard, the interiors are colorful and decorative. Le Vau built his own home adjacent to the Hôtel Lambert, and after his death the facades of the two buildings were joined, creating one grand estate.

Baroque 1550–1790

Louis Le Vau was trained by his mason father and i[...] enced by Italian styles as well as the architecture of P[...] Berrettini da Cortona (p. 234). He worked with Clas[...] French and Baroque styles to build townhouses and [...] teaux for the wealthy on the Île Saint-Louis, includin[...] own. His masterpiece, Vaux-le-Vicomte, is where[...] supervised the decorator Charles Le Brun and lands[...] gardener André Le Nôtre. Le Vau helped to create[...] Louis XIV style and was one of the chief architects at [...] sailles. He remodeled the garden facade, including [...] elaborate Escalier des Ambassadeurs. He also worke[...] the Louvre and Collège des Quatre-Nations. He ha[...] own style and used varying decorative techniques [...] emphasized space. His style was useful for French re[...] sentation, as it resembled the glory of ancient Rome[...]

nt-Sulpice, 1646, Paris

Sulpice is the second larg-
urch in Paris after Notre
. The large arched win-
allow light in, and two
shells frame the front
The 328-foot (100-meter)
wer, the stained glass,
e spiral staircase all add
grandiose appearance.
nni Niccolo Servandoni
he facade, and Le Vau's
ns were completed by
Marie Oppenord. The
ation is Italian, while the
n is French.

her Works by Le Vau

d de Bautru, 1634, Paris

eau of Livry, 1645,
y

re Wings, 1654, Paris

d de Fonteney, 1656, Paris

-le-Vicomte, 1657–61,
nte

ie d'Apollon in the
re, decorated by Le Brun,
–63, Paris

deling of Versailles, first
1669, Versailles

■ **Vincennes Castle**, 1654,
Vincennes

Vincennes is a formidable 13th-
century stone fortress that Le
Vau worked on after completing
Vaux-le-Vicomte, before being
interrupted by the work on Versailles. He built the southern pavilions for the queen mother
and Cardinal Mazarin. The two
Classically styled pavilions are in
perfect symmetry with each
other, and the remodeling
leaves wide, open spaces surrounded by six towers.

Louis Le Vau

Versailles

Located outside of Paris, Versailles was built and expanded upon by the Fre[...] royalty. Begun as an extension of Louis XIII's hunting lodge in 1623, the palac[...] came France's most elaborate Baroque building and a symbol of the absolu[...] and decadence of the monarchy. The château itself is only part of the large [...] scaped grounds, which include the Grand Trianon (1687–88), the Pavilion [...] çais (1749), the Petit Trianon (1762–68), and the Jardin du Petit Trianon (1775[...] There are also five chapels in the complex. The main architects, Louis Le [...] (p. 240) and Jules Hardouin Mansart (p. 238), worked together with landscap[...] chitect André Le Nôtre and painter Charles Le Brun. Together they interprete[...] lian Baroque aesthetics to French tastes. In 1682 Louis XIV moved the cour[...] nobility away from the civil trouble of Paris to Versailles, and the palace at one [...] housed up to 3,000 people. Throughout the 17th century the palace went thr[...] six different building campaigns that coincided with the Louis XIV Wars.

■ **Jules Hardouin Mansart and Charles Le Brun: Hall of Mirrors**, 1678, Versailles Palace

The Hall of Mirrors was the pièce de résistance of the third building stage. The hall is a thematic trompe l'oeil, depicting the king in allegorical scenes. Magnificent mirrored arches reflect all 17 windows that look out over the gardens. Altogether, 578 mirrors, 17 crys[...] chandeliers, and 41 silver delabras display the mona[...] chy's extreme wealth.

■ **Louis Le Vau and Jules Hardouin Mansart: Marble Court**, 1669, Versailles Palace

The original hunting lodge that stood on the present-day grounds of Versailles was enveloped into a three-floor château with a flat roof and new wings added to it for the king and queen. The impressive black-and-white marble courtyard gave it the name Marble Court. Classic columns support gilded wrought iron balconies. There is no pediment on the courtyard side; instead the facade terminates in a monumental clock, surrounded by the *petits apartments*.

Versailles

French Castles and Gardens

1610–1678

■ The 17th century was an age of French lavish palaces, châteaux, and g
dens ■ The king's residences symbolized the monarch's power ■ Garde
implemented geometry and water mechanics ■ Architects, landscape
gardeners, and interior decorators often worked together

■ **1610–43** Reign of
Louis XIII, who commis-
sions Baroque buildings

1615–31 The Palais du
Luxembourg, with its sub-
ordinated wings, sets the
standard for French
Baroque châteaux

1643–1714 Reign of
Louis XIV, who uses extravagant Baroque archi-
tecture to glorify himself

1661–78 After seeing
Vaux-le-Vicomte, the king
employs Louis Le Vau,
André Le Nôtre, and
Charles Le Brun to work
on Versailles

Other Works

Château de Blérancourt,
by Salomon de Brosse,
ca. 1614, Blérancourt

Château de Maisons-
Lafitte, by François
Mansart, 1651, near Paris

Garden Plan of Tuileries
Palace, by André Le Nôtre,
1664, Paris

Versailles Palace, by Louis
Le Vau, Jules Hardouin
Mansart, André Le Nôtre,
Charles Le Brun, begun
1669, Versailles

Terrace of Saint-Germain-
en-Laye, by André Le
Nôtre, 1673, near Paris

With its castles and gardens, 17th-century France riv
Rome in architectural splendor. Most of the palaces
country châteaux belonged to the monarchy, and
Maison du Roi ("household of the king") appointed
perintendents to oversee all royal building works. Th
chitecture was influenced by Italian Baroque but inco
rated French elements inherited from medieval tir
The three-sided courtyard was popularized, and
wings scaled down. Royal architects Louis Le Vau (p.
and Jules Hardouin Mansart (p. 238) collaborated
landscape gardeners like André Le Nôtre. French Barc
gardens were renowned and included in estate plans
desire to subordinate nature to reason was emphas
by using Cartesian geometry throughout designs.

■ **Louis Le Vau: Vaux-le-
Vicomte**, 1658–61, Vicom

Vaux-le-Vicomte is the mo
significant French château
the Baroque period and w
built for the wealthy finan
minister Nicolas Fouquet.
Classical characteristics of
order, balance, and symm
and the monumental form
convey a powerful impres
A large pediment and ova
dome dominate the garde
facade and have alternatir
patterns of pilasters and
windows. The moat and w
add to the aggrandizemer
the building. Le Nôtre des
the gardens and fountains

lomon de Brosse: Palais de Luxembourg, –31, Paris

'alais de Luxembourg was planned by Marie edici in the Florentine style, but the rusticated e is more in the style of French Classicism. It nusually large corner pavilions that thrust rd, elevated roofs, and an impressive three-entrance.

■ André Le Nôtre: Gardens of Château de Saint-Cloud, 1664–65, Hauts-de-Seine

The Grande Cascade in the gardens at Saint-Cloud was the most magnificent fountain of Baroque France and had two arches accompanied by urns and figurines from which water would spout. The elevation offered vast views over the grounds, and the avenues were superbly planned, despite the steep and hilly decline.

Urban Planning in Paris

1589–1715

■ The new middle class settled in *hôtels particuliers* ■ Speculative developments failed and were sold off to the rich ■ Political power and the court tr[an]-
ferred to Versailles ■ Defense fortifications moved, making the city open fo[r]
new squares and boulevards ■ Urban designs and gardens glorified Louis X[IV]

1589–1610 Reign of
Henri IV

1605–12 Place des Vosges
(originally Place Royale) is
built under Henri IV and
becomes Europe's first city
square as well as the first
royally commissioned city
planning project

1610–43 Reign of
Louis XIII

1618 Fire of Paris and the
destruction of a large
number of buildings

1643–1715 Reign of
Louis XIV, also known as
the Sun King, and the Versailles court

Paris in the 17th century witnessed the rise of a n[ew]
middle class, called the *noblesse de robe*, who reside[d in]
the newly built *hôtels particuliers*, grand private hou[ses.]
Architects such as Jules Hardouin Mansart were [em]-
ployed to construct the new Parisian skyline and pu[blic]
squares. During the reign of Louis XIV, known as the [Sun]
King, the city's population reached over 400,000. Des[pite]
the growing masses, all architecture and landscape [de]-
sign had to complement the king's absolutism. As [the]
center of political power moved to Versailles, the ci[ty's]
medieval fortifications were demolished. Walls w[ere]
transformed into grand tree-lined boulevards as the [city]
moved westward. Old quarters, such as the Marais, w[ere]
rebuilt, and the Île Saint-Louis was urbanized. [These]
changes were a precedent to Haussmann's (p. 3[xx])
sweeping urban reforms of the 19th century.

■ **Jean Androuet du Cerc[eau,]
Hôtel de Sully**, 1625–30, P[aris]

The Marais townhouse Hôt[el de]
Sully is attributed to du Cer[ceau]
and follows the popular *hô[tel]
particulier* formula. It consis[ts of]
three-story pavilions and a[n]
orangerie. Separated from [the]
street by a courtyard, the si[de]
wings are the same height [as]
the main building and deco[r]-
rated with elaborate carving[s]
and detailed friezes. The co[urt]-
yard is decorated with figur[es]
celebrating the elements a[nd]
four seasons.

Other Works

■ Jules Hardouin Mansart: Place Vendôme, 1698, Paris

The Vendôme square was begun by Loius XIV to house the royal academies and libraries, but financial problems halted the development. In 1698, with only the facades built, the back plots were sold off to the rich to build *hôtels particuliers* as they pleased. Jules Hardouin Mansart's designs and roofs are evident, as are the Baroque and classic Roman features, such as Corinthian columns adorning the double-story facades. Access is via two entrances into the octagonal square. The centerpiece column was erected by Napoleon in 1807.

■ Jardin des Tuileries, 1664, Paris

The gardens of Tuileries were designed for Catherine de Medici's palace and remodeled in 1664 by André Le Nôtre to glorify the Sun King's return. Perspective techniques, such as adding steps to the palace and lengthening the 1.4 mile (2.3 km) avenue of trees to reach the horizon, were used to accentuate the grandness of the space.

Urban Planning in Paris

Johann Bernhard Fischer von Erlach

1656, Graz–1723, Vienna

■ Leading architect during the Hapsburg era ■ Brought Italian Baroque sty
to central Europe ■ Combined influences from antiquity, Europe, and the O

■ **1656** Born near Graz

1672 Travels to Italy, where he meets Bernini and studies sculpting and architecture

1687 Returns to Austria and is appointed court architect

1696 Knighted

1704 Travels to Germany, the Netherlands, the UK, and Venice

1707 Builds Palais Clam Gallas in Prague

1721 Publishes *Entwurf einer historischen Architektur*

1723 Begins Vienna Hofbibliothek, which is completed by his son

1723 Dies in Vienna

Other Works

Schloss Frain, 1690–94, Moravia

Dreifaltigkeitskirche, 1694–1707, Salzburg

Stadtpalais, 1695–98, Vienna

Ursulinenkirche, 1699–1705, Salzburg

Batthyany Palais, ca. 1700, Vienna

Palais Trautson, 1710–16, Vienna

One of the most prominent Austrian architects, Fis
von Erlach came from an artisan family, and his
Joseph, completed his final buildings after his death.
young age he moved to Italy, where he trained
sculptor. There he was also exposed to the architectu
Borromini (p. 232), Bernini (p. 230), and Palladianism,
this was to affect his building style. Following the de
of the Turks at the Battle of Vienna, the Hapsburg in
rial family wanted an architecture that would display
power. Fischer von Erlach's grand facades and Baro
splendor encapsulated their aspirations. As court a
tect for three emperors he built many triumphal pal
and churches. He also built spectacular secular buildi
such as the Vienna Hofbibliothek, or Ce
Library, with its grand main room. He
published an influential book recor
world architecture.

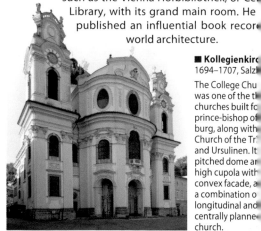

■ **Kollegienkirc**
1694–1707, Salzl

The College Chu
was one of the th
churches built fo
prince-bishop of
burg, along with
Church of the Tr
and Ursulinen. It
pitched dome ar
high cupola with
convex facade, a
a combination o
longitudinal and
centrally planne
church.

urch of St. Charles,
30, Vienna

arles is one of the grand-
urches of the Baroque pe-
n his design, Fischer von

Erlach referenced other
structures, such as the the
dome from St. Peter's and the
portico from the Parthenon.
The central bulk is framed by

two Trojan pillars, with spiral reliefs, creating a dramatic entrance. The low, wide front and
huge dome also create vertical
and horizontal movement.

Johann Bernhard Fischer von Erlach

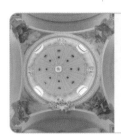

Johann Dientzenhofer

1663, St. Margarethen–1726, Bamberg

■ Part of the Dientzenhofer architecture family ■ Influenced by the Baroque styles of Italy and France ■ Built palaces for the prince-bishops Bamberg and churches for the bishop of Fulda
■ *left:* **Fulda Cathedral**, interior view of dome, 1704–12

1663 Born in St. Margarethen, Bavaria

1693–1729 Reign of his patron, Lothar Franz von Schönborn

1699–1700 Studies in Prague and Italy

1704–12 Builds for the prince-bishop of Fulda

1707 After the death of his brother Leonhard, Johann takes over the work at Banz Abbey

1711 Begins work on Weissenstein Castle

1711–19 Builds for the prince-bishop of Bamberg

1720–23 Works with Johann Neumann and Christoph Dietzenhofer on the Würzburg Residence

1726 Dies in Bamberg

Other Works

Fulda City Palace, 1707–12, Fulda

Bieberstein Castle, 1709, near Fulda

Abbey Church of Banz Abbey, 1710–18, Banz

Parish Church of St. Wenceslaus, 1715–18, Litzendorf

Bibra Palais, 1716, Bamberg

Johann Dientzenhofer designed German Baroque pala and churches famous for their lavish interiors. He was youngest son of the architect Georg, and the brothe Georg, Leonhard, Wolfgang, and Christoph, who, gether with Christoph's son Kilian Ignaz, comprised famous Dientzenhofer family of architects. He traine Prague and Italy, and went on to be the court architec several ecclesiastical princes. Lothar Franz von Sch born, the highest-ranking elector of the Holy Roman pire, was his greatest patron, and commissioned gr residences at Bamberg, Pommersfelden, and Re mannsdorf comparable to the palaces of his contem raries in France and Italy. Dientzenhofer also designed the prince-bishop of Fulda, and his design of the I buildings brought much elegance to the town.

■ **Weissenstein Castle**, 1711–18, Pommersfelden

The Weissenstein Castle was built as a summer residence and contains lavish rooms and surprising

features, including one of the grottoes built in Germany. Th staircase, influenced by that Würzburg Residence, has de ceiling frescoes.

...da Cathedral, 1704–12

...ulda Cathedral was ...ructed on the remaining ...ations of the abbot ...r's basilica from the 9th ...ry. The cathedral and ... were part of the larger Baroque rebuilding of the entire city and are inspired by the styles of Italian Baroque, in particular the Roman churches of Borromini's St. Giovanni in Laterno and St. Peter's Basilica. The nave has three main sections and a Baroque altar. The building's interior is white, and the marble staircase ascends toward the heavily frescoed ceiling. The east facade is made up of a number of turrets, domes, towers, and obelisks.

Johann Dientzenhofer

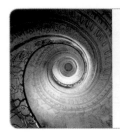

Jakob Prandtauer

1660, Stanz bei Landeck–1726, St. Pöltan

- Leading Austrian architect and master mason ■ Created his own style
Baroque by adding elements of traditional Austrian design to the style
- Also influenced by Italian styles
- *left:* **Melk Abbey**, staircase to library, 1702–36, Melk, Austria

- **1660** Born in Stanz bei Landeck, Austria
- **1677–88** Studies sculpture and masonry with Hans Georg Asam
- **ca. 1680** Is greatly influenced by the Italian family of sculptors and masons the Carlones, and begins using frescoes and stuccoed vaulting in his work
- **1690s** Builds in the St. Pöltan area of Austria, including engineering projects such as bridges
- **1708** Following the death of Carlo Antonio Carlone, Prandtauer begins work on the St. Florian Abbey and Library
- **1726** Dies in St. Pöltan

Jakob Prandtauer trained as a master mason with Georg Asam and utilized his artistic skills in his architecture. He combined his knowledge of traditional Austrian designs with Italian Baroque elements, such as the use of stucco and frescoes, to create his own style of architecture and ornamentation. He lived and worked in Pöltan, Austria, at the beginning of the century and built country palaces, bridges, and large abbeys. In his later life he worked on the restoration of many churches, an activity that corresponded with his religious beliefs. Abbey was his life's work and, like most of his works that were uncompleted by the time of his death in 1726, completed by his assistant, student and cousin Joseph Munggenast.

Other Works

Pilgrimage Church, 1706–32, Sonntagberg

Pilgrimage Church, 1706–14, Christkindl

Kremsmünster Abbey, 1710–15, Kremsmünster

Abbey Church at Dürnstein, 1717

St. Pölten Cathedral, 1722

Pfarrkirche, 1725, Wullersdorf

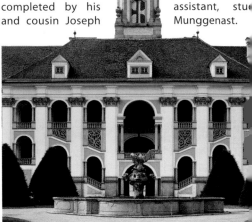

…k Abbey, 1702–36, Melk, …a

…tauer's life work, Melk … is one of the most dra-…examples of Austrian …ue architecture. Situated …n the cliffs above the …e River, it was originally a …and fortification, and of-…ectacular views of the

…Florian Library,
…26, Linz, Austria

…he death of Carlo Antonio …e, Prandtauer con-…d a number of Baroque …ons to the St. Florian … near Linz, including his …n the library with Got-…Hayberger. He also de-…the stately staircase, …compares to those of the

river below. The church, with its high dome and double towers, is situated between the two main arms of the abbey, which extend outward. The exterior is a mass of undulating facades and soaring towers and turrets, which make the building appear to rise out of the rocky outcrop. Prandtauer collaborated

architect Sanfelice in Naples. During his construction of the library, he was also involved in the building of several other monasteries in the area. As was the custom in the Baroque period, Prandtauer not only served as the architect for these projects, but was also in charge of all of the aspects of construction, including the exterior and

with many of the leading artists at the time on the interiors, frescoes, and hallways. The complex also includes the famous Marble Hall, a school, the Imperial Staircase, an extensive library of rare medieval texts, a vast courtyard, abbey terrace, and the southern high wall that overlooks the town.

interior decorations. His training as a mason and sculptor aided him in creating the designs, and he was greatly influenced by the Italian stucco and fresco work of his predecessor Carlone. These dynamic ornamentations and embellishments give his monasteries and the St. Florian Library a dynamic Baroque aesthetic.

Jakob Prandtauer

Johann Balthasar Neumann

1687, Eger—1753, Würzburg

- Leading German Baroque architect ■ Helped in developing the elab[
rate Rococo style of interior design ■ Built churches, palaces, and abbe[
- Also worked on civil projects ■ Royal architect to the Schönborn fam[
- Was involved in the imperial forces ■ Famous for his elaborate stairc[

- **1687** Born in Bohemia (now Czech Republic)
- **1711** Moves to Würzburg
- **1717** Visits Milan and Vienna; comes under the patronage of the Schönborn family
- **1731** Builds the staircase at Schloss Bruchsal
- **1732–41** Works on Würzburg Chapel with the Austrian Baroque architect Johann Lukas von Hildebrandt, and assists in the decoration
- **1733** Builds utilitarian factories for glass and mirrors
- **1737** Builds the staircase at the Würzburg Residenz
- **1740** Draws plans for the church at Gaibach, although work only begins three years later
- **1753** Dies in Würzburg

■ Wallfahrtskirche, 1730–39, Gossweinstein

The Wallfahrtskirche, or Pilgrims' Church, in the town of Gossweinstein is a monumental sandstone building that was one of the largest in Swiss Franconia (now part of Bavaria, Germany). It replaced a medieval church that was not big enough to accommo-

Johann Balthasar Neumann was a late Baroque arch[
who worked mainly in the German towns of Würz[
and Bamberg. His father was a clothier, and after [
dying engineering, he joined the imperial force[
which he remained active throughout his life. Early i[
career he assisted on the Würzburg Residenz, along [
his contemporaries the Dientzenhofers (p. 250). Afte[
laborating on it for more than 20 years, the final res[
chiefly his design. Although his buildings were care[
planned, they are frivolous, playful, and colorful t[
counter. Due to his preciseness Neumann is know[
the "architect's architect." The Schönborn prince-bis[
were his lifelong patrons, and he built courtly reside[
for them throughout their munic[
ity of Swiss Franconia.[
mann was famous fo[
elaborate staircases, v[
often took center s[
in a building, v[
at the same tim[

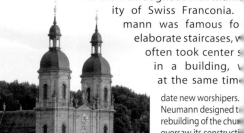

date new worshipers.
Neumann designed t[
rebuilding of the chu[
oversaw its constructi[
Two high towers on t[
west facade face the t[
The church has a serie[
triangular corners and[
rior walls that represe[
Trinity. The church un[
went another recon-
struction in 1746 afte[

Augustusburg Palace Staircase,
48, Bruhl

ugustusburg Palace was rebuilt on the ince of the archbishop of Cologne. The mag-
nt staircase is typical of Neumann's use of
design, and is highly decorative yet metic-
y constructed. Made of marble, the two
cal stairways are stunning examples of the
style and have elaborate sculptures,
, and frescoes integrated into the forms.

rrkirche, 1740, Gaiback

nall Trinity church in Gaiback is deceptively
. On the outside it is minimally decorated
w and green ocher sandstone, and has
gle tower. However, the interior is one of
est examples of German High Baroque. It is
d into a long nave and vaultlike rotunda.
nters from the arch-shaped windows,
g a heavenly atmosphere.

Johann Balthasar Neumann

showing his genius in the field of engineering, and his talents in manipulating space. The interiors of his buildings were spacious and elegant. Neumann built over 70 churches and developed extravagant Rococo interiors, such as his masterpiece at Vierzehnheiligen. Multiskilled, he managed town and water planning, factories, houses, monasteries, hospitals, gardens, and even fireworks. He also taught military and civil engineering at the University of Würzburg. Neumann used sophisticated vaults and oval ground plans in his churches. He also employed large windows to let in light and emphasize the splendor of his buildings. Toward the end of his career, he preempted the shift to a more Classicist style.

Other Works by Neuma

Schönbornkapelle, 1721–3
Würzburg

Haus des Architekten, 1722
Würzburg

Klosterkirche Holzkirchen,
1724–32, Holzkirchen

Wiesentheid Church, 1727,
Wiesentheid

Schloss Werneck, 1734–45,
Werneck

Parish and Mortury Church
Sts. Cecilia and Barbera,
1739–56, Hesse

Käppele, 1740–52,
Würzburg

Augustinerkirche, 1741,
Würzburg

Holy Cross Chapel, 1741,
Etwashausen

Schloss Bruhl,1743–48, Bor

Mariankirche, 1747–52,
Limbach

■ Benedictine Abbey,
designed in 1747, Nereshe

The Benedictine Nereshei
Abbey in Baden-Württem
southern Germany, is base
Neumann's designs but w
completed after his death
takes the form of a longitu
plan, and the nave is brok
into seven ovals, or ellipse
largest of which is over th
crossing. The domes are s
ported by thin columns, a
large windows allow both
rect and indirect light in,
increases the impression
unified space. One does n
tice the separated areas, a
the domes seem to float.
frescoes on the seven cup
were painted by Martin K.

erzehnheiligen, 1742–74, near Bad Staffel-

ann's masterpiece was built on an already-
undation, which he used to his advantage.
tar, where 14 saints are believed to have ap-
d, is at the center of a Latin cross. The ground
s based on three ovals above the long nave
vo above the transepts, which create move-
The curves are also reflected in the vaults in
of. An abundance of gold columns, statues,
, and gilding creates an intense array of co-
nd textures.

rzberg Residenz, 1720–44, Würzburg

ately home and court at Würzburg is a mon-
tal building based on a C-shaped plan. The
l block has an octagonal dome, and the *cour
eur* is surrounded by three pavilions. The
r is gilded and painted. Rooms include the
e room with adjoining state apartments, four
courtyards, and an enclosed entrance for
es, which all demonstrated the wealth of the
borns. The magnificent staircase has a
that is unobstructed by supports and deco-
with colorful frescoes by Tiepolo.

Baroque in Germany and Austria

Johann Balthasar Neumann

Bohemian Baroque

1655–1751

■ Bohemian or "radical" Baroque buildings were built throughout Bohe[mia] and Moravia ■ Churches were lavish and dramatic ■ Christoph and Ki[lian] Ignaz Dientzenhofer were the central figures ■ Secular architecture wa[s] greatly influenced by French Baroque styles

● **1655** Christoph Dientzenhofer is born

1678 Christoph moves to Prague from Germany

1689 Kilian Ignaz Dientzenhofer is born in Prague

1699 Château Liblice is designed by Giovanni Alliprandi

1719–27 Jan Santini Aichel builds the star-shaped church of Jan Nepomucky

1722 Christoph Dientzenhofer dies

1751 Kilian Ignaz Dientzenhofer dies

As a result of the Thirty Years War and the Cou[nter]-Reformation, Bohemia and Moravia, today the C[zech] Republic and Slovakia, embraced Catholicism and [its] accompanying architectural styles. The resulting Bar[oque] style was introduced to their ecclesiastical and secular a[rchi]-tecture with vigor. Rich nobles invited architects t[o the] eastern provinces, and the dramatic regional style be[came] known as Bohemian Baroque. Prominent Bohemian a[rchi]-tects included Jan Santini Aichel and Giovanni Allipra[ndi. In] particular, the legacy of Bohemian Baroque was due t[o the] Dientzenhofer family. Kilian Ignaz and his father Chris[toph,] brother of Johann (p. 250), lived in Prague and built for [royal] and neighboring patrons. Christoph designed and re[built] many churches, and Kilian Ignaz, who trained under Jo[hann] Lukas von Hildebrandt, brought a variety of Baroque inn[ova]-tions to his churches, such as concave and convex wal[ls.]

■ **Kilian Ignaz Dientzenhofer: St. Nicholas**, 1732–37, Prague

Inspired by Paris's Saint-Louis-des-Invalides, St. Nicholas on the Old Town Square reflects Christoph's earlier St. Nicholas Church, located just nearby. Two identical towers frame the 263-foot- (80-meter-) high lanterned dome. The south-ern facade is decorated with saintly statues. It is one of the largest Baroque churches in central Europe.

Baroque 1550–1790

Kilian Ignaz Dientzenhofer: America, 1712–20, Prague

Villa America functioned as summer palace and was the

Christoph and Kilian Ignaz Dientzenhofer: Loreto Church, Prague

Loreto Church is inspired by Italian Santa Casa of Loreto. Like the Italian church, here *santa casa* (holy house) is indoors in the courtyard. The first phase construction was begun by Christoph but passed to his son and grandson to complete. The large bell tower, with 30 bells, crowns the octagon tower and dome. The bells ring on the hour—a complicated mechanical feat for the time.

first to be built independently by Kilian Ignaz Dientzenhofer. The style is French but clearly influenced by the Austrian

architect Hildebrandt—it is small, with decorative pieces on the window arches and detailed busts and vases.

Other Works
Church of the Holy Trinity, by Giovanni Alliprandi, 1708–10, Kuks
St. Klara, by Christoph Dientzenhofer, 1708–11, Cheb
St. Margaretha, by Christoph Dientzenhofer, 1708–15, Brevnov
Karlova Koruna, by Jan Santini Aichel, 1721–23, Chlumec nad Cidlinou
Palais Sylva Taroucca, by Kilian Ignaz Dientzenhofer, 1749, Prague

Baroque Dynamism

Much of the Baroque style was about creating spectacle and illusion with new methods of design and construction. The straight, rigid lines of the Renaissance were replaced by flowing curves, projections, and recesses. Domes and roofs were enlarged, and frescoes used complicated trompe l'oeil techniques to create the illusion of height and depth on flat surfaces. Light and shadow were used to create dramatic effects on virtually every type of surface. Buildings were full of dark niches, narrow enclaves, and corners. Contrastingly, well-lit protruding pilasters, high windows, and hidden sources of illumination produced light, shadow, and undulating surfaces, which created the Baroque aesthetic.

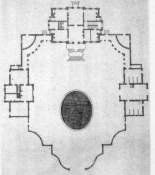

■ **Roehampton Great House**, 1625, London

English architects who learned Baroque styles and techniques while in Italy on a grand tour tended to apply them less extravagantly once they returned home. The curved facades of Borromini and Bernini are used here for secular architecture, creating a complex floor plan.

Baroque 1550–1790

■ **Borromini: St. Carlo all[e] Quattro Fontane**, 1638–41[?]

The innovative use of com[pli]cated interlinking ovals, ra[ther] than circles or lines, in gro[und] plans was reflected in the [un]dulating walls. Simple cruc[i]form layouts were also trea[ted] anew—lengthening naves [and] placing ellipses or triangle[s] over the crossings. This res[ul]ted in a combination of co[n]cave and convex surfaces [that] created dynamism in stati[c] walls. These bulges appea[r] both on the interior and e[xte]rior facades. At St. Carlo, t[he] placement of columns, sta[t]ues, and decorations emp[ha]sizes the movement of the curves.

**ernini: Cornaro Chapel in
aria della Vittoria**, Rome,
–52

ni's talents as an artist en-
him to work with sculp-
nd color in a remarkable
er. Inside the St. Maria
Vittoria lies Bernini's

Cornaro Chapel, with his remarkable sculpture depicting
St. Theresa of Avila in a state of
religious ecstasy. The mood and
exhalation of the work is emphasized by different sources of
light. Bernini placed hidden
windows with yellow glass to

reflect the gilded rays penetrat-
ing the statue, so that they
appear to glow. The colored
marble contrasts with the an-
gelic white of the sculpture. The
chapel is set up like a stage,
with figures of the Cornaro family watching from the sides.

Baroque Dynamism

Iberian Baroque

ca. 1665–1755

■ During the 18th century the Churrigueresque style became popular throughout the Iberian Peninsula ■ Portugal's wealth enabled large-scal building projects and the use of expensive materials ■ Italian-born archi tect Niccolo Nasoni worked in Portugal

● **ca. 1665** Eufrasio López de Rojas builds an early Baroque cathedral at Jaen

1667 The facade of the Granada Cathedral is built, laying the groundwork for the Churrigueresque style

1706–50 Reign of King John V, who commissions large Portuguese palaces

1725 Nasoni settles and works in Oporto and influences local design

1755 Earthquake in Lisbon leads to massive rebuilding

Spanish Baroque architecture began as a reserved st but gained momentum in the 18th century and peak with the emergence of the Churrigueresque st Named after an architect family from Salamanca, Chu gueresque is recognizable by surface areas and faca that are elaborately detailed and decorated v sculpted features incorporated into the architecture. towns of Salamanca and Seville and the Andalusian a have many examples of religious and civic Baro buildings. Portuguese Baroque was more restrained t Spanish Baroque and incorporated classic French a Italian elements. King John V used the wealth gai from colonies to finance architect projects such as Mafra and the Que residence. In the north of the cou buildings were fashioned out of l granite, and wood carvings were o coated in Brazilian gold. The lead Portuguese architect was the Ital born Niccolo Nasoni.

■ **Santiago de Compostela**, obradoiro, 1738–50, Cazas y Nova, Galicia, Spain

The large cathedral of Santiago de Compostela an architectonic mix of Gothic, medieval, Rom esque, Plateresque, and Baroque styles. The fo dations were laid in the 9th century, but the he ily ornamented Baroque *obradoiro* (or goldsm work) facade was added in the 18th century. T central spire forms an arch with the statue of t apostle James, whose relics are said to be buri the crypt. Two interlinking external staircases to the elevated entrance.

⬛ Carlos da Cruz Amarante:
Bom Jesús do Monte Stairway,
1725, Braga, Portugal

The most striking Baroque feature of the pilgrimage church of Bom Jesús do Monte, near Braga, is the elaborate zigzag staircase that ascends the 380 feet (116 meters) to the main sanctuary. The stairs were part of the design of a new building in 1722 under the order of the archbishop of Braga, Rodrigo de Moura Telles. Each level represents one of the five senses—smell, taste, sight, touch, and hearing—and each level also has a fountain symbolizing purity and cleanliness. The three chapels in the rear are octagonal and surrounded by more fountains and sculptures of saints. A further staircase was added later to symbolize the three theological virtues—faith, hope, and charity. The Bom Jesús do Monte influenced many other Baroque sites in Portugal, as well as the Congonhas in Brazil. The main church was redesigned in the late 18th century.

Other Works

ada Cathedral, by Alonso
, 1667, Granada, Spain

ital de los Venerables
rdotes, by Leonardo de
roa, 1687–97, Seville,

dos Clérigo, by Niccolo
ni, 1754, Oporto, Portugal

ch of the Carmelite Third
r, by José Figueiredo de
s, 1756–68, Oporto, Por-

⬛ João Frederico Ludovice:
Mafra Monastic Palace,
1711–30, Mafra, Portugal

The abbey of Mafra was designed by the German-born architect João Frederico Ludovice. Mafra consists of a palace, church, monastery, and convent. The grand facade, with its two towers, is constructed out of limestone, and the church itself is a mix of pink and white marble. Mafra was influenced by St. Peter's and the Carlo Fontana school.

Iberian Baroque

Sir John Vanbrugh

1664, London–1726, London

- Never formally trained in architecture ■ Writer of satirical plays and politically active ■ Built large estates for the Earl of Marlborough and for t[ ] Earl of Carlisle ■ Served as comptroller at the Royal Works with Sir Christ[ ] pher Wren ■ His work was met with both positive and negative reviews

1664 Born in London

1690 Arrested for espionage in France

1702 Appointed as comptroller of the Royal Works; designs Castle Howard in Yorkshire

1703 Works on the Haymarket Theater

1714 Returns to England from Europe

1723 Knighted by King George I

1726 Dies in London

The son of a Flemish refugee, John Vanbrugh led a [col]orful and controversial life as an architect, playwright, [and] politician. Most of all he was the leader of the short-li[ved] English Baroque architectural style and designed mo[nu]mental country estates. He was imprisoned in Franc[e for] espionage, where he may have been exposed to the [de]signs of Louis Le Vau (p. 240) and French Baroque. U[pon] his return, although untrained, he worked with [Sir] Christopher Wren (p. 292) at the Royal Works. He [was] always assisted by fellow Baroque architect Nich[olas] Hawksmoor, who was said to have provided the pra[cti]cality needed to realize Vanbrugh's grandiose vision[s.]

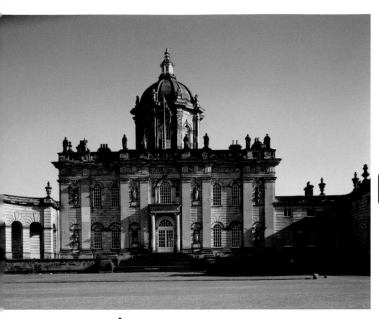

...nheim Palace, 1705–22, ...stock, Oxfordshire

...eim Palace is both a
...y home and a monument
... victory of the Earl of Marl-
...gh. It is a monumental
...ruction of stone, with a
...ing portico and grand
...ard. There are two large
...ings, and allegorical stat-
...e the palace's extensive
...ns.

🏠 Castle Howard, 1702–12, Yorkshire

Although Castle Howard was
Vanbrugh's first commission, it
earned him a great reputation
as a Baroque architect. A
domed central tower domi-
nates the facade, which has columns of the Doric order on
the north and Corinthian
on the south. The west
wing was completed,
after Vanbrugh's
death, in a Palladian
style.

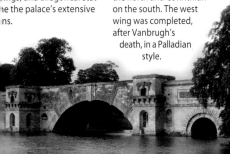

Other Works by Vanbrugh

Kimbolton Castle, 1707–09, Cambridgeshire

Kings Weston House, 1710–25, Bristol

Seaton Delaval Hall, 1720–28, Northumberland

Grimsthorpe Castle, 1722–26, Lincolnshire

◀ Grand Bridge at Blenheim Palace, 1705–22, Woodstock, Oxfordshire

The landscaping at Blenheim
complements the scale of the
palace. The massive Picturesque bridge was said to
contain 30 rooms.

Sir John Vanbrugh

Rococo Architecture

1715–1789

■ Decorative style popular during the late Baroque ■ Named for its curving shell-shaped forms ■ Began in France but spread to Germany, Austria, Italy and Russia ■ Stucco was the main decorative material ■ Architects include Johann Michael Fischer and Johann Lukas von Hildebrandt

1715–23 Régence period; the French court is located in Paris

1715–74 Reign of King Louis XV

ca. 1723 Hildebrandt uses Rococo details, introducing Rococo to Austria

1760s Voltaire denounces the excessiveness of Rococo

1789 French Revolution

Rococo is a style of elaborate decoration developed in last phase of Baroque and popular during the reign of Louis XV. A style of art, architecture, furniture, and e music, the word comes from the French *rocaille*, mean "rock," and *coquillage*, meaning "shells," because of abundance of flowing, curved forms. In churches palaces, skilled architects, artists, and sculptors collabor to create a complete aesthetic encounter. Opposing the terity of Baroque, light colors and airy atmospheres v used. Surfaces often incorporated mirrors and jewels,

■ **Filippo Juvarra: Basilic Superga**, 1715–18, Turin,

The Surperga Basilica was Baroque church built by th Sicilian architect Filippo Juvarra, who had experien with set design and theate decoration. The basilica ha many historical references the facade and portico are gantly Classical, but the hi dome and cupola are clea spired by the Baroque dra Borromini and Bernini. Tw ferent colors highlight the columns and pillars on the exterior. Six heavily decora chapels surround the circu nave, which contains exte work in marble. The entra to the Savoy family tomb i further decorated with ma reliefs and gilded stucco.

[Fran]çois de Cuvilliés: Amalienburg in the [Nymp]henburg Castle Park, 1734–39, Munich, [German]y

[...a sm]all hunting pavilion was built for Arch-[duches]s Amalia, an avid hunter. The Hall of Mir-[rors is t]he interior centerpiece and is decorated [in silver]e and blue, the Bavarian national colors. [The wa]lls are painted with images of the hunt, [and the]e ceiling has blue chinoiseries. The artists [Johann] Baptist Zimmermann and Joachim [Dietric]h worked on the interior.

[Joh]ann Michael Fischer: Zwiefalten Abbey, [1739–6]7, near Reutlingen, Germany

[Zw]iefalten Abbey is one of Fischer's largest and [most ex]quisite interiors. The high alter and balus-[trades r]adiate light from their gilt ornamentation. [The ela]borate frescoes merge with the stucco [figures] through the asymmetrical frames that [surroun]d them. The figures seem alive and in action, and [emer]ge effortlessly from the painted frames to [gilded] ornament. The gilded Corinthian columns [are dec]orative rather than functional.

and there was an abundant use of white stucco, with asymmetrical and unbalanced elements. Lines were arabesque—curved like the organic growth of flowers and plants—and filigree—intricately designed from gold or silver wire. Oriental designs, or chinoiseries, were incorporated onto buildings, and gardens had small intimate areas and water features. Rococo first appeared in France and, due to the relative peace in Europe, spread easily. It was embraced with vigor in Germany and Austria. Rococo reached its zenith in southern Germany, and traveling artisans spread the style throughout Italy and Russia. In England, Rococo was limited to furnishing, and small decorative items. The French Revolution signaled an end to the excessive style and heralded a return to Classicism.

■ **Philippe de La Guêpière: Solitude Palace**, 1764–69, Stuttgart, Germany

French architect Philippe de La Guêpière brought Rococo to southern Germany. Built as a hunting retreat for Duke Carl

Eugen von Württemberg, this elegant Rococo palace is directly linked to the large Baroque Ludwigsburg Palace by a long avenue. The building's focal point is the two grand curving staircases that lead to the

central entrance. The gard
had typical Rococo landsc
features, such as intimate
ners, pools, and an Orient
house. The facade of Solit
similar in appearance to t
Sanssouci Palace at Potsd

**ŋçois de Cuvilliés:
iés Theater**, 1751–53,
ı, Germany

trance to the theater was
ı the royal palace, there-
owing Cuvilliés to focus
interior and furnishings
than the facade. The four
e a splendid combina-
carved wooden orna-
and Rococo furnishings.

**ann Michael Fischer:
euren Abbey**, 1737–66,
uren, Germany

ouilding of this large
took many years to
ete. It has three Baroque
s and an ornate Rococo
r. Polished stucco angels
o the elaborate pulpit.

Rococo Architecture

Bartolomeo Rastrelli

1700, Paris–1771, St. Petersburg

■ Prominent architect in Russia ■ Worked in High Baroque and Rococo
styles ■ Court architect during the reign of Peter the Great ■ Favorite
tect of the empresses Anne and Elizabeth ■ Designed facades with bri
colors and lavish decoration ■ Fell out of favor with Catherine the Grea

1700 Born in Paris

1715 Moves to Russia

1722–30 Travels to Italy and France to study architecture

1730 Appointed senior court architect

1730s Earliest independent building in Mitau (now Jelgava, Latvia)

1764 Catherine the Great prefers the Neoclassical style, and his commissions decline

1771 Dies in St. Petersburg

Of Italian origin, Francesco Bartolomeo Rastrelli
chiefly responsible for the style that came to be kno
Russian Baroque. Son of the architect and sculptor
Bartolomeo Rastrelli, he arrived in Russia from Fran
the age of 15. He was appointed senior court arch
and was popular with Empresses Anne and Elizabet
style was influenced by French and Italian Baroque
the monumental linearity of his designs and his g
colored facades were fitting for the royal building
powerful new nation under Peter the Great. His inte
as well as his exterior stucco decorations, were in a
Rococo style. He often used light and mirrors, and
structed a large school of artisans.

Other Important Works by Rastrel	
St. Petersburg Summer Palace, 1741, St. Petersburg	Voronostrov, 174 St. Petersburg
Hermitage at Catherines Palace, 1746–52, near St. Petersburg	Stroganov Palace 1753, St. Petersbu
St. Andrew's, 1747–67, Kiev	Grotto at Catheri Palace, 1755–56, near St. Petersbu

■ **Smolny Cathedral**, 1748–57, St. Peters

The Smolny Cathedral, on the banks of the
River, is the center of a convent complex a
constructed as a residence for Empress Eliz
The blue and white color-washed stucco s
out on the perfectly proportioned structur
playing with the senses. It is surrounded by
domed churches, which form a cross. Rast
plans for a tiered belfry were never execut

Baroque in Russia

...ter Palace, 1754–62,
...ersburg

...and Winter Palace
...dies the rising greatness
...Russian court through
...lli's design and spatial

planning. By adding a double layer of columns, the height of the three-story palace seems to increase. Stone statues adorning the balustrade and decorative vases on the vertical axis

add to the visual effect. Many artisans were employed on this large-scale building project. Three large arches lead from the palace square through to the inner ceremonial courtyard.

■ **Catherine's Palace**, 1756, near St. Petersburg

First built by J. F. Braunstein, Catherine's Palace was given an elaborate Baroque redesign by Rastrelli in 1756. The palace was extended, and stucco decorations and gilded columns were built onto the exterior facade. It was said that 220 lbs (100 kg) of gold was used. The interior was given a Rococo finish, and included grand rooms such as the Mirrored Ballroom and the famous Amber Room.

Bartolomeo Rastrelli

Islamic Architecture

1527–1722

■ Islam spread throughout the world ■ Mosques were heavily ornamented, decoration included calligraphy, geometric patterns, and mosaics, but there strict ban on human representation ■ Minarets were both utilitarian and deco
■ *left:* **Blue Mosque**, interior, 1609–16, Istanbul

● **1527–1858** Reign of the Mughal Empire in India

1587–1629 Reign of Shah Abbas I (Abbas the Great), of the Safavid dynasty, who reunites Persia

1590–1602 Naghsh-i Jahan Square in Isfahan, Iran, is constructed

1591 The Charminar Gate in Hyderabad, India, has minarets built into the main structure, different from the Taj Mahal

1722 Fall of the Safavid dynasty

During the Mughal dynasty in India, many mosques monuments were built, and in Persia the reign of the Sa dynasty saw innovative town planning and the constru of new places of worship. The third powerful Islamic en was that of the Ottomans in Turkey. Structurally, do dominated mosques, while arcades, tunnel vaults, and ca portals linked interior spaces. Minarets, tall towers use calling worshippers to prayer, often had balconies an polas on them. Fountains and reflective pools were com in the entrance courtyards, because worshippers wash b prayer. The technique of *synching*—connecting a sc base to a round dome—was improved upon during this by using bricks and complicated systems of arches.

■ **Taj Mahal**, 1630–53, Agra, India

The Taj Mahal was commissioned as a mausol by Mughal emperor Shah Jahan for his favori Thousands of laborers were needed to erect t monumental shrine, made from white marble inlaid with semiprecious stones. The central b bous onion dome dominates the building, an smaller repetitions of the shape, on each corn hance the mirroring of the building.

Other Important Works	
Qolsharif Mosque, ca. 1500, destroyed 1522, Kazan, Russia	Shaykh Lutfallah Mosque, 1603–19 Isfahan, Iran
Ali bin Yusuf Madrasa, 1564–65, Marrakech, Morocco	Qarawiyyin Mos 1613–14, Fez, Mo
Mosque of Sinan Pasha, 1571, Cairo	Badshahi Mosqu 1674, Lahore, Pak

**defhar Mehmet Ağa: Sultan Ahmed
que (Blue Mosque)**, 1609–16, Istanbul

lue Mosque earned its name from the blue
at decorate the interior. The architect,
har Mehmet Ağa, was influenced by the
Ottoman architect Sinan. Small domes and
omes ascend harmoniously above the
base to the large central dome, 140 feet
ters) high, and 260 windows allow light in.
rge courtyard leading to the entrance has
ins for decoration and for ablutions. Unusu-
has six minarets instead of four.

**Akbar Isfahani, Fereydun Naini, Shoja'
ni: Shah Mosque (Imam Mosque)**,
1611, Isfahan, Iran

s capital was moved to Isfahan by the Safavid
ty. Shah Abbas the Great commissioned a se-
connecting mosques, parks, and monu-
leading to Isfahan being nicknamed "half
rld." The Shah Mosque is on the north side of
at Naghsh-i Jahan Square. The entrance
is framed by high minarets, and the largest
is decorated with pink and turquoise tiles.

Ottoman Empire

1512–1770

■ During the 16th and 17th centuries, the Ottoman Empire included Turke the Middle East, and parts of North Africa ■ Süleyman the Magnificent oversaw many new building projects ■ Sinan was the best-known archite of the Ottoman era ■ The mosque complex was an integral part of Islamic

■ **1512** The architect Mimar Sinan goes to Istanbul and learns engineering

1530s Sinan's miltary experience exposes him to the architecture of the Middle East, Africa, and Rhodes

1539 Sinan is appointed architect of Istanbul by the grand vizier

1588 Sinan dies

1703–57 Turkey's Tulip era, in which public spaces were built, and the beginning of Baroque mosques

1770 Westernized tastes change architecture

Other Works

Köse Hüsrev Pasa Mosque, by Mimar Sinan, 1536–37, Van, Turkey

Sultan Süleyman Mosque, by Mimar Sinan, 1563, Damascus

Sokollu Mehmed, by Mimar Sinan, 1570–74, Istanbul

Laleli Mosque, 1760–63, Istanbul

Zeynep Sultan Mosque, by Mehmet Tahir Ağa, 1769, Istanbul

Under Süleyman the Magnificent (1520–1566), both Ottoman Empire and the arts and architecture flouris Architecture was a combination of Byzantine in ences—such as domes and colored glass—and Europ influences—the Italian Renaissance. Mosques were b in the Islamic style and were often inside a larger c plex, or *camii*, consisting of minarets, domes, and the facing Mecca, the *kibla*. Decoration consisted of intri tiling and limestone carvings. Mimar Sinan, the grea toman architect, built over 300 buildings and helpe create the dramatic skyline of Istanbul with his sle minarets and staggered domes. Sinan aimed for a un interior space and experimented with supports, vaul and arches. Secular buildings included bazaars and ki

■ **Mimar Sinan: Süleyma Mosque**, 1551–58, Istanbu

Following in the grand sty the Fatih complex, the Sül maniye Mosque is a large c plex for prayer, culture, an education. It consists of sy metrical groups in geomet shapes. Four minarets star the four corners, and a lar main dome is flanked by tw half domes. As in the Byza Hagia Sophia, the Süley-maniye's dome is separate from its supports by a row windows. The mosque sym izes the grandeur of the en and of Istanbul.

274

Architecture of the Ottoman Empire

Baroque 1550–1790

mar Sinan: Selimiye Mosque, 1569–75,
e, Turkey

elimiye Mosque is considered Sinan's mas-
ce, because its interior is a unified space of
geometry. The massive dome is supported
ght pillars, and four semidomes round off
uilding's corners. The complex was unique

in that its minarets were the tallest in the Ottoman era, and the interior has an innovative
mihrab, a niche in the kibla wall, which can be
observed from everywhere in the prayer hall. The
mihrab is large enough to allow for windows,
which illuminate the glazed tiles on the interior
with natural light.

**mar Sinan: Şehzade
ue**, interior, 1544–48,
ul

ehzade complex was
Sinan's earliest works
architectural ingenuity.
osque exhibits his work-
hip and advanced con-
ion skills. Created on a
e plan, four half domes
he large central domed
ng. Four tall piers round
ches and assist in the
s support. The asymmet-
entral plan is repeated in
urtyard.

Japanese Architecture

1568–1657

■ Predominant Japanese architectural styles are *Shoin* and *Sukiya* ■ The re[
tionship between exterior and interior spaces was an important stylistic
element that influenced structural elements ■ Gardens and water were im[
portant ■ Sliding doors and screens were often incorporated into residenc[

● **1568** During the Azuchi-
Momoyama period, forti-
fied architectural elements
are prominent due to the
political climate

1603 The Edo period
begins, under which structural and stylistic innovations appear in traditional
architecture

1614 Christianity is for-
bidden, and the construc-
tion of Christian
churches ends

1641 All foreigners are
banned from Japan until
1853, ending cultural
exchange between the
East and West

1642 Toshitada renovates
the Katsura Imperial Villa

1657 Great Fire of Meireki
destroys most of Edo
(today Tokyo)

In 17th-century Japan, the Shoin and Sukiya styles de[
oped in the defensive designs of castles, temples[
prayer, and private residences. Sukiya architecture c[
sists of simple materials and proportions creatin[
harmonious relationship between interior and exte[
spaces, and was heavily influenced by the designs of[
houses. During Japan's Edo period, a series of fires in[
capital required massive rebuilding campaigns. In o[
to construct easily rebuilt houses, the government sp[
sored the building of simple wooden houses. In the[
gious sector, Shoin architecture was employed[
Buddhist monasteries, which had functional requ[
ments such as contemplative areas with water and[
dens. The structures often had sliding decorated scre[
and wooden floors. In 1868 castles were destroyed,[
Hikone Castle is one of the few remaining example[
fortified architecture.

■ **Katsura Imperial Villa**, interior a[
exterior, 1620, Kyoto

This villa was first built by Prince[
Toshihito as a moon-watchin[
treat, and its constructio[
was continued by h[
sons. The building is[
composed of untrea[
wood and tree trun[
Sukiya-style elemen[
such as the balance[
proportions of the v[
panels were added [
give the building a h[
monious aesthetic.

kone Castle, 1603–22, Shiga

riginal five-floor *tenshu*, or "tower,"
e Hikone Castle was removed,
ng only three floors. The
ling has three moats,
arkable roof gables,
otus-shaped
r windows.

Japanese Architecture

Baroque in Latin America

1650–ca. 1770

■ The Baroque style was brought to Latin America with European coloni
lism ■ In Mexico, the Spanish introduced the Churrigueresque style, wh
was adapted and used widely ■ Mining towns like Ouro Preto had many
Baroque churches ■ Style retained its popularity until Neoclassicism

■ **1650–60s** Spiral pilasters
are introduced to Peru
from Spain

1657–73 Monastery of St.
Francisco precedes a new
wave of the Mudéjar style

1664 Jesuit shrine on
Plaza des Armas is the first
in the late Baroque style

1698 First example of an
independent Peruvian-
Bolivian mestizo in La
Compañía Church

1730s Architect Aleijadinho, or "Little Cripple,"
born in Brazil

1749 Metropolitan Sacristy has tapering pilasters

ca. 1770 Most Baroque
projects are completed

Baroque architecture was brought to Latin America
the colonizing powers of Spain and Portugal. Fran
cans, Dominicans, and Jesuits were all to leave their m
on the ecclesiastical architecture and religious art of
region. The discovery of gold and silver played a la
role in bringing European architectural styles to w
were previously remote villages. The Brazilian schoo
Baroque was heavily influenced by Portuguese sty
Antonio Francisco Lisboa, known as Aleijadinho, w
leading Brazilian architect, sculptor, and painter w
built many churches in the Ouro Preto region. Mexi
Baroque architecture was especially influenced by
adaptation of the Spanish Churrigueresque style, w
resulted in highly decorative facades. Late Baroque sp
columns (*salomónica*) were imported from Spain,
tapering pilasters (*estípite*) were widely used. In

■ **Catedral Metropoli-
tana**, 1667, Mexico City,
Mexico

The Catedral Metropoli-
tana is one of the largest in
the Western Hemisphere.
The lower levels of the
facade, with their twisted
columns, volutes, and statues, are High Baroque,
while the Classical towers
were added later. The side
chapel is in Churrigue-
resque style. There are five
naves, and the church
forms a cross.

Baroque

. Domingo, 1731,
ca, Mexico

5t. Domingo de Guzmán
ch consists of a complex of
lings and was founded in
570s by the Dominican
r. The sober Baroque
de conceals an elaborate
ior, which is one of the
examples of Mexican High
que. The many chapels sit
gside gilded plaster orna-
ts and towering columns.
:eiling decoration shows
neage of St. Dominic.

**. Francisco Church at
epec**, 1730, Cholula,
:o

e 16th century, nearly 400
:hes were built to replace
\ztec temples destroyed by
xploratory party of Hernán
\s in the town of Cholula.
it. Francisco Church was

built in nearby Acatepec in
Puebla, a region famous for its
local ceramics. Made from the
local *azulejos,* or hand-painted
tiles, the *talevera* ceramics can
be seen on many of the remarkable facades and domes of the
buildings in the area. St. Francis,
in particular, elevates the use of

local materials to an art form.
Yellow, blue, and green tiles
adorn the red-brick facade of
this Churrigueresque church.
Even the large doorway is covered in tiles and carvings.
The interior is excessively ornate, with gilded and plaster
decoration.

Baroque in Latin America

Puebla, hand-painted ceramics, stone, and gold leaf led to a local, indigenous style that was used in m churches, both in the facades and in riors. Local artisans developed a s of white stucco decoration called *ñique* in the 18th century. In Peru Bolivia, indigenous carvings were in duced to church ornamentation, cr ing a style known as *mestizo*. Ot countries to be influenced by the roque style were Ecuador, Colum and Argentina. The style remained p ular in Latin America for longer tha did in Europe.

■ **St. Iphigenia, or Our Lady of the Rosary**, 1730, Ouro Preto, Minas Gerais, Brazil

St. Iphigenia was built for the the African community of Ouro Preto, a town named after "black gold" but famous for its elegant Baroque churches. The architect Aleijadinho and sculptor Francisco Xavier de Brito collaborated on the project. It has the oldest stone clocks in the city.

Other Important Works	
Puebla Cathedral, 1551–64, Puebla, Mexico	Ocotlan Sanctuary 1745, Ocotlan, Mex
St. Francisco Monastery, 1657–73, Lima, Peru	St. Francis of Assisi begun 1772, Ouro Preto, Brazil

Baroque

Prisca Cathedral,
58, Taxco, Mexico

vo towers of the St. Prisca
dral are the highest
in the city of Taxco. The
olored church is elabo-
constructed, and the
ned dome lies at the
of the cross. St. Prisca
hanced by Don Jose de la
a French Spaniard who
ered silver in the hills. It is
the finest examples of
an Churrigueresque.

■ **Aleijadinho: Congonhas
do Campo**, 1757–77, Minas
Gerais, Brazil

The Congonhas do Campo is
considered to be Aleijadinho's
masterwork and was designed
and constructed toward the
end of his life. It is typical of the
Brazilian school of Baroque,
with an elongated plan and
double facade towers. However, its unique beauty lies primarily in the remarkable statues
encountered as one ascends

the stairs to the sanctuary.
Sixty-six carved and painted
wooden figures occupy the
chapels on the lower level,
signifying the stations of the
cross. At the top of the stairs, 16
life-size statues of the prophets
are symmetrically arranged. The
interior is Rococo and has gold
and white altars and ornately
decorated pulpits. The church
was commissioned by the Portuguese adventurer and patron
Feliciano Mendes.

Baroque in Latin America

Neoclassicism

1640–1850

Sir Christopher Wren: St. Paul's Cathedral, 1674–1710, London

Neoclassicism

1640–1750
Early Neoclassicism

After the austentatious Baroque and Rococo styles, Neoclassical architecture develops as an ordered return to rational architecture

Inigo Jones
Sir Christopher
Wren p. 292

p. 304

1600

1650

1700

1750–1850
French Neoclassicism

Neoclassicism develops in France as the result of French architects educated in Italy

Claude Nicolas Ledoux
p. 304

p. 299

1750–1850
Neoclassicism in the UK

Neoclassical styles ar incorporated into pu and religious buildin

William Kent p. 294
Robert Adam p. 296
John Nash p. 298
John Soane p. 300
Sir Robert Smirke p

50–1850
rman
oclassicism

man architects
sform Prussia with
classical styles

Gotthard Langhans
6

Friedrich Schinkel
8

p. 307

| 1800 | 1850 | 1900 |

50–1850
ssian
oclassicism

co styles remain popular in
ia for a long time, but some
ents of Neoclassicism are
ted under the patronage
atherine the Great

les Cameron

p. 317

1750–1850
Neoclassicism in
the United States

Neoclassical architecture is
a popular style for American
government buildings

Thomas Jefferson p. 318
Benjamin Henry
Latrobe p. 314

Neoclassicism

■ Jacques Ge
main Soufflo
Panthéon,
1756–97, Pari

After the theatrical undulation of the Baroque and
Rococo eras, the 17th and 18th centuries witnessed a
return to Classicism on a monumental level. There
was a renewed interest in antiquity, which was seen
as a lost, pure era. The designs of the Renaissance architect Andrea Palladio were repopularized, and this
new Palladianism spread throughout Europe and the
United States as a rational method of building, associated with great empires.

Study scholarships as well as the fashionable grand
tour of Europe allowed architects to study ruins and
Classical structures firsthand. Columns of the Ionic,
Doric, Corinthian, and Tuscan orders were again used
for buildings, sometimes in monumental proportions
known as the Colossal order. Columns were multiplied
and stacked, accentuating the impression of height.
Colonnades, rotundas, and porticoes completed the

facades. New construction innovations like layered cupolas and inner cores added strength to domes and their size increased, aggrandizing the civic buildings, churches, educational facilities, and large private homes that they topped.

Neoclassicism originated in France, where Classic elements had begun appearing in architecture at the end of Louis XVI's reign. These styles were taken up during the first Napoleonic Empire. High society embraced the style for their private homes, and experimental architects tried it out on municipal structures by redesigning urban areas.

Landscapers collaborated with architects, and the UK's Picturesque movement created grand vistas like those found in the paintings of Nicolas Poussin. Picturesque architecture played with light, texture, and color. This was emphasized by faux ruins, follies, grottoes, and fountains in the landscapes.

Introduction

■ Robert Sm
British Muse
ca. 1854, Lon

In the UK, where Baroque had not been as popular, the Neoclassical style was used from banks to museums to post offices. British royalty were especially privy to its grand forms, commissioning the architect John Nash to redesign entire city blocks and parks. Lord Burlington, known as "the Architect Earl," wrote, commissioned, and built in the Palladian style, and was integral in the popularization of the theories and work of Inigo Jones (1573–1652), another early Neoclassical English architect. Wealthy estate owners embraced the style, and country mansions were renovated with new porticoes and columns.

In Germany, Karl Friedrich Schinkel and Carl Gotthard Langhans transformed the Prussian capital of Berlin, under the patronage of Friedrich Wilhelm II, into a city to rival Paris or Rome in Classical splendor. The Brandenburg Gate, based on the Propylaea on the Athenian Acropolis, is a monumental construction

of pillars and columns. The opening of the Bauakademie in 1830 spread the style further.

Neoclassical styles spread to Russia, where they helped to define the power and might of the czars through impressive facades. Catherine the Great was a great benefactor of the Classical lines and reacted against the High Rococo tastes of her predecessors.

Despite the style's popularity in Europe, it was in the United States that Neoclassicism was taken up with the most enthusiasm, as the newly formed country began building civic buildings to define the aesthetics of the country. The United States Capitol in Washington, DC, is a Neoclassical masterpiece, echoing the power of past empires in its impressive dome. The first universities were built based on Greek temples, a reference to learning. President Thomas Jefferson supported and built in the clear geometry of the Neoclassical style.

Introduction

Neoclassical Styles

Although Neoclassicism was influenced by the Classical styles of Greece and Rome, these were adapted and developed in Neoclassical architecture. During the 17th century, discoveries in science, mathematics, and astronomy influenced building techniques. It is no wonder that one of the first great Neoclassical architects, Christopher Wren (p. 292), was a renowned scientist and physicist. Wren's St. Paul's Cathedral in London used an innovative three-layered construction to support the weight of the dome. Experiments in perspective and optics also resulted in new ways of planning. Light and color were used with mirrors and skylights.

■ **Giovanni Paolo Pannini: Gallery Displaying Views of Ancient Rome**, 1758

Giovanni Paolo Pannini's paintings show the public fascination with the ruins and temples of ancient Rome. Antiquity was seen as an age bound to reason, and the return to Classicism was a reaction against the excesses of Baroque and Rococo styles. Columns and domes were often used, and there was a renewed focus on remaining Classical buildings, such as the Pantheon and Colosseum.

■ **Karl Friedrich Schinke** **Altes Museum**, 1823–30,

Schinkel learnt to draw de perspective drawings as a of his study trips to Italy. H drawings of the Altes Mus had great influence on the chitecture of the time.

■ **Karl Friedrich Schink Friedrichswerder Chure** 1824–30, Berlin

Schinkel's perspective dr only assisted in the planr the church, but give the v an impression of its size f human-scaled point of vi

**rl Friedrich Schinkel:
Museum**, 1823–30, Berlin

ome and rotunda were
lent features in Neoclas-
rchitecture, but unlike the
popular during the
ue and Rococo eras, they
used for buildings other

than solely ecclesiastical ones.
The rotunda and dome of
Schinkel's Altes Museum in
Berlin is directly influenced by,
and refers to, the Pantheon in
Rome. However, in this instance
the drum, rotunda, and dome,
although painted like a Roman

temple, are instead used as a
place to venerate art and culture—the museum. Inside the
rotunda, pillars and Greek
sculptures are displayed among
the art, and the square cof-
fering lightens the weight of
the dome.

Neoclassical Styles

Sir Christopher Wren

1632, Wiltshire—1723, London

■ Renowned British architect ■ Respected scientist, mathematician, and astronomer ■ Influenced by Bernini and Vitruvius ■ Oversaw the construction of 51 new churches following the Great Fire of London ■ Built under four British sovereigns ■ Designed academic, royal, and church buildings

■ **1632** Born in East Knoyle, Wiltshire

1661 Appointed Savilian Professor of Astronomy at Oxford

1665 Travels to Paris and sees Bernini's designs for the new Louvre

1665 Builds College Chapel at Cambridge, his first commission

1666 Great Fire of London

1669 Appointed king's surveyor of works

1670 Appointed surveyor for building the city churches

1685 Enters Parliament and House of Commons

1723 Dies in London

Christopher Wren was born in Wiltshire and studied Oxford. Most renowned as an architect, he also succe fully engaged in mechanics, biology, optics, and astr omy and was a founder of the Royal Society. Having r Vitruvius, he developed an interest in architecture visited Bernini in Paris. Shortly after his redesign fo Paul's Cathedral was accepted, the Great Fire destro both the church and much of London. Wren was selec to rebuild not just the church, but also the city. Fo years he was the king's surveyor and approved 51 churches. Although not all were built to his designs, t were all Classical in form. Wren built Kensington Pa and Hampton Court Palace for William of Orange. He able to combine constructive ingenuity and rea with aesthetics. He was knighted and is burie St. Paul's, under his own spectacular dome

■ **Sheldonian Theat** 1663, Oxford

The Sheldonian Theat was only Wren's secor completed building, b nevertheless typifies style. Designed in the of a classic Roman ten the theater is based o theater at Marcelles. Wren's ingenuity and draftsmanship can be in the roofing, where developed a new kind timber truss with a sp 72 feet (22 meters).

Paul's Cathedral,
-1710, London

had to modify his plans
. Paul's Cathedral many
to satisfy the medieval
s of the church. The final
: differed from his original
n and is constructed on a
cross with a large dome

crowned by a spire. Crowning
the intersection of the church's
transepts, the dome includes
three layers. The external aesthetic wooden dome, which
stands 365 feet (111 meters)
high, is supported by an inner
brick core that separates it from
the interior cupola.

🛡 **Old Royal Naval College**,
1696–1712, Greenwich

The Old Royal Naval College at
Greenwich was originally built
as a navy hospital. It is in the
English Baroque style, with four
blocks centered around a courtyard and views of the Queen's
House.

Sir Christopher Wren

William Kent

1685, Bridlington—1748, London

■ Father of English landscape gardening ■ Architect and interior, stage, garden, and couture designer ■ Influenced by Andrea Palladio and Inigo Jones ■ Used the Picturesque method of composition and opened up formal gardens ■ Combined nature and architecture to create a work of

- **1685** Born in Bridlington, Yorkshire
- **1710** Sent by patrons to study painting in Italy
- **1714** Meets 1st Earl of Leicester Coke and Lord Burlington
- **1719** Returns to London
- **1722** Designs the Cupola Room in Kensington Palace
- **1726** Designs Holkham Hall in a style strongly influenced by Palladio
- **1727** Edits *The Designs of Inigo Jones*
- **1748** Dies in London

William Kent was an English painter, architect, and signer most renowned for his elaborate landscape dens. Trained as a coach painter, it was in Italy tha met his patron, Lord Burlington, "the Architect Earl," encouraged him to design in the Classical style of Palla (p. 190) and Inigo Jones. His manor houses and inter were sought after by the nobility. In his "natural" la scapes, Kent opened up enclosed gardens and rejec formal, rigid structures in favor of connecting the gar with the surrounding terrain. His work incorporated tique and Classical elements, and he placed objects s as follies, obelisks, hermitages, and grottoes into the lish countryside. His compositional technique aime the Picturesque by utilizing shape, light, and color.

■ **Rousham Gardens**, 1737, Oxfordshire

The Rousham Gardens are inspired by Classical mythology. Within the gardens, the River Cherwell transforms into ponds

and fountains as it winds past grottoes and follies. Lookout create a theatrical landscape focus out toward the surroun meadows while including the viewer in the panorama.

Other Works by Kent
Kensington Palace Interiors, 1722–27, London
Houghton Hall Interiors, 1725 Norfolk
Claremont Gardens, ca. 1730, Surrey
Royal Mews, 1731–33, Charine Cross
Holkham Hall, 1734–65, Norfo

◀ **Chiswick House**, 1726, London

Chiswick was a collaboration between Kent and Lord Burlington. The rotunda-like villa, statues, obelisks, and urns represent the Neopalladian style. Roman cypresses and cedars evoke an Italian landscape, and the sloping lawns and natural lakes were highly original for the time.

■ **Stowe Landscape Gardens**, 1744, Buckinghamshire

At Stowe, Kent placed neo-antique and political architectonic elements throughout his gardens. The Elysian Fields, Temples of British Worthies, and Palladium Bridge combine 18th-century cultural life and popular styles with the arcadian and orderly ideals of Palladian architecture.

William Kent

Robert Adam

1728, Kirkcaldy—1792, London

■ Born into a famous Scottish architectural family that included his fath■
William and two brothers ■ Popular architect inspired by Classical antic■
uity and Palladianism ■ Often designed interiors, furnishings, and déco■
■ *left*: **Ceiling of Syon House**, 1762–69, Brentford

■ **1728** Born in Kirkcaldy
1743–45 Studies at the University of Edinburgh
1754 Grand tour
1758 Elected member of Royal Society of Arts
1764 Publishes his study of the Diocletian ruins
1773 Publishes the highly influential *The Works in Architecture of Robert and James Adam*
1792 Dies in London

Born in Scotland, Robert Adam rose to fame in Engl■ His father was the architect William Adam. After a g■ tour of Italy, France, and the Damaltian Coast, Ro■ opened a practice in England with his brothers John ■ James. He redesigned many castles and villas and ■ though influenced by Palladio (p. 192), he experime■ and reworked his style, adding Greek, Byzantine, ■ Gothic elements to create the Adam style. His comb■ tion of Neoclassical features with self-designed inter■ often down to the smallest detail, resulted in a grand ■ unified architectural style.

Other Works by Adar■
Syon House, 1760–69, Middlesex
Osterly Park, 1767–68, Middlesex
Kenwood Library, 1767–69■ Hampstead
Adelphi, 1768–72, London
Headfort House, 1771–75, County Meath
Theater Royal, 1775–76, London
Charlotte Square, 1791–92, Edinburgh

■ **Culzean Castle**, 1777–92, Ayrshire

Built atop a cliff in Scotland, this romantic castle complements its surroundings, just as Adam believed a building should. He built a large drum tower and a circular saloon with sweeping views of the western Scottish coast. The centerpiece of the castle is a■ staircase, illuminated from a■ cupola that allows light to b■ off its arrangement of Ionic a■ elaborate Corinthian column■

wood House, 1763,
hire

n added an orangery and
the menagerie and mau-
m for the Earl of Shelburne

ndleston Hall, 1760–61,
yshire

ed by Lord Burlington's
dianism, the north face of
uilding has a rusticated
nd floor and larger windows
e piano nobile. On the
ern end, Adam incorpo-
Classical designs based on
rch of Constantine and the
of the Pantheon. The vast
or has typical Adam de-
g, from the huge apses in
ning room to the ceiling
d on the Palace of Augustus
Farnese Gardens.

on the Bowood estate. He decorated the main rooms, and his
elaborate staircase and high ceilings add Classical grandeur to
the building. He also altered the

pedimented portico and designed the Diocletian wing based
on observations from the ruins of
the palace of the emperor Diocletian at Split in Croatia.

Robert Adam

John Nash

1752, Lambeth—1835, Isle of Wight

■ Favorite architect of the prince regent ■ Part of the Picturesque movement in England ■ Influential in the town planning of London ■ Mixed Classical, Gothic, and Oriental styles ■ Used stucco facades
■ *left:* **Cumberland Terrace**, 1828, London

● **1752** Born in Lambeth

1780s Works on country houses and castles with Humphry Repton

1792 Returns to London to work

1811 Begins Marylebone designs for the prince regent

1812 Heads Regent's Canal Company

1820s Trafalgar Square town planning

1830 Dismissed from Buckingham Palace

1835 Dies on the Isle of Wight

John Nash, son of a millwright, designed large part[s of] London during the Regency era, giving the city a gr[and] quality. He was part of the Picturesque movement, c[om]bining irregular views with Neoclassical structures. N[ash] trained with Robert Taylor but went on to open a prac[tice] with landscape gardener Humphry Repton. Nash ca[me] to the attention of the prince regent, who later beca[me] King George IV, because of his "garden city" plans [for] Marylebone (now Regent's Park), which included la[rge] terraces, and a summer palace. The layout of Lond[on's] West End, including St. James's Park, Trafalgar Squ[are] and the Royal Mews, owes much to his often unortho[dox] designs. His work on Buckingham Palace was uns[uc]cessful, and he was dismissed when the king died. N[ash] died on the Isle of Wight, in East Cowes Castle.

Other Works by Nash

East Cowes Castle, 1789, Isle of Wight

Ravensworth Castle, 1808, North Durham

Trafalgar Square Town Planning, 1820s, London

Haymarket Theater, 1820, London

Buckingham Palace, 1821–35, London

All Souls, Langham Place, 1822–25, London

Royal Mews, 1825, London

■ **Blaise Hamlet**, 1810–11[,] Bristol

Blaise Hamlet epitomizes th[e] Nash style and the Pictures[que] school's style. These small a[nd] asymmetrical cottages diffe[r in] style and materials. They w[ere] built to house estate worke[rs] on the property of J. S. Harf[ord.] The single- and two-story dwellings include seating nooks and oversize chimne[ys] and are sheltered by either thatched or stone-tiled hip[ped] roofs. They are laid out aro[und] an open green and have a c[en]tral sundial.

...mberland Terrace, 1828, ...on

...umberland Terrace is part ...Regency residential de-...ment. The three blocks

are of a High Classical style and are connected by archways with Doric columns. The central building utilizes Ionic columns and has a triangular pediment

decorated with statues. Allegorical figures adorn the white stucco building, which offers sweeping views of the park from the terrace.

...lton House Terrace, ...32, London

...arlton House Terrace con-...f two large, white, stucco-...blocks, with nine houses

that face onto St. James's Park. The houses are of the Roman Classical style, with Corinthian column facades and Doric columns at street level. The end

terraces have an extra level, which gives the building a grand effect. Nash also designed the interiors for many of the apartments.

John Nash

Sir John Soane

1753, Goring on Thames—1837, London

■ An innovative Neoclassical architect ■ Attended the Royal Academy Schools ■ Experimented with light, form, and space ■ Used shallow do[me] instead of semicircular domes ■ Surveyor and architect of the Bank of E[ng] land ■ Built country residences and financial and political institutions

- **1753** Born in Goring on Thames
- **1776** Wins gold medal at the Royal Academy for bridge drawing
- **1780** Returns to London from traveling and opens practice
- **1788** Becomes surveyor of the Bank of England
- **1800** Appointed professor of architecture at Royal Academy
- **1831** Is knighted
- **1837** Dies in London

The son of a brickmason, Sir John Soane was one o[f] UK's most innovative architects during the Neoclas[sical] period. Trained by George Dance the Younger and H[enry] Holland, he also attended the Royal Academy. An [able] student, Soane was awarded the school's gold meda[l and] a scholarship to Italy. There, he became familiar with [clas]sical architecture. As architect of the Bank of Engl[and,] Soane's reputation grew, and he landed many new c[om]missions. He built numerous country houses, inclu[ding] his own, and was sought after by ministers and the p[ublic] alike. He also designed the first purpose-built picture [gal]lery, at Dulwich. Stylistically, Soane was able to mi[x the] Classical orders and utilize referenc[es to] the past, while managing to kee[p in] touch with the emerging indus[trial] times. He is famed for his experime[ntal] use of lighting, dramatic angles, an[d re]cesses. When he died, he donate[d his] house and extensive private colle[ction] of antiques to the public.

■ **Pitshanger Manor**, 1800–03, London

Pitshanger Manor was the country villa rebu[ilt by] Soane and previously designed by his tutor [George] Dance. The villa epitomizes the Picturesque [style] that Soane often used, and the gardens incl[uded] fake ruins and a bridge. The central facade h[as] four columns and demonstrates Soane's em[pha]phasis on line over form. The refined Classic[al] details include arched windows and shallow [cupola] domes. The villa's interior was an idiosyncra[tic] mix of colors.

■ Bank of England, 1792, London

After the death of Sir Robert Taylor, Soane took over his position and set about building and expanding the Bank of England, a job which was to last thoughout his working life. He designed a new rotunda and stock office for the bank. Although the building was inspired by the Temple of the Sibyl at Tivoli in Italy and was Classical in style, Soane also acknowledged the changing times and the civil significance of financial institutions. The interior included fountains, arches, and gardens as well as heating—radically combining functionality with the picturesque. Always an innovator, Soane utilized a skylight in the large, shallow dome of the main room to allow for light.

John Soane's Museum, 1812–13, London

er 13 Lincoln's Inn Fields was Soane's per-
esidence. It functioned as a laboratory to
t architectural ideas and to store and dis-
ughly 30,000 artifacts and books. The
ng itself was designed with odd angles and
ar shapes, utilizing an unorthodox mani-
n of mirrors, lighting, and domes to high-
he collection.

Other Important Works by Soane

agton Hall, 1785, rdshire	Stables at Chelsea Hospital, 1814–17, London
erhanger e, 1790–1812, rdshire	Dulwich Picture Gallery, 1817, Dulwich
field House, Wales	Pell Wall House, 1822–28, Staffordshire
oe Park, 1795, dshire	St. Peter's Church, 1823–25, Walworth

Sir John Soane

Sir Robert Smirke

1780, London—1867, Cheltenham

■ Medieval and Neoclassical styles ■ Contemporary of Sir John Soane
John Nash ■ Built castles for earls and lords ■ Active in Cumbria and
London ■ Included Doric and Ionic orders in his buildings ■ Rebuilt th
British Museum, which was completed by his brother Sydney Smirke

■ **1780** Born in London to a historical painter and illustrator

1801–05 Travels to Greece and Italy

1806 Publishes his architectural sketches in *Specimens of Continental Architecture*

1808 Builds Covent Garden Theater, the first Greek-inspired building in London, and subsequently popularizes Neoclassical architecture in England

1813 Elected to the Board of Works

1832 Knighted

1858 Receives RIBA Royal Gold Medal

1867 Dies in Cheltenham

Other Works

The Citadel, 1810, Carlisle

Appelby Cloisters,1811, Appelby, Cumbria

St. George's Church, Brandon Hill, 1821, Bristol

Edenhall Mansion, 1824, Edenhall, Cumbria

General Post Office, 1824–29, London

Edmond Castle, 1824–29, Hayton

Royal College of Physicians, 1825, London

Sir Robert Smirke was the son of a scholar and pai
studied at the Royal Academy, and trained briefly wit
John Soane (p. 300). He published a book of sketche
lowing his Mediterranean travels and became one o
major Classical revivalists in the UK. Smirke's early b
ings were grand country residences and castle
wealthy lords and earls, designed in the Romantic
medieval styles. Castles such as Eastnor and Lowthe
pealed to the decadent tastes of the British aristoc
His theater in London's Covent Garden was the fir
demonstrate his Classical Greek influences and to us
Doric order. Smirke's Neoclassical style culminated
the rebuilding of the British Museum, albeit usin
Ionic order. Other buildings in London include the
eral Post Office and Royal College of Physicians. He
elected to the Board of Works with his contemporari
John Soane and John Nash (p. 298).

🏰 **Eastnor Castle**, 1810, Eastnor

One of Smirke's earlier castles, the plan of Eastnor was more symmetrical and orderly than that of Lowther Castle. Resembling a medieval fortress, Eastnor was built in a style known as Norman revivalism.

ᵂther Castle,
Cumbria

ᵊr Castle was
when Smirke was
ᵌ5 years old and
peak of the

ᵊitish Museum,
ᵊ 1823, London

ᵊitish Museum is
ᵊgest and grand-
ᵊample of Smir-
ᵊeoclassical style
ᵊcorporates the
ᵊal orders into its
ᵊn. The south
ᵊe has a Ionic
ᵊnade fronted by

Romantic movement.
An extravagant
Neo-Gothic castle,
Lowther's turrets and
battlements are only
decorative.

a portico. The pedi-
ment is supported by
another row of eight
columns. Smirke's 1823
plan of a quadrangle
was completed by his
brother Sydney, who
covered the quad-
rangle with a large
domed reading room,
completed in 1857.

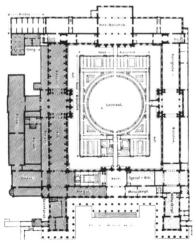

Sir Robert Smirke

Claude Nicolas Ledoux

1736, Dormans–1806, Paris

■ Prominent Neoclassical architect in France ■ Used extended and monumental porticoes and columns ■ Designed both private buildings for the aristocracy and government buildings ■ Imprisoned during the French Revolution, but released ■ Considered a visionary with utopian and mythical ideas

● **1736** Born in Dormans

1749–53 Studies in Paris

1764 Appointed architect of the waters and forests

1769–71 Visits the UK and is influenced by Palladian ideas

1773–79 First stage of the Royal Saltworks at Arc-et-Senans

1791 Imprisoned during the French Revolution

1794 Released from prison

1804 Publishes a volume of engravings

1806 Dies in Paris

Claude Nicolas Ledoux was a prominent French Neoclassical architect who designed monumental structures for private commissions as well as for civic functions. His buildings used bold geometric shapes and often employed columns of a Colossal order. As architect of the waters and forests he was technically minded. His marriage into aristocracy made him a popular architect with the society ladies, including Madame du Barry, which often led to extravagant commissions. Called a utopian, his uncompleted saltworks inspired his plan for the ideal city of Chaux. Despite his visionary outlook, Ledoux symbolized the ancient regime and was imprisoned during the French Revolution. He avoided the guillotine and published a volume of engravings after he was released.

■ **Royal Saltworks**, 1773–9, Arc-et-Senans

This remarkable and unfinished semicircular collection of buildings is both a saltworks and a speculative city where mythology mixes with function. Built during the Enlightenment in France, the Royal Saltworks strove to create rational architectural layout for industry that was based in geometry. The semicircular layout was meant to reflect the hierarchy of the industrial work sector. Buildings such as the central director's house, with its rustic columns made of cubes and squares, took on templelike forms.

Ronde de la Villette, Paris

...d Paris, Ledoux built the ...mental Wall of the Farm- ...neral and 60 buildings ...e considered his propy- ...r entrances to a temple ...or the collection of salt ...These buildings extolled his Neoclassical style. The toll-houses took on archetypal forms such as rotundas, porticoes, Greek temples, and apses. They were constructed hastily due to the revolutionary unrest and abandoned after 1788. La Villette is a rotunda that occupies the center of the crossing.

Other Works by Ledoux

Cathedral of Saint-Germaine, 1762–64, Auxerre

Pavillion de Musique de Mme du Barry, 1770–71, Louveciennes

Hôtel Montmorency, 1771–73, Paris

Theater of Besaneon, 1771–73, Paris

Hôtel Thelusson, 1778–83, Paris

■ Château de Bénouville, 1770–80, Bénouville

The château was built for the Marquis de Livry, one of Ledoux's many high-society customers. The striking staircase and the large portico, supported by wide columns, complement the gardens through their combination of city life and nature.

Claude Nicolas Ledoux

Carl Gotthard Langhans

1732, Kamiennej Gorze—1808, Wroclaw Dabie

■ Early Neoclassical architect ■ Inspired by British Neoclassicism and th...
Adam brothers ■ Used elements of Baroque, Classicism, and Greek antic...
in his buildings and did not follow one style ■ Worked for Berlin's royal
court under King Friedrich Wilhelm II

1732 Born in Landeshut, Silesia, today Kamiennej Gorze

1753–57 Studies law

1764 Gains recognition as an architect, becomes building inspector for Count Hatzfeld

1766 Designs the stairwell in Castle Rheinsberg as his first royal commission

1768–69 Sponsored by Count Hatzfeld and goes on grand tour

1788 Moves to Berlin

1789–91 Works on Brandenburg Gate

1799 Joins the faculty of the Bauakademie

1800–02 Builds the German National Theater, which burns down in 1817

1808 Dies in Wroclaw Dabie

Perhaps most famed for his design of the symbol of Ber...
the Brandenburg Gate—Carl Gotthard Langhans did...
train as an architect, but rather studied law and mathe...
tics. A studious youth, he independently taught himse...
chitecture and building. Though most of his buildings w...
fashioned in the late Baroque style, he was greatly insp...
by Classicism, Palladio (p. 192), and his travels to the...
where he saw the work of the Adam brothers (p. 296...
work as building inspector for Count Hatzfeld resulte...
his working for the royal court and moving to Berlin. As...
as late Baroque buildings, he also designed more c...
structures like the theaters in Potsdam and Gda...

Langhans's buildings were the first to introduce elements from antiquity into German architecture, a style that was later popularized by Karl Schinkel (p. 308).

■ **Belvedere Schlosspark**, 1788–90, Berlin

The teahouse and palace theater were Langhans's contribution to the large Charlottenburg Palace in Berlin and were built for King Friedrich II. The Belvedere now lies in the northern end of the expansive gardens, but was originally designed to be constructed on an island. The ground plan is laid out in the shape of an oval, with open balconies and pilasters on three levels. The cupola, with its three gold figures holding a basket of flowers, tops off this Classical Baroque building.

andenburg Gate,
–91, Berlin

of the original 18 gated en-
es to Berlin, the Branden-
Gate is the city's first
ture based on Greek antiq-
Modeled on the propy-
n from the Acropolis, the

atomical Theater, 1790,

heater for the veterinary
ol on the grounds of a
tal exhibits Langhans's
dian style at its finest. The
ior resembles a temple,
Tuscan columns and an
lature joining the low
. The stairs visually match
omplement the portico as
ascend into the lecture
vhich is designed as a
ed circular amphitheater.

entablature is inspired by the
Parthenon. The five openings are
separated by Doric columns. The
crowning quadriga, the goddess
of Victory, was completed in
1793 by Johann Schadow. Reliefs
show the goddess, her assistants,
and Hercules.

Other Works by Langhans

Rheinsberg Conversion, 1769,
Rheinsberg

Theaterhouse, 1795, Potsdam

German National Theater,
1800–02, Berlin

Carl Gotthard Langhans

Karl Friedrich Schinkel

1781, Neuruppin–1841, Berlin

- Architect, painter, and set designer ■ Helped to define the look of the German capital ■ Used Gothic Revival and Classical influences to create Neoclassical style ■ Held Romantic perceptions of nature and existence ■ Designed and directed at the esteemed Building Academy in Berlin

■ **1781** Born in Neuruppin

1794 Moves to Berlin

1803 Tours Italy, France, and Austria

1816 Builds royal guard-house in military style with Doric portico

1821 Publishes *Erste Vor-bilder für Fabrikanten und Handwerker* with Peter Beuth

1826 Goes to England and is impressed by industrial technology

1836 Building Academy opens in Berlin

1840 Reign of Friedrich Wilhelm IV, the "architect king"

1841 Dies in Berlin

Karl Friedrich Schinkel designed churches, theaters, academies in a Neoclassical style, symbolically elevat not just religious buildings but also places of cult learning, and public life. He lived and studied archi ture with David Gilly and his son Friedrich, who ha large influence on his work and ideas. A remarka painter, he depicted idyllic landscapes based on his Eu pean travels. These images were published and gre influential for later generations of artists and archite During Napoléon's occupation, Schinkel painted thea sets, including for the acclaimed *Magic Flute* by Moz and spectacular dioramas and panoramas for the Grop family. His theater experiences would later inform plans and buildings. He came to the attention of Prussian court and Friedrich Wilhelm IV, and recei commissions for royal furnishings as well as for Queen

■ **Altes Museum**,
1823–30, Berlin

Built between the Prussian Palace and the cathedral, the New (now referred to as Old) Museum has a colonnade of 18 Ionic columns sheltering its staircase. The second-floor rotunda is connected to a cubic attic and a monumental hall. The Altes Museum takes the form of a loggia, from which one can look out over the *Lust-garten* (pleasure garden).

19th Century

onzerthaus on Gendar-
nmarkt,1819–21, Berlin

t on the foundation of the
ghans Theater after it burnt
rn, Schinkel's *Schauspiel-*
s, or "theater," (now a con-
house) was based on the
gns of the Parthenon and
vily influenced by Hel-
tic architecture. By refer-

encing these styles, he
therefore elevated a cultural
building to a position of historic
importance. It is situated between two churches and accessed by grand stairs leading
up to a portico of the Ionic
order. The interior was a simplification of earlier extravagant
Baroque ele-
ments and

uses multiple perspectives and
illusions to enliven the Classical
design. Whereas earlier theaters
were laid out in a hierarchical
manner, with attention focused
on the perspective from the
king's seating area, at the Konzerthaus on Gendarmenmarkt
the seating was arranged in
a circular shape, providing
great views.

■ **Tegel Palace**, 1821–24,
Berlin

Schinkel remodeled the original
palace of 1550 for the wealthy
Humboldt family. Not only did
he add Classical elements to the
building itself, but he also
worked on the landscaping,
changing the original Baroque
gardens to Neoclassical ones.
The Neoclassical style was
better suited to the building's
purpose—showcasing the
family's extensive collection of
sculptures and objects from
antiquity.

Karl Friedrich Schinkel

Louise's Memorial, where he experimented with iron for artistic purposes. He built summer residencies for the king's three sons and was soon appointed to the Prussian Building Commission, which he would later go on to become director of. Not only was Schinkel famous in the Prussian Empire, but he was also involved in many international architectural associations. He utilized the historic knowledge gained from his trips and sketches but reworked Classical architecture, appropriating it for a new era in a rational and dignified way. Schinkel undeniably helped to create much of the look of the urban landscape of Berlin.

Other Works by Schinke

Pomona Temple,1800, Potsdam

Palace Bridge, 1822–24, Berli

Castle Glienecke, 1825, Berli

Lighthouse, 1825–27, Kap Arkona, Germany

Nikolai Church, 1830–37, Potsdam

Town Hall, 1832, Koblenz

Römische Bader, 1833–40, Potsdam

■ **Friedrichswerder Church**, 1824–30, Berlin

A restoration to replace a former ruin, the Friedrichs-werder Church was planned as a Classical Roman temple but was changed on the suggestion of the king into a Neo-Gothic building. It was the first church to be built in this style in Berlin and set a national trend. The facade is in the style of the German brick Gothic, and the interior and exterior décor was constructed from terra cott The main section has a cen ized cube form and single r and the high windows and double towers soar above surrounding rooftops in a r dieval manner.

belsberg Castle, 1833,
lam

sberg Castle was built as a
mer residence for Prince

William I and Queen Augustus.
Schinkel constructed its first
phase using the English Tudor
style, popularized by Nash,

mixed with Neo-Gothic towering turrets. The surrounding
gardens were designed by
Peter Joseph Lenne.

■ **Building Academy**,
1831–35, Berlin

Schinkel designed the first
building academy in the center
of Berlin. The decorative elements, such as the relief sculptures, depict the history of
architecture. Various shades of
rough red brick and terra-cotta
panels around the entrance are
Neo-Gothic, and the use of non-
supporting wall elements and
supporting piers was a pre-
cursor to modern building techniques and industrial skeleton
building.

Karl Friedrich Schinkel

Russian Neoclassicism

1762–1850

■ Catherine the Great brought Neoclassical architecture to Russia ■ Scott architect Charles Cameron was influential in St. Petersburg ■ Czar Alexander I and Czar Paul I commissioned large Neoclassical buildings ■ The Palace Square in St. Petersburg had Neoclassical and Baroque features

● **1762–96** Reign of Catherine the Great, who favors Neoclassical styles

1779 Charles Cameron moves to Russia, bringing with him the Adams style

1787 Vincenzo Brenna becomes architect in chief at the Russian court

1796 Catherine the Great dies of smallpox

1812 Cameron dies

1830–50 Neoclassical style falls out of favor

Other Works

Senate Building, by Matvey Kazakov, 1776–87, Moscow

Alexander Palace Pavilions, by Giacomo Quarenghi, 1780s, near St. Petersburg

Razumovsky Palace, by Charles Cameron, 1802, Baturyn, Ukraine

Alexander Palace, interiors, by Charles Cameron, 1812, near St. Petersburg

■ **Pavlovsk Palace,** 1782–86, near St. Petersburg

The Pavlovsk Palace was built for the grand duke Paul by Charles Cameron

Catherine the Great despised the excessive Baroque Rococo styles and indulgent spending of her prede sors czarinas Anne and Elizabeth. Classically educa she felt Russia, particularly St. Petersburg, should b the grand Neoclassical style and sent for the Scot architect Charles Cameron, who was famous for his tailed documentation of the Baths of Rome. Cameron built for the later czars Paul I and Alexander I. Follow Cameron, his student Vincenzo Brenna took over as c architect. Other notable architects of the period are como Quarenghi and Matvey Fyodorovich Kazakov.

and Vincenzo Brenna. It was inspired by the Adams brothers' Kedleston Hall, but was built on a far grander scale. A large Corinthian colonnade indicates the design's Classical influences.

Rooms include the Grecian H filled with antique statues in niches, and the Grand Hall an Pilaster Room, all with Classic motifs. The surrounding gard are in the English style.

Neoclassicism 1640–1850

**meron Gallery,
erine Palace**, 1783, near
tersburg

rine the Great opposed
vhipped cream" style of
que and Rococo, and had
es Cameron add Neoclas-
extensions to her palace.
ron built private apart-
s for Catherine, including
techamber with Roman
beneath. The green
g room, one of the first
ons, had carved wooden
ers. The Agate Pavilion
ameron Gallery were also
d, with a vaulted ramp and
d windows. In the gardens
ron added picturesque
caping and lakes, and
d Classical objects such
nples and obelisks.

■ **Palace Square**, 1806–33,
St. Petersburg

Palace Square in St. Petersburg
is a combination of historical
styles that were tailored to the
times. At the north of the
square is the blue and white
Baroque Winter Palace, which is
surrounded by the Neoclassical
buildings of the square. Despite
the differences in style, the
Neoclassical buildings are able
to match the palace's Baroque
rhythm and grand scale. The
Alexander Column in the center
is made from red granite.

Russian Neoclassicism

Benjamin Henry Latrobe

1764, Yorkshire—1820, New Orleans

■ First professional architect in America ■ Worked with Thomas Jeffers
■ Built in the Neoclassical style ■ Introduced Gothic elements into his
buildings ■ Worked on the United States Capitol in Washington ■ Buil
private residences, churches, colleges, and banks

● **1764** Born in Yorkshire, UK

1788 Incorporates Gothic features at Sedgely Mansion in Philadelphia

1792 Hammerwood House in Sussex is his first independent work

1795 Moves to the United States

1797 Works on Virginia State Penitentiary

1803 Appointed surveyor of public buildings; begins work on the US Capitol

1812 Outbreak of war results in a pause in the Capitol's construction

1815–17 Work on the Capitol resumes

1820 Dies in New Orleans from yellow fever

■ **Baltimore Basilica**, 1806–21, Baltimore

The Baltimore Basilica was the first Roman Catholic cathedral in the United States. The ground plan is a rectangle with a shallow dome on one side and two spired towers on the other. The entrance is covered by a projected portico with columns. Skylights provide interior illumination, and the dome is double layered for durability.

Neoclassicism 1640–1850

Benjamin Henry Latrobe was born in the UK to a Mora
minister and educated in Europe. His training inclu
architecture and engineering. He emigrated to Ame
living first in Virginia, where he assisted Thomas Jeffe
(p. 318) on the Virginia State Capitol, and then in Phila
phia. He is considered the first professional archite
America and was appointed surveyor of public buildi
In his Neoclassical buildings, he introduced both G
and Gothic features to American architecture and o
used the Doric and Ionic orders. His most renowned
largest project is the Washington Capitol, which
worked on over two building stages. Due to his e
neering skills, Latrobe was capable of municipal arch
ture and worked on water projects, town planning,
even penitentiaries. He was also interested in landsca
in the English manner. Latrobe was influential and wi
copied. He died from yellow fever while workin
New Orleans.

...rmount Waterworks, begun 1799, ...elphia

...e was responsible for much of the initial ...eering at the Fairmount Waterworks, on ...huylkill River. The main pump houses are ...n the style of Greek temples, with columns ...Ionic order. Latrobe's ap-
...ce Fredrick Graff took
...e design work after

Latrobe's engineering proved unsatisfactory, but Latrobe's architecture remained. Along with the Bank of Philadephia, which he also designed, Latrobe's design of the waterworks had a lasting influence on the architectural development of the city of Philadelphia.

■ **Nassau Hall**, 1802, Princeton

Nassau House is the oldest building at Princeton University, in New Jersey, and still bears Latrobe's additions. Following the Battle of Princeton in 1777 and a fire in 1802, Latrobe experimented with fire-

proof materials, using brick flooring, stone stairs, and an iron roof. He added a pediment and raised the entire roof of the building 2 feet (0.6 meters), thereby improving both the building's interior and exterior.

Benjamin Henry Latrobe

The US Capitol

The United States Capitol's dome is an American icon. William Thornton's winning plan centered the building on a grand entrance, accentuated by jecting wings that add a horizontal element to the building. The centermost projects outward, supported by vertical elements—columns— that draw the up to the crowning pediment. The pediment itself leads to the massive dome building's design was inspired by both the eastern facade of the Louvre in and by the Pantheon in Rome. Neoclassical designs and the architectural syn ism of antiquity were appropriated to the young country's capital in ord assert the government's power and relate it to that of the Roman Empire.

Several architects and building campaigns have contributed to the buil that we see today, including Benjamin Henry Latrobe (p. 314), Stephen H and Charles Bulfinch. After the War of 1812 and the burning of Washing Latrobe resumed the building's construction. The dome and rotunda were nally constructed of wood, but were later rep by more durable and classical materials. In extensions and a new cast-iron dome added. The current dome has a two- drum with a double-shell interior, cir vented by 36 columns, and topped b Statue of Freedom.

United States Capitol, begun
Washington, DC

terior of the Capitol is a combina-
halls and rooms constructed
ghout the nation's history,
monstrates advance-
in building materials.
d Senate Chamber,
ed by Latrobe and
ch, is now a
m. Decorated
h dark red
old fabrics,
large canopy
uishing the
n of the
ent of the
, the
er is

shaped like a semicircular amphitheater with a
half-domed, coffered ceiling. The Classical orders play an important role in the assertion of
the government's power, by recalling
great empires of the past. The Visitors'
Gallery is supported by eight
marble Ionic columns, while the
Ladies' Gallery is supported by
iron and steel Corinthian columns. Bulfinch's design for the
crypt, which was built in
1827, supports the floor of
the rotunda above with
stone columns of the
Doric order. A star in the
center of the floor indi-
cates the point where
all the roads in
Washington orig-
inate.

The US Capitol

Thomas Jefferson

1743, Shadwell—1826, Monticello

■ American president, architect, planner, and educator ■ Self-taught a
interested in Palladianism ■ Lived in France as an ambassador ■ Work
with Latrobe and Clerisseau ■ Built in Virginia ■ Responsible for desig
of the United States Capitol ■ Passionate about education and learnin

● **1743** Born in Shadwell, son of a wealthy surveyor

1779–81 Governor of Virginia; facilitates the move of the Capitol from Williamsburg to Richmond

1784–89 Minister to France, where he travels and is exposed to European architecture; develops an interest in Palladio

1792 As secretary of state, he approves plans for the new federal capitol in Washington

1801–09 President of the United States

1819 Founds the University of Virginia

1826 Dies on the Fourth of July in Monticello

Other Works by Jefferson

George Divers House, (Farmington Country Club), ca. 1802, Charlottesville, Virginia

Poplar Forest, 1806, Lynchburg, Virginia

Farmington, 1815–16, Louisville, Kentucky

The Lawn (Academical Village), 1826, University of Virginia, Charlottesville

Thomas Jefferson, third president of the United State
author of the Declaration of Independence, was als
accomplished architect. Jefferson was extremely well
cated and, after studying law, entered politics. Largely
taught, he was introduced to European Neoclass
while serving as minister to France. Greatly influence
Palladio's (p. 192) theories on the relation of archite
and the state, his style was based on architecture from
tiquity. He was involved in the design of the United S
Capitol as secretary of state and as president, and ass
in city planning. His designs for the University of Vir
were the first to separate academia and the church.

■ **Monticello House**, 1768–1809, Monticello, Virginia

Jefferson built his own residence at Monticello. The house has two Palladian-inspired porticoes and a large forecourt. Jefferson experi-

mented with semi-octagon
rooms that maximized the u
space. He was also responsi
the surrounding landscapin
English gardens, used to tes
growing techniques.

[Vir]ginia State Capitol, [Richmond]

[Vi]rginia State Capitol is [mode]led after one of the best-[prese]rved Roman temples in [exista]nce today—the Maison [Carré]e at Nîmes in France. One [of the] first buildings in the [United] States to be built in the [form] of a classic temple, the

Capitol was received with great acclaim and set a fashion for Classical, rather than Federal or Georgian architecture, for government buildings. The Neoclassical-style Capitol provides visitors with an impression of strength and permanence, which is emphasized by its hilltop location. By building

in the manner of the Romans, Jefferson associated the young American government with the great Roman Empire. Although the Maison Carrée was built with Corinthian columns, Jefferson, working with C. L. Clérisseau, decided to use columns of the less ornate, more stoic Ionic order instead.

[Rot]unda, 1822–26, Univer-[sity of] Virginia, Charlottesville

[The U]niversity of Virginia is [design]ed as an academic village, [where] 10 utilitarian and resi-[dentia]l pavilions surround a [large] grassy quadrangle. The 10 [pavilions r]esemble Neopalladian [villa]s and are connected by [colonn]ades. A large rotunda in [the no]rth is based on the Pan-[theon,] and the library, rather [than th]e church, is the main [focal p]oint.

Thomas Jefferson

19th Century

Henri Labrouste: Bibliotèque Sainte-Geneviève,
1845–50, Paris

19th Century

p. 331

322

1800–1900
Greek Revival

Focuses on Hellenistic architecture and the Doric and Ionic orders

1810–1900
Gothic Revival

Revives medieval styles by restoring Gothic structures and building new ones in the style; often combines medieval aesthetics with modern materials

1840–1880
Neo-Renais-sance and Richardsonia Romanesque

Revival of Classically influenced architectu from the Renaissance a return to Romanesc styles

| 1800 | 1810 | 1820 | 1830 | 1840 |

p. 340

1850–1900
Industrial Architecture

New, industrial materials are used on public buildings

350–1880
econd Empire

France, sweeping anges in politics and

hitectural styles
ead to the United
tes, where the man-
d roof and appro-
ated French styles
come popular; Beaux-
s styles also come to
e United States

ron Georges-Eugène
ussmann p. 352
hard Morris Hunt
58
red B. Mullet
liam Boyington
ob Weidenmann
. Elletson
n McArthur Jr.

1800–1900
Exoticism

Moorish, Egyptian, and Asian styles are popular with wealthy patrons

Eduard Knoblauch
Ludwig Foerster

Henri Labrouste p. 366
Charles Garnier p. 364
Joseph Paxton
W. H. Barlow
Gustav Eiffel
Ferdinand Dutert

p. 365

19th-Century Revivals

19th-century architecture was greatly influenced by earlier architectural movements and foreign, exotic styles, which were adapted to the new technologies of the early modern age. The revivals of Gothic, Greek, and Renaissance styles were combined with contemporary technologies and materials. In the Western world, Historicism idealized past empires and cultures and used motifs inspired by them to spark national nostalgia.

Mediterranean exploration and an interest in antiquity led to the revival of ancient Greek architecture. Similar to Neoclassicism, the Greek Revival movement was more decorative and ornamental. Because of ancient Greek intellectual culture, it was a popular style for colleges and cultural institutions. Greek Revival was also at times combined with traditional ecclesiastical architecture.

■ **Federal Hall**
1700, New York
painting by
Bernard Boutet
de Monvel, 193

alpole's Villa,
–76, Straw-
Hill, London

Gothic Revivalism

Perhaps because of their long Gothic traditions and the power of their empires during the Middle Ages, the revival of Gothic and medieval architecture was embraced in the UK and France in all art forms. The style was used for churches, and many Gothic churches were restored and converted to Neo-Gothic structures. Stately homes and mansions used Gothic elements, as wealthy landowners wanted romantic castles. The writings of James Ruskin, Horace Walpole, and Victor Hugo were influential to its popularity. In Victorian England, the formation of the Ecclesiological Society argued for the Gothic aesthetic.

In France, Viollet-le-Duc argued for the combination of the use of new industrial materials in Gothic structural plans. The final defeat of the French monarchy in the second half of the 19th century and the reign of Napoléon III created the "Second Empire" style, not just in the capital but internationally.

Introduction

Beaux-Arts, Neo-Renaissance, and Richardsonian Romanesque
The École des Beaux-Arts in Paris was influential in creating a generation of architects working in a cohesive style. Beaux-Arts architecture is a lavish combination of Neo-Baroque and Neo-Renaissance that symbolized the Belle Époch. International students who studied at the school spread the style abroad. Haussmann's Parisian urban planning, based on rationalized consistency, aesthetics, and infrastructures, was also exported.

In America, architecture developed a local flair, and architects such as Henry Hobson Richardson and Richard Morris Hunt developed their own adaptations of Second Empire and Beaux-Arts styles, and Romanesque and Renaissance styles were repopularized. Meanwhile, 15th- and 16th-century Italian styles were used in the United Kingdom by Charles Barry for conveying a Classical environment.

■ **Edward Ried and Georg von Dollman: Neuschwanste Castle**, 1886, Bavaria

19th Century

dwig
ster: New
gogue,
Budapest

Exoticism and Empire

Increased travel and colonialism introduced both architects and the public to the styles of the Orient and Middle East. The fascination with exotic lands and cultures grew, and wealthy patrons commissioned works in foreign styles to assert their worldliness. Motifs such as obelisks, pyramids, and onion-shaped domes became popular throughout Europe and the United States.

The Industrial Revolution and the increased speed of the production and distribution of new materials enabled construction techniques to improve in leaps and bounds. Architecture became larger, stronger, and more durable. Buildings demonstrated their structural elements with exposed beams, braces, and cast-iron pillars. The World Exhibitions created a forum for greater exchange of designs and technical innovations between countries.

Introduction

Industrial Architecture

With 19th-century advancements in coal and steam energy, new materials such as cast iron, glass, and steel were being produced at an accelerated rate. This signaled the birth of industrial architecture, as architects and engineers had easier access to materials. Utilitarian, public venues became more important, and needed to be durable. The popularity of World's Fairs resulted in spectacular temporary exhibition halls in Paris and London. Art Nouveau and Neo-Gothic styles adorned these new temples of the future, as cities spread outward and upward, supported by new and robust materials. Architects and engineers collaborated, paving the way for modern high-rises and skyscrapers.

The Galerie des Machines the 1889 Paris World's Fair showcased the new method construction. Ferdinand Du and Victor Contamin built a 374-foot (114-meter) hall o metal and glass. The tall roo had no central supports, bu was created using a three-hinged arch structure.

An icon of industrialization, Joseph Paxton's Crystal Palace was constructed to house the first Great Exhibition in London. A testament to industrial materials, it was composed of nearly 300,000 panes of glass on wrought iron framing, and was assembled on-site from prefabricated elements.

Building Techniques

**...ustav Eiffel and Stephen
...vestre: Eiffel Tower**,
...–89, Paris

...Eiffel Tower was originally
... as a temporary attraction
...he World's Fair of 1889, yet
...s come to be the most rec-
...zed landmark in Paris. Engi-
...Gustav Eiffel collaborated
...the architect Stephen
...estre. The tower is a cele-
...on of iron as a building tool
...set a precedent in demon-
...ing the durability and ele-
...e of the material. The
...r is 1,010 feet (308 meters)
...nd weighs 7,000 tons. The
...ht is evenly distributed to
...ur supports.

**Construction techniques for
the Eiffel Tower** came from ex-
pertise learned from the rail-
road industry. The tower is a
large replica of a viaduct pylon
and consists of a system of
girders. It was prefabricated
and riveted together on-site
using cranes.

William Wilkins

1778, Norwich–1839, Cambridge

- Traveled to Greece and Turkey ■ Worked in the Greek Revival style
- Designed many university buildings at Cambridge ■ Designed the National Gallery at Trafalgar Square in London ■ Experimented with Got styles ■ Published his work and drawing plans

- **1778** Born in Norwich
- **1801** Tours the Mediterranean, where he is exposed to Classical architecture
- **1807** Publishes *Antiquities of Magna Graecia*
- **1819** Designs the Theater Royal, Bury St. Edmunds, with a horseshoe-shaped layout that implements Classical lines and proportions
- **1827** Designs University College, London, in a refined Classical style, with a Corinthian portico
- **1837** Publishes *Prolusiones Architectonicae*
- **1839** Dies in Cambridge

■ **Downing College**, 1807–20, Cambridge

Wilkins introduced the Greek Revival style to his university buildings at Downing College. The layout consists of Classical structures, resembling temples to knowledge, in a large grassy main court. It is considered one of the first university campuses of the kind, preceding Jefferson's University of Virginia.

19th Century

William Wilkins was the son of an architect and plaste Educated at Cambridge, he studied mathematics a later taught himself architecture. An avid member of Society of Antiquities, he was awarded a traveling sch arship to the Mediterranean, and his time in Greece a Turkey was to have a profound effect on his appreciat of Classical Greek architecture. Upon his return, he se an architecture practice, and he received commissions country houses, theaters, art galleries, and academic ir tutions. His design for the National Gallery was cho over John Nash's (p. 298). Wilkins incorporated anci Greek symbols and construction techniques, such porticoes and columns, into his buildings, with vary degrees of success. He was responsible for the appe ance of many UK university buildings, whose Class style would influence university architecture such Thomas Jefferson's (p. 318) University of Virginia. Late his career he began working in the Gothic Revival st using turrets and towers on country mansions. Similarly, Wilkins brought Gothic Revivalist styles to university architecture.

tional Gallery, 1832–38,
on

ormer Kings Mews (sta-
on Trafalgar Square were
en as the site for the Na-
l Gallery, as it was a site
ed accessible to all.
ns used eight of the
nns from the recently de-
hed Carlton House, but
were too short for the
l main portico, and were
quently used for the east
est porticoes.

her Works by Wilkins

ybury and Imperial
ce College, 1806–09,
ord

heny House, 1817, near
ourgh

ter Royal, Bury
dmunds, 1819, Suffolk

house and Porter's Lodge
ng's College, 1824–28,
bridge

ersity College, London,
–32

Court of Corpus Christi
ge, 1827, Cambridge

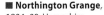

331

Greek Revival in the UK

■ **Northington Grange**,
1804–09, Hampshire

Wilkins built a new Classical facade onto the Northington Grange manor house, which was originally designed by William Samwell. Northington Grange is one of the earliest ex-amples of Greek Revival archi-tecture in Europe and takes the form of an antique temple. A double row of six Doric col-umns support the portico and triangular pediment. Square columns can be found on the sides of the building.

William Wilkins

The Inwood Family

1771–1843

■ British family of architects ■ William Inwood and his son Henry William Inwood were the most prominent architects ■ Strong proponents of the Greek Revival style ■ Added authenticity to their buildings through carefully modeling their designs on Greek buildings

● **1771** William Inwood born

1794 Henry William Inwood born

1799 Charles Frederick, designer of the Church of All Saints in Marlow, born

1802 Edward is born

1818–19 Henry William travels to Italy and Greece

1819–22 St. Pancras is built

1827 Henry William publishes *The Erechtheion at Athens: Fragments of Athenian Architecture and a Few Remains in Attica, Megara, and Epirus*

1834 Henry William publishes *The Resources of Design in the Architecture of Greece, Egypt, and Other Countries*

1840 Charles Frederick and Edward die

1843 William and Henry William die

Other Works

St. Peter's Church, 1822–25, Regent Square, London

St. Mary's Church, 1824–27, Somers Town, London

Church of All Saints, 1832–35, Marlow, Buckinghamshire

William Inwood and his sons, Henry William, Charles Frederick, and Edward composed the Inwood family of architects, who worked in the Greek Revival style. Henry William Inwood traveled to Greece, bringing back objects from antiquity that were to influence his buildings. He also published his studies in the highly influential *Erechtheion at Athens: Fragments of Athenian Architecture and a Few Remains in Attica, Megara, and Epirus*. St. Pancras Church in London is William and Henry William's most famous collaboration and is based on ancient Greek styles. The structural features of Greek temples and monuments were combined with the British ecclesiastical architectural styles. The Inwoods added round porticos and decorative motifs to traditional lanterns and cupolas favored by British architects. In some of the Inwoods' later works, Gothic Revivalist ornamentation and structural features were incorporated into the designs.

■ **All Saints Church**, 1822–24, Camden Town, London

The All Saints Church in Camden Town is a juxtaposition of Greek Revival and traditional British styles. Though the traditional British lantern remains, a small circular protruding portico circumvented by a row of Ionic columns is added, with Greek decorative motifs along the roof.

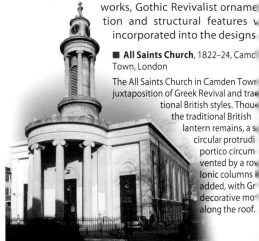

Pancras New Church, 22, London

ncras New Church is the enowned Greek Revival church in the UK. The Inwoods directly referenced the Athenian Erechtheion temple and the Choragic Monument of Lys- icrates in Athens. Draped *cary-atids* support the rear porches. The building is built of brick and clad in stone.

The Inwood Family

Gottfried Semper

1803, Hamburg–1879, Rome

- Lived in Dresden, Paris, London, and Vienna ■ Friend and collaborator composer Richard Wagner ■ Design theorist who studied industrial art and materials ■ Helped redefine theater layout ■ Worked in Neo-Renaissance style ■ Forced to leave Dresden after the May Uprising

- **1803** Born in Hamburg, Germany
- **1834** Appointed chair of Dresden Academy
- **1845** Participates in the May Uprising in Dresden, after which he flees to Paris
- **1851** Works on Great Exhibition in London
- **1851** Publishes *Die vier Elemente der Baukunst* (*The Four Elements of Architecture*)
- **1852** Publishes *Wissenschaft, Industrie und Kunst* (*Science, Industry, and Art*)
- **1855–71** Teaches at the Polytechnikum in Zurich
- **1879** Dies in Rome

■ **Festival Theater**, 1876, Bayreuth, Germany

Wagner adapted Semper's designs for the unbuilt Richard Wagner Theater in Munich to build the Festival Theater. Instead of the traditional theater layout of a tiered horseshoe shape, the plan resembles a wider amphitheater, and emphasized the antibourgeois, nonhierarchical views of the composer. The orchestra pit was also lowered out of sight.

19th Century

Gottfried Semper was an influential German architect design theorist who worked in the UK, Austria, Switzerland. Born in Hamburg, he studied law, ma matics, and architecture. His published work includes ories on polychromy in Greek architecture, an analys decorative functions, and the materiality related to a tectonic forms. His *Four Elements of Architecture* was i nationally respected. After the failed May Uprisin Dresden he fled to Paris—where he was influence Hittorf—and then later to London. There he worke the 1851 Great Exhibition and as an adviser to Princ bert. Later he taught at the Zurich Polytechnikum worked on the new buildings on the Imperial Ringstr in Vienna. Semper's architecture was a combinatio large-scale Neo-Renaissance styles. His later buildin Vienna were completed by Karl von Hasenauer.

mperoper (Semper
a House), 1841, 1869–78,
den

of Semper's first and most
y regarded buildings, the
er Opera House was origi-
built in Neo-Renaissance

style. Following a fire in 1869,
Semper was commissioned to
redesign the replacement theater, but was not able to
oversee the construction because he was in exile for his part
in the May Uprising. His son,

■ Museum of Natural
History, 1872–81, Vienna

The Museum of Natural History
collated the imperial collection
for the first time and made it
available to the public. Its architecture, interior design, and

Manfred Semper, oversaw the
reconstruction of the opera.
The redesign is considered the
prime example of the Dresden
Baroque Revival style and has
decorative elements from Classical architecture.

the collection itself work together to create a *gesamtkunst-
werk*, a building in which the
parts function together as an
integrated whole, a
grand homage to
history.

Gottfried Semper

Scottish Baronial

1811–1876

■ Large manor houses and castles were built and renovated ■ Traditional Scottish architectural styles from the Renaissance were revived ■ Began in rural areas but later spread to cities ■ The main architects were William Burn and David Bryce ■ Features include towers, turrets, battlements, and crowstep gables

■ **1811** Sir Walter Scott buys property on which to build Abbotsford

1822 King George IV visits Scotland, evoking national pride

1825 David Bryce begins working with William Burn

1829 Milton Lockhart, in Lanarkshire, by Burn, shows traditional Scottish traits

1844 Burn and Bryce part ways

1847–52 Robert William Billings publishes *The Baronial and Ecclesiastical Antiquities of Scotland*, an inspiration to local architects

1854 Kinnaird Castle, by Bryce, has elements of French manor houses

1870 William Burn dies

1876 David Bryce dies

Other Works

Taymouth Castle, by James Elliot, 1806–09, Aberfeldy

St. John's Church, by William Burn, 1816–18, Edinburgh

Stenhouse, by William Burn, 1836, Stirlingshire

Kinnaird Castle, by David Bryce, 1854–57, Angus

Scottish Baronial was a form of medieval and Gothic revival popular in the 19th century. The style appealed Scottish national pride by relating the progress and affluence of the Renaissance to the wealth of contemporary Scotland. Scottish Baronial buildings had castle towers, stone turrets, crowstep gables, steep roofs, large windows, and a portcullis. Begun as a way to demonstrate prestige in large country residences, the style spread to urban centers such as Edinburgh after 1850. The leading architect of the style was William Burn. His partner, David Bryce, was known for his mature Baronial style and built more than 200 buildings, often incorporating French features. Scottish Baronial spread to England and Ireland.

■ **William Smith: Balmoral Castle**, 1853, Aberdeenshire

Balmoral Castle was purchased by King Albert for Queen Victoria and used by the British royal family as a summer retreat. The previous castle was demolished and rebuilt in Scottish Baronial style, which helped to solidify the style's popularity even more.

William Atkinson: Abbotsford, 1818–24, near Melrose, Scottish Borders

Abbotsford, the home of Scottish novelist Sir Walter Scott, embodied the Romantic nostalgia and national pride of the author. The house was built by Atkinson with contributions from Edward Blore and Scott himself. There were many rooms filled with Scottish memorabilia, antiques, armor, and an impressive library that contained many of Scott's writings.

■ William Burn: Brodie Castle, ca. 1824, Moray

Brodie Castle was originally a 16th-century fortified manor house laid out on a Z-shaped plan. In 1645 the original castle was partially burned in attacks. Three centuries later William Burn designed extensive alterations, including adding an eastern wing onto the house. By this time there was no need for the defensive battlements of traditional castles, and the additions were purely decorative. Picturesque landscaped gardens surround Brodie.

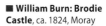
Scottish Baronial

Egyptian Revival

1802–1884

■ Influenced by an interest in the culture and designs of ancient Egypt
■ Used in cemeteries and mausoleums ■ There is a long history of obe
being captured and relocated as bounty from war ■ Features included
tered walls, reed-shaped columns, pyramids, and lotus flowers

■ **1802** Publication of the illustrated *Voyage dans la basse et haute Egypte*

1809 Publication of *Description de l'Egypt*

1811 Plans drawn up for the Egyptian Hall by P. F. Robinson in London

1822 Jean-François Champollion deciphers hieroglyphics and the Rosetta Stone is made public

1827 The Egyptian collection at the Louvre opens

1836–84 The Washington Monument, a large obelisk, is designed, but takes nearly 40 years to be built

Egyptian Revival was a decorative and architectural that was influenced by ancient Egypt. Napoléon's paign into Egypt in 1798 and the findings of expl and researchers brought images and information Egypt back to Europe. As with other exoticist cr Egyptian Revivalism manifested in the furniture, inte and cemeteries of wealthy European and Ame patrons. In architecture, motifs included obelisks pyrus-reed-shaped columns, lotus flower capitals, moldings, and flat roofs. Egyptian Revivalism was e used for educational institutes and cemeteries, bec of ancient Egyptian advancements in science and k in the afterworld. It was also sometimes mixed witl ments of Greek Revivalism. A second wav Egyptian Revival occurred following the covery of Tutankhamen's tomb in the 19

■ **Wilhelm von Traitteur and Basil Christianowicz: Egyptian Bridge**, 1825–26, St. Petersburg

Built by engineers Wilhelm von Traitteur and Basil Christianowicz, the Egyptian Bridge was the first metal bridge in Russia and is ornamented with iron sphinxes and a giant iron obelisk. Because of faulty engineering with iron, which is a rather heavy metal, the bridge collapsed in the early 20th century. Some of its Egyptian ornamentation, which is anchored to land by granite supports, was salvaged and used in the bridge's reconstruction. Originally the bridge had cast-iron gates fashioned after Egyptian columns with hieroglyphic reliefs.

Other Works

Rue de Sevres Fountain, by Beauvallet, 1809, Paris

Egyptian Hall, by P. F. Robinson, 1812, London

Egyptian Quay, by Konstantin Thon, 1832–34, St. Petersburg

Sharrow Vale Cemetery, 1836, Sheffield

Grove Street Cemetery, by Henry Austen, 1845, New Haven

...omas Stewart: Medical ...ge of Richmond (now ...gyptian Building of the ...ical College of Virginia), ...Richmond

...Medical College of Rich-...d, now known as the ...tian Building, was con-...ted with reference to the ...tian healer and architect ...ep and his ancient medic-...owers. The building's ...known as "battered

walls," narrow at the top, and the towering reedlike columns have palm fond capitals. Other motifs include winged sun discs with cobras, lotus flowers, and hieroglyphics. The five-story building's monumentality is emphasized by its near total lack of windows.

■ H. H. Richardson: Ames Monument, 1882, Wyoming

The Ames Monument is a pyramid dedicated to the memory of Oakes and Oliver Ames. It is made from pale local granite and irregularly shaped bricks arranged in a random ashlar manner, or so that their positioning appears unplanned. Pyramid forms were popular shapes, used in monuments and tombs.

Egyptian Revival

Sir Charles Barry

1795, London–1860, London

■ Gothic and Greek Revival architect in the UK ■ Leader of the Anglo-Italian Renaissance Revival ■ Built in London, Manchester, and Brighton ■ Collaborated with A. W. N. Pugin ■ Designed the UK Houses of Parliament ■ Utilized classic Italian ground plans ■ Designed elaborate inter

● **1795** Born in London

1817–20 Travels to Europe and the Middle East and studies Italian architecture

1823 Begins St. Peter's in Brighton, which would be one of the first Gothic Revival churches in the area

1834 A fire at the Palace of Westminster destroys much of the building

1835–36 Wins competition to build the new Houses of Parliament

1850 Awarded the RIBA Gold Medal

1851 Works on the Great Exhibition

1859 Begins Halifax Town Hall

1860 Dies in London

Sir Charles Barry was an esteemed architect during Victorian era. His style was a mix of Gothic, Greek, Italian Neo-Renaissance, which were greatly influer by his Mediterranean travels. In particular, his studie Italian palazzi were to be influential. In his designs country houses and gentlemen's clubs, Barry develo the Neo-Renaissance style. The Travellers Club evo 15th-century Italian styles, while the nearby Reform (incorporated 16th-century styles into its design. B also designed churches in London, Brighton, and M chester in the Gothic Revival style. His most famous ation is the UK Houses of Parliament, for which he later knighted. Barry was accepted into many inte tional architecture academies.

■ **UK Houses of Parliament**, 1839–52, London

Barry was awarded the prize of reconstructing the UK Houses of Parliament, made up of the House

of Lords and House of Comm He worked with Pugin on the tailing and interiors. The Got clock tower (Big Ben) is harm nious with the former mediev remains of the Victoria Tower

■ **Trafalgar Square**, 1840–45, London

Barry remodeled London's Trafalgar Square after Sir John Nash, but it was not completed to his plans. He designed the northern terrace, steps, and fountains. Four octagonal plinths with lanterns stand at each corner of the square. The central Corinthian column has a statue of Viscount Nelson at its summit and four bronze lions at its base. The central mounted figure is a monument to Charles I.

eform Club, 1837–41,
on

Reform Club was a liberal
r-class gentlemen's club
gned by Barry on Pall Mall.
g with the Bridgewater and
den houses, the club

demonstrates Barry's Italian Renaissance influences. The layout is based loosely on the Palazzo Farnese in Rome and is centered around a glass-domed central salon, which is connected to all other rooms, in-

cluding the map room, audience room, and parliamentary library. Barry supervised the interior decorations, which used rich fabrics, white marble, and dark wood, emphasizing the Renaissance appearance.

Sir Charles Barry

Augustus Welby Northmore Pugin

1812, London–1852, Ramsgate, Kent

■ Influential writer, draftsman, and architect ■ Influenced the Gothic Revival through his designs and books ■ Known for his interior designs

- **1812** Born in London
- **1834–55** Converts to Catholicism, which is to have a profound effect on his architectural style
- **1836** Publishes *Contrasts*
- **1837–42** Provides Sir Charles Barry with drawings and designs for the Palace of Westminster
- **1841** Publishes *True Principles of Christian Architecture*
- **1852** Dies in Ramsgate

Augustus Pugin began his career early by assisting French father, a draftsman, and illustrating medie buildings for publication. At the age of 15 he was desi ing furniture for Windsor Castle. His conversion to Catl icism cemented his belief in the superiority of Gothic medieval styles. In his short life Pugin worked on over ecclesiastical and secular buildings and wrote 8 bod The first book, *Contrasts*, was highly influential for Gothic Revival. Pugin was able to re-create authe Gothic details that included wallpaper, tiles, carvings, metalworks. Pugin was employed by Sir Charles B. (p. 340), including desi ing the interiors for Palace of Westmins but died after a bre down the year Barry knighted for his work.

■ **Church of St. Giles**, 184(Cheadle, Staffordshire

The Earl of Shrewsbury paic the elaborately decorated S Giles, which was one of the largest of Pugin's commissi The interior is a rich and dec dent juxtaposition of wallpa carvings, and metalwork. Ea pillar has a differing patterr and there are colorful and o nate tiles throughout. Arche lead from the nave to the ch els, and the rood screen is h carved from oak.

George's Cathedral,
–48, Southwark, London

n's renovation of St.
ge's Cathedral in South-
was largely destroyed by
ds during World War II.
ltar, three chapels, two
tries, and facade ornamen-
n survived the war. These
es are decorated with stone
ngs and gold ornamenta-
in stark contrast to the
restorations of the church.

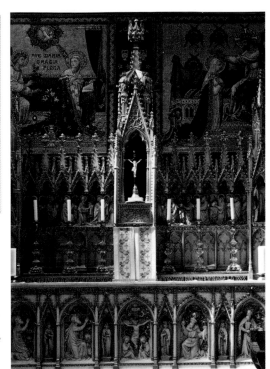

🔺 **Altar for the Church of the Immaculate Conception (Farm Street Church),**
1844–49, London

The Jesuit Church of the Immaculate Conception, on Farm Street in London, was built between 1844 and 1849 by Joseph James Scoles in the highly ornate Gothic Revival style. The style served to affirm that the Catholic Church maintained a significant place in British society. By using the imagery of Gothic England in the altar's carving, brasswork, and decoration, Pugin recalls the grandeur and power of the church and the piety of the masses. Pugin's French father exposed him to the delicate styles of French moldings, reliefs, and traceries, which he later incorporated into his altars, screens, railings, and pulpits. Pugin's religious fervor, extravagances, eccentric ideas, and wholesale condemnation of all forms except for those of the Gothic were not always accepted during his time.

Augustus Welby Northmore Pugin

Sir George Gilbert Scott

1811, Buckinghamshire–1878, London

■ Prominent British Gothic Revival architect and restorer ■ Influenced I
A. W. N. Pugin ■ Developed Collegiate Gothic ■ St. Pancras Station com
bined Gothic Revival with the innovations of industrial architecture
■ *left:* **St. Mary's Church**, 1872, London

1811 Born in Bucking-
hamshire
1837 Reign of Queen Victoria begins
1844 Builds St. Nicholas in
Hamburg with a German
Gothic spire
1849 Appointed surveyor
of Westminster Abbey and
completes restorations
1858 Publishes *Remarks
on Secular and Domestic
Architecture*
1859 Awarded RIBA Gold
Medal
1878 Dies in London

Sir George Gilbert Scott was born into an intensely
gious British family, which most likely influenced hi
terest in Gothic architecture. He was a prolific archite
the Victorian UK and worked on more than 800 build
in his lifetime, both home and abroad. A leading pro
nent of the Gothic Revival style, he was inspirec
Augustus Welby Northmore Pugin (p. 342) and the in
national Gothic developments in both architecture
restoration from Continental Europe. He initially built
itarian buildings but soon received ecclesiastical, rc
and academic commissions. Scott studied medieval st
closely and was a respected medieval church restorer
styles were innovative for the Gothic Revival mover
in that they incorporated designs f
Gothic traditions outside of the U
staunch supporter of the Gothic m
in both secular and religious archi
ture, his published architectural th
ries were influential.

■ **St. Pancras Station**, 1868–74, London

St. Pancras Station in London is made up of t
buildings—the large train shed, built by indu
trial engineer W. H. Barlow, and the Midland
Grand Hotel by Scott. Not only a masterpiece
Gothic Revival, St. Pancras Station was also a
credible technological feat for the time, utiliz
iron, steel, and glass. The hotel was inspired
international Gothic trends and has grand sp
pointed arches, and numerous towers. The r
brick facade has heavily decorated windows
the interior walls are gilded. The Grand Hote
had early elevators.

Prince Albert Memorial,
1864–76, London

The Prince Albert Memorial in Hyde
Park was commissioned by
Queen Victoria for her late husband Prince Albert following his
death from typhoid. The memorial takes the *ciborium* form of a
Gothic shrine, or tabernacle,
which shelters the large bronze
statue of the seated prince. The
ornate canopy is supported by
pink and gray granite columns
and made from gilded bronze
with glass mosaics and colored
stones, crowned with a crucifix.
A marble frieze of Parnassus
below the podium depicts 169
characters from the history of
the Victorian arts and sciences.
At each corner of the polished
white steps are a group of
statues representing the continents of Asia, the Americas,
Europe, and Africa. The main
sculptors were Henry Armstead
and John Bell, and together
with Scott they achieved a
remarkable synthesis of architecture and sculpture.

Durham Cathedral, interior
restoration, 1859

Scott was responsible for the
19th-century Gothic restoration
of the Gothic cathedral at
Durham, one of the first to use a
ribbed vault system. The "Scott
Screen" stands at the entrance
to the choir and is made from
marble and alabaster. Scott also
built the marble pulpit, which is
supported by decorated
columns, and the historically
accurate brass lectern, covered
in filigree designs and inlaid
crystals.

Other Works by Scott
Royal Wanstead School, 1840, Essex
St. Giles Church, 1841–43, London
Chesterfield Church, restoration, 1841, Chesterfield
Doncaster Parish Church, 1854, Doncaster
Exeter College,1854–60, Oxford
Hereford Cathedral, restoration, 1857–63, Herefordshire
St. Mary Abbot's Church, 1872, London

Sir George Gilbert Scott

William Butterfield

1814, London—1900, London

■ High Victorian Gothic architect and restorer ■ Influenced by Ruskin and Pugin ■ Member of the Ecclesiological Society and built for the Tractarians ■ Developed Collegiate Gothic architecture ■ Created polychromatic surfa of bricks and tiles and used unconventional combinations of natural colors

■ **1814** Born in London

1833–36 Studies under E. L. Blackburne, but his architectural style is largely self-taught

1840 Opens own practice

1844–45 Builds his first noteworthy church—the St. Saviour at Coalpit Heath

1853–56 Builds Milton Ernest Hall in Bedfordshire, a large Gothic country house

1871 Completes Rugby School Chapel, the epitome of his use of colors

1884–85 Restoration work at St. Cross Hospital

1900 Dies in London

Other Works

St. Savior, 1844, Coalpit Heath, Gloucestershire

St. Augustine's College, 1848, Canterbury

St. Ninian's, 1850, Perth, UK

St. Matthias, 1850–52, Stoke Newington

Balliol College, 1856, Oxford

St. Peter's Cathedral, 1878, Adelaide, Australia

William Butterfield was the son of a chemist and work in the Gothic Revival style. He was a devout man a renowned for his religious buildings that celebrated t Anglican Church. He was influenced by Augustus We Pugin (p. 352) and the writings of James Ruskin. Butt field studied under E. L. Blackburne, but was largely s taught, drawing influence from Gothic architecture. A member of the Ecclesiological Society, or the Cambric Camden Society, he contributed to *The Ecclesiologis* journal that extolled Gothic Revivalism as the only leg mate Christian architecture. His buildings are noted their diverse colors and prolific use of brick. Butterfi used polychromatic bricks, tiles, and stones and believ that all combinations of natural colors were allowed.

original use of color w point of critique, but was commissioned as afield as Australia.

■ **All Saints (Margaret Str Church)**, 1849–59, London

All Saints Church was the ce of worship for the Tractarian who set out to revive the Catholic elements of Christi anity. Despite the small urba plot, Butterfield managed to clude a church, clergy house courtyard, and school on the grounds. The facade is of red and black brick, and the inter is a mass of colored tiles, gla and mosaic.

...ble College, 1867–83, Oxford

...rfield built Keble College (named after ...d Movement founder John Keble) and the ...rsity chapel. Due to both financial restraints ...ersonal taste, red, white, and blue bricks ...used for the construction. The result was ...rfield's typically unorthodox polychromatic ...e. The buildings are High Victorian Gothic, ...tall towers and arched windows. The chapel ...tricate mosaics, tiles, and stained glass, and ...nowned W. H. Hunt painting *The Light of* ...orld.

...rton College Chapel Restoration, ...-51, Oxford

...on College is one of the oldest colleges at ...d and was built in the 13th century. Butter-...along with G. G. Scott and Edward Blore, ...esponsible for the 19th-century restoration ...e chapel. Yellow and red tiles were added to ...uilding, and the northern transept received ...nate Gothic facade. Butterfield also built the ...e Building residence at Oxford, which was ...a leafy location and had a high-pitched ...ed roof, which was later altered.

William Butterfield

Eugène Viollet-le-Duc

1814, Paris—1879, Lausanne

■ Writer, theorist, architect, and restorer ■ Applied Gothic principles to mod[
building renovations ■ Predominantly restored Gothic and medieval buildin[
to his own designs ■ Published his ideas on steel rib vaults and skeletons
■ Influenced industrial architecture internationally

● **1814** Born in Paris, France

1836–37 Studies in Italy

1840 Commissioned by writer and minister Mérimée to restore Basilique Sainte-Marie-Madeleine at Vézelay Abbey

1853 Designs for Napoleon III

1854–68 Publishes the *Dictionnaire Raisonne de L'Architecture Française*

1858 Tomb for Duc de Morny is Gothic Revival

1858–72 Publishes the illustrated *Entretiens sur l'Architecture*, in which he discusses the skeleton frame structure applied to iron

1879 Dies in Switzerland

Other Works

Sainte-Marie-Madeleine, restoration, 1840, Vézelay

Château de Roquetaillade, restoration, 1850–70, Mazères

Saint-Louis, restoration, 1852–65, Poissy

Château de Vincennes, restoration, 1860, Paris

Lausanne Cathedral, restoration, 1874

Château de Coucy, restoration, 1875, Aisne

Eugène-Emmanuel Viollet-le-Duc was an unconventi[
theorist, designer, builder, and writer. He worked on m[
eval restorations, which often went well beyond histo[
authenticity, and his writings inspired the Gothic Reviv[
France. He rejected the École des Beaux-Arts and inst[
traveled and studied monuments from the French Mi[
Ages. Employed by the Ministry of Historical Monument[
also worked with Lassau on the restoration of Sainte-C[
pelle and Notre Dame de Paris. Viollet-le-Duc held a st[
belief in Gothic not merely as a style, but as a functional
rational architectural philosophy, which could be applie[
new materials. His work was widely read and influenti[

■ **Renovation of Notre Dame de Paris**, 1845, Paris

Inspired by Victor Hugo's *Hunchback of Notre Dame* and his own personal historical studies, Viollet-le-Duc renovated Notre Dame[its former medieval glory, pla[a new spire above the crossin[and restoring the cathedral's doors and gargoyles.

...âteau de Pierrefonds,
...–85, Oise, France

...efonds was a 12th-century
...e that had been in ruins for
...years when Napoléon Bon-
...e bought it. After visiting
...hâteau in 1850, Napoléon III
...missioned a limited
...ration by Viollet-le-Duc,
...ing to retain the pictur-
...e quality of the ruins. The
...nce and two main towers
...restored to their original
...eval style. Napoléon III was
...pressed that he upscaled
...roject into an imperial resi-
...e. Three hundred workers
...brought in to reconstruct
...ouble terrace wall and
...unding buildings. The ex-
...r retained its military archi-
...re of defensive battle-
...s and small garrisons,
...e the interior was con-
...ted and decorated in the
...ic Revival style. There are
...owers in each corner and
...n each wall. Work was
...d by the Franco-Prussian
...nd the departure of the
...eror in 1870, and Viollet-le-
...died before its completion.

■ Illustrations from *Entretiens sur l'Architecture*, 1858–72

In the 19th century, the fortified city of Carcossonne was in structural decline. As chief architect, Viollet-le-Duc's initial work was the renovation of the cathedral and restorating gargoyles and other Gothic motifs throughout the city. He restored the entire town based on his historical research, which he catalogued in *Entretiens sur l'Architecture*. In this publication he included historic drawings based on his research that served to systematize his restoration work and architectural theories. These two volumes opposed the École des Beaux-Arts, which emphasized that architectural styles and drawings should use the buildings of antiquity as a model. After Viollet-le-Duc's death, his pupil Paul Boeswillwald completed the restoration of the city according to his designs.

Eugène Viollet-le-Duc

James Renwick Jr.

1818, Bloomingdale—1895, New York

■ Leading proponent of Gothic Revival ■ Built mansions and private residences around New York ■ Retained Romanesque elements ■ Combines technical advances in ventilation and structure with decorative features ■ Built churches, colleges, and civil buildings ■ Internationally influential

■ **1818** Born in Bloomingdale, New York

1830 Enters Columbia University at age 12

1843 Gets his first major commission, the Grace Protestant Episcopal Church in New York

1847 Begins buildings at Vassar College

1855 Visits France to study architecture

1858 Builds Charity Hospital, based on Tuileries Palace in France

1859 Begins Corcoran Gallery and introduces the Second Empire style to the United States

1895 Dies in New York

■ **Smithsonian Institute**, 1847–55, Washington, DC

The Smithsonian Institute was known as "the Castle" because of its romantic turrets, round arches, and tapering towers. While the vaulting construction is Gothic Revival, the red sandstone building has strong Romanesque elements, and its proportions refer back to the Picturesque tradition.

19th Century

James Renwick Jr. was the well-educated son of a Columbia College professor. He traveled widely and came into contact with many building styles. Renwick initially worked as an engineer on civil projects. His design for Grace Church, where he introduced Gothic Revival features, was his starting point as an architect. He went on to build many college buildings, private residences, public buildings such as hospitals, the facade on the New York Stock Exchange, and many striking churches. He was a founder of the Delta Psi secret society and designed their fraternity house, St. Anthony Hall. Renwick was a leading architectural figure in the United States, and many of his protégés went on to successful careers. Although he favored Gothic Revival, his buildings include influences from many styles. He introduced the mansard roofs of the early Second Empire in his mansions, as well as using Romanesque features such as round arches.

■ St. Patrick's Cathedral, 1858–79, New York

This Roman Catholic cathedral is one of the largest churches in the United States. Standing on the corner of Fifth Avenue and 51st Street, it showcases Renwick's interpretation of the Decorated style, inspired by the cathedrals at Reims and Cologne and Westminster Abbey. It is a refined example of ecclesiastical workmanship, and has been praised for its purity of style and harmony of proportions.

Other Works by Renwick

Grace Protestant Episcopal Church, 1843, New York

Charity Hospital, 1854–56, Roosevelt Island, New York

Corcoran Gallery, 1859, Washington, DC

Vassar College Main Hall, 1861–65, Poughkeepsie, New York

St. Bartholomew's Church, 1871–72, New York

ty College of York, 1849

City College of York, originally vn as the Free lemy, was said to e first Gothic Re- college building e East Coast. Ren- based his plans arly 14th-century pean centers of ing, such as Cam- e University. He ed for the use of the Gothic style, as it could combine both the decorative and beautiful with the functional. This can be seen in the tall chimneys (for ventilation) and the dormer windows (for light). This design displayed Renwick's mastery of Gothic forms before he began his finest work, St. Patrick's Cathedral.

James Renwick Jr.

Haussmannization of Paris

1852–1870

- Haussmann and Napoléon III renovated Paris ■ Overcrowding had resulted in unhygenic conditions ■ Much of the medieval city was demolished and rebuilt ■ Grand boulevards and avenues were built ■ Haussmann's actions were expensive and controversial ■ The planning was very influential

---

Sidebar:

- **1852–70** Second Empire; Napoléon III decides to modernize Paris
- **1852** Napoléon III creates regulations allowing Baron Haussmann to seize property and demolish large portions of medieval Paris
- **1853** Haussmann is appointed prefect of the Seine Department
- **1854–58** Avenues are carved out of Paris to create symbolic vistas
- **1859** The maximum height of buildings is regulated to 65.6 feet (20 meters)
- **1870** Haussmann is dismissed from his post

By the 1840s the population of Paris had reached aro[und] 1 million and outbreaks of cholera were common in ov[er]crowded urban areas. Baron Georges-Eugène Haussma[nn] was prefect of the Seine Department and responsible [for] the changes to urban Paris under Napoléon III. He focu[sed] on restructuring traffic and improving Paris's sanitary c[on]ditions. Haussmann created large boulevards and av[]enues by widening the main east-west and north-so[uth] roads. Whole medieval districts were demolished, a[nd] boulevards were built in long, straight lines to prov[ide] grand views. He also lengthened the boulevards to cre[ate] rings around the city. Strict rules applied to facades b[uilt] along the new boulevards, and slum areas were clea[red] to the city's outskirts. The Paris model for the city w[as] highly successful, influential, and copied throughout [the] world, but also controversial for its brutality.

■ **Boulevard Haussmann,** ca. 1860–70, Paris

The wide, tree-lined boulev[ard] was designed by and name[d] after Haussmann, and is repre[]sentative of his ideal style. Because of strict regulation[s re]garding the width of streets and sidewalks and the heig[ht of] buildings, most of Paris's bu[ild]ings are uniform in style and size. Boulevard Haussmann [is] typically Parisian and, havin[g] appeared in Impressionist a[rt,] one of the most iconograph[ic] images of the remodeled P[aris.]

352

Urban Planning in France

19th Century

■ 16th Arrondissement, Avenue Foch, 1854, Paris

Haussmann further developed an earlier plan to implement long, straight traversing boulevards. The avenues were meant to create grand vistas through the city and often terminate at major landmarks. Slums and houses, which had grown organically one next to the other to create winding medieval streets, were demolished to make way for the new axes across the city. In order to encourage movement north of the city, the Champs Élysées, Boulevard Malesherbes, and Avenue de l'Impératrice were created. As a result wealthy residents built hotels and apartments in this area.

■ Place de l'Étoile with Arc de Triomphe, 1853, Paris

Haussman redesigned the Place de l'Étoile, from which 12 avenues now radiate. The Arc is the western focal point of the Axe Historique, which forms a straight line along the Champs Élysées to the Louvre.

Other Works

de Boulogne, 1852

de Rivoli, 1852–58

e la Cité, extensive demolition and rebuilding works, –70

e du Châtelet and Crossing of Paris's n-South and East-West s, 1854–58

de Vincennes, 1860

el Dieu, begun 1866

ue de l'Opéra, 1867

Haussmannization of Paris

The Louvre

The Louvre was not heavily used by Louise XVI, who focused on Versailles, b[...] the 18th century it was taken up by Napoléon I and his successors, who nee[...] an ambitious Parisian court. A series of architects were put to work. The grea[...] achievement was the completion of the Grand Dessein and the large C[...] Napoléon, which would link the Tuileries Palace and the Louvre, creating [...] large complex in the heart of Paris.

Under Napoléon I, the construction of the Cour Carrée, the Grande Galerie, [...] a museum began. Corinthian columns were added along the existing colonn[...] During the downfall of the First Empire, Fontaine and Percier continued to v[...] on the interiors, decorating them in a Neoclassical style. When Napoléon III came to power in 1848, he employed L. T. Visconti to draw up new plans, which were passed on to his successor Hector-Martin Lefuel. Lefuel greatly impacted the Louvre's look.

The Cour Napoléon was built by L. T. Visconti and H. M. Lefuel. Lefuel completely remodeled the western facade and, in 1857, the Grand Dessein was completed. The Tuileries burned in 1871, and gardens were designed in its place. Luckily the Louvre's art galleries and new wings survived.

At the Louvre Leufel was uncompromising in the splendor of his designs, using freestanding columns and an abundance of sculptures for the elevated facades. He also used twinned orders to create a grand Neo-Renaissance atmosphere to rival the previous empire.

■ **L. T. Visconti and H. M[...] Lefuel: Cour Napoléon**, 1853–57, Paris

Lefuel demolished houses [...] streets by continuing the R[...] de Rivoli so that the two ch[...] teaux would be connected [...] vast courtyard. The large C[...] Napoléon had cordoned-o[...] gardens and the Place du C[...] rousel, which was used as [...] rade ground. The new Rich[...] Wing contained accommo[...] tion for the ministry and p[...]

19th Century

PAVILLON RICHELIEU

Second Empire in the USA

1855–1880

■ The Second Empire in France during the reign of Napoléon III spread Fren[ch]
styles to the United States ■ Used in mansions, hospitals, government buil[d]-
ings, and cottages ■ The mansard roof gained popularity and was adapted [to]
American tastes ■ The style ended with the economic depression

■ **1855** The Great Exhibition in Paris showcases the Second Empire style and spreads it internationally, inspiring designs in the United States

1857 Additions to the Louvre by Le Vau draw the attention of American architects

1859 Corcoran Gallery, a very early Second Empire–style building in America, is built by J. Renwick Jr.

1867 Second Great Exhibition in Paris

1869–77 General Ulysses S. Grant's administration

1880 Economic depression brings an end to the Second Empire style

■ **Alfred B. Mullet: Old Executive Office Building**, begun 1871, Washington, DC

The Old Executive Office Building in Washington is the masterpiece of archi[tec]t Alfred B. Mullet. Con[structed] from cast iron, [granite and s]late, it took [eleven years to comple]te.

[... and
le Louvre]

Second Empire was an architectural style that coincid[ed]
with the reign of Napoléon III in France and was enthu[si]-
astically applied in America. It was implemented in g[ov]-
ernment buildings, stately homes, asylums, hospitals, a[nd]
private houses. The most recognizable feature of the Sec[-]
ond Empire style is the mansard roof—a steeply pitch[ed]
slated roof developed by François Mansard (p. 236) a[nd]
popular in the time of Louis XIV—which had come b[ack]
into fashion in Napoléon III's Paris. Other prominent f[ea]-
tures of the style include square towers, dormer windo[ws,]
decorative brackets, and the use of paired columns [to]
give the impression of height. Protruding central faca[des]
and pavilions were also common in larger buildi[ngs.]
Because the style's popularity coincided with the admi[nis]-
tration of General Ulysses S. Grant, it was also someti[mes]
referred to as the General Grant style, or simply the M[an]-
sard style.

■ **John McArthur Jr.: Philadelphia City Hall**, begun 1871, Philadelphia

The Philadelphia City Hall is made from granite and brick and is the tallest occupied masonry building in the United States. The steep tower was an innovative architectural feat for its time.

■ **Gridley James Fox Bryant and Arthur Gilman: Old City Hall**, 1862–65, Boston

One of the first government buildings to be built in the Second Empire style, the Old Town Hall has a steep mansard roof and a projecting stepped central bay. The three levels have paired columns, which, with their tall windows, create an imposing facade.

Other Important Works

xander Ramsey
se, by Monroe
ire, 1868, St. Paul,
nesota

w York City Court-
se and Post Office,
Alfred B. Mullet,
9–75

el Vendome,
William G. Preston,
1, Boston

nilton Mansion,
. D. Hall, 1873,
annah

Old Post Office,
by Alfred B. Mullet,
1873–84, St. Louis,
Missouri

South Hall, by David
Farquharson, 1873,
University of California,
Berkeley

Harker Hall,
by Nathan Clifford
Ricker, 1878, University
of Illinois at Urbana-
Champaign

■ **William Boyington, Jacob Weidenmann, J. T. Elletson: Terrace Hill**, 1866–69, Des Moines, Iowa

The large governor's residence is a splendid example of American Second Empire, with its central tower, arched entrance, and attic dormer windows.

Second Empire in the USA

Richard Morris Hunt

1827, Brattleboro—1895, Newport

- Studied in Europe and was inspired by the French Renaissance ■ Brough the Beaux-Arts to the United States ■ One of the founders of the American Institute of Architects ■ Built homes during the United States' Gilded Age
- Set up a workshop in New York ■ Used new industrial materials

Other Works by Hunt

Richard Morris Hunt was born into a wealthy Americ family and moved to Paris with his mother. He was first American to study at the École des Beaux-Arts a trained under Hector Martis Lefuel. After serving as spector of the Louvre extensions and traveling throu out Europe, he returned to the United States and set u workshop in New York based on the French practic Hunt was responsible for bringing the style of the Bea Arts to America and was influenced by Continental sty especially Neorenaissance. He built large, stately hom for wealthy clients such as the Vanderbilts and Asto who had become rich during America's Gilded Age. O of the founders of the American Institute of Architec he became its president in 1888. Hunt was respected the City Beautiful movement, and his Tribune Build was one of the first to have modern-day elevators.

■ **Biltmore Estate**, 1888–95, Asheville, North Carolina

The French Renaissance–inspired summer estate was built for George Washington Vanderbilt II at the height of the Gilded Age.

The estate borrows elements, such as the exposed front stair tower and steeply pitched roof from the famous Blois, Chenonceau, and Chambord châteaux France's Loire Valley.

■ **Pedestal of Statue of Liberty**, 1886, New York Harbor

The Statue of Liberty was given to the people of America by France, on the anniversary of the Declaration of Independence. The conditions were such that while the statue *Liberty Enlightening the World* was being created in France by Frederic-Auguste Bartholdi, a pedestal would be constructed on the American side to support the figure. It is fitting that Hunt, who had lived in both countries, was chosen to design this base. Following initial financial difficulties, the pedestal was completed, standing at 153 feet (47 meters) high and made from 6 tons of granite. It is an integral component to the statue's durability and wind resistance. Two sets of four iron girders run up through the pedestal and join with the statue's internal framework, itself constructed by the great engineer Gustav Eiffel.

etropolitan Museum of Art, drawing by n Fieldhouse, 1890–1902, New York

redesigned the new Metropolitan um when it was moved to Central He updated the museum's Victo-acade, which he based on designs s unbuilt Ministry of Justice. Al-gh he wanted a marble facade, a tone facade was built instead.

Richard Morris Hunt

Henry Hobson Richardson

1838, Priestly Plantation—1886, Brookline

■ Studied at the École des Beaux-Arts in Paris ■ Interpreted Romanesque styles for American towns ■ His architecture was widely copied and came be known as Richardson Romanesque ■ Used rounded circular arches, turrets, and red brick ■ Built churches, domestic houses, warehouses, and ja

1838 Born on the Priestly Plantation in Louisiana, the great-grandson of Joseph Priestly

1860 Studies at the École des Beaux-Arts in Paris

1865 Sets up a practice in Boston with Charles Dexter Gambrill

1871 Builds Brattle Street Church, with a remarkable frieze by Frédéric-Auguste Bartholdi

1881 Builds Austin Hall at Harvard on a cross-axial, classic French plan

1882 Travels to Europe again and sees original Byzantine architecture

1886 Dies in Brookline, Massachusetts

Henry Hobson Richardson trained in engineering at H vard Universtity in Boston and was the second Ameri ever to attend the École des Beaux-Arts in Paris. There worked with Theodore Labrouste and J. I. Hittorf. On return to America he settled in Boston. Instead of work in the grand Beaux-Arts style or the Gothic Revival of peers, Richardson developed his own individual s based on Romanesque forms. He used large semicirc arches, single towers, and rusticated brick facades on buildings, which were monumentally heavy, yet simpl line. He built many nonresidential projects such a braries and warehouses. In his domestic buildings, ma in New England, he championed the Arts and Cr movement and demonstrated his skills and workm ship. His style was extremely popular, and spr throughout America and Europe. Named after him, style is known as Richardson Romanesque.

■ **Sever Hall at Harvard University**, 1840, Boston

The large red facade of the Sever Hall at Harvard University contains 60 different types of molded and carved bricks. The buildings' two unique turrets are built into both the exterior wall and the hipped roof. While stone was traditionally used in Romanesque buildings, brick creates a strong yet subtle look.

19th Century

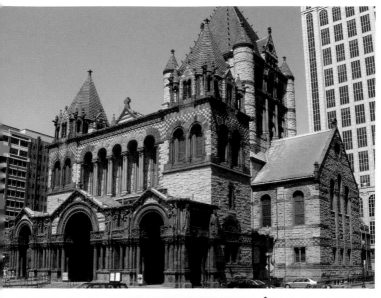

Works by Richardson

ttle Square Church,
71–73, Boston

liam Watts Sherman
use, 1876, Newport,
ode Island

es Free Library, 1877–79,
rth Easton, Massachusetts

any City Hall, 1880–82,
any, New York

homas Crane Public
ary, 1882, Quincy,
achusetts

library is one of Richard-
s smallest works, yet his
t refined. There are
es on the east and west
s, and one more lying
metrically to the axis.

Trinity Church, 1872–77, Boston

Boston's Trinity Church is the embodiment of Richardson Romanesque. With its large crossing tower and deep-set arches, the structural thickness recalls traditional Romanesque styles. The layout is based on a Greek cross and draws influences from the floor plan of St. Mark's in Venice and the Salamanca Cathedral in Spain. Its interior demonstrates the expert craftsmanship common to the Arts and Crafts movement. Because the church was built on soft ground, it rests on wooden supports to prevent sinking.

Henry Hobson Richardson

Exoticism

1757–1878

■ Exoticist architecture included elements from Moorish, Near Eastern, Egyptian, Indian, and Oriental styles ■ Colored brick, arched or round windows, cupolas, bulbous domes, and towers were popular ■ Moorish aesthetics were internationally adopted for synagogue designs

● **1757–62** Chambers builds the Pagoda in the Royal Botanic Gardens, Kew

1832 *Tales of the Alhambra* by Washington Irving publicizes Moorish design

1858 The elephant house at Antwerp Zoo is built in the style of an Egyptian temple

1866 Isaac M. Wise Temple is built, the first Moorish-style temple in the United States

1867 A mosque is exhibited for the first time by the Ottoman Empire at the World's Fair in Paris

1878 Algeria exhibits various national monuments at the World's Fair

Among the many revival movements of the 19th cent there was an increase in the attention given foreign cultures following colonialism. Exoticism and C entalism were explored in the architectural designs of Western world. The Moorish Revival drew from the Isla architecture of North Africa, Spain, and Portugal, and e ments such as colored tiling, onion domes, and reflect metals were incorporated into the architecture of Euro and the United States. As the medieval Moorish, or N dejar, age had been relatively peaceful and product for European Jews, this style was taken up internation for synagogue design. There was an ongoing fascinat with Eastern aesthetics. Styles from the Far East and In were brought back and adapted by colonists, and wealthy classes often built teahouses and ornate leis rooms in the Asian style.

...uard Knoblauch and ...rich August Stuehler: ...ynagogue, 1859–66,

...'s New Synagogue was ...d Knoblauch's last build- ...nd was completed by ...ich August Stuehler after

...n Nash: Royal Pavilion, ...-23, Brighton, UK

...oyal Pavilion, remodeled ...ummer retreat for the ...e regent, displays a mix of ...h and Far Eastern influ- ... The white exterior, with ...bous domes and mina- ...esembles the Taj Mahal, ...the luxurious chinoiseries ...riental designs of the inte-

his death. The gold dome dominates the 164-foot- (50-meter-) high structure and has gilt ribs to accentuate the arabesque structuring. On each side of the dome are two smaller domed towers that resemble the minarets of a mosque. The building

rior are based on popular styles in the Far East. Exotic objects and styles were popular during the Regency era for showing off wealth. Nash adopted the use of iron and, through the design of the Royal Pavilion, demonstrated its use as a malleable yet durable material, thereby embracing both exoticism and the advancements of the Industrial Revolution.

itself is made from different colored and shaped terra cotta bricks, and the entrance arcades are exact copies of those at the Alhambra in Granada. The building's frame is constructed of iron, a new building material for its time.

Other Works

Pagoda, Royal Botanic Gardens, by Sir William Chambers, 1757–62, Kew, London

Munich Synagogue, by Friedrich von Gartner, 1832

Dresden Synagogue, by Gottfried Semper, 1837

Isaac M. Wise Temple, by James Wilson, 1866, Cincinatti

Charles Garnier

1825, Paris—1898, Paris

■ French architect who built in the time of Napoléon III ■ Studied at the É[cole] des Beaux-Arts and winner of Grand Prix traveling scholarship ■ Worked w[ith] Eiffel and Viollet-le-Duc ■ Built operas and casinos in a Neo-Baroque style ■ His architecture was often elaborate and focused on Parisian high society

Jean-Louis-Charles Garnier attended the École de De[ssin] and studied at the École des Beaux-Arts in Paris, wher[e he] won the Grand Prix scholarship to Rome. He also trave[led] to Turkey and Greece, where he was greatly influence[d by] Byzantine aesthetics. He studied with L. H. Lebas [and] worked briefly with Viollet-le-Duc (p. 348) and Ballu. [Gar]nier did not receive many private commissions, but [the] elegant and glamorous designs of the Paris Opéra [and] Monte Carlo Casino epitomize Second Empire archi[tec]ture in France. Although he expertly used industrial [ma]terials for structural support, Garnier always maintai[ned] a paramount level of style and décor.

**ris Opéra (Palais
ier)**, exterior and interior
h, 1860–75

aris Opéra displays the
influences of the di-
ng movements prevalent
École des Beaux-Arts. The

nte Carlo Casino,
–85

on the Riviera, this river-
eo-Baroque building con-
of a casino, an opera
e, a hotel, and colorful
g gardens. The opera is
act, albeit smaller, dupli-
f the Paris Opéra, and is
ated in rich reds and gold,
murals and chandeliers.
asino itself has Rococo tur-
opper cupolas, and an or-
marble interior. The atrium
rounded by 28 onyx Ionic
ns.

dramatic Baroque foyer and
grand staircase provided a
space for the high society to be
seen in, and Neo-Gothic details
fuse seamlessly with the new
materials used in its construction. Cast-iron girders reinforce

the great weight of the dome,
interiors, facade, and lighting
fixtures, which include a seven-
ton crystal and bronze chande-
lier. The Opéra heralded a new
era of construction possibilities
using new materials.

Other Works by Garnier
Villa Bordighera, 1874, Bordighera, Italy
Cercle de la Librairie, 1878–79, Paris
Tomb of Bizet, 1880, Père-Lachaise Cemetery, Paris
Vittel Casino and Thermal Spa, 1882–85, Provence
Panorama Français, 1882, Paris
Tomb of Offenbach, 1883, Montmartre Cemetery, Paris
Nice Observatory, 1886, Provence

Charles Garnier

Henri Labrouste

1801, Paris–1875, Fontainebleau

■ Renowned French industrial architect ■ Was a Rationalist ■ Set up a
workshop in Paris ■ Famous for his two acclaimed large libraries ■ Use
cast iron for structural and aesthetic purposes ■ The publishing of his
ideology gained him critical esteem

■ **1801** Born in Paris

1819 Attends École des
Beaux-Arts at the age of 18

1823 Works on Saint-
Pierre-du-Gros-Caillou
with E. H. Godde

1824 Wins Prix de Rome

1825–30 Stays in Rome
and studies at the Villa
Medici

1828 Writes on the reconstruction of the Paestum
Temples (published later,
in 1877)

1839 Receives the commission to build Biblio-
thèque Sainte-Geneviève

1875 Dies in Fontainbleau

Henri Labrouste came from a family of French archit
that included his brother Theodore. Extremely taler
he studied at the École des Beaux-Arts under A. L. T.
doyer and L. H. Lebas, and attended the French Acad
in Rome. He wrote a groundbreaking dissertation or
Doric temples at Paestum, which challenged the cla
ideology and examined the environmental, social,
historical factors that affect architectural developm
Influenced by engineer Émile Jacques Gilbert and his
temporary Félix Duban, Labrouste emphasized a Ra
nalist approach to architecture, and on his return to
established a workshop. Labrouste's major contribu
was his revolutionary use of exposed cast iron, not jus
structural support and durability, but as an elegant
ornamental resource material. His libraries in Paris s
worldwide standard.

Other Works

Saint-Pierre-du-Gros-
Caillou, 1823, Paris

Tombe Brunet et Ri-
dèle,1837, Montparnasse,
Paris

Asylum, 1837–38, Lau-
sanne, Switzerland

Prison, 1840, Alessandria,
Italy

Le Grand Séminaire,
1853–72, Rennes

Hôtel Fould, 1856–58,
Paris

Hôtel Thouret, 1860, Paris

■ **Bibliothèque Sainte-G
viève**, 1845–50, Paris

The Saint Geneviève Librar
was the first nonutilitarian
lic building to show expose
metalwork. Sixteen slende
cast-iron columns support
scrolled arched canopy. Th
columns also separate the
oblong building into two b
vaults. The result is both el
gant and functional. The ex
rior is in Cinquecento style
round-arched windows. Th
plan became a model for o
libraries.

bliothèque Nationale de ce, 1854–75, Paris

buste's extensions to the nal Library continued the sure of industrial and cast- iron construction. The reading room has nine interlinking terra- cotta domes, supported by thin columns, and is illuminated through glass openings in the apex of each dome. The book- stack area is five levels high, and grilled floors allow light to pen- etrate down. Latticework and rivets function as decoration.

Henri Labrouste

20th Century before 1945

Walter Gropius: Bauhaus, 1925, Dessau

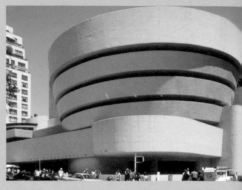

1900–1920
Art Nouveau

The organic designs of Art Nouveau mix industrial materials with ornamentation

Otto Wagner p. 394
Antoni Gaudí p. 390
Victor Horta p. 386

p. 387

1900–1925
Early Modernism

Development and availability of materials allows for the new shapes of Modernism

Louis Sullivan p. 378
Frank Lloyd Wright
p. 382
Peter Behrens p. 400
Adolf Loos p. 398

1900–1930s
Architecture Totalitarian States

Political upheaval lea to styles that reflected the strength of the government

Marcello Piacentini
Boris Iofan
Werner March
Giuseppe Terragni
Albert Speer

900 to 1945

910–1925
xpressionism, De Stijl,
nd Neue Sachlichkeit

rchitectural movements develop
uickly with diverse theories on purpose
nd aesthetics

alter Gropius p. 406
rich Mendelsohn p. 402
homas Gerrit Rietveld p. 404

p. 403

| 1925 | 1930 | 1935 | 1940 | 1945 |

925–1940
odernism
nd Art Deco

aterials and craft are
eveloped by various
hools, which deal with
namentation in differ-
t ways

uno Taut
illiam van Alen
rl Ehn
ik Gunnar Asplund
418
ans Scharoun
var Aalto p. 418

p. 419

1930–
International
Modernism

Simple, unornamented
buildings are constructed
of glass and steel

Le Corbusier p. 412
J. J. P. Oud
Pierre Jeanneret

Early 20th Century

When Otto Wagner published his *Moderne Architektur* in 1896, the developments of modern architecture over the next 50 years were simply inconceivable. For Wagner, absolute beauty was the essence of architecture. The idea of a "categorical imperative" for building implied an objective and attainable architectural perfection. It took only two decades for this ideal architectural bubble to burst in light of the economic, political, and social realities of 1920s Europe. Yet what Wagner and his American counterpart Louis Sullivan did for Modern architecture cannot be underestimated. By addressing structure and ornament together, they created a new functionally conscious architecture, which was acceptable to the general public because it took the aesthetics of the city into consideration. Without compromising the Modern client's needs, they achieved a functional beauty.

**einhard &
meister,
rison &
cmurray, and
od & Fouil-
ux: Rockefeller
ter, RCA
lding**, mainly
2–39, New York

**rank Lloyd
ght: Price
ver**, 1952–56,
lesville, OK

Reconfiguring the American City: from Chicago to Suburbia

Two opposing trends have governed American architecture since the late 19th century. The first was
indiscriminate densification, initially realized in
Chicago after the Great Fire and later in New York.
The cost of land rose dramatically and the only way to
stay competitive was to build up. The automobile had
not yet become dominant and centrality meant
business. The economic booms and busts of early
20th-century America made speculative construction
profitable but dangerous. With the popularization of
the car, suburbia became a feasible alternative to the
inner city. Yet without organized government support, suburban development was in the hands of the
middle classes. With the efforts of Frank Lloyd Wright,
suburbia went from a housing solution to a national
ideology. In decentralized suburban living, Wright
saw the ultimate in moral democratic existence.

The House Exploded: Wright, Mies, and Le Corbusier

Suburban development in Europe never reached American proportions, but on both continents it was the single-family home, rather than apartment buildings, that became a forum for architectural experimentation. The early villas of Wright, Mies, and Le Corbusier were studied sculptures for living, where Functionalism catered to the needs of wealthy clients. In some ways the Tugendhat and Savoye houses were an ultimate synthesis of function and beauty. Only later did these experiments in residential planning lead to a reconceptualization of mass housing. The free plan, propagated by all three architects, was scaled down to apartment size. Members of the Bauhaus produced detailed studies of minimal requirements for functional living that, aided by mass production, suddenly made Modernist housing the cheapest path to residential equality.

■ **Walter Gropi**
Houses for Bau
haus Masters,
1925–26, Dessau
Germany

■ **Mies van der**
Rohe: Apartme
Block at the We
senhofsiedlun
1927, Stuttgart

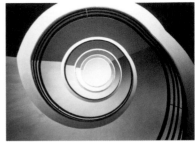

ntoni Gaudi:
nia Güell
pel,
3–1914,
elona

rich Mendel-
n: Metal
kers Union
ding, staircase,
9–30, Berlin

Regionalism: from Gaudí to Aalto

Parallel to the Functionalist approach, a generation of European architects had developed who either rejected the maxim of "existence minimum" altogether or tended toward a more humanistic approach. These individuals often found inspiration in traditional styles and their work had strong political connotations. Antoni Gaudí took the Catalan vernacular and transformed it into a magical world of dragons and warriors, producing some of the most structurally innovative work of the early 20th century. Following Gunnar Asplund, architects like Aino and Alvar Aalto took the Nordic vernacular and mainstream Modernism, transforming the two into a style that was universal enough to be exported throughout the world. In Germany, Mendelsohn was able to build quirky anthropomorphic buildings with sophisticated contributions from the sleek International style.

The International Style

Modernism was defined by two sets of principles that were extrapolated over the entire body of architectural production—the concepts outlined in 1920s luxury villas and industrial architecture. Peter Behrens's work gave German industrial infrastructure a new face. Design began to apply to industry and consequently industrial design was invented as a way to reconcile mass production with artistic ambition. At the Bauhaus, this knowledge was synthesized and Functionalism emerged as the architectural and ethical stance of the European avant-garde. Yet the word *Functionalism* was often insufficient to explain Modernist preoccupations with form and aesthetics. Thus Philip Johnson, an influential American architect and critic, coined the term *International style* to describe the efforts of a group of influential Modernists working between 1922 and 1932.

■ **Peter Behren** **Technical** **Administration** **Building, Höch** **Dye Factory,** 1920–25, Frankf am Main

**Mies van der
Rohe: Crown Hall**,
1950–56, Chicago

**Marcel Breuer:
Wassily Steel
Tube Chair**, 1925

New Realities

Within a few years of Philip Johnson's New York Exhibition of 1932, many of the European architects featured were either forced or chose to move to the United States in the wake of World War II. The Bauhaus was shut down in 1933 and by 1938 Mies van der Rohe, Walter Gropius, and Marcel Breuer had all accepted influential posts at major American universities. Erich Mendelsohn followed in 1941, by which point avant-garde architectural production in Germany had ceased. North America thus became the hub of Modernist architectural and educational practice. The new cultural and geographic reality of American cities was the perfect setting to perform architectural experiments, and the strong American economy allowed for monumental and comprehensive projects. Only Le Corbusier stayed behind in Europe to develop a unique and personal style.

Introduction

Louis Sullivan

1856, Boston–1924, Chicago

■ Father of American Modernism ■ Endeavored to establish an appropriate aesthetic for the skyscraper ■ Used terra cotta, brick, and stone to clad his steel buildings ■ Interested in organic architecture and ornamen[t] ■ Teacher and employer of Frank Lloyd Wright

■ **1856** Born in Boston
1872 Studies at MIT
1874 Studies at the École des Beaux-Arts in Paris
1879 Joins Dankmar Adler as an assistant
1880 Becomes partners with Adler and forms Adler and Sullivan Architects
1893 Participates in the World's Columbian Exposition held in Chicago
1896 Publishes *The Tall Office Building Artistically Considered*
1924 Dies in Chicago

Louis Sullivan and his partner Dankmar Adler (1844–19[0?] may not have invented steel frame construction, but th[ey] were the first to put convincing cladding and steel stru[c]tures together, designing high-quality skyscrapers [in] Chicago. For Sullivan the skyscraper was not only an [ex]ercise in efficient capitalist building, but also an aesthe[tic] and formal problem. Relying on the Classical division [of] the facade into base, middle, and top, or cornice, he i[so]lated the base, giving it an intense decorative treatme[nt.] The middle was used to emphasize either the vertica[lity] of the composition, as in the Wainwright Building, or [its] horizontality, as in the Carson, Pirie, Scott Departme[nt] Store. The top was where Sullivan's id[eas] of organic ornament really triumph[ed.] From its roots at the base, the vege[tal] ornamentation twined up the slen[der] piers, blooming around the windo[ws] of the cornice.

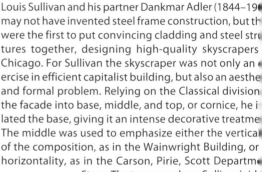

■ **Guaranty Building**, 1894–95, Buffalo, New York

Built with Dankmar Adler, at the Guaranty Building Sullivan fused ornamentation with cladding so that they represented a unified skin. Verticality was expressed effectively here, because instead of

having the piers en[d] abruptly, they elegantly merged wit[h] the cornice and we[re] subtly ornamente[d.] The building typifi[es] Sullivan's mantra t[hat] "form follows function." After th[e] Guaranty Building[,] of construction, Dankmar Adler an[d] Sullivan dissolved their partnership.

hlesinger and Mayer
artment Store (now
on, Pirie, Scott),
–1904, Chicago

ough Carson, Pirie, Scott
wed Sullivan's typical tri-
te facade division, it was a
nct step away from his ear-
ffice buildings, which were
d forms that emphasized
cal hierarchy. The depart-
store posed a different
al problem: the articulation
e main volume had to be
titive enough so that the
e could easily grow and
ge. Also, each floor is de-
ed as a continuous horizon-
ublic space and needed to
xpressed as such. The result
ystem of vertical and hori-
al steel members of almost
l thickness, which allow for
e window surfaces. Sul-
's design foreshadowed
niform grids of Modernist
tecture that would make
crapers possible.

🏛 **Wainwright Building**, 1890–91, St. Louis

Sullivan understood that to stress verticality he
needed to strengthen the vertical pier and sup-
press the spandrel, the horizontal connecting elements. The wall is eliminated in favor of a grid of
pronounced structural verticals and recessed
ornamented horizontals.

Other Important Works by Sullivan	
Auditorium Building, 1885–89, Chicago	National Farmers' Bank (now Norwest Bank), 1907–08, Owatonna, Minnesota
Walker Warehouse, 1888–89, Chicago	People's Federal Savings & Loan Association, 1917–18, Sidney, Ohio
Getty Tomb, 1890, Chicago	
Wainwright Tomb, 1892, St. Louis, Missouri	

Louis Sullivan

379

Early Modernism in the United States

Steel Frames

Iron and, later, steel had been used for bridges and in larger public buildings throughout the 19th century, but it was not until the 1880s in Chicago that the structural steel frame was invented. After the fire of 1871, investors needed to increase their usable floor area in order to remain competitive. Conventional masonry allowed for tall buildings, but at 16 stories the wall thickness at ground level exceeded five feet. The answer was to replace load-bearing masonry with a uniform and flexible steel skeleton.

◀ **Cass Gilbert: Woolworth Building**, under construction, 1912, New York

Steel frame construction and elevators meant that height was no longer a limiting factor. Although by 1910 steel had been in use for two decades, a 50-story building posed new challenges—wind loads, foundation stability, and fire safety were all factors needing thorough research.

🏛 **Daniel Burnham and Charles Atwood: Reliance Building**, 1890–95, Chicago

One of the earliest and most elegant incarnations of the skyscraper, a wall of glass and white terra cotta hangs from the riveted, wind-braced steel frame. Thin vertical members rest on continuous spandrel panels, emphasizing the stacked horizontality of skeleton construction.

▶ **William Le Baron Jenney: Second Leiter Building**, 1889–91, Chicago

The second incarnation of the Leiter Building was a mature example of steel frame construction. A self-supporting, fireproof metal frame was draped in a comparatively light masonry curtain wall. With no load-bearing masonry left, all the loads had to be carried by the steel skeleton. It was erected before cladding and partition walls were added, determining the building's layout.

20th Century before 1945

**...aniel Burnham: Flatiron Build-
...Fuller Building)**, 1901–03,
...York

...ough Louis Sullivan had
...dy addressed questions of
...position in tall buildings, the
...alent Beaux-Arts movement
...ll prepared to deal with a
...building type. Historical
...els had to be reinter-
...ed to accommodate the
...ortions of the office
...r.

Frank Lloyd Wright

1867, Richland Center—1959, Phoenix

■ Iconic figure of American architecture ■ Spanned generations and style
■ Developed the Prairie style ■ Used local materials and adapted his pl
to the surrounding landscape ■ Published utopian urban planning
projects ■ Influenced the development of American suburbs

In the late 1890s Frank Lloyd Wright was building
stract, geometric forms while the Beaux-Arts moven
dominated Europe and North America. In Europe, Wrig
Art Nouveau contemporaries were grappling with the
lationships between ornament and structure, but v
much less interested in the complex spaces and in
secting volumes that Wright began to explore at
outset of his career. Influenced by the Shingle style, v
its sprawling porches and sheltering roofs, as well a
Louis Sullivan's (p. 378) clarity of volume and unique
namentation, Wright developed his own manner, kno
as the Prairie style. "Prairie" proved only a symbolic na
for Wright's houses were almost exclusively suburb
built on relatively small and regular plots. The
encompassing horizon of the true prairies led Wrigh
an exaggerated horizontality that creates an illusio
space, which otherwise is unavailable within the

■ **Robie House**, 1908–10,
Chicago

In the center of the Robie
House, the hearth—an area
consisting of the fireplace a
staircase—stands out amid
open floor plan. Dramatic c
tilevered roofs shelter the
rooms, large courts, and
porches. Low walls, a burie
garden, and views in all dire
tions give a feeling of both
freedom and protection by
corporating open-air space
into the shelter of the hom

■ **Unity Temple**, interior view, 1905–08, Oak Park, Illinois

Inside the temple, two levels of balconies hover over the central square seating area on the main level, enabling the entire congregation to sit in close proximity to one another. Protected from the noisy street behind the building, the space is discreetly entered from below and lit only from the top with a combination of clerestory windows and stained glass skylights. The interior is not ornamented, but rather unified with sets of intersecting volumes, planes, and lines.

383

Other Important Works by F. L. Wright

ight House and dio, begun 1889, Park, Illinois

nslow House, 1894, er Forest, Illinois

kin Building, 2–06, Buffalo, w York

esin East, 1911, ing Green, consin

perial Hotel, 1915, yo

Hollyhock House, 1919–21, Los Angeles

Ennis House, 1923, Los Angeles

Rosenbaum House, 1939, Florence, Alabama

Price Tower, 1954–55, Bartlesville, Oklahoma

Annunciation Greek Orthodox Church, 1959–61, Milwaukee, Wisconsin

allingwater, 5, Mill Run, nsylvania

ngwater stirred the gination of a ety yearning for a uded, utopian life. n pillars rising out e rock, ocher- red reinforced crete trays hover

over each other and the waterfall below. In elevation, the entire composition appears flat. The volumes are arranged so masterfully that the walls seem to slide past each other in an abstract manner, like a de Stijl graphic.

Frank Lloyd Wright

confines of the suburban plot. After a period of divergent trends between 1914 and 1936, Wright returned to design in a completely new context. Unable to practice in Nazi Germany, leaders of the European Modernist movement like Walter Gropius (p. 406), Erich Mendelsohn (p. 402), and Mies van der Rohe (p. 434) resettled and took influential positions at North American universities. Wright adapted to this new face of American Modernism, designing one of the most celebrated houses of the 20th century—Fallingwater. The house was an essay on site-specific or "organic" architecture, as Wright called it. Despite the stress he put on integrating architecture with the natural environment, Wright's utopian schemes for suburbs were environmentally devastating, promoting single-family acreages and requiring a heavy reliance on cars. In his late career, Wright's designs turned to intensely futuristic imagery. The swelling spiral of the Guggenheim Museum in New York was the conclusion of his architectural journey.

■ **Johnson Wax Administration Building**, interior view 1936–39, Racine, Wisconsin

The consistent logic of Wright residential projects is also seen in his public and commercial buildings. From the Larkin Building through Unity Temple and Johnson Wax to the Guggenheim, Wright always drew energy from a top-lit central atrium. In most cases, these atria were not used as lobby or circulation spaces, but rather served as main workrooms for administrative staff. In the ceiling of the Johnson Wax building, the relationships between solid and void, load and support are reversed. Defying structural logic, tapered columns with blooming capitals float up to a glass ceiling.

**Solomon R. Guggenheim
Museum**, atrium with spiral
ramp, 1956–59, New York

The Guggenheim sparked a discussion on museum architecture that still continues today. Should museums provide neutral rooms for artwork to speak alone, or should architects create unique exhibition spaces

**Solomon R. Guggenheim
Museum**, exterior, 1956–59,
New York

Accentuating the elevation of the building, the exterior of the Guggenheim reflects the spiral-ing interior ramp. Rather than diminishing in size with height, as most buildings do, the museum instead grows larger. The crowning coil sits precariously on a horizontal plinth, which itself bulges restlessly, adding to the alien, almost alive feeling of the whole composition.

that in and of themselves are works of art? For the Guggenheim, Wright chose to design a ramp where paintings spiral down a continuous curving wall. In no other museum is the exhibition space entirely uninterrupted and therefore perfectly suited to chronological exhibitions. Transcending time

and gravity, the visitor takes an elevator to the top floor and then leisurely strolls through the narrative of art back down to reality. In relation to the sloping floor, and indeed to the viewer, each work hangs crooked—its proper alignment dictated only by the immutable power of gravity.

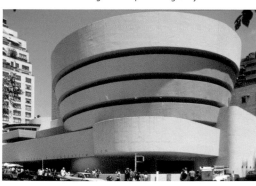

Frank Lloyd Wright

Victor Horta

1861, Ghent–1947, Brussels

■ Leading Art Nouveau architect ■ Designed luxurious homes for the Belgian industrial and political elite ■ Used iron extensively in residential buildings ■ Modeled his stone, metal, and woodwork in plaster ■ Worked in a variety of styles to create both avant-garde and conservative buildings

■ **1861** Born in Ghent, Belgium

1881 Enrolls at the Academy of Fine Arts in Brussels

1889 Visits the Exposition Universelle in Paris, including the Eiffel Tower

1892–1911 Professor at the Université Libre de Bruxelles

1894 President of the Belgian Architectural Society

1913–16 Serves as director of the Academy of Arts in Brussels

1916–19 Political exile in the United States

1947 Dies in Brussels

More than any other Art Nouveau architect, Victor Horta maintained an impeccable continuity of line in his designs. His serpentine ornamentations in paint, metal, and glass flow as freely as the innovative spaces they adorn. Horta's comprehensive design process was widely misunderstood in the years following his death. After public opinion shifted against Art Nouveau, his buildings were considered to be collections of superfluous ornament and their remarkable spatial qualities were ignored. After the demolition of several of his buildings, including Maison du Peuple, there was a positive shift in the public opinion of his work. Horta's principal contribution to architectural history lay neither in revolutionary planning techniques nor in the use of totally new structural systems, but was simply intensely personal—he designed with an irreproducible delicacy and beauty.

Other Important Works

Hôtel Autrique, 1893, Brussels

Hôtel Tassel, 1894, Brussels

Hôtel Solvay, 1895–1900, Brussels

Magasins Waucquez, 1903, Brussels

Palais des Beaux-Arts, 1928, Brussels

Brussels-Central Railway Station, 1937

■ **Dubois House and Studio**
1901, Brussels

The tensile qualities of steel gave Horta the opportunity to structurally explode his house, creating large open spaces with minimal supports. In the 19th century iron had been used in combination with glass in totally glazed structures like the Crystal Palace. On a residential scale, this allowed for very large openings in the facade, such as the unique windows of the Dubois House.

ôtel van Eetvelde,
rior, 1895–98, Brussels

Hôtel van Eetvelde follows
same additive logic as Hor-
own home and studio. The
ding consists of the house
er, a corner rental building,
a small addition. The
de, therefore, is a result of
e separate additive con-
ction phases. The main
se betrays Horta's interest
on and glass frames, which
ould later develop in his
er public buildings. Horta
the first architect to use
liberally in domestic inte-
. The metal had been em-
ed extensively in the 19th
ury, but was considered
propriate for residential
Horta's use of iron, how-
, such as in the entrance
here, showcased it as a ma-
l of both strength and deli-
, of structural function and
tlessly elegant decoration.

■ **Horta Museum**,
main stair, 1898–1902,
Brussels

Through his precise
detailing, Horta mas-
terfully joined building
and ornamental
materials with different
physical and structural
properties. In Horta's
own former home,
wood, iron, and glass
all flow seamlessly
around the skylight in
the main stair. The mal-
leability of iron allowed
Horta to experiment
with flowing tendrils
on columns, capitals,
and balustrades, which
are echoed by delicate
wall finishes and floor
mosaics. The tensile
qualities of iron gave
him the opportunity to
structurally expand his
houses, creating large
open spaces with min-
imal supports. Now the
Horta Museum, the
building contains
Horta's and his con-
temporaries' Art Nou-
veau interior designs,
designs for furniture,
utensils, and objects.

Victor Horta

Hector Guimard

1867, Lyon—1942, New York

■ One of the most famous Art Nouveau architects, designers, and writers who helped to popularize the movement ■ Designer of the Art Nouveau metro stops in Paris ■ Inspired by Viollet-Le-Duc and Victor Horta ■ Fus abstract and new ornamental lines with engineering ingenuity

1867 Born in France

1882 Studies at the École des Arts Décoratifs

1885 Studies at the École des Beaux Arts in Paris

1889 Becomes a professor at the École des Arts Décoratifs

1895 Visits Victor Horta's Hôtel Tassel, where he is greatly inspired

1898 Designs the Castel Béranger, which is criticized for its abstract forms

1928 Builds his last work, the apartments on Rue Greuze

1938 Flees to New York

1942 Dies in New York

Hector Guimard's sinuous works meld architecture w design. Greatly inspired by the work of Viollet-Le-D (p. 348) and the expressive lines of Victor Horta (p. 3 Guimard transformed Paris. Also a great designer of jects, he brought industrial materials such as steel, ir glass, and prefabricated elements to the French public though famed for ornamentation, Guimard was also an complished engineer. The Humbert-de-Romans Con Hall in Paris employed a structurally innovative frame t created excellent acoustics. Despite his ingenu Guimard's work was met with heavy criticism. His highly stract shapes shocked Parisians, and the use of green s in his designs for the Paris metro was deemed too Gerr in style and unworthy of gracing the French capital; m were demolished in the early 20th century.

■ **Entrance Gate of the Castle Béranger,**
1894–98, Paris

Along with his Paris metro entrances, the Castle Béranger is Guimard's most famous work. He headed both the structural design and the interior design, creating a total work that resembles a twisting garden. The apartment building was one of the first Art Nouveau buildings in France and helped to popularize the style.

19th Century

Other Works by Guimar

Maison Coilliot, 1899–1900, Lille

Castel Henriette, 1903, Sèvres

La Sapinière, 1903, Hermanville-sur-Mer

Castel d'Orge, 1904, Villemoisson-sur-Orge

11 Rue François-Millet, 191(Paris

Hôtel Mezzara, 1911, Paris

Synagogue at 10 Rue Pavée 1913, Paris

■ **Hôtel Guimard**, 1912, Paris

Guimard's own residence, built as a wedding present for his wife, was constructed on an irregular, triangularly shaped plot. Because of this, the building had to be structurally and compositionally innovative. Guimard arranged the interior rooms in an unconventional manner, shifting the layout from floor to floor so as not to load the asymmetrical exterior walls with too much weight. Guimard designed most of the objects and interior fixtures, including the Art Nouveau fabrics. When the work was completed, Guimard's contemporaries condemned his abstract lines.

Métro Station at Porte Dauphine, 1899, Paris

Guimard's metro entrances brought the flowing lines and shapes of Art Nouveau decoration into the urban realm. Constructed in the same manner as London's Crystal Palace—from prefabricated pieces—the design undermines the strength of the structure's materials, appearing delicate because of its graceful lines. By using iron and enameled steel in public, infrastructural buildings, Guimard reinvented the materials as part of the public sphere, releasing them from their industrial nature. Many of his gates, map displays, flowering lights, and curved canopies remain, and these are synonymous with the Paris Métro.

Antoni Gaudí

1852, Reus—1926, Barcelona

■ Greatly influenced by Eugène Viollet-le-Duc ■ Interested in botany as well as biomorphic and geomorphic forms ■ Built with stone, concrete, steel, and ceramics ■ Used symbolic sculpture as a didactic tool ■ Drew upon Catalan styles and Islamic architecture from the Iberian Peninsula

1852 Born in Reus, near Barcelona

1873–77 Studies at the newly opened Faculty of Architecture at the University of Barcelona

1877 Opens his first office in Barcelona

1883 Appointed chief architect of Sagrada Família

1887 Studies traditional ceramics with Domènech i Montaner

1888 Contributes to the Exposición Universal in Barcelona

1906 Moves into the showhouse in Park Güell

1914 Declines all commissions, to focus on the Sagrada Família

1926 Dies in Barcelona

■ **Casa Milà**, 1906–10, Barcelona

At the Casa Milà, simple roof vents are transformed into groups of masked guardians keeping watch over the hills of Barcelona. Inside, complex apartments with polygonal rooms resembling a honeycomb change from floor to floor, responding to the undulating shape of the facade.

Antoni Gaudí synthesized a multitude of influences i a magnificent style that is so personal it defies categozation. Parallel to Art Nouveau and incorporating organic forms of the style, his work is part of the Cata Modernisme movement, developed in the context of Gothic Revivalist training and love for medieval Medi ranean architecture. Reinterpreting early Modernist m tors, like John Ruskin and Eugène Viollet-le-Duc (p. 3 Gaudí studied structure as a way to convey imaginat forms. In the end Gaudí's architecture was a product of intense Catholic faith, his dedication to Catalan cultu and his obsession with nature's structural logic.

Sagrada Família, 1883–,
Barcelona

In Sagrada Família Gaudí reinterpreted the structural principles of Gothic architecture. He eliminated buttresses and substituted them with slanted columns that could take the lateral loads created by his parabolic vaults. He tested the system with brilliant hanging models made of wire, sandbags, and canvas that when inverted gave the proper distribution of forces. Gaudí projected that it would take 200 years to build the Sagrada Família. No other architect since the Middle Ages had attempted a building of such magnitude. Gaudí understood that to build a church surpassing the achievements of Gothic masters was to respect the medieval process. Paradoxically, as construction on the church continues, the institution devoted to funding this medieval undertaking posts progress reports on their foundation Web site.

■ **Park Güell**, 1900–14,
Barcelona

Eager to replicate the English garden style in the city of Barcelona, Count Güell commissioned a large park and a development of villas for the Catalan bourgeoisie. The residential district was never completed, but the park attests to Gaudí's romantic imagination. Mosaic dragons guard a caricatural Doric colonnade, as viaducts of piled stone weave

Other Works by Gaudí
Finca Güell, 1883–85, Barcelona
Casa Vicens, 1883–88, Barcelona
Palau Güell, 1886–90, Barcelona
Palacio Episcopal, 1889–93, León, Spain
Casa Calvet, 1898–1900, Barcelona
Colònia Güell Chapel, crypt, 1898–1915, Barcelona
Villa Bellesguard, 1900–05, Barcelona

Antoni Gaudí

Charles Rennie Mackintosh

1868, Glasgow—1928, London

■ Architect, furniture designer, and painter ■ Influenced by Jan Toorop's Symbolist art ■ Formed the Glasgow Four ■ Argued for stone rather than steel and glass construction ■ Created a unique language of ornament, fusing Celtic symbolism with the pragmatics of the Arts and Crafts design movement

1868 Born in Glasgow
1884–89 Apprenticeship with architect John Hutchison
1889 Draftsman at Honeyman and Keppie (H&K) in Glasgow
1896 Glasgow Four exhibition in London; H&K wins Mackintosh-designed Glasgow School of Art competition
1901 The Glasgow Four exhibit at the Vienna Secession Building
1914–27 Moves to the UK and later France, devoting himself almost entirely to painting
1928 Dies in London

Other Important Works

Glasgow Herald Building, 1893–95, Glasgow

Queen's Cross Church, 1898–99, Glasgow

Windyhill, 1899–1901, Kilmacolm, Renfrewshire

The Daily Record Building, 1900, Glasgow

Willow Tea Rooms, 1903–04, Glasgow

Scotland Street School, 1904, Glasgow

Together with his wife and compatriots at the Glasgow School of Art, Charles Rennie Mackintosh formed the Glasgow Four. The group exhibited graphics and decorative art in the UK concurrently with the Art Nouveau and Secession movements of continental Europe. Like Antoni Gaudí (p. 390), Mackintosh worked with a powerful vernacular aesthetic. Coupled with his Art Nouveau sensibilities, his background in Scottish Gothic Revival resulted in an architecture free from the formal constraints of the Beaux-Arts. Mackintosh's ornament was encoded in Celtic symbolism and an erotic sensibility akin to the paintings of Georgia O'Keeffe.

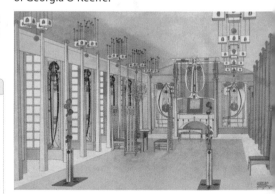

■ **House for an Art Lover**, drawing of the reception and music room, 1901

Mackintosh remained largely unrecognized until Postmodernists such as Venturi began to praise his work. As a result, his competition entry for the House for an Art Lover was built in Glasgow in 1990 from original drawings.

ill House, 1902–03, Helensburgh

ne of his most famous buildings, Mackintosh
tinued Charles F. A. Voysey's process of simpli-
g traditional domestic architecture. At the Hill
se, slight openings in a white mass protect
delicate interiors, which
progress from dark en-
trance rooms to airy salons
and bedrooms.

■ Chair for the Argyle Street Tea Rooms, 1898–99, Glasgow

Mackintosh designed fur-
niture for many buildings,
including the interior elements for many of his
own. The excessively tall
backrests of his slim, iconic
chairs continue
down to the
floor, visually
supporting the
entire composi-
tion and accen-
tuating the chair's
verticality.

▇ Glasgow School of Art, 1897–1909

At the School of Art Mackintosh mixed Scottish
medieval traditions with the severity of industrial architecture, unifying them with tense and
eerie Art Nouveau ornamentation. For the second phase of construction, from 1907 to 1909,
he reworked his drawings and plans, designing a
dramatic western elevation with a double-
height library behind.

Charles Rennie Mackintosh

Otto Wagner

1841, Penzing—1918, Vienna

■ Educator, academic, and influential Viennese architect ■ Felt that struc ture was the essence of architecture ■ Concerned with the relationship between structure and ornament ■ Integrated infrastructure into the city fabric ■ Developed a highly recognizable style called the Wagner School

1841 Born in Penzing

1860–63 Studies in Vienna and Berlin

1886 Builds his first sub-urban villa

1894 Appointed professor at the school of archi-tecture of the Academy of Fine Arts in Vienna

1894–1901 Works on the Vienna Stadtbahn

1896 Publishes the first edition of *Moderne Architektur*

1899 Joins the Vienna Secession

1910 Publishes *Grossstadt*, an urban plan

1918 Dies in Vienna

■ **Karlsplatz Stadtbahn Station**, 1898, Vienna

Wagner was not a true functionalist. He did not believe, like Adolf Loos, that all ornament must be eliminated in favor of cul-tural honesty. Instead, in his metropolitan railway projects, he looked for ar-tistic solutions to the chal-lenges posed by new forms of urban infra-structure that incorporated these structures into the city's architectural fabric.

Although Wagner built relatively few large buildings, left behind a chain of delicate interventions through Vienna. He designed metro stops, pavilions, bridges, a railings that appear unexpectedly, dotting the city with light green and gilded metalwork so typical of his aesthe Wagner was able to combine structural precision and propriate ornament with a keen understanding of Mod urban planning. Like Louis Sullivan (p. 378) or Peter Behr (p. 400) for Modernism, Wagner was the father figure hind the Vienna Secession. Supportive of his studen stand against the establishment, Wagner had his own st that evolved on an independent trajectory. Where app priate, he incorporated J. M. Olbrich's (p. 396) more fri lous manner or Josef Hoffmann's abstract volumes, fin joining his students and their Secession movement in 18

■ St. Leopold's Church,
1905–07, Steinhof Asylum, near Vienna

What is most striking about the section of St. Leopold's is that the interior space is not incorporated with the dome—the dome is fake. Unlike the Secession Building, where the golden sphere is clearly empty and only symbolic, the Steinhof dome is a solid structure with a remarkable spatial potential. How could an architect so loyal to the concept of structural clarity propose such a dishonest solution? This question, posed by a 21st-century critic, is fundamentally different from the concerns of the Belle Époque. For Wagner, the building is to read as a clear, unified object—clarity lies not in exhibiting all the structural elements, but rather in creating a consistent, legible whole. Inside, St. Leopold's simple white surfaces are contrasted with golden angles, wreaths, and colorful stained glass.

▶ Majolika House, 1898, Vienna

The Majolika House was Wagner's first demonstration of solidarity with the Vienna Secession. In one sophisticated move he created cladding and ornament, proving that decoration could be practical. Ceramic tiles with a large-scale flower motif were assembled along the surface of the facade. The entire building became a canvas—a giant billboard for Wagner's new functionally aesthetic approach to architecture.

Otto Wagner

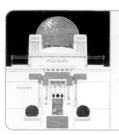

Joseph Maria Olbrich

1867, Opava—1908, Düsseldorf

■ Founding member of the Vienna Secession with Gustav Klimt, Koloman Moser, and Josef Hoffmann ■ Designed the Secession Building ■ Secession movement was parallel to Art Nouveau in France and Belgium, and Jugends... in Germany ■ Influenced by Otto Wagner ■ Worked in Austria and German...

1867 Born in Troppau (now Opava, Czech Republic)

1890 Enrolls in School of Architecture at the Vienna Academy of Fine Arts

1893 Begins to work for Otto Wagner

1893 Wins the Prix de Rome and travels to Italy

1894 Returns to work with Wagner on the Vienna Stadtbahn

1897 Secession movement established in Vienna

1899 Joins Darmstadt Artists' Colony

1906 Wins competition for Tietz store

1908 Dies of leukemia in Düsseldorf

With Gustav Klimt at the helm, the members of the Wie... Sezession (Vienna Secession) combined intense or... mentation and blank spaces with a search for geome... clarity. Instead of flowing freely through the struct... floral embellishment was in constant tension with lin... ornamentation and the hard edges of the architectu... frames. As a founding member of the group, Olbrich's f... major commission was the Secession Building. Fr... there he avoided refining and narrowing his style, exp... imenting instead with the new forms, bizarre proportio... and awkward angles typical of his playful Darmstadt A... ists' Colony houses. His last project for the colony, t... Hochzeitsturm (Wedding Tower), signified a distinct s... in Olbrich's understanding of Modern architecture. W... the plain walls, hard lines, and lack of symmetry in his ... signs came a sense of the irreversibility of the Moder... movement in architecture.

■ **Secession Building**, 1897–98, Vienna

The exhibition building for t... Vienna Secession was com- posed of two basic spaces w... very different symbolic func- tions. The entrance hall, like ... entrance of a church, was se... as an intermediary space be- tween the profanity outside ... and the art within. The exhib... tion space behind the entrar... was treated like an industria... warehouse—white, top-lit, a... flexible.

Other Works by Olbrich

Friedmann House, 1898, Hinterbrühl (near Vienna)

Vienna Room, 1900, Paris Exhibition

Olbrich House, 1900, Artists' Colony, Darmstadt

Glückert House I, 1901, Artists' Colony, Darmstadt

Provisional Exhibition Pavilions, 1901, Artists' Colony, Darmstadt

Opel Workers' House, 1908, Artists' Colony, Darmstadt

Feinhals House, 1908, Cologne

rnst Ludwig House, Artists' ony, 1900–01, Darmstadt

399 Grand Duke Ernst wig invited Olbrich to de- a utopian artists' colony r Darmstadt. The Ernst

Ludwig House was the centerpiece of a complex that consisted of houses for the artists and various temporary pavilions. A heavily symbolic axial entrance was embedded in an

otherwise plain volume. In section, the roof dropped down from the front facade in three separate slopes, glazed to let light into the artists' work spaces behind.

Wedding Tower, 1908, Darmstadt

Wedding Tower was built on the occasion of st Ludwig's marriage to his second wife. Al- ugh the building's exterior is stark, the inte- was richly decorated with scenes from the ory of the grand duke's family history and of the city of Darmstadt. The asymmetrically ed windows visible on the exterior corre- sponded to consecutive levels of exhibition spaces, culminating in a private chapel under the finger-shaped gables. While the task of developing Expressionist architecture went to people like Behrens or Mendelsohn, Olbrich used abstract forms to symbolize the flow of time and space.

Joseph Maria Olbrich

Adolf Loos

1870, Brno—1933, Vienna

■ Cultural theorist and architect ■ Believed art and architecture were sep-
rate disciplines ■ Influenced by Louis Sullivan's *Ornament in Architecture*
■ Impressed by the simplicity of American middle-class society compared
the European bourgeoisie ■ Recognized for his interiors and cubical hous

■ **1870** Born in Brno, Czech
Republic
1889–93 Studies architecture in Dresden
1892 Louis Sullivan's
Ornament in Architecture
published
1893 Travels to America
1900 Begins writing for
the liberal magazine *Neue
Freie Presse*
1908 Publishes *Ornament
and Crime*
1920–22 Chief architect at
the Housing Department
of Vienna
1922 Moves to Paris after
resigning from his
post
1933 Dies in
Vienna

Adolf Loos's early work transcended many different sty
but he is most known for his theoretical work, *Ornam*
and Crime, which paved the way for European Modern
to eliminate ornament from architecture altogether. B
the Arts and Crafts movement in the UK and the Secess
in Vienna reacted against the eclecticism of the 19th c
tury, but by no means shunned the decorative arts.
though Loos preached a break with expensive bourge
habits, the interiors of his own houses were finished w
rich materials. Perhaps incongruous with his a
eclecticism, Loos's logic for contrasting luxurious interi
with stark exterior elevations was quite simple: a hou
should make a Modern statement, but inside, the hom
fundamentally about the clients', comfort and theref
should be furnished and inhabited as they wish.

■ **Müller House**, 1928–30,
Prague

For Loos, rooms were volum
rather than areas. He combi
the benefits of an irregular p
with the satisfaction of achie
ing exterior clarity in his layo
Moving through the Müller
House is an exercise in compression and decompression
From the small, finite waitin
room a concealed staircase
leads upstairs, giving no ind
tion of the openness of the
main floor. The building's ex
rior responds, jutting out to
commodate special rooms o
terraces.

■ **Loos House**, 1910–11, Vienna

The Goldman and Salatsch Building, also called the Loos House, is a striking example of Loos's dichotomous approach to architecture. What later appeared as a contrast between interior and exterior was manifested here in one elevation. The very simplified residential stories above sit on a marble-clad plinth containing the commercial levels. Developing his *Raumplan* concept, Loos introduced split levels inside.

Early Modernism

Other Works by Loos
Café Museum, 1899, Vienna
Loos Apartment, 1903, Vienna
Villa Karma, 1904–06, Vienna
Steiner House, 1910, Vienna
Rufer House, 1922, Vienna
Chicago Tribune Tower Competition (not built), 1922
Villa on Lido, 1923, Venice
House for Dadaist Tristan Tzara, 1926–27, Paris
Khuner House, 1930, Kreuzberg, Austria

merican Bar, 1907, na

ing at the American also called the Kärtner it may seem that Loos simply preoccupied materiality. Yet the al purpose of the intri- weaving of reflective nonreflective surfaces create the illusion of e. The bar is extremely l, and the dark stones woods combined with rs, all of which are set arious grids and

planes, create exaggerated perspectives that visually explode the space. The long counter, checkered floor, layered marble ceiling, and delicate brass fittings all add to the effect by pulling the eye in and out of the room. Outside, three beautifully proportioned openings are surmounted by a projecting mosaic of a stylized American flag, with the words "Kärtner Bar" dotted in between the stripes.

Adolf Loos

Peter Behrens

1868, Hamburg–1940, Berlin

■ Painter, architect, professor, and pioneer of industrial design ■ Father [of?]
the early Modernist movement ■ Founding member of the Deutscher
Werkbund ■ Influenced Mies van der Rohe, Gropius, and Le Corbusier
■ Expressed the spirit of the age through monumental buildings

■ **1868** Born in Hamburg
1886–89 Studies painting in Hamburg, Düsseldorf, and Karlsruhe
1899 Joins the Darmstadt Artists' Colony
1907 Founds the Deutscher Werkbund
1936 Becomes the director of the Prussian Academy of Fine Arts in Berlin
1940 Dies in Berlin

Other Works by Behrens

House at Artists' Colony, 1901, Darmstadt

Eduard Müller Crematorium, 1905–06, Hagen

Product and Graphic Design for AEG, from 1907

Small Motors Factory, 1910–11, Berlin

Wiegand House, 1911–12, Berlin

German Embassy, 1911–12, St. Petersburg

House at Weissenhof Housing Estate, 1927, Stuttgart

■ **AEG Turbine Factory**, 1908–09, Berlin

Although its structure and layout were standard for

Peter Behrens influenced some of the greatest archite[cts]
of the 20th century. Mies van der Rohe (p. 434), Wa[lter]
Gropius (p. 406), and Le Corbusier (p. 412) all worked a[t his]
office. At that time, Behrens was involved with the A[EG]
(German General Electric Company), designing not o[nly]
the factory and office buildings, but also the indust[rial]
products, stationary, and company logos—in essence [the]
entire corporate identity. Behrens founded the Deutsc[he]
Werkbund to tackle the effect of mass production on [the]
arts and achieved just that, inventing the discipline of [in]-
dustrial design in the process.

great industrial halls, the building
brought factory design to the
forefront of architectural debate.
The AEG factory raised the question of whether it is appropria[te to]
use the architectural styles pre[-]
viously reserved for temples a[nd]
palaces in an industrial contex[t.]

chnical Administration ding, Höchst Dye ory, 1920–24, Frankfurt am

ens contributed to most of tylistic movements of the 20th century, from Art /eau at his house in Darm- to Functionalism with the senhof Housing Estate. His Factory was a key building e German Expressionist ement. Its fortresslike qual- ith tower and bridge, were istent with Behrens's ex- ents at the AEG factory. time the element of histor- nalysis was not temples, ather the medieval brick es of northern Germany.

🏠 Alexander and Berolina Houses, 1929–32, Berlin

Behrens once again used an industrial aesthetic, this time in

the context of a commercial building, with boxy utilitarian forms and repetitive large-scale glazing.

Peter Behrens

Erich Mendelsohn

1887, Olsztyn–1953, San Francisco

- Successful Modernist architect ■ Part of the Expressionist movement ■
a member of the Jewish community, was forced to emigrate from Germany
■ Designed numerous commercial buildings ■ Influenced the American A
Deco movement ■ Worked in Germany, the UK, Israel, and the United State

Expressionism

- **1887** Born in Allenstein, East Prussia (now Olsztyn, Poland)
1906 Studies economics in Munich
1908–12 Studies architecture at technical universities in Berlin and Munich
1912–14 Starts architectural practice in Munich
1915–18 Serves in the military; produces expressive sketches
1919 Opens office in Berlin; first sketches for the Einstein Tower
1933 In light of growing anti-Semitism, immigrates to the UK and opens a London office
1936 Opens an office in Jerusalem
1941 Immigrates to the United States
1945 Establishes practice in San Francisco
1947 Begins teaching at the University of California, Berkeley
1953 Dies in San Francisco

■ **Columbus House**, 1932, Berlin

The Columbus House was an exercise in infinity—the ends of the structure remained undefined as its

Erich Mendelsohn's architecture was powerful with
being monumental. Throughout his career, his w
evolved from the sculpted Expressionist buildings like
Einstein Tower to the delicate High Modernism in
Columbus House. Mendelsohn was able to reconcile
pragmatics of Functionalism with the Expressionist in
est in a mystical time and space. In Mendelsohn's har
Expressionism was an energy, not a style. He drew u
the language of International Modernism, but gave
quality of infinity and irresolution, as if he had someh
internalized Einstein's theory of relativity.

slightly curved horizontal lines flowed alongside one of the busiest intersections of interwar Europe. A thin shell was folded around the top and sides of the entire glass volume, almost as if to

stop the expansion of the buil
only for a moment. One could
imagine the facade rhythmica
enveloping the city fabric—a
bolic manifesto for the moder
ization of Germany.

20th Century before 1945

■ Schocken Department Store, 1926, Stuttgart

In contrast to Modernist icons such as those of the Bauhaus or even his own Einstein Tower, Mendelsohn's department stores were urban. Their design was meant to make people associate the brand with the modern energy of the city. During the day, the facade's glass reflected the surrounding traditional architecture, but at night, the expressive interior staircase was lit, and could be seen shining through the building's curves. Mendelsohn's store seems to flow, despite its horizontal nature created by the store spaces and lines of windows. The whole building pivots on the cylindrical corner section, which creates a diagonal thrust in the repetitive structuring.

Other Works by Mendelsohn

osse Publishing ouse, 1922–23, erlin	Mendelsohn Residence, 1929, Berlin	Cohen House, 1935–36, London
oga Cinema Complex, 1926–31, Berlin	De La Warr Pavilion, 1934, Bexhill-on-Sea, Sussex, UK	Hebrew University Buildings, 1937–39, Jerusalem

Einstein Tower, 1919–24, near Potsdam, Germany

e of Mendelsohn's first projects, the stein Tower was built as an observa- y. For Expressionists, architectural ms were not to be derived from his- ical precedents or architectural ions, but, as Hans Poelzig phrased it, t of the mystic abyss" of intuition. e Einstein Tower may make no refer- ce to architectural styles, but it is d to avoid comparing its profile to t of a sphinx. At the base of the lding's vertical mass are the living d working quarters for scientists and laboratory. Above, stairs lead to observatory's telescope. Mendel- n wanted to carve and mold the cture out of reinforced concrete, with technological limitations, entire structure had to made of brick covered h stucco.

Gerrit Thomas Rietveld

1888, Utrecht–1964, Utrecht

■ Cabinet maker, furniture designer, and architect ■ Believed in reconceptua[lizing] living space ■ Influenced by Frank Lloyd Wright ■ Founded the de Stijl movement ■ His work impacted architects like Mies van der Rohe, Gropius, and Le Corbusier ■ Later in life followed principles of International Modernis[m]

Rietveld thought that reality could only be experienced [as] a matter of delimitation and contrast. Undefined spa[ce] cannot be understood, while space that is given a huma[n] scale becomes perceivable. Rietveld physically demo[n]strated the idea of de Stijl with only a few furniture piec[es] and the modest Schröder House. The movement w[as] founded in 1917 by several artists and writers includi[ng] Piet Mondrian, Theo van Doesburg, and Rietveld himse[lf.] De Stijl was based on a complex utopian philosophy th[at,] in architectural terms, translated into using element[ary] forms and primary colors to create open, interactive, a[nd] unified environments.

Schröder House, 1924,
echt

ther than architecture con-
ting of a facade and walls
at act as an envelope and an
erior, the Schröder House is
nceived as a large cabinet
ere intersecting planes and
es appear to move on the
tside and really do move in-
e—nearly all the interior
lls can be retracted, result-
in an open floor plan.

■ **Sculpture Pavilion**, 1955
(rebuilt 1965), Kröller-Müller
Museum, Otterlo

Rietveld's Sculpture Pavilion
owes much to Mies van der
Rohe's Barcelona Pavilion. Although the typical de Stijl primary color scheme is gone, the
building's concrete block and
glass partitions are tied
together with a steel roof and
columns. Following de Stijl
logic, elements radiate from a
central point in the composition and reach out into the
nearby space so as to unify the
interior spaces with the surrounds on different planes.

■ **Red-Blue Chair**, ca. 1918

Like a painting by Piet Mondrian, the Red-Blue
Chair is "elementarized," or distilled to its basic
components and painted with primary
colors to accentuate the parts.
The ends of the black rectangular
sections composing the frame
are painted yellow, as if to
show that they were cut
from one continuous
piece and by extension
embody a series of infinite
intersecting axes in space.
Conceived as a "universal"
chair, it could theoretically
be reconstituted into almost any
other object.

Gerrit Thomas Rietveld

Walter Gropius

1883, Berlin–1969, Boston

■ Director and designer of the Bauhaus ■ Believed in the unity of visual arts and architecture ■ Defined the course of Modern design ■ Worked in academies in both Europe and North America ■ Profoundly influenced the curricula of art and architecture schools ■ Used color in his buildings

1883 Born in Berlin

1903–07 Studies at the Technische Hochschule in Munich, then in Berlin

1908 Employed by Peter Behrens on AEG Turbine Hall

1910 Opens an office near Berlin with Adolf Meyer

1919–28 Director of the Bauhaus in Weimar, and in Dessau from 1925

1938 Director of the Department of Architecture at Harvard University

1969 Dies in Boston, Massachusetts

■ **Fagus Factory**, 1911–25, Alfeld an der Leine

This factory building is clearly an inversion of the monumental industrial logic of Peter Behrens's AEG Turbine Hall in Berlin-Moabit. Instead of glazing the center of the building, Gropius hung the corners of the structure with large sheets of glass from a projecting steel frame. In contrast, the center was a solid, windowless volume containing only the entrance and a small clock. In a factory, time is of the essence.

20th Century before 1945

Walter Gropius followed one simple principle: insert creative elements at key points in an otherwise repetitive elevation. Entrances, staircases, and junctions between building functions all provided opportunities to introduce moments of craft into an industrial framework. According to Gropius's philosophy, facade treatment only needed to be consistent around a specific function. One building could have multiple, even contradictory, elevations if they served their respective functions appropriately. At the Fagus Factory, the structural logic was also completely new. The staircase was placed behind a precarious glass corner that did not hide its floating white landings. The effect was an architecture of paradox-monumental and fragile at the same time.

Other Works by Gropius

Deutscher Werkbund Exhibition, Office and Factory Buildings, 1914, Cologne

Sommerfeld Residence, 1920–21, Berlin

Bauhaus Building and Masters Houses, 1925–26, Dessau

Siemensstadt Housing Estate, 1929–30, Berlin

Gropius Residence, 1938, Lincoln, Massachusetts

Graduate Center, Harvard University, 1948–50, Cambridge, Massachusetts

Housing Block, 1955–57, Hansaviertel, Berlin

■ Chicago Tribune Tower Competition, 1922

The simple guidelines and the goal of building "the most beautiful office building in the world" generated hundreds of entries and much discussion about the future of high-rises. Unlike Mies van der Rohe's revolutionary 1921 skyscraper design, Gropius proposed a feasible building with a structural grid based on the famous Chicago window. With staggered verticals, definite horizontals, and large cantilevers, the building was a synthesis of trends in Modernism. The winning entry was a Neo-Gothic tower typical of American architecture of the era.

Walter Gropius

Bauhaus

In 1919 Walter Gropius (p. 406) fused the Weimar Academy of Fine Arts and t
Weimar School of Arts and Crafts to establish the Bauhaus in Weimar, Germany. T
school, supported by leading artists, was a success, and a new Bauhaus openec
Dessau in 1925. Based on the Deutscher Werkbund
concept of reconciling craft and industry, the Bauhaus
trained professionals to be equally comfortable with
design, craft, and methods of mass production. Theater, metalwork, woodwork, ceramics, architecture,
furniture, and object design were included in the cur-
riculum. The Bauhaus was closed by the Nazis in 1933.

◀ **Walter Gropius: Director's Study**, 1927, Weimar

Walter Gropius's study was
symbolically located at the absolute center of the Bauhaus
school in Weimar, on a bridge
overlooking all of the elements
of the complex. The simple furniture, tubular metal fixtures,
and painted colorful rectangles
were influenced by the designs
of de Stijl.

■ **Herbert Bayer: Font and Workshop Building**, 1927, Weimar

Graphic design, including
typography, was a key eleme
in the publicity of the Bauha
The school's books, publica-
tions, and posters dissemina
ideas of Constructivist or de
origin to the wider public. Th
Bauhaus font appears on the
side of the workshop buildin

▶ **Walter Gropius: Main Stairway of the Workshop Building**, 1925, Dessau

In the Bauhaus, color played a
didactic role in identifying
structure, services, and movement patterns. The focus on
essentials aimed not to strip
architecture of aesthetic or
sculptural value, but to increase
the purity of that value by
exposing functional elements.
In the stairways, light is used to
highlight the structural composition, and windows orient the
user within the complex.

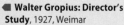

Walter Gropius: Workshop Building and the Vocational School, 1925, Dessau

Bauhaus buildings all involved new and untested innovations. Some experiments failed: the glass curtain wall was visually superb, but led to severe heat gain and loss. A curtain wall means that the interior structure, not the wall, supports the building.

Bauhaus

Social Housing Estates

1918–1930

■ Lack of new construction, political strife, and inflation led to a massive housing shortage in interwar Europe ■ Overcrowding and poverty in traditional tenement housing led architects, politicians, and workers to search for new architectural solutions

■ **1918** World War I ends

1918 J. P. P. Oud becomes the city architect for Rotterdam, the Netherlands

1923 Inflation sends Germany into economic crisis

1925 Le Corbusier introduces the Plan Voisin for Paris

1926 Le Corbusier builds the Pessac Housing Estate near Bordeaux, France

1927 Mies, Oud, Gropius, Le Corbusier, and others build houses at the Weissenhofsiedlung in Stuttgart, Germany

1930 Gropius designs an apartment block for Siemensstadt in Berlin

■ **Karl Ehn: Karl Marx Hof**, 1930, Vienna

In interwar socialist Vienna, the construction of cooperative housing was widespread. Karl Marx Hof turned workers' housing into an institution and gave it a monumental aesthetic that was appropriate to workers' new position in society. Close to 1,400 apartments were arranged in a seemingly endless, unbroken line.

20th Century before 1945

After the stagnation of World War I and the economic crises of the 1920s, Europe desperately needed new housing. It was clear that the 19th-century system of tenement blocks was outdated both in sociopolitical and functional terms. Modernists like Walter Gropius (p. 414) and Bruno Taut had spent the war years developing radically new minimal-cost housing solutions and were eager to try them out on a mass scale in government-sponsored social housing estates. There were disagreements as to the form these estates were to take, but several basic schemes were developed that persist in urban planning to this day. The choice was between single-family and multifamily dwellings. The former were more popular in the UK, in the form of traditional terraced houses, but mainland Europe opted for large-scale apartment blocks as the solution to the housing crisis. Workers' estates and low-cost housing projects sprang up throughout Europe.

**uno Taut: Britz
eshoe Estate,
ter Plan**, 1925–33,
n

e Britz Estate,
ng planning
mes were adopt-
he central horse-
-shaped building
organized around
in courtyard that
d as a social
enser. Other
lings were widely
ed and arranged
rth-south parallel
for maximum
exposure.

emensstadt,
–30, Berlin

emensstadt, sev-
architects worked
e different areas
eir own style.
, only the most
: elements of ar-
cture are used.
curving white wall
ains two window
s, one for the
tments and one
e staircases.
le brick portals
: the entrances.

■ Hans Scharoun: Siemensstadt Master Plan, 1929–30, Berlin

At this Siemensstadt block, Hans Scharoun
joined the exterior elements—the staircases and
balconies—to form a working core that runs up
each unit of the block. The combination
is also treated as an object of formal
design that adds variation to the
monotonous facade. Plain, uncan-
opied doors and a bare, light
rooftop betray the Minimalist
tendencies of the Func-
tionalist movement.

Other Works

Eigen Haard Estate,
by Michel de Klerk,
1920, Amsterdam

Workers' Housing Es-
tate, by J. P. P. Oud,
1924, Hoek van Hol-
land, the Netherlands

Bruchfeldstrasse Es-
tate, by Ernst May,
1925–27, Frankfurt am
Main, Germany

Weissenhofsiedlung,
by Mies van der Rohe,
master plan and apart-
ment block, 1927,
Stuttgart, Germany

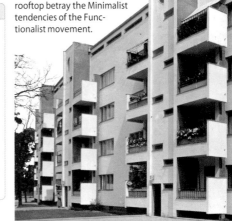

Le Corbusier

Charles Edouard Jeanneret
1887, La Chaux-de-Fonds–1965, Roquebrune-Cap-Martin

■ Modernist architect and ideological urban planner ■ Influenced by Auguste Perret ■ Proponent of reinforced concrete ■ Saw the house as a machine for living ■ Interested in new housing solutions

■ **1887** Born Charles-Edouard Jeanneret in Switzerland

1902–7 Studies at the Chaux-de-Fonds School of Decorative Arts

1908–9 Works for Auguste Perret in Paris

1910–11 Visits Peter Behrens in Berlin

1920 Takes on the pseudonym "Le Corbusier" in an article for his new periodical *L'Esprit Nouveau*

1923 Publishes *Towards a New Architecture*

1935 Publishes *The Radiant City*

1965 Dies in Roquebrune-Cap-Martin, France, while swimming

■ **Villa Savoye**, 1928–31, Poissy-sur-Seine, France

At the Villa Savoye, *pilotis* raise the structure's main volume above ground level, enabling visitors to arrive at the very center of the building. The entrance ramp creates a continuous route from the semicircular ground floor pavilion, past the apartment in the main volume, and up to the screened roof garden.

In 1927 Le Corbusier announced his *Five Points for a New Architecture*. The manifesto mapped out his own concept of architectural forms. It stated that structures should raised upon stilts, or *pilotis,* to free the ground for circulation; that a roof garden should be created by the use of roofs; a free plan and facade should be allowed by an independent frame structure; and ribbon windows should used to allow more light than would possible with a load-bearing wall. Architectural historians argue that despite Corbusier's idiosyncratic style, he was able to determine the evolution of building for years to come by inventing imitable architectural language. He reduced architecture its main functional elements: window, ramp, stair, column or slab, redefining and renaming them in light of new functional and aesthetic requirements. His architectural components were not always successful and were often replicated without refinement, but have permanently

20th Century before 1945

nité d'Habitation, Interbau Fair, '–58, Berlin

r five decades Le Corbusier's Unité lings are still provocative, chal- ing the relationships between the vidual and the collective. As the of the nuclear family and later the vidual grew, so did the need to re- communities shattered by World II. Le Corbusier accommodated

by designing interlocking cellular s. These long split-level apartments e the depth of the building and coustically and visually separate one another, yet at the same time of a tight community of over 300 s. Communal facilities in the form id-air" shopping streets, day cares, nasiums, and swimming pools e inserted between myriad unit s, arranged like a puzzle in the t creeping frame of the Unité bitation so as to create a close-knit munity.

Assembly Hall at Chandigarh, 1952–58

The urban plan for Chandigarh, the new capital of the Punjab province, ultimately failed but the Assembly Hall is a good example of Le Corbusier's Brutalist architecture. The hyperbolic shell over the entrance portico of the column-free space illustrates the great potential of concrete.

Semi-Detached House, Weissenhofsiedlung, 1926–27, Stuttgart

Conceptually, the Semi-Detached House was similar to Villa Savoye. In fact, Le Corbusier drafted his *Five Points for a New Architecture* to specifically illustrate the principles behind its design. *Pilotis*, ribbon windows, and a roof garden are all clearly visible in the Semi-Detached House. A symbolic partition divides the two units.

413

International Modernism

Le Corbusier

entered architectural vocabulary. Some examples of Le Corbusier's influence on architectural vocabulary include: *pilotis*, free-standing columns, and *brise soleil*, a sun shade that, together with other elements used for ventilation and light control, constitutes an *ondulatoire*, or a module for climatic control. To give these elements a framework, Le Corbusier invented his own system of proportions, known as the *Modulor*, which he rigorously applied to most of his buildings in his late career. His housing units were based on the *Domino* model—the name for a structural system composed of six columns, three slabs, and a stair resting together on simple footings.

■ **La Tourette Monastery**, 1953–57, Eveux-sur-l'Arbresle

The basic language for a dwelling unit established by Le Corbusier at the Unité d'Habitati is repeated here with the effect that the monks' spartan living quarters are easily distinguisha The U-shaped building touches its fourth sid the church. Complete, the severe fortress of prayer perches uneasily over the landscape.

■ **La Tourette Monastery**, side chapels, 1953–57, Eveux-sur-l'Arbresle

At the Dominican monastery, Le Corbusier reshaped and re-arranged the basic elements of ecclesiastical architecture. The

chapel, choir, and the vestry are all there, but are distributed according to an entirely different logic. An undulating volume projects from the church and contains seven descending side chapels surmounted by three enormous light tubes.

Other Works

Villa Schwob, 1916,
La Chaux-de-Fonds

Villa La Roche/Jeanneret,
1923, Paris

Centrosoyuz Building,
1929–33, Moscow

Unité d'Habitation, 1946–5
Marseille

Jaoul Houses, 1951, Neuilly-sur-Seine

Shodhan House, 1951–56,
Ahmedabad, Gujarat

Master Plan for the city of
Chandigarh, 1952–58, Chan
garh, Punjab

Philips Pavilion, 1958
(demolished), Exposition
Universelle, Brussels

National Museum of Weste
Art, 1959, Tokyo

Carpenter Center for the
Visual Arts, 1959–62,
Cambridge, Massachusetts

Notre Dame du Haut,
1–54, Ronchamp

...power of Notre Dame du
...t lies in its multiplicity of
...anings. It is at once per-
...ly stable and just moments
...y from collapse—solid,
...ted in the ground, with

Notre Dame du Haut, inte-
...view, 1951–54, Ronchamp

...massive roof of Notre
...ne du Haut seems to
...athe, sagging under its own
...ght as it inhales. The
...logy of breath is pertinent
...:e the roof is actually hollow,
...tched on an internal frame
... supported by columns
...den within the walls. A slit of
...t separates the walls and
... shell of the roof.

thick walls and a looming roof
that are in fact all hollow. The
building is defensive, like a
castle, but pulls space directly
into its heart. The unifying roof
dips down to pick up the earth
while at the same time reaching up to the sky. The crude

finishes and basic detailing
seem to have nothing of the
machine-produced aesthetic
of Villa Savoye; however the
Cartesian logic that governed
Le Corbusier's early houses remains in the floor pattern of
Notre Dame du Haut.

Le Corbusier

Nordic Modernism

1916–1976

■ Nordic Modernism combined Neoclassical and Regional influences ■ Mod[...]
fied by Alvar Aalto, the movement was included in International Modernism
■ Aalto and his wife, Aino Marsio, were pioneers in furniture and object desi[...]
■ *left:* **Lighting Fixtures**, by Alvar Aalto, 1956–61, Bazoches-sur-Guyonne, Fran[...]

■ **1916–21** Alvar Aalto studies architecture at Helsinki University of Technology

1924 Aalto marries architect Aino Marsio and travels to Italy, developing an interest in Italian styles

1930 Erik Gunnar Asplund has his architectural breakthrough at the Stockholm Exposition

1940 Asplund dies in Stockholm

1976 Aalto dies in Helsinki

The two key figures of Nordic Modernism were Swed[...] architect Erik Gunnar Asplund and his Finnish colleag[...] Alvar Aalto. Asplund was older than Aalto by 13 yea[...] and his work provided the young architect with a point [...] departure for a wholly alternative aesthetic. Althou[...] Aalto was interested in economical architecture and m[...] production, his attachment to Finnish architectural d[...] sign history tempered his work and gave it a human fa[...] that other functionalist architecture lacked. A prece[...] for Aalto, Asplund's Woodland Chapel was a Classi[...] temple fused with a "primitive hut," creating [...] unexpectedly Modern effect.

Other Works

Woodland Cemetery, by Erik Gunnar Asplund and Sigurd Lewerentz, 1917–20, Stockholm, Sweden

Lister County Courthouse, by Erik Gunnar Asplund, 1917–21 Sölvesborg, Sweden

Tuberculosis Sanatorium, by Alvar Aalto, 1929, Paimio, Finland

Villa Mairea, by Alvar Aalto, 1939, Noormarkku, Finland

Finlandia Hall, by Alvar Aalto, 1971, Helsinki, Finland

■ **Erik Gunnar Asplund: Stockholm Public Library**, 1918–27, Stockholm

A U-shaped building surrounds the main cylindrical reading room. Inside, three tiers of books encircle the room. Light enters through vertical windows set high in the curv[...] wall. There is little ornamenta[...] tion apart from the entrance portal and facade banding.

20th Century

Alvar Aalto: Viipuri City Library, 1935, Vyborg, Russia (formerly Viipuri, Finland)

...composition of two offset rectangles, with the entrance at their juncture, the library is lit from above by numerous tubular skylights, while the lecture hall has long windows and is lined with a folding wooden ceiling. Aalto designed many of the technical aspects of the building, including the forced-air ventilation shafts within the building's walls.

Alvar Aalto: Finnish Church of the Holy Ghost, 1960–62, Wolfsburg, Germany

...Church of the Holy Ghost is ...of a large community ...center. Aalto's unusual church ...brings Minimalist architectural ...ideas to the ecclesiastical ...form. It features an enormous ...tower which, despite its ...Modernist aesthetics, resembles ...a stepped Italian campa... ...The interior is well lit and ...a fan-shaped roof provides ...excellent acoustics. Aalto also ...designed many of the interior ...elements, such as collection ...plates and candelabras.

Nordic Modernism

Art Deco in New York

ca. 1900–ca. 1940

■ New materials such as stainless steel, aluminum, and plastics were introduced into architecture ■ Occupancy in a high-revenue area and visibility on the city's skyline meant that skyscrapers were advantageous to both developers and businesses

■ **ca. 1900** Skyscraper construction enters a mature phase and the New York skyline grows

1916 New York passes a restrictive zoning ordinance that enforces setbacks past a certain building height

ca. 1920 Tubular steel begins to replace traditional wood scaffolding

1929 The stock market crash triggers the Great Depression; funding problems give rise to innovative methods of financing buildings

1931 The Empire State Building becomes the tallest building in the world

ca. 1940 The style loses popularity

Art Deco architecture is derived from a mix of variou[s] [in]fluences, including the aesthetics of Africa, Egypt, C[en]tral and South America, and the Futurists and Cub[ists]. New building materials were manipulated into stepp[ed,] radiating styles that contrasted sharply with the f[loral] motifs of Art Nouveau. It is striking how a zoning law [can] determine not only a city's skyline, but an entire archit[ec]tural style. In accordance with the law passed in New Y[ork,] the Art Deco skyscrapers were defined by staggered [pro]files, one of the most potent architectural images of [the] early 20th century. The power of capitalism was flaun[ted] throughout the city in the designs of one skyscraper a[fter] another. The American economy seemed invincible [and] the society bound for a mechanized future that had[n't,] yet, only been imagined by the Futurist architects in [Italy] or Russia, who were seldom able to realize project[s. In] New York, towers counting 40, 50, or even 60 floors w[ere] built in a matter of months.

■ **Reinhard & Hofmeister[,] Harrison & Macmurray, a[nd] Hood & Fouilhoux: Rocke[-] feller Center**, entrance pla[za,] mainly 1932–39, New York

As an urban ensemble, Roc[ke]feller Center is more signifi[cant] than any of its buildings tak[en] separately. Grouped aroun[d] a sunken public plaza, narr[ow] towers are slotted into an urban matrix. The interiors [and] entrances are geometricall[y] Art Deco.

■ William van Alen: Chrysler Building, 1928–30, New York

The Chrysler Building required only a few typical floor plans, which were then repeated throughout the elevation, cutting both design and construction costs. Sequencing, layering, and reiteration became design tools in order to use economic hardship to best advantage. In response to the negligent building habits that were turning the city's streets into dark alleys, the city implemented a zoning ordinance that regulated the height of buildings by lot size and street width. Past a certain height, the building needed to step back from the street in successive increments. The new laws meant that a site was considered in terms of available cubic space rather than pure area, and buildings were designed to read as volumes instead of surfaces, shaping the city's skyline for the next four decades.

Modernism in the United States

Other Important Works	
Chanin Building, by Sloan & Robertson, 1927–29, New York	1929–30, New York
McGraw-Hill Building, by Raymond Hood,	News Building, by Raymond Hood with John Mead Howells, 1929–30, New York

Shreve, Lamb & Harmon: Empire State Building, 1929–31, New York

The Metropolis of Tomorrow Hugh Ferriss envisioned the perfect "set-back building." Reminiscent of a ziggurat, it is heavy and monumental. But New York was interested in pure height. Efficiency was sacrificed for glamour, and the Empire State Building was built as a monument to the optimism of the 1930s.

Art Deco in New York

Totalitarian Architecture

1922–1953

■ Totalitarian architecture was an expression of nationalism ■ Used monumental Classical and Modernist models ■ Contemporary to the Art Deco movement ■ Key architects working under totalitarian regimes included Albert Speer in Berlin, Boris Iofan in Moscow, and Marcello Piacentini in Rome

■ **1922** Mussolini becomes prime minister of Italy; Stalin is made general secretary of the Communist Party Central Committee in the Soviet Union, a position he would hold until his death

1929 Stock market crash triggers worldwide economic depression

1933 Hitler becomes chancellor of Germany and closes the Bauhaus

1939 World War II begins

1945 World War II ends; Hitler commits suicide in Berlin; Mussolini executed at Lake Como, Italy

1953 Stalin dies in Moscow

■ **Albert Speer: German Pavilion for the World Exhibition**, 1937, Paris

The centerpiece for Albert Speer's 1937 master plan for Berlin was not the proposed Führer's Palace, facing an enlarged Reichstag, but rather an enormous domed hall intended for rallies of over 150,000 people. If built, it would have been 16 times the size of St. Peter's Basilica in Rome.

After almost 20 years of Modernist architecture, the totalitarian states of Europe converged upon the same stripped Neoclassical aesthetic. The context for this distillation of form was different for Germany, Italy, and the Soviet Union, but all three aimed to establish a national style that could express totalitarian rhetoric. The Neoclassical model suited an ideology of long-standing power, while Modern failed in that capacity, because it was a language of commerce, which responded primarily to the energy of the free market economy, not to the glorification of state power. Only in Italy was Rationalist architecture accepted in the fascist canon. In Italy, the architect Guiseppe Terragni managed to fulfill the party rhetorical needs, while at once maintaining a clear C

Albert Speer: German Pavilion for the World Exhibition, 1937, Paris

The pavilion at the Paris Exhibition proved not only that Nazi Germany was disinterested in Functionalist architecture, but also that similar Neoclassical buildings had become the only accepted form for representing national power. Functionalist architecture lacked the iconographic means to convey national propaganda and was often too abstract to be understood by a wider public. Unable to withdraw from the simplification of ornament that Modernism had already proposed, this new Classicism was austere and monumental. At the Paris Exhibition, the German Pavilion faced off with a similarly heavy entry from the Soviet Union.

Albert Speer: Mosaic Hall, New Reichs Chancellery, 1938–39, Berlin

Finding the existing palaces and administrative buildings either too small or laden with unwanted symbolism, Hitler commissioned a new Chancellery in the administrative district of

Berlin. However imposing, the building was only to house him until the larger, strategically placed Führer's Palace was completed. The building was built on a grand scale, to flaunt the power of the Third Reich. Primarily ceremonial in function, it included richly finished but empty halls leading to Hitler's reception room. The complex, including Hitler's infamous bunker, was damaged during the Allied offensive and later leveled, after the war.

Totalitarian Architecture

Rationalist expression. In the Soviet Union, Constructivism was part of revolutionary thought, until Stalin's paradoxical decree that only Classical architecture was appropriate for expressing proletarian ambitions. In Germany—the country then at the forefront of Modernism—Hitler closed institutions like the Bauhaus, which were, in his mind, propagating a decadence that he despised. Yet there was an underlying Modernity to both fascist and Soviet logic. Le Corbusier (p. 412) had proposed the destruction of 19th-century Paris to make room for La Ville Radieuse, and certainly each dictator succeeded in demolishing large parts of his historic capital for megalomaniacal developments. Yet in stylistic terms, totalitarian regimes looked mainly to the past for architectural models that could assert and sanctify their power. In Berlin, Albert Speer produced a new master plan that eliminated entire neighborhoods in favor of a ceremonial axis mimicking (and enlarging) the Champs Élysées. In Italy the French capital became a model for Mussolini's "Haussmannization" of Rome.

■ Giuseppe Terragni: Casa del Fascio,
1932–36, Como, Italy

The Casa del Fascio combines de Stijl ideas of an infinite Cartesian space with Classical notions of proportion. A three-dimensional grid of columns and beams is bound by a perfect half-cube.

**e Corbusier: Palace of the
iets**, competition entry
del, 1931

orbusier's scheme for the
ce of the Soviets was an

**oris Iofan: Project for the
ce of the Soviets**, 1934,
cow

ies for the Moscow competi-
poured in from all over Eu-
e, especially from the mem-
of the Modernist avant-
e who sympathized with
the Russian Constructivists
their socialist program. The
ernist entries were rejected
he grounds that they were
abstract to be understood by
general public. Instead, a
ect by Iofan was modified to
e emerging Social Realist

assemblage of distinct shapes,
each representing a separate
programmatic element. A giant
parabolic arch was to support
two stacked auditoriums, that

would stand opposite a separate administrative wing. In
between, a covered public
forum would serve as a place
for political discussion.

state-sanctioned aesthetic. In
1931 Stalin demolished a major
Moscow landmark, the Cathedral
of Christ the Savior, to make
room for the palace. Yet the
building was never finished, because preparation for World
War II became a priority. The
crater made by excavations was
left untouched for decades, until
it was turned into Moscow's
largest outdoor swimming pool.
With the breakup of the Soviet
Union the pool was once more
covered up, and the cathedral
faithfully reconstructed.

Totalitarian Architecture

Architecture
After 1945

**Future Systems: NatWest Media Center at Lords
Cricket Ground**, 1994–99, London

1945–1970
Late Modernism

Postwar Europe and Japan require massive rebuilding and the United States' strengthened economy creates a new aesthetic that spreads around the world

1945–Present
Corporate Modernism and High Tech Architecture

p. 474

Luxury offices reflect the power of capitalist economies, while High Tech architecture exposes structural elements

1960–Present
Postmodernism

Combinations of differen styles create unique and referential buildings

1945   1950   1960

p. 442

p. 466

After 1945

1980–Present
Deconstructivism

Deconstructivist architecture bends traditional building frames, distorting the popular rectilinear conception of buildings

p. 493

427

1980   1990   2000

970–Present
inimalist
odernism and
ate Modernism

chitects influenced by
e International style
ip buildings of
namentation

Denys Lasdun
ul Rudolph
varo Siza Viera p. 454
oshe Safdie
dao Ando p. 452

Frank Gehry p. 486
Peter Eisenman p. 484
Daniel Libeskind p. 494
Zaha Hadid p. 490

New Directions

Technological innovations have created seemingly endless possibilities

Rem Koolhaas p. 496
Lars Spuybroek
NIO Architecten
Herzog & de Meuron p. 498

p. 497

Architecture after 1945

After World War II, many architects set about disman-
tling the prevailing notions of form, material, and
function in step with a rapidly changing, future-
focused, and increasingly urban society. Architects
looked to philosophy, theory, and history to liberate
their forms from the strict Functionalist aesthetic of
Modernism. A pluralism of styles developed, often in
direct contrast to each other, as architecture entered
into a dramatic dialogue with itself.

In the late 1940s and early 1950s, this new language took the form of the allegorical and Rationalist
works of Eero Saarinen and Kenzo Tange, who ex-
ploited the sculptural possibilities of materials like
reinforced concrete, while Mies van der Rohe forged
a new aesthetic with his use of exposed industrial
steel and glass. Mies's designs illustrated the importance of simplicity and elegance, while experimenting

■ Kenzo Tange
St. Mary's Cath
dral, 1955, Toky

■ Alison and
Peter Smithson
The Economist
Building, 1964,
London

with diverse and inventive structural elements. This approach was perhaps best encapsulated in the iconic Seagram Building (1958), a testament to Mies's insistence that a building's structural elements should not only be visible, but indeed a focal point of a building.

Meanwhile, as late Modernists integrated the industrial with the functional, the poetic, emotionally expressive approach of Louis Kahn searched for new, site-sensitive and sculptural forms with materials like brick and concrete. Kahn's Modern Expressionistic approach combined philosophy with a rigorous examination of the possibilities of engineering, and had a dramatic influence both in the United States and around the world.

In the wake of World War II, particularly in the UK, huge building projects had to be undertaken at minimal cost. Brutalism, was by nature quick and inexpen-

sive, and seemed the ideal choice for a nation looking to rebuild in the 1950s and 1960s. With their utopian philosophy of integration and transparency, Brutalists like Paulo Mendes da Rocha and Alison and Peter Smithson emphasized structural forms through the use of exposed beams and raw concrete. Similarly, Tadao Ando's Minimalist designs melded stripped elements to geometric shapes and angles that relied heavily on natural elements and negative space.

By the 1960s, I. M. Pei's and SOM's pairing of contemporary Classicism with technological innovation saw a move away from bulky masonry facades to glass, aluminum, and stainless steel. Norman Foster's High Tech approach continued this trend by accentuating the technical aspects of his designs, resulting in a machinelike aesthetic that rejected the static forms of Modernism and the soft curves of Expressionism in favor of repetitive geometry and minimal detail.

Architecture after 1945

Zaha Hadid:
Bergisel Ski Jump,
2002, Innsbruck,
Austria

In response to this paring back of ornamentation, American architects like Michael Graves and Robert Venturi began to experiment with new aesthetics by turning to architectural history. Borrowing elements such as columns and decorative edifices, their Postmodern style created referential, witty, and ornamental forms. History became a feeding ground for new ideas, and these borrowed forms were given a new context through their relationship with contemporary life.

Peter Eisenman's designs signaled a decisive shift away from ornamental, user-friendly designs to mathematical, gridlike forms that highlighted architecture as *pure form*—a self-referential language in which design, rather than function, is absolute. Similarly, Deconstructivist architects like Daniel Libeskind, Zaha Hadid, and Frank Gehry aimed to disassemble and disjoint spaces through new

Introduction

experiments in 3-D geometry. Great colliding planes and fragmented, non-rectilinear shapes were used to provoke disorientation and curiosity, and by the mid-1980s, Deconstructivism's ambitions of an entirely new and non-Functionalist aesthetic were recognizable the world over.

Sustainable architecture, or "green designs," have become an increasingly prevalent theme in contemporary architecture. In an effort to engineer better spaces for living and working, architects such as Norman Foster and Zaha Hadid incorporate design elements that lower the buildings' overall impact on the ecosystem. New heating and cooling systems and alternative energies maximize the building's ability to be environmentally friendly. Common aspects of green buildings include the channeling of wind for cooling, and rainwater for landscaping and washing. Architects are now able to make use of the elements

■ **Daniel Libes-kind: Imperial War Museum**, 2002, Manchester

■ **Future Systems: Selfridge** 2003, Birmingham UK

Architecture after 1945

that would normally negatively impact their buildings, so that they instead benefit both the aesthetic design and the environment.

In the latter part of the 20th century, innovations in materials and design techniques created exciting and previously unimaginable possibilities. Blobitecture became a byword for the creation of unthinkable forms. Herzog and de Meuron, Lars Spuybroek, and Rem Koolhaas, among others utilized new techniques to create buildings that responded in a more sympathetic way to the natural forms found in the environment. Whereas Deconstructivism aimed to take apart form through geometry, Blobitecture became a tool for creating shapes that could be molded and sculpted to fit any need, allowing infinite possibilities for form, function, and individuality, illustrating contemporary architecture's seemingly limitless manifestations.

Introduction

Mies van der Rohe

Maria Ludwig Michael Mies
1886, Aachen–1969, Chicago

■ Modernist architect ■ Author of the phrase "less is more" ■ Influenced b
Karl Friedrich Schinkel and Peter Behrens ■ Greatly changed the look of co
mercial city centers ■ Used predominantly steel and glass in his buildings

■ **1886** Born Maria Ludwig
Michael Mies in Aachen,
Germany

1907–11 Works for Peter
Behrens in Berlin

1921 Joins the Deutscher
Werkbund

1929 Designs the German
Pavilion for the Interna-
tional Exhibition in
Barcelona

1930–33 Serves as the last
director of the Bauhaus

1938 Immigrates to the
USA; becomes director of
architecture at the Armour
Institute in Chicago (later
the Illinois Institute of
Technology)

1954–58 Designs and
builds the Seagram Build-
ing in New York

1969 Dies in Chicago

■ **Lakeshore Drive
Apartments**, 1948–51,
Chicago

Known as the "glass
houses," these two 26-
story towers were Mies's
first steel and glass high-
rise buildings. Revolutionary in their structure, the
towers introduced Amer-
ica to an elegance based
on order and clarity rather
than opulence.

20th Century before 1945

His famous aphorism "less is more" describes only one
pect of Mies van der Rohe's multifaceted style. M
changed the popular conception of built forms and p
foundly influenced the evolution of American cit
Skeletons of steel and glass replaced the traditional lo.
bearing walls. The boundary between interior and ex
rior space blurred, as the glazed curtain wall became

■ **Glass Skyscraper**, designed 1921, Berlin

A truly visionary project, the Glass Skyscraper betrays Mies's early fascination with glass. Its complex plan—like a blown-up snowflake—produces an undulating and almost crystalline volume. The project was designed for a triangular site near Friedrichstrasse in Berlin, but was never built. The emergence of new materials such as reinforced concrete and steel and the production of glass on an industrial scale allowed architects to imagine structures that would only become technically feasible decades later. For Mies, this building was more an experiment in material and form, reflection, and transparency than a structural concept. The design forecasts his glass-box structures.

Mies van der Rohe

a filter instead of a barrier. Mies was directly involved in most of the intellectual movements that contributed to the International Modern style. Through Peter Behrens (p. 400), Mies was exposed to the Deutscher Werkbund and was the director of its influential 1927 Stuttgart Exhibition. His Barcelona Pavilion of 1929 was one of the most sophisticated applications of de Stijl's experiments in form. Sometimes to the detriment of other ideas, Mies pursued structure as the answer to the problem of Modern architecture. Through constant reduction, he created the modern organization of commercial buildings. Unfortunately, misinterpretions of his style have led to the drab high-rises that populate our cities.

■ **Barcelona Pavilion for the International Exhibition (German Pavilion)**, 1928–29, Barcelona

20th Century before 1945

Built as part of an exhibition demonstrating a new way of living and heavily influenced by F. L. Wright's Prairie houses and

de Stijl, Mies replaced the wa and windows with ephemera partitions, inviting the exteric into the house.

Villa Tugendhat, 1930, Brno

sponding to changing needs
the modern lifestyle, Mies
ovided the Tugendhat family
with a composition of luxurious
spaces that flowed effortlessly
between interior rooms and exterior terraces. Spaces were no
longer divided into traditional
rooms but could now be
changed to suit the needs of
the Tugendhats.

■ **Neue Nationalgalerie**,
1962–68, Berlin

Thanks to a system of only six
structural columns, the exhibition floor is column free and
completely flexible for a variety
of curatorial uses. Inside the
building, one experiences only
a roof floating overhead, integrating the surrounding city
with the interior. Underneath,
hidden within a massive plinth,
additional gallery spaces spill
out onto a sculpture garden.

Mies van der Rohe

Seagram Building

The absolute pinnacle of the International style, the Seagram Building achieve a logic and clarity unmatched before or since in Modern architecture. Much of th was due to the financial abilities of the client. Owner Samuel Bronfman asked n more than that the new headquarters of his massive distillery operation be "th crowning glory of everyone's work" and provided $45 million to accomplish th end. This was more than twice the average budget for a skyscraper project at th time, and it allowed the principal architect Mies van der Rohe (p. 434) and his in terior designer Philip Johnson to spare no expense when it came to either cra

or materials. The Seagram Building wa enormously influential: It marked th emergence of the International style i America and established the templat for corporate Modernist architecture fo the next 20 years. But this crucial finan cial factor would be missing from th high-rise projects that followed it, an none would come close to the meg lithic elegance of the Seagram Buildin itself. The office building's use of stru tural innovations with organization clarity make it stand out among th other tall buildings of New York City.

Mies van der Rohe sought to reduce buildings to the absolute evocation of their idea. This was achieved through a strict sense of proportion and a commitment to structural minimalism. In both these aspects, the Seagram Building is a masterpiece. Expertly balanced, the structure occupies less than half of its site. The remaining space is planned as a large granite plaza, bordered by reflecting pools and ledges made of pink marble. The plaza has a double

function: firstly employed as a pedestrian gathering area, it is among the most popular public spaces in the city; it is also employed as a plinth, lending the building itself a space to stand in and be seen from. The building is set back from the street on bronze-clad pillars. Composed of a steel-frame skeleton, the building externalizes this frame in bronze, according to the Miesian logic of conceptual structure shadowing actual structure. The idea

was to deduce the external ap pearance of a building from it necessary structural propertie rather than imposing them ar bitrarily. The building's 38-sto facade consists of alternating bands of bronze plating and brown-tinted glass. With floor to-ceiling windows, the build ing's interior walls are true cur tains of glass. Between the windows, bronze I-beams frame the mullions—structura window divisions—emphasiz ing the verticality of the facad

Seagram Building

Louis Kahn

Itze-Leib Schmuilowsky
1901, Kuressaare—1974, New York

■ Known for his geometric forms and use of technical innovations ■ Turned away from pure Modernism after touring Egypt and Greece ■ Sought to give his buildings a timeless, eternal quality

1901 Born Itze-Leib Schmuilowsky in Kuressaare, Estonia
1906 Emigrates to the United States
1935 Starts his own practice in Philadelphia
1947 Becomes a professor at Yale
1955 Appointed professor of architecture at the University of Pennsylvania
1974 Dies of a heart attack in Pennsylvania Station, New York

The Estonian-born, Philadelphia-based Louis Kahn w acclaimed by his peers as "a philosopher among arch tects." Kahn drew from the ruins of the ancient world imbue the International style with an architecture th felt silent and light. Divided between his extensive teac ing and speaking commitments and his elaborate pe sonal life, the meticulous Kahn completed relatively fe buildings during his lifetime. Several of these, howeve are now esteemed as being among the most epic co structions of the 20th century. "Truly," Kahn once wro "a work of art is one that tells us that nature cannot ma what man can make."

Other Works by Kahn

Yale University Art Gallery, 1951–53, New Haven, Connecticut

Jewish Community Center (Trenton Bath House), 1954–59, Ewing, New Jersey

Richards Medical Research Laboratories, 1957–65, Philadelphia, Pennsylvania

Indian Institute of Management 1962–74, Ahmedabad, India

Phillips Exeter Academy Library, 1965–72, Exeter, New Hampshire

■ **Jatiyo Sangshad Bhaban (National Assembly Building)**, 1961, Dhaka, Bangladesh
Kahn's Modern design for

the main building of the capital complex consists of different levels of interlocking functional spaces. Constructed from concrete and marble and laced with

blue lakes and green lawns, his sunlight-flooded design draws from regional archetypes to create an elemental harmony m roring a democratic political on

Architecture after 1945

Salk Institute, 1960–66, La
~~l~~la, California

~~:~~tuated at the edge of the
~~:~~ific Ocean, the Salk Institute
~~:~~nsists of two geometrically
~~:~~aped laboratory blocks, di-

Kimbell Art Museum,
~~19~~67–72, Fort Worth, Texas

~~Th~~e Kimbell Art Museum is a
~~co~~mposite of parts that them-
~~se~~lves stand as wholes. Through
~~Kah~~n's organization, these
~~wh~~oles work in harmony with
~~on~~e another. His concrete and
~~an~~d barrel-vault design provides
~~a c~~lear aesthetic appropriate
~~for~~ a gallery space, while filtering
~~na~~tural light down the curved
~~wa~~lls to illuminate the exhibi-
~~tio~~n area.

vided by a cventral courtyard.
Kahn conceived of the building
as a kind of Modern monastery
and sought to infuse it with a
sense of calm and serenity
through its structural order,

while at the same time maintaining it's Modernist feel. The
exteriors of the cubic office
spaces are fashioned out of
concrete while wood and
marble is used on the interiors.

Louis Kahn

Sydney Opera House

Located on Sydney Harbor, the Opera House is one of the 20th century's most iconic buildings. Designed by Danish architect Jørn Utzon and built in the Expressionist Modernist style, the Opera House was an innovative and ambitious design that required new technologies to build and stabilize. In order to accommodate the design to the waterside location and plan the unique roof of the building, it became one of the first designs to utilize computer-aided analysis—techniques that have been further developed and are now used in the designs of Frank Gehry (p. 486) and in Blobs (p. 500). The triumph of the Opera House is the roof, which consists of a series of shells resembling sails made of concrete and supported by precast concrete ribs. The shells are covered in 1,056,056 tiles imported from Sweden, whose texture is visible only at close range.

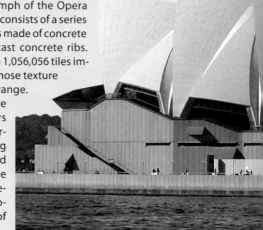

The serialistic use of pure curving shapes mirrors the shapes of the surrounding harbor, creating aesthetic balance and harmony. Platforms are used to create and segregate spaces and to provide dramatic views of the waterside.

Jørn Utzon: Sydney Opera House, 1958–73, Sydney

The Sydney Opera House is supported by 580 concrete piers that have been sunk up to 82 feet (25 meters) below the sea. It was one of the first buildings to use industrial-strength Araldite adhesive to glue precast structural elements together. Because the roof is the central focal point of the structure, the traditional elements of walls—columns, divisions, and windows—have been almost completely dispensed with. The interior, composed of local pink granite, contains five theaters, five rehearsal studios, two main halls, four restaurants, and six bars. The vaulted concrete ribs create a fan motif on the building's interior. These ribs and the roof shells are further held together by prestressing tendons.

Sydney Opera House

Eero Saarinen

1910, Kirkkonummi–1961, Ann Arbor

■ Architect and product designer ■ Son of the architect and educator Eliel Saarinen ■ Grew up in the Cranbrook Academy of Art in Michigan, a progressive educational community designed by his father ■ Explored a different vernacular for each of his projects, rather than developing a personal style

1910 Born in Kirkkonummi, Finland

1923 Emigrates to the US with his family

1940 Becomes a naturalized United States citizen

1940 Wins a furniture-design competition and begins his long association with the Knoll Furniture Company

1949 Designs his first major building, the General Motors Technical Center in Warren, Michigan

1950 Becomes principal partner of the firm established by his father

1954 Marries Aline Bernstein, an art critic

1961 Dies in Michigan

The life of the Finnish-born Eero Saarinen closely parallels the 20th-century transformation of America itself—an immigrant nation initially looking back to its European roots turning into Kennedy's New Frontier, and a society where innovative vitality and technological prowess would come to triumph. The only son of the influential architect, planner, and educator Eliel Saarinen, Eero initially worked with his father in a partnership that blended the elder's simplified Classicism with the younger's commitment to Modernism. After Eliel's death in 1950, Eero took charge of the practice and created much of his signature work, including the swooping TWA terminal and the graceful St. Louis Gateway Arch. Criticized for not having a definitive style, he was able to adapt his architecture to the needs of his clients. Sadly, Eero himself did not live to see most of his major works built, dying prematurely of a brain tumor in 1961, at the age of 51.

Architecture after 1945

■ TWA Flight Center,
1956–62, Kennedy Airport, New York

The most advanced of his sculptural forms, the TWA Flight Center in New York creates a fluid continuity of space, shape, and surface to celebrate the grandeur of flight. Fusing together a series of thin-shelled slices of concrete to create an ultramodern display of curves, the building was acclaimed upon its completion, and quickly labeled "Eero's Bird."

Kresge Auditorium at MIT, 1953–55, Cambridge, Massachusetts

Designed at the same time as the Kresge Chapel, the Kresge complex as a whole extends the community planning techniques that Saarinen learned from his father. Similar to Eliel's design of Cranbrook in its civic emphasis on open space,

Eero's innovative thin-shell concrete plan for the Kresge Auditorium departs from his father's aesthetic in its stark appreciation of Modernist formalism. The structure resembles a slice from a copper-clad glass circle. The concert hall provides ample seating, and the absence of interior supports gives every seat an unobstructed view.

■ **The Jefferson National Expansion Memorial**, 1947–66, St. Louis, Missouri

More commonly called the Gateway Arch, the Jefferson National Expansion Memorial was built to commemorate the spread of the US West. Built from reinforced concrete and clad with a stainless steel skin, the arch derives its shape from a mathematical function. The interior is hollow and contains an innovative tram system, giving visitors access to an observation deck at the top. Rising to a height of 630 feet (192 meters), the arch is the tallest building in St. Louis and is viewed as the city's definitive icon.

Other Important Works by Saarinen	
General Motors Technical Center, 1949–55, Warren, Michigan	Yale Hockey Rink, 1956–58, New Haven, Connecticut
Kresge Chapel, 1955, Cambridge, Massachusetts	Dulles Airport, 1958–62, Chantilly, Virginia
Thomas J. Watson Research Center (IBM), 1957–61, Yorktown, New York	John Deere and Company Headquarters, 1964, Moline, Illinois

Eero Saarinen

Kenzo Tange

1913, Sakai—2005, Tokyo

■ Fused traditional Japanese styles with Modernism ■ Designed buildings
five continents ■ Influenced a new generation of architects from his teachin
post at Tokyo University ■ Aided in the rebuilding of Hiroshima, conceived
an ambitious urban plan for Tokyo, and redesigned Skopje after an earthqua

- 1913 Born in Sakai, Japan
  1949 Wins commission to design Hiroshima's Peace Center
  1964 Achieves international recognition with his Yoyogi National Gymnasium Complex, his contribution to the 1964 Tokyo Olympics
  1987 Becomes the first Japanese architect to be awarded the Pritzker Prize
  2005 Dies in Tokyo; his funeral is held in his own St. Mary's Cathedral

Other Works by Tange

St. Mary's Cathedral,
1961–64, Tokyo

Master Plan for the
Reconstruction of Skopje,
1966, Skopje, Macedonia

Master Plan for Expo '70,
1970, Osaka

American Medical
Association Headquarters Building, 1987–90,
Chicago, Illinois

Arabian Gulf University,
1988, Manamah, Bahrain

Fuji Television
Building, 1993–96,
Tokyo

Perhaps the central figure in 20th-century Japanese
sign, the architect, author, and urban planner Ker
Tange combined the International style with High Te
architecture and traditional Japanese forms to creat
visionary synthesis that helped to define the identity
postwar Japan. Arguing that architecture should reflec
be an expression of social structure that always advan
from the past to the future, Tange first achieved pro
nence with his hugely symbolic Hiroshima Peace Cent
a peacetime fusion of traditional Japanese tomb arc
tecture with a concrete hyperbolic parabola, whose sha
signaled at once an acceptance of history and a cou
geous rebirth.

■ **Hiroshima Peace Center**,
1949–55, Hiroshima

Drawing from both the 8th-
century Shosoin Storehouse, near

Nara, and the work of Le Corbu
sier, the Hiroshima Peace Cente
set the agenda for postwar Japa
nese architecture.

Yamanashi Press and Radio Center, 1967, Kofu, Japan

Regarded by some critics as Tange's most impressive achievement, the Yamanashi Press and Radio Center is an example of the new structure—

National Gymnasium Complex, 1961–64, Yoyogi, Tokyo

The National Gymnasium Complex was hailed in Tange's citation for the Pritzker Prize as being one of the most beautiful structures of the 20th century. Tange claimed that his 1964 gymnastics arena represented a significant break with his earlier regionalism. In a radical break with traditional Japanese styles, he sought to divorce modern Japan from the constraints of its historical architecture.

the megastructure—that Tange was experimenting with at the time. Based on an innovative space-grid frame designed to increase flexibility by maximizing connections between units, Tange himself saw the

project as a smaller-scale prototype for an ideal city of the future, which he hoped would eliminate the isolation between individual buildings and turn urban space into a single integrated area.

Kenzo Tange

Oscar Niemeyer

1907, Rio de Janeiro

■ Created a regional variation of Modernism specific to Brazil ■ Used concrete in innovative ways to produce new forms ■ Promoted Modern architecture as a means of moving beyond a nation's colonial history, particularly in it use for government buildings ■ Designed the new utopian city of Brasília

■ **1907** Born in Rio de Janeiro

1929–34 Studies at the Escuela Nacional de Bellas Artes, Rio de Janeiro

1936 Works with Le Corbusier in designing Capanema Place

1939 Designs his World's Fair pavilion with Lúcio Costa

1947 Travels to New York to design the UN Headquarters with Le Corbusier

1957–68 Design and construction of Brasília

1967–85 Exiled to Paris due to dictatorship in Brazil

1988 Awarded the Pritzker Prize

Other Works

Capanema Place, 1936–43, Rio de Janeiro,

Pampulha Complex, 1940–43, Pampulha

Canoas House, 1953–54, Rio de Janeiro

French Communist Party Headquarters, 1967–72, Paris

Maison de la Culture, 1972–82, Le Havre

Museu de Arte Contemporânea, 1996, Niterói

Architecture after 1945

Niemeyer was a pioneer in his adaptation of western European Modernism to the Southern Hemisphere, and the most renowned Brazilian architect of the 20th century. Curvilinear concrete forms, as well as large expanses of glass, typify his work. Early in his career he was influenced by Le Corbusier (p. 412), rejecting the dogmatic Functionalism of Bauhaus. He developed an agenda of "aesthetic functionalism," in which "form follows beauty" creating buildings that reflected the natural environment of Brazil. He designed the new capital Brasília, where his monumental buildings created a new cultural identity for modern Brazil.

■ **Palácio do Itamaraty**, 1962–70, Brasília

Niemeyer skillfully contrasts lightness and heaviness in the Ministry of Foreign Relations. The building appears to float serenely above reflecting pool, while the rough concrete arches invoke a commanding Roman Classicism suitable for a government building.

■ **Metropolitan Cathedral**,
1959–70, Brasília

This heavily symbolic and
sculptural cathedral is
Niemeyer's crowning
achievement in Brasília. With
all of its functions located underground, the architecture

reaches up toward the sky.
Concrete ribs evoke both
Gothic cathedrals and the palm
fronds native to Brazil. Colored
glass spanning between the rib
structures creates a dramatic
and heavenly lighting effect in
the interior.

■ **Praça dos Tres Podres**,
1958–60, showing the Federal
Supreme Court, Brasília

The vastness of the plaza, designed as the seat of government, represents a new utopian
vision for Brazil, yet is also

highly Classical in its axial composition and the balanced
asymmetry of the surrounding
buildings. Its two major buildings are glass boxes hovering
above the ground, suspended
from a white sculptural frame.

Oscar Neimeyer

Brutalism

1952–1975

■ Derived its name from French *béton brut*, meaning "raw concrete" ■ Especially prominent in reconstruction projects in the UK after World War II ■ Fell out of favor after the failure of positive communities to form in many Brutalist structures, possibly due to broader processes of urban decay

1952 Le Corbusier devises his Unité d'Habitation principle and builds the Cité Radieuse in Marseille

1954 The term *Brutalism* is coined by the British architects Alison and Peter Smithson

1954 Publication of Reyner Banham's book *The New Brutalism*, which becomes the movement's manual

1960s Brutalism is popular in university campus expansions across the United States

1975 J. G. Ballard publishes his novel *High-Rise*, which argues that Brutalist architecture causes murderous chaos

Other Works

Barbican Estate, by Chamberlin, Powell, and Bon, 1965–76, London

Tricorn Center, by Owen Luder, 1965–66, demolished 2004, Portsmouth, UK

Trellick Tower, by Ernő Goldfinger, 1966–72, London

Robin Hood Gardens, by Alison and Peter Smithson, 1969–72, London

The Brutalist movement in architecture stems from the French *béton brut*—meaning "raw concrete"—a term used by Le Corbusier to describe his choice of material. Associated with social utopianism, the movement sought to use architecture to engineer a more rational urban environment. This was to be accomplished through the construction of high-density housing blocks based on Corbusier's vision of the Unité d'Habitation. The idea was to engender more collective and functional patterns of living by reducing ornament and distraction. Highly controversial, this plan achieved only mixed success, although some aspects of Brutalism have managed to be incorporated into later styles.

■ **Paul Rudolph: Yale Art and Architecture Building,** 1958–63, New Haven, Connecticut

The most renowned example of Brutalist architecture in the United States, the Yale Art and Architecture Building is made of ribbed bush-hammered concrete.

Sir Denys Lasdun: National Theater, 1967

...scribed by Prince Charles as a clever way of building a nuclear power station in the middle of London without anyone objecting," Denys Lasdun's National Theater regularly places among the ten most hated and the ten most loved buildings in the UK. The complex achieves a structural balance, smoothing out the horizontal spaces to match its vertical axis.

■ **Moshe Safdie: Habitat '67**, Montreal, Canada

Built as part of Expo '67, Moshe Safdie designed Habitat '67 when he was just 24, for his master's thesis at Montreal's McGill University. Composed of a series of modular, interlocking forms, Safdie hoped his dynamic vision would become popular among architects around the world. Sadly, his several attempts to construct similar structures elsewhere have all failed due to lack of funding.

Brutalism

Tadao Ando

1941, Osaka

■ Never received formal training ■ Pioneer of critical Regionalism ■ Bases his work on the premise of "using walls to defeat walls" to create sanctuaries that are removed from the chaos of the late Modern world
■ *left:* **Kidosaki House**, staircase, 1986, Tokyo

■ **1941** Born in Osaka, Japan

1969 Begins his architectural practice, Tadao Ando and Associates

1976 Decorated by the Japanese Architectural Association for the Azuma House in Sumiyoshi, Japan

1992 Awarded the Carlsberg Architectural Prize

1995 Awarded the Pritzker Prize and donates the prize money to orphans of the 1995 Kobe earthquake

1996 Awarded the Praemium Imperiale

2002 Awarded the Kyoto Prize

Other Works by Ando

Koshino House, 1981, Kobe, Japan

Chapel on Mount Rokko, 1986, Kobe, Japan

Church on the Water, 1988, Tomamu, Japan

Water Temple, 1991, Awaji Island, Japan

Naoshima Contemporary Art Museum Annex, 1995, Kagawa, Japan

Awaji-Yumebutal, 2000, Awaji Island, Japan

Tadao Ando worked first as a professional boxer and then as a carpenter before turning to architecture in 1969. Unusual among architects for being entirely self-taught—an achievement he shares with Frank Lloyd Wright (p. 382)—at present Ando remains the only architect ever to have won the discipline's four most prestigious prizes—the Carlsberg Architectural Prize, Pritzker Prize, Praemium Imperiale, and the Kyoto Prize. On account of his austere use of concrete and his profound ability to texture light, Ando has been compared to Louis Kahn (p. 440) and Le Corbusier (p. 412), yet his style also retains a strong aspect of Japanese traditionalism, especially in his strategic use of spatial enclosure and his reverent treatment of nature. Acclaimed by critics as "a poet of vertical movement," his buildings have been described as "land art that struggles to emerge from the earth."

■ **Church of the Light**, 1989, Ibariki, Osaka, Japan

Tasked with the problem of designing a building using light as the only material—to create an architecture of light—Ando sliced a cruciform into the eastern wall of his raw concrete construction. The interior was kept coldly bare, like a giant cement box. The result turned the play of sunlight and night into the central event of the building, emphasizing the spiritual power contained within natural cycles.

Minimalist Modernism

452

Architecture after 1945

■ **The Fort Worth Museum of Modern Art**, 2002, Fort Worth, Texas

Built from his signature reinforced concrete, surrounded by 11 naturally landscaped acres (4.5 hectares), and encircled on three sides by water, Fort Worth's Museum of Modern Art is both the second largest gallery space in the United States and Ando's largest US commission to date. The project also had an important personal dimension for Ando: it directly faces his hero Louis Kahn's 1972 Kimbell Museum, a building seen by many critics and architects—including Ando himself—as the finest art museum of the century. Ando felt it was his duty to extend Kahn's ideas and to use the sense of order and harmony that he learned from him. To do this, he created an oasis where people can gather in peace and encounter art and architecture as well as the surrounding nature.

Teatro Armani Milan, 00–2002, Italy

e renovation of a disused colate factory into a global hion headquarters saw Ando ting his talents to work for brand interests of a large poration. The result is an imsing neofeudal cathedral t strives to cement Armani's ce at the apex of Milanese . Rather than wrapping the sting framework in rich terials, Ando's renovation kes use of rough concrete to w the harmony of its protions to take center stage.

Tadao Ando

Álvaro Siza Vieira

1933, Matosinhos

■ Works out of the organic conditions of an existing site, rather than imposing his own designs on them ■ Renowned for his coherent, understated designs and absence of rhetoric

■ *left:* **Schlesisches Tor Apartments**, 1980, Berlin

The sculptor and architect Álvaro Siza Vieira was born 1933 in a coastal town in the mountainous northe region of Portugal. Siza's fresh, lucid buildings take the inspiration from the long light and quiet of his birthplac and his work is characterized by a sensitivity to th specificities of local contexts. Utilizing a tactile ar material-focused approach, rather than an overtly visu or graphic one, Siza has been called a Minimalist for h emphasis on simplicity, balance, and scale. Nevertheles there is also a strong current of sensuality in his work th is revealed by the cool delicacy with which he manip lates texture. Siza has designed swimming pools, housir developments, private residences, banks, office building restaurants, art galleries, shops, and almost every oth type of structure.

■ **Banco Borges e Irmão**, 1978–86 Vila do Conde, Portugal

This small bank branch gave Siza the chance to realize some of the formal ideas that he had developed for his unbuilt works in Berlin. Both expansive ar compact, colossa and delicate, hea set and limpid, Siza's design play with the paradoxe of space itself.

College of Education, 1986–94, Setubal, Portugal

Striking a balance between rigor and flexibility, Siza's design for the college tethers a series of outlying volumes to a central U-shaped foundation, like boats moored to a quay. The idea was to create a series of freely calibrated, semi-autonomous spaces that would remain at the same time linked to a central whole.

Other Works	
Boa Nova Tea House, 1963, Leça da Palmeira, Portugal	Faculty of Architecture at the University of Porto, 1995, Portugal
Leça Swimming Pool, 1966, Leça da Palmeira	Serpentine Gallery Pavilion in Hyde Park, 2005, London
Duarte House, 1981–85, Ovar, Portugal	

Centro Gallego de Arte Contemporaneo, 1988–93, Santiago de Compostela, Spain

Unusual among contemporary art museums in that it strives to merge with its surroundings rather then dominate them, the Centro Gallego de Arte Contemporaneo achieves a harmonious relationship with its urban setting, allowing the city's traditional and modern styles to converge. Siza's clear-headed, granite-clad design reflects his admiration for Rationalism and his sensitivity to local conditions.

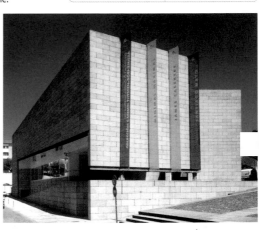

Álvaro Siza Viera

Urban Utopias: Theoretical Urban Planning

1949–Present

■ A genre of architectural thought rather than a unified movement ■ Ofte
guided by a strong commitment to technologically guided social reform

■ **1949** Constant Nieu-
wenhuis, a member of the
Situationists, publishes the
first sketches of his project
The New Babylon

1960 Kenzo Tange helps
to launch the Metabolist
movement with *A Plan
for Tokyo*

1961 Publication of
Archigram 1 pamphlet by
the radical British architectural group Archigram

1967 Jacques Tati releases
his film *Play Time*, popu-
larizing the futuristic city

2002 Archigram awarded
the RIBA Royal Gold Medal

After World War II, and partly as a result of the explosiv
growth of advanced technologies that occurred as a co
sequence of the war, an increasing number of architec
and urban planners began designing for utopian citie
Recognizing that society was changing, and believir
that it was changing for the better, these designe
argued that urban space should be reshaped so as to b
better suited to take account of these social changes.
practice, the designs involved a strong moral commi
ment to the virtues of connectivity, dynamism, and flex
bility, together with a championing of technologic
solutions to social and political problems. In this wa
urban utopian planning has had an important impact c
subsequent capitalist development, because many of i
designs were dictated by pro-consumer beliefs.

Architecture after 1945

Yona Friedman: Spatial City, model, 1958–60

Spatial City is the most significant model of Yona Friedman's theories of mobile architecture and have greatly influenced the work of Archigram and the Metabolists. A 3-D spanning structure, which has minimal contact with the ground, the

design allows for dwellings to be dismantled and moved, as well as altered as the occupant desires. A response to housing shortages in postwar Europe, Friedman's designs were multifunctional and made use of natural sunlight. Spatial models were designed for several cities around the world.

Arata Isozaki/Metabolist: Clusters in the Air Project, model, 1962

In an effort to deal with overpopulation and urban sprawl, the Japanese Metabolist group proposed the creation of megastructures, and argued that the city should not be static, but capable of under-

going organic change. The Clusters in the Air Project sought to revolutionize the way that cities used space and how they built upward. Spaces were conceived of as modular and subject to Functionalist rules. Modules were cantilevered from a central spine creating one of the most futuristic aesthetics in modern architecture.

Other Works

Marine City, model,
by Kiyonori Kikutake, 1958–63

Box-Type Mass Produced Apartments, model,
by Kisho Kurokawa, 1962

Plug-In-City, model,
by Peter Cook/Archigram, 1964

Instant City Airship, model,
by Archigram, 1968–70

The Continuous Monument, model,
by Superstudio, 1969

No-Stop City, model,
by Archizoom, 1969–72

Berlin City Edge, model,
by Daniel Libeskind, 1987

Walking City, model, by Ron Herron/Archigram, 1964

Urban Utopias: Theoretical Urban Planning

Complex Curvature

The use of curvature in architecture dates from antiquity. The Parthenon demon strates an upward curvature of its platform and steps, continuing up into the superstructure and the delicate inclination of its columns' seemingly vertica surfaces. Nevertheless, it was only with the development of modern building materials and modern engineering techniques that more sophisticated curva tures became possible. Following World War II, an Expressionist and humanisti revolt against the flat planar dominance of the early Modernist period began t take shape. Employing a variety of methods, these architects sought to extend th sense of fluidity and flux that curvature can instill. Modern computer program aid in the complex planning of the shapes.

■ **Pier Luigi Nervi: Palazzett dello Sport**,1956–59, Rome

Nervi was among the few structural engineers to have established major reputations for their independent architectural works, and the ribbed shell dome of the Palazzetto represents the jewel of his ca reer. Made from reinforced cor crete and encircled by a series of Y-shaped supporting beams the dome possesses a 197-foo (60-meter) span.

■ **Eladio Dieste: Church of Christ the Worker**, 1958–60, Atlantida, Uruguay

Evolving out of a commission for a simple vault in 1952, the church was Eladio Dieste's first architectural work. The building is very unusual in that its sinusoidal—or wavelike, curvaceous— structure is achieved through an extremely novel use of brick, skill- fully manipulated to create a cathedral-like

effect, normally reserved for expensive stone and stucco.

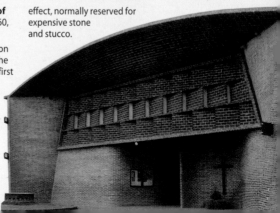

Architecture after 1945

Félix Candela: Church of the Miraculous Virgin, interior, 1953–55, Mexico City

A pioneering work, the design of the church demonstrates that reinforced concrete can be twisted and turned without losing its structural essence.

Félix Candela: Church of the Miraculous Virgin, 1953–55, Mexico City

Candela's major stylistic achievement was the synthesis of the scientific, naturalist, and artistic expressions of architectural design, as seen at the Church of the Miraculous Virgin. Though Candela saw himself as a Structural Rationalist, his buildings harbor a sense of lightness, and the grace of his thin-shelled hyperboloids has often been described as poetic.

This represented both an economic advance and a stylistic one. The benefit of Candela's model was that its realization required neither a skilled labor force nor expensive materials like structural steel, but instead only unskilled labor and concrete. The ease of the design was an attractive proposition for modernizing nations that needed economical, standardized building designs, and, from India to Brazil, Candela's construction plans have been widely applied.

Complex Curvature

Skidmore, Owings & Merrill

1936–Present

■ Interested in technological and structural advancements ■ Concerned with architecture, design, urban planning, and structural engineering ■ Create a corporate identity in which individual architects come under the general name of SOM ■ One of the largest architecture firms in the world

■ **1936** Louis Skidmore and Nathaniel Owings found an architectural firm

1937 First office is opened in New York City

1939 John Merrill becomes a member and the firm becomes Skidmore, Owings & Merrill (SOM)

1952 The structurally innovative design of the Lever House in the International Modernist style sets a new standard for the firm

1970s Involved in the redesigning of Boston's infrastructure systems, using innovative technology

2004 Groundbreaking for Burj Dubai

■ **Jin Mao Building**, 1998, Shanghai

The Jin Mao Building skillfully blends traditional Chinese aesthetics like upturned eaves and pagoda forms with the skyscraper. SOM designed the building's proportions around the number eight, which symbolizes prosperity in China. Structural innovations absorb shock from typhoon winds and earthquakes.

Architecture after 1945

Skidmore, Owings & Merrill is one of the largest architecture firms in the world. Founded in 1936, the company has a long tradition of multidisciplinary design and research projects, involving more than 10,000 campaigns in over 50 countries. After World War II, the firm received worldwide recognition for its cutting-edge corporate design of the Lever House in New York. The firm's research and commissions span the fields of architecture, product design, urban planning, infrastructural planning, and structural engineering, stressing teamwork under the SOM name. Famous for their inventive design and structural research, SOM's architects and designers are renowned for

立邦漆

■ Vasco da Gama Tower at Expo 1998, Lisbon

Leonor Janeiro and Nick Jacobs worked with SOM to create this steel framework tower for the Expo 1998 World's Fair. At the tower's base is a three-story building, used as the European Union Building during the fair. The tower, shaped to resemble the sail of a Portuguese ship, leads up to a luxury restaurant and an observation deck.

■ John Hancock Center
1967–70, Chicago

When the John Hancock Center was completed, it held the record for being the tallest building in the world outside New York City. Structural engineer Fazul Kahn's 100 stories are made possible by an innovative technique of using X-shaped braces to support the building's height.

Other Important Works

ever House, 1952, Jew York	Wachovia Financial Center, 1984, Miami
ir Force Academy hapel, 1956–62, olorado Springs	Time Warner Center, 2000–2004, New York
laj Terminal, 972, Jeddah, Saudi rabia	San Francisco International Airport, 2001
irst Wisconsin Plaza, 974, Madison	Ben Gurion Airport Terminal 3, 2004, Tel Aviv
ears Tower, 1974–76, hicago	Burj Dubai, 2004–, Dubai
nerplex North uilding, 1982, rinceton	Pearl River Tower, 2006–, Guangzhou
	Freedom Tower, 2006–, New York

their innovative approach to top-end commercial projects. Since the 1950s SOM has catered to corporate clients and has achieved international success around the world. SOM's design for Burj Dubai, which is currently under construction and scheduled for completion late in 2008, will make it the world's tallest building, surpassing even the Taipei 101.

Time Warner Center, 2003–07, New York

[D]avid Childs and Mustafa Kemal Abadan of SOM [d]esigned New York's Time Warner Center. The [s]yscraper is a multiuse structure and consists of [m]all, office spaces, luxury condominiums, a [h]otel, performance theaters, and broadcasting [st]udios. Atop a seven-story base, two towers are [su]pported by steel frames and clad in a rectan-[g]ular-patterned curtain wall. The building's twin [to]wers stand on trapezoidal floor plans, and their [w]eight is supported by 65 columns and a wall of [th]ick, reinforced concrete that runs through the [ba]se building.

Sears Tower, 1970–74, Chicago

[S]OM has long been at the forefront of technolog-[ic]al advancements and record-breaking designs. [In] 1973 the Sears Tower was the tallest building [in] the world, until the Petronas Twin Towers in [M]alaysia surpassed it. The building's elevation is [m]ade possible by a series of sharp setbacks that [re]duce the load of the uppermost portions. The [to]wer is further supported by an innovative [st]eel-tubing technique, making it possible for [ad]ditional heightening.

Corporate Modernism

■ **Burj Dubai**, 2004–, Dubai

The Burj Dubai is currently the tallest structure in the world, and it is still growing. The building's design resembles a needle. Its vertical massing is carefully manipulated so as to provide sufficient protection and strength against wind, while at the same time recalling the designs of Islamic architecture in its floor plan. The building's base is Y-shaped, maximizing views, and it is positioned to minimize wind impact. The lower portion, from the 155th floor down, will be constructed of reinforced concrete. Above 1,922 feet (586 meters) the tower will finish in a steel frame. It will be clad in aluminum and stainless steel to help defend it from the desert's intense summer heat.

Skidmore, Owings & Merrill

I. M. Pei

Ieoh Ming Pei
1917, Guangzhou

■ Pursues a technological approach to design, often letting structural solutions dictate architectural form ■ Promotes Modernism as a pure aesthetic ■ Established the renowned Pei, Cobb, Freed, and Partners firm

■ **1917** Born Ieoh Ming Pei in Guangzhou, China

1940 Receives bachelor of architecture from MIT

1946 Receives master of architecture from Harvard, Walter Gropius is among his teachers

1955 Forms I. M. Pei and Associates

1962 Receives FAA commission for 50 air traffic control towers

1968 Receives AIA Architectural Firm award

1975 Elected to American Academy

1983 Receives Pritzker Architectural Prize

1989 Forms Pei, Cobb, Freed, and Partners

■ **Grand Louvre**, 1983–98, Paris

Mostly underground, the new main entrance to the Louvre allows the museum to deal with the large crowds. Although Pei's addition entirely reorganized the museum's space, visually the project treads lightly upon the great historic building, adding only an iconic glass pyramid to create an entrance atrium.

Architecture after 1945

Although many architects pioneered the discourse an forms of Modern architecture before him, I. M. Pei broug Modernism to the attention of the general public. H commissions employed the stylistic innovations prewar Modernism—such as large expanses of glass, un ornamented surfaces, geometrical purity, and expresse structure—for public and institutional buildings tha were expected to convey their importance throug monumental architecture. Pei's works, particularly his ac ditions to the Louvre and the National Gallery in Wash ington, DC, helped to establish Modernism, which ha often been understood as too cold and stark to conve grandeur, as an appropriate style for prominent publ buildings. Along with that of his partners Henry Cobb an James Freed, I. M. Pei's creative genius has made him on of the most favored architects of governments, museum universities, and corporations in the 20th century.

Bank of China Tower,
82–89, Hong Kong

e tower uses a diamond motif
organize its surface and mass-
g. Expressed cross bracing set
a reflective glass curtain wall is
signed to resist high winds.
gether with its triangulated,
pped form, the visual bulk
d the actual weight of this
10-foot (369-meter) tower is
ninished. The Bank of China
wer was the tallest building
tside of the United States at
e time of its completion.

Other Works by Pei

ational Center for
tmospheric Research,
961–67, Boulder

hn F. Kennedy Library,
965–79, Boston

hn Hancock Building,
967–76, Boston

agrant Hill Hotel,
979–82, Beijing

eyerson Symphony Center,
982–89, Dallas

ock and Roll Hall of Fame,
987–95, Cleveland

xtension to the Deutsches
istorisches Museum, 2003,
erlln

■ **East Wing of the
National Gallery of
Art**, 1968–78,
Washington, DC

In the East Wing of the
National Gallery, built
as an addition to the
existing Neoclassical
museum, Pei overlaps
triangular forms in the
plan to create a series
of galleries flanking a
large, central open
space. The building is
clad in marble, allow-
ing for the simple
geometry of the plan
to be clearly legible on
the exterior, and form-
ing sharp edges that
are the celebrated hall-
mark of the building.

I. M. Pei

Sir Norman Foster

1935, Manchester

■ Pioneers new materials, structural and environmental controls, and construction technologies ■ Projects are often characterized by the extensive use of glass ■ Emphasizes constructability, materiality, and an adherence to time and budget constraints ■ Forgoes historical conventions

■ **1935** Born in Manchester

1961 Receives degree from Manchester University; wins Yale scholarship

1967 Founds his own firm, Foster + Partners

1979 Begins Hongkong and Shanghai Bank headquarters

1983 Wins RIBA Gold Medal

1994 Wins AIA Gold Medal

1998 Awarded the Stirling Prize for Imperial War Museum, Duxford

1999 Wins the Pritzker Prize

2004 Awarded the Stirling Prize for 30 St. Mary Axe

2007 Wins the Aga Khan Award

■ **30 St. Mary Axe**, 1997–2004, London

Known as "the Gherkin," 30 St. Mary Axe is London's first ecological tall building. Its unique shape and triangulated structural surface is designed to resist wind, while double glazing allows for passive solar heating and natural cooling. Designed to maximize the use of natural light, the building is fitted with sensors to minimize energy waste.

Architecture after 1945

The architecture practice of Sir Norman Foster is renowne for its pursuit of and Modernist belief in technological inn vation. One of the most famous contemporary architectu practices in the world, Foster + Partners often works close with engineers and has designed a vast number of larg scale, institutional, and infrastructural buildings around th world that are characterized by their use of glass, stainle steel, and exposed and aestheticized structures, often in iconic and metaphoric forms. Since the 1970s, the firm has been internationally recognized for its environmentally sustainable designs, which make use of natural daylight and passive climate-control strategies, thus revolutionizing the typology of tall buildings in this a embracing ⌧

Corporate Modernism

■ Hongkong and Shanghai Bank Headquarters, 1979–86, Hong Kong

The Hongkong and Shanghai Bank building significantly revolutionized the tall building typology. Constructed from five structural modules that were prefabricated in Glasgow, UK, the building was designed to allow for flexibility in its internal configuration. With structure and service cores pushed to the periphery, the deep, open floor plates and a 10-story atrium are naturally lit by a mirrored central sun-scoop. Although all of the building's technology fulfills functional requirements, Foster also allowed the structural elements of the building to be the primary motifs of its aesthetics, as well as its organization—particularly the V-shaped suspension trusses on the exterior, which are a prominent symbol of the building and that also form double-height spaces inside. This relationship between aesthetics and technology makes the Hongkong and Shanghai Bank one of the icons of High Tech architecture.

■ Reichstag Dome, 1992–99, Berlin

Foster's glass dome on top of the existing Neo-classical Reichstag building was conceived as a visual metaphor for the transparency and openness of the newly unified German government. In addition to serving as the primary attraction for visitors to the German parliament, with a spiral ramp providing panoramic views of the city, the interior cone of the dome provides reflected daylight to the chambers below, with an automated sunshade to reduce heat gain during the warmer summer months.

Other Important Works by Foster

Willis Faber & Dumas Headquarters, 1971–75, Ipswich, UK	Chep Lap Kok Airport, 1992–97, Hong Kong
Sainsbury Center for Visual Arts, 1974–78, Norwich, UK	The Great Court at the British Museum, 1994–2000, London
Canary Wharf Underground Station, 1991–99, London	Masdar Initiative Master Plan, 2007–, Abu Dhabi

Sir Norman Foster

Modernity and High Tech innovations, both his architectural and infrastructural designs maintain a level of cultural sensitivity. His work spans 40 years, adapting to technological and social changes, maintaining his status as a leader in the world of architectural design.

■ Clyde Auditorium, 1997, Glasgow

Nicknamed "the Armadillo," the Clyde Auditorium is a massive addition to the Scottish Exhibition and Conference Center, extending its use for concerts and public events. The structure, shaped like sails, references the shipping tradition of the area, and it is now one of Glasgow's most recognizable

■ Essen Design Center, 1992–97, Essen, Germany

The Essen Design Center is located on the site of the former Zeche Zollverein, a decommissioned coal-mining complex. The center uses the architectural bones of the old powerhouse, exposing the functional, industrial aspects o the inside concealed behind a sleek geometric facade. The entire complex of buildings is united by its use of brown wall and red exposed I-beams. The center contains galleries and work spaces within the contex of a 1930s factory—juxtaposing Modern designs with early technologies. The building offers design and display space of over 43,000 square feet (4,000 square meters), making it the largest design center in the world.

forms. Flat aluminum sheeting is fixed to hull-shaped frames. The overlapping shells create an arced canopy at the entrance. Inside, the center's facilities are multifunctional.

Chesa Futura, 2000–04,
St. Moritz, Switzerland

The Chesa Futura apartments
were constructed using state-
of-the-art computer design

Millau Viaduct, 1993–2004,
Millau, France

Spanning nearly 1.5 miles (2.5
kilometers), the Millau Viaduct
is taller than the Empire State
Building, making it the tallest
vehicular bridge in the world.
Aesthetically, the horizontal
deck of the bridge appears light
in comparison to the massive
masts, accentuating its span.
The deck employs an innovative steel material that allows
for flexibility and resistance to
wear and wind.

techniques mixed with
traditional local timber on the
building's framing and facade.
The wooden shingles, from
local trees, are extremely

durable in the cold climate and,
despite an eventual change in
color from exposure to the elements, will not need mainten-
ance for many years to come.

Sir Norman Foster

High Tech Architecture

1969–Present

■ First developed in the UK by the brief pairing of Richard Rogers and Renzo Piano ■ Named after the design book *High Tech: The Industrial Style and Source Book for the Home* ■ Distinguished by an aesthetic use of industrial and structural elements and a revitalization of Functionalism

■ **1969** Neil Armstrong walks on the moon, and public interest in new technologies increases

1971 The previously little-known Piano and Rogers are awarded the prize to design the Centre Georges Pompidou

1977 Completion of the Centre Georges Pompidou

1978 Publication of Joan Kron and Suzanne Slesin's influential style manual *High Tech: The Industrial Style and Source Book for the Home*

1999 The Media Center at Lords Cricket Ground is the first-ever all-aluminum building with a semi-structural skin

The futuristic look of High Tech architecture first appeared as a distinctive style at the beginning of the 1970s. The style, developed most by the brief pairing of Richard Rogers and Renzo Piano, was greatly influenced by the ideas of the 1960s group Archigram. As with Postmodernism, the style grew out of a dissatisfaction with a Modernist Functionalism that was now considered to be exhausted. Unlike the Postmodernists, however, Rogers and Piano held the view that the idea was not to abandon Functionalism, but to update and revamp it by infusing it with the spirit and energy of the space age. Drawing on the theories of Buckminster Fuller as well as the ideas of Kenzo Tange (p. 446), the Smithsons, and Archigram, they crafted a new synthesis, prizing efficiency, flexibility, and technological sophistication over symbolism and citation, and affirming its own technological aesthetic through the exposure of structural systems. As with 🖙

■ **Nicholas Grimshaw, Channel Tunnel Railway Terminal, Waterloo Station**, London, 1993

Famous for its 1,312-foot (400-meter) prismatic curved glass roof, Grimshaw's International Terminal provided a stunning sight for railway travelers arriving in London. With Eurostar's relocation of its London operation to St. Pancras, the fate of the building is uncertain.

Architecture after 1945

■ **Renzo Piano and Richard Rogers: Centre Georges Pompidou**, 1971–77, Paris

Inspired by Cedric Price's unbuilt designs for the Fun Palace, the Centre Pompidou turned the architectural world upside down. With its exposed skeleton of brightly colored tubes for mechanical systems, the building represented a new form of museum, now no longer an elite institution, but instead a place of exchange in the heart of the city.

Other Important Works

Enerplex, North Building, by SOM, 1982, Princeton, New Jersey

Hysolar Building, by Gunter Behnisch, 1986–87, Stuttgart

Rue de Meaux Housing, by Renzo Piano, 1988–91, Paris

Hôtel du Departement, by Alsop and Stormer, 1994, Marseille

Kansai Airport Terminal, by Renzo Piano, 1994, Osaka, Japan

Eden Project, by Nicholas Grimshaw, 1996, Cornwall, UK

■ **Richard Rogers: Lloyds of London**, 1978–86

Similar to the Centre Pompidou in removing its essential service conduits to the outside of the structure, Rogers nevertheless achieved a much more elegant vertical form for his

Lloyd's of London building by drawing from the designs of the Soviet Constructivist movement. The irony of applying these designs to a bank notwithstanding, the work forms a stunningly original element of the London skyline.

High Tech Architecture

turn-of-the-century architects who incorporated then new industrial materials and styles into their designs, architects of the High Tech movement appropriated common exposed metal plating, shelving, industrial lighting fixtures, and fabrics into their residential and corporate buildings. The style was the next step in industrialized Modernism, redirecting the forms of postwar architecture.

■ **Žižkov Television Tower**, 1985–92, Prague

The unconventional television tower is a startling addition to the medieval city of Prague and is a controversial remnant of the Communist era. Supported by three massive concrete pillars, the futuristic tower reaches 708 feet (216 meters) into the air. Often associated with Brutalist architecture because of its disjointed and Cubistic levels, the tower was fitted with sculptures of babies crawling up its pillars by the Czech artist David Černý in 2000. Although greatly criticized, the tower succeeds in the High Tech ideal of asserting the role of technology in society. The tower features observation decks as well as transmission devices.

▶ **Foster + Partners: Stansted Airport**, 1991, London

Foster + Partners' design for the new terminal at Stansted Airport displays its structural support elements. The building's innovative roof is nonstructural and functions only as a sheltering canopy. The building's simple interior allows for easy usage and movement. Services that are usually found within the building's walls and atop it have been relegated to a subterranean sector, clarifying the building's structural aesthetic. Because these services are located beneath the building, the terminal is able to fully display its light structure. The roof is supported by Y-shaped pillars and, in an effort to incorporate sustainable building techniques into the design, is transparent enough to allow the building to be lit by natural light on most days.

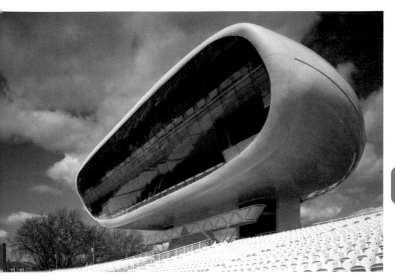

Future Systems: NatWest Media Center at Lord's Cricket Ground, 1994–99, London

One of the most innovative media centers in the world, Future Systems' design is the first fully aluminum structure semi-supported by its skin. Built using technology derived from the boat-building industry, it is aerodynamic and seamless. The windows provide excellent views of the field and are slightly inclined to avoid glare.

High Tech Architecture

Venturi & Scott-Brown

1925, Philadelphia, and 1931, Nkana

■ Heavily criticized Modernist Functionalism and laid the foundations for Postmodernism in architecture ■ Venturi is especially well known for coining the maxim "less is a bore," as a response to Mies van der Rohe's Modernist dictum that "less is more"

■ **1925** Robert Venturi is born in Philadelphia

1931 Denise Scott-Brown is born in Nkana, Zambia, as Denise Lakofski

1960 Venturi founds his professional practice in Philadelphia

1966 *Complexity and Contradiction in Architecture* is published

1967 Scott-Brown and Venturi marry in Santa Monica, California

1969 Scott-Brown joins Venturi's firm as partner in charge of planning

1991 Venturi is awarded the Pritzker Prize

Other Works

Allen Memorial Art Museum at Oberlin College, 1976, Oberlin, Ohio

Seattle Art Museum, 1991

Museum of Contemporary Art, 1996, San Diego, California

Mielparque Nikko Kirifuri Resort, 1997, Nikko, Japan

Provincial Capital Building, 1999, Toulouse, France

Architecture after 1945

Arguably the most influential American architects of the second half of the 20th century, the husband and wife team of Robert Venturi and Denise Scott-Brown are renowned for their embrace of populism and vernacular design. Their architectural style was developed at a time in which many felt that Modernism had run out of steam. Their innovative ideas effectively gave birth to what became known as Postmodern architecture. As with the emergence of Modernism itself, this would be a stylistic shift achieved as much through the medium of writing as through the medium of built architecture—Venturi in particular was a brilliantly effective polemicist, and his 1966 text *Complexity and Contradiction in Architecture* represents perhaps the most seminal architectural manifesto since Le Corbusier's (p. 412) 1923 statement of intent, *Towards a New Architecture*.

■ **Guild House Retirement Home**, 1961–66, Philadelphia

Full of peculiar details, it was originally topped with a non-functioning antenna to commemorate the elderly's appreciation of television. The antenna was seen as a cynical joke and removed.

Sainsbury Wing of the National Gallery, 1985–91, London

Venturi and Scott-Brown were hired to build London's Na-tional Gallery extension after Prince Charles described an ear-lier Modernist design as "a monstrous carbuncle on the face of a much-loved and ele-gant friend." Their own design strives for similarity rather than difference, using similar mate-rials and quoting many of the original building's details.

Vanna Venturi House, 1961–64, Chestnut Hill, Pennsylvania

The built component of Ven-turi's *Complexity and Contradic-tion in Architecture,* and his first major project, Venturi designed this house for his mother. Cen-tralized around the chimney, the Vanna Venturi House radi-ates warmth. The geometric layout of the house, and its use of vaulted, separated spaces and fractured pediments recalls historical styles and Palladian geometric designs.

Venturi & Scott-Brown

Sir James Stirling

1926, Glasgow—1992, London

■ Sought to prioritize the artistic aspect of architecture over its functionalist side ■ Widely seen as a Postmodernist, but rejected the label, preferring to call himself "Post-International" ■ Gave his name to the Stirling Prize, a major British award for architectural excellence that was started after his death in 1996

One of the most influential architects of the postwar period, James Stirling employed a style of eclectic citation that aimed to bury the stagnant International style and to create a revitalized Modernism in architecture. His designs were often built in the traditional styles common to the area, or with local materials. Stirling's work was consistently playful and ironic, an effect achieved through his deliberately ambiguous mingling of Modernist and Classicist elements. Chiefly concerned with the Modernist problem of humanizing the environment, Stirling drew freely from historical models to develop his own varied architectural language. His sensitivities to tradition and his cultural depth have attracted the attention of major architectural critics and theoreticians, and literature examining his architecture is published around the world.

■ **Engineering Building of Leicester University**, 1959–6

Built in the last days of their dissolving partnership, Stirling and Gowan's Engineering Building at Leicester University combined red brick and tile with aesthetics from greenhouses, references to vent pipes from steamships, industrial glazing, engineering brick, and other faceless industrial aspects of building. The work jokingly dismisses the earnestness of much architectural austerity, and challenged the meaning of Modernism.

Neue Staatsgalerie, 1977–84, Stuttgart, Germany

Modeled after Karl Friedrich Schinkel's Neoclassical Altes Museum, Stirling's Neue Staatsgalerie boldly omitted the building's facade to achieve a much more dynamic effect. The building's interiors are lined by walls of warm marble and tiled with floors of green rubber.

Other Important Works by Stirling	
Ham Common Flats, 1955–58, near London	Clore Gallery, Tate Britain, 1980–87, London
Infill Housing, 1957–59, Preston	Tate Liverpool, 1984–88
Faculty of History at the University of Cambridge, 1964–68, Cambridge	Bibliothèque de France, 1989, Paris
	Kyoto Center, 1991, Kyoto

■ **No. 1 Poultry**, 1988–98, London

Among the last buildings Stirling designed, No. 1 Poultry was completed after his death by his partner Michael Wilford. The work remains controversial and was once voted London's fifth most hated building. Despite the controversy, the structure has also been seen as the city's Postmodernist crown jewel.

Sir James Stirling

Aldo Rossi

1931, Milan–1997, Milan

■ Achieved international recognition across the three separate fields of architectural theory, building, and drawing ■ Formulated the principles of Neo-Rationalism ■ Stressed the importance of monuments ■ Also designed objects, including a series of coffeepots for Alessi

Most famous in architecture for his part in the develop ment of Neo-Rationalism, a Postmodernist school th sought to reinvigorate Classicism, Aldo Rossi accom plished the unusual feat of gaining international recogni tion across three separate fields: theory, architecture, an drawing. As a theorist, Rossi is best known for his stud *The Architecture of the City,* a book that criticized the Mod ernist understanding of urban space and argued th cities were entities that evolved over time, and that de pended upon the forms of shared memory concentrate in monuments to provide them with structure an meaning. As an artist, Aldo Rossi drew from the work Italian landscape painters to produce haunting images which both his buildings and others in the city shrin while everyday objects, such as coffeepots and cigaret packs, swell to fill the frame. His drafts of projects hav also garnered much success.

Gallaratese Apartment Block, 1969–74, Milan

Built as part of the response to an urgent postwar Milanese housing shortage, the Gallara- tese Apartment Block is a satel- lite community, housing around 2,500 people, split across five buildings—one by Rossi and four by his friend Carlo Aymonino. In contrast to Aymonino's typologically di- verse slabs, Rossi's contributio is simple and almost entirely repetitive, rational, and white.

St. Cataldo Cemetery, 1971–84, Modena, Italy

One of his earliest major public buildings, Rossi's addition to the existing cemetery emphasized its role as a repository of social meaning. Whereas the city housed the living, he felt the cemetery should house the dead. This caused controversy, with some critics objecting that Rossi's stress on monumental collectivity sacrificed the feelings of individuals.

Other Works

■ **Hotel il Palazzo**, 1987, Fukuoka, Japan

Mainly by virtue of its pink-hued stone facade, Rossi's Hotel il Palazzo became an instant design icon upon its completion in 1987. More strongly than the color of its surface, the Palazzo's clear geometric simplicity emphasizes solidity, Classical order, and harmony. Like much of Rossi's work, the building possesses an important monumental aspect and expresses a sense of power—sitting atop a stepped stone base, the structure has a facade of carved columns and is lined with massive copper lintels. Notably devoid of windows, Rossi explained this absence by invoking the E. M. Forster novel *A Room with a View*: "At the beginning of the novel, the view of Florence is very important," he said. "But at the end, what is really important is the stay at the hotel, the love, the life of the hotel."

Aldo Rossi

New York Five

1967–2000

■ Composed of Peter Eisenman, Michael Graves, Charles Gwathmey, John Hejduk, and Richard Meier ■ First grouped together in a 1967 MoMA exhibition organized by Arthur Drexler ■ Advocates of European architectural Modernism in a famous conflict with Robert Venturi and his Postmodern school

1967 Arthur Drexler hosts the Five Architects exhibition at the Museum of Modern Art in New York

1972 Publication of *Five Architects: Eisenman, Graves, Gwathmey, Hejduk, Meier*, the book that would be mistaken for the New York Five's manifesto

1973 *Five on Five*, a counterblast against the supposedly Modernist excesses of the New York Five by Robert Stern, Jaquelin Robertson, Charles Moore, Allan Greenberg, and Romaldo Giurgola

2000 Hejduk dies and the Five's styles become increasingly divergent

■ **Michael Graves: Benacerraf House Addition**, 1969, Princeton

Michael Graves's Benacerraf House addition recalls the early work of Le Corbusier, such as Villa Savoye. He created a minimal and functional space for living. The expansive use of fine walls and cutaway spaces is designed to accomplish a panoramic exposure, inviting the outside in.

Architecture after 1945

Also known as "the Whites," the New York Five were on side of a rhetorical war waged in 1970s American architectural theory. Presented as theoretical, intellectual, European, and Modernist, they fought for these ideals with their rivals, "the Grays," five Philadelphia-based architectural theorists. The Grays were unofficially led by Robert Venturi (p. 480), and defined themselves as pragmatic, American, populist, and Postmodern, by comparison. In truth, the dichotomy was never as clear cut as this, and major differences always existed between the New York Five members. Nevertheless, the polemic was important in the battle for the meaning of Modernism.

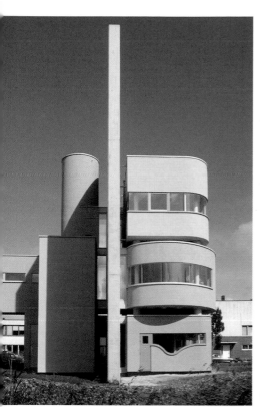

Modernism

■ **John Hejduk: Wall House 2**, front view, 2001, Groningen, the Netherlands

Described by Hejduk as "an architectural meditation on the passage of time," Wall House 2 is on a lakefront in the Netherlands. A rare example of a realized Hejduk structure—most of his highly theoretical work exists only on paper—it was completed after his death and over 25 years after its original conception. Used mainly for exhibitions and performances, the unit is also employed as a residency site for artists.

Other Works

Gwathmey Residence and Studio, by Charles Gwathmey, 1967, Amagansett, New York

House II, by Peter Eisenman, Hardwick, 1969–70, Vermont

The Getty Center, by Richard Meier, 1984–97, Los Angeles

Museum of Contemporary Art, by Charles Gwathmey, 1996, North Miami

Richard Meier: Barcelona Museum of Contemporary Art, 1987–95

Richard Meier's geometric design for the renovation of the Barcelona Museum of Contemporary Art offers new perspectives from every angle that simultaneously unite and divorce it from its setting. The layers of flat white surfaces and glass are pierced by natural light, creating a disjointed aesthetic that is united by the rectangles of light and shadow. The interior organization of the museum is a maze of paths and Minimalistic rooms that allow for a variety of exhibition possibilities.

New York Five

Postmodern Classicism

1964–Present

■ Aims to liberate architecture from a purely functional role ■ Provides new treatments for elements from architectural history ■ Establishes a dialogue with history ■ Utilizes nonfunctional decorative elements ■ Unusual color palates and combinations ■ Playful and sculptural

■ **1964** Construction of Vanna Venturi House

1966 Robert Venturi publishes *Complexity and Contradiction in Architecture*, laying the groundwork for Postmodern Classicism

1972 Robert Venturi, Denise Scott Brown, and Steven Izenour publish *Learning from Las Vegas*, exploring urban sprawl and architectural theories

1983 Construction of Les Espaces D'Abraxas

1995 Construction of San Antonio Library

Postmodern Classicism is an international style that was developed in response to the largely formal, functionalized language of Modernism. In order to alleviate the rigidity and rules of Modernism, Postmodern Classicism returns to the past, collecting elements of pre-Modern designs such as pillars and decorative facades, and recreating them in a contemporary climate alongside other styles in order to make them sensitive to their context. Postmodern Classicism is characterized by stark ornamentation, eclectic and decorative iconography, symbolism, wit, and irony. Ideologically, it suggests that knowledge cannot be understood without a consideration of context, and thus aims to give rise to a dialogue between ideas, styles, and history.

Other Works

Vanna Venturi House, by Robert Venturi, 1964, Philadelphia

Brion-Vega Cemetery, by Carlo Scarpa, 1972, St. Vito d'Altivole, Italy

Abteiberg Museum, by Hans Hollein, 1982, Mönchengladbach, Germany

San Antonio Public Library, by Ricardo Legoretta, 1995, San Antonio, Texas

■ **Charles Moore: Piazza d'Italia**, 1978, New Orleans

Piazza d'Italia is a playful, arousing structure that borrows design elements from Roman antiquity. These styles are given new treatments with loud colors and modern materials such as platinum tiles and polymer resin. The piazza's unconventional elements and historical references create one of the most well-known examples of Postmodern Classicism.

■ **Ricardo Bofill: Les Espaces D'Abraxas**, 1983, Marne-la-Vallée, France

Constructed of prefabricated concrete, this gigantic co-lumnar structure was designed in response to the banality of large-scale, often rectangular housing designs. Consisting of 591 dwellings, the D'Abraxas blends the language of Classi-cism with contemporary urban life. Within the structure, which resembles the Colosseum, a central lawn-covered plaza links the design together and creates a dynamic public theater.

■ **Philip Johnson and John Burgee: Sony Tower (formerly AT&T Building)**, 1984, New York

The 37-story Sony Tower chal-lenges the Modernist preoccu-pation with stark Functionalism through its use of a highly vis-ible, Classically-referenced pediment and a spectacular seven-story arched entrance-way. The iconic Manhattan high-rise defies traditional skyscraper design by being playful and ornamental, while remaining functional and Modernist in its lack on ornamentation and height. Not only does the Sony Tower reference Classical structures, but it also recalls the popular 18th-century furniture designs of Thomas Chippendale.

Postmodern Classicism

Peter Eisenman

1932, Newark

■ Influenced by philosophy ■ Attempts to expand architectural language by creating "pure" forms ■ Uses fragmented and opposing elements ■ Associated with the Deconstructivist movement ■ Challenges aesthetic notions of beauty ■ Interested in mathematics, grids, and multiple geometric orders

■ **1932** Born in Newark

1955 Studies architecture at Cornell University

1963 Receives his PhD from the University of Cambridge

1970 Construction of Eisenman's House III

1982–85 Teaches at Harvard and the University of Illinois

1987 Eisenman Architects is formed

1988 Participates in the Deconstructivist Architecture exhibition

1989 Construction of the Wexner Center

■ **City of Culture of Galicia**, 1999–, Santiago de Compostela

Expected to be completed in 2012, the City of Culture is composed of the street plan of the ancient city of Santiago, superimposed on a modern Cartesian grid, and the topography of the hillside, which is allowed to distort both designs, creating an entirely new landscape. The design is so complex that every windowpane must be custom shaped.

Eisenman Architects is the architectural firm established by Peter Eisenman, who first achieved notoriety in 1967 as a member of the New York Five (p. 480). His early work was preoccupied by the desire to embrace architecture as a self-referential and pure form—a largely academic exercise that often resulted in structures that were antagonistic or disorienting to users when actually built. His early use of fragmented, disjointed forms and colliding planes has labeled him as one of the founding members of the Deconstructivist movement, despite Eisenman's repeated attempts to distance himself from this collective. His designs exercise the expansion of architectural forms and ideas and are particularly influenced by philosophy and architectural theory, especially the writings of Jacques Derrida.

■ **Wexner Center**, south facade, 1989, Columbus, Ohio

Cited as one of the first examples of Deconstructivist architecture, this curious, disorienting design features large

brick towers inspired by the Armory Building, a castlelike structure that burnt down on the location in 1958. In contrast to the Armory's shapely edifices, white scaffoldlike beams

are imposed on the facade, creating fragmented, partial forms. The building received extensive restoration work in 2003 as a result of leaks and damage done by excessive sunlight.

Other Works by Eisenman

Project Romeo and Juliet, 1984, Verona

Koizumi Sangyo Building, 1990, Tokyo

Nunotani Corporation Headquarters Building, 1992, Tokyo

BLF Software Administration Building, 1996, Bangalore

Memorial to the Murdered Jews of Europe, 2005, Berlin

Arizona Cardinals Stadium, 2006, Glendale

■ **Eisenman's House III (Haus Miller)**, 1970, Lakeville, Connecticut

Designed as a self-referential structure, Eisenman's House III is a mathematical and formulaic representation of architecture as pure form. Its rectilinear, boxlike design exists independently of human context, challenging traditional ideas of comfort and aesthetic beauty. The angular planes and blunt forms create an environment of dislocation and curiosity.

Peter Eisenman

Frank Gehry

1929, Toronto

- Rejects both the restraints of Modernism and the historical reference of Postmodernism ■ Drew attention to the Los Angeles architecture scene in the 1980s and 90s, which also included Morphosis and Eric Owen Moss ■ First architect to use digital technology to fabricate previously unrealizable forms

Deconstructivism

1929 Born in Toronto

1954 Graduates from University of Southern California School of Architecture

1962 Opens Frank O. Gehry & Associates in Los Angeles

1969–73 Develops the Easy Edges cardboard furniture line

1985–91 Collaborates with Claes Oldenburg and Coosje van Bruggen on Chiat/Day building in Venice, California

1989 Awarded the Pritzker Prize

2001 Exhibition of his work at the Guggenheim Museum, New York

■ **Vitra Design Museum**, 1987–89, Weil am Rhein

The white stucco and zinc cladding of the Vitra Design Museum blurs distinctions between horizontal and vertical planes, as well as interior and exterior spaces. Unlike Gehry's earlier work, this building is no longer an assemblage of parts, but instead a unified, sculptural whole that bends into and moves out of itself.

Architecture after 1945

With his innovative use of materials and expressive, recognizable forms, Canadian-born Frank Gehry is the most popularly celebrated contemporary American architect. Gehry's early work was inspired by the fast pace and artificiality of Los Angeles, the city in which he has always been based. He assembled ordinary materials such as plywood, chain-link fence, and corrugated metal to create Cubist-inspired buildings, including many houses that are often associated with the Deconstructivist movement. As he moved on to larger projects, his buildings became increasingly curvilinear. His later works incorporate Deconstructivist elements with flowing lines. Gehry's firm pioneered the use of software from the aerospace industry for the design and fabrication of his buildings, many of which employ high-tech materials. Although his works have been associated with a variety of movements, he has managed to create a distinguished personal

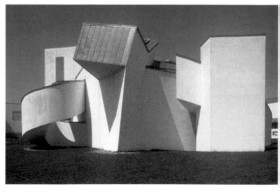

■ **Guggenheim Museum Bilbao**, 1991–97, Bilbao

Clad in titanium, the Guggenheim Bilbao is a culmination of Gehry's form-making and techno-logical pursuits. The building is both a work of sculpture and of urbanism. It was carefully de-signed to integrate with the surrounding urban fabric, including the neighboring bridge. The museum supported F. L. Wright's concept of the first Guggenheim in New York, in which the ar-chitecture is as dazzling as the art within.

Other Works by Gehry
Gehry House, 1977–78, Santa Monica
Walt Disney Concert Hall, 1988–2003, Los Angeles
Weisman Museum, 1990–93, Minneapolis
Gehry Tower, 2001, Hanover, Germany

■ **Nationale Neder-landen Building**, 1992–96, Prague

Also known as "Fred and Ginger," a name referencing the dance-like nature of the two forms, this building adopts the regularity of its historic surround-ings to Gehry's trade-mark curves.

Frank Gehry

style that at once draws from Classical themes and an explosive Modernism. His most recent works have seen a shift away from the metallic surfaces, such as those used at the Guggenheim Museum Bilbao. Despite his fame for such sculptural metal designs, he is now attempting to create buildings with equally complex shapes and lines using other materials. Gehry's buildings stand out as defining aspects of their surroundings. Rather than incorporating or reflecting their setting, they redefine it. His architecture has become so famous that several cities around the world have commissioned him as a means to encourage tourism. Despite his popularity and wealth of commissions, Gehry is also criticized for his sometimes lack of sensitivity to local architectural traditions or climates. Some of his daring buildings have had problems resulting from faulty designs and engineering.

■ Apartments of the DG Bank Berlin, 1995–2001

The DG Bank's headquarters is composed of a commercial area and a residential area. The building's facade is outfitted in pale limestone, matching the nearby Brandenburg Gate. Behind the 39 apartments, the tubular glass ceiling encases a sculptural, metal conference room shell and cafeteria. The facade of the apartment building is relatively tame in comparison with Gehry's work in Bilbao or Seattle because of strict building regulations in Berlin, but still has a curving facade.

■ Experience Music Project, 1999–2000, Seattle

As with many of Gehry's other works, the Experience Music Project in Seattle is clad in metal. The building is composed of separate Blobitectural

Architecture after 1945

multicolored parts modeled with 3-D computer programs. The five colors of the separate areas are meant to evoke different tunes. Some of the areas of the facade are painted—like the blue wing, which was painted with auto body paint—while others achieve different tones and colors by special treatments on their metallic skin. Despite its stark super-modern appearance, the facade recalls the drapery of sculpture from antiquity in its folds and seemingly hanging nature. The building is often associated with Jimi Hendrix's music for its revolutionary, explosive nature, and is an architectural meta-phor for rock and roll.

Frank Gehry

Zaha Hadid

1950, Baghdad

■ Works in diverse mediums including furniture and interiors ■ First female architect to receive the Pritzker Prize ■ Interested in theory, teaching, and practice ■ Associated with the Deconstructivist movement ■ Unconventional and visionary use of shape and form

■ **1950** Born in Baghdad

1972 Moves to London after studying mathematics at the American University in Beirut

1977 Graduates from the Architectural Association in London

1977–87 Collaborates with Rem Koolhaas and Elia Zenghelis at the Office of Metropolitan Architecture in London

1980 Establishes her own firm in London

1988 Participates in Deconstructivist Architecture Exhibition in New York

2004 Awarded the Pritzker Prize

Zaha Hadid was the first female recipient of the Pritzker Prize. She uses strong, arched shapes that appear to stretch the limits of their materials. Hadid's work encompasses all fields of design, ranging from urban planning to products, interiors, and furniture. Her work experiments with new spatial concepts, intensifying existing urban landscapes in the pursuit of a visionary aesthetic. Her buildings' designs make use of multiple perspective points that at times seem confusing, but the overall effect absorbs viewers and the surrounding environment, uniting both through her Modernist designs. Her early work makes use of asymmetrical sharp angles; tiered, flat-planed levels; and seemingly hermetic forms that create new and unexpected spaces and angles. In designing her buildings and plans, Hadid combines preliminary sketches and applies computer design programs to unite glass and metals, ▭

■ **LFone Pavilion**, 1999, Weil-am-Rhein, Germany

A fluid yet geometrical extension of a network of surrounding paths, this cement structure is an amalgamation of organic and inorganic solid planes, blunt edges, and tiered levels.

Vitra Fire Station, 1993, Weil-am-Rhein

One of Hadid's first infrastructural projects, the Vitra Fire Station appears impenetrable from the front, but reveals its interiors from a perpendicular viewpoint. Constructed of exposed, reinforced concrete, it uses sharp edges and layered walls that bend and break in accordance with their structural functions. The building is now used as a showcase for designer chairs.

Phaeno Science Center, interior, 2005, Wolfsburg, Germany

Within the Phaeno Science Center a craterlike interior creates diagonal sectional views to the different levels of the exhibition space, while protruding volumes allow for diverse functions. The structural ground supports also provide space for both cultural functions associated with the science center and commercial functions.

Phaeno Science Center, exterior, 2005, Wolfsburg, Germany

Allowing for maximum transparency and porosity at ground level, the science center appears as a mysterious, strange object. The design generates curiosity and discovery in its visitors. The bulk of the building is elevated on stilts, creating a public space for visitors. As with her other buildings, Hadid constructed an intricate network of pedestrian and vehicular paths throughout the structure.

Zaha Hadid

plastics, and concrete in unconventional ways that push the boundaries of architecture and urban design. Her most recent works and winning designs for future projects involve more organic, less geometric shapes and prove that Modern architecture can accomplish the seemingly impossible. Her central concerns are her simultaneous engagement in practice, teaching and research, and her conceptual plans are widely acclaimed.

■ Furniture Design

Zaha Hadid's furniture designs create new spaces within their architecture. The forms often stand apart from the walls as sculptural pieces. Conventional furniture objects are treated anew, and Hadid endows these works with the same type of multiple-viewpoint, curvaceousness and yet angular aesthetic that many of her buildings have. Through developing both the enclosing space and the furniture inside, Hadid molds entire experiences with her fluid shapes.

■ Museum of Nuragic and Contemporary Art, scheduled completion 2007, design, Cagliari, Italy

The prestigious winning design for the waterfront museum is an interconnected, sinuous shape that provides a multifaceted landmark for Cagliari. The museum's fluid white exterior is pierced by negative space, recesses, and open pedestrian ways, while the interior includes exibition spaces, a library, a congress hall, offices, and a shopping area that are all interconnected by different paths and spaces. Hadid was particularly sensitive to the surrounding environment and designed the museum so that it would geometrically

mirror the seafront. It has axes that both spacially and historically link to the city, while reaching out to existing landmarks in the area. The design's shape is Functionalist in that it allows the building to maximize its use of recyclable energy sources. The rounded rooftop channels rainwater down into reservoirs for use within the building.

Energy for heating and cooling is drawn from solar panels, geothermic pumps, and ground-based cooling and air circulation devices that use the dynamic shape of the building to harness natural energies. The circulation of visitors is also enhanced by the building's shape, creating waterfront promenades and internal paths.

Zaha Hadid

Daniel Libeskind

1946, Lodz

■ Famous Deconstructivist architect ■ Combines memorials with functional museums to enhance the symbolism of his designs ■ His design of the Freedom Tower won the 2003 competition for the reconstruction of the World Trade Center site in New York City

■ **1946** Born in Lodz, Poland

1965 Becomes a US citizen, studies music

1970 Graduates with an architecture degree from Cooper Union in New York

1972 Receives his postgraduate degree in architecture from the University of Essex

1988 Participates in the Deconstructivist Architecture Exhibition, New York

1989 Wins the design competition to build the Jewish Museum in Berlin

2004 Appointed first US Cultural Ambassador for Architecture

■ **Eighteen Turns Serpentine Gallery Café in Hyde Park**, 2002, London

Designed as a temporary, movable structure, this angular and jumbled composition showcases architecture as a sculptural and artistic form. No fully enclosed spaces exist within the bold, flat-planed design. The irregular geometric shapes create a constantly changing and fluid environment.

Architecture after 1945

Libeskind, a Polish-born American Jewish architect, first came to prominence in the late 1980s, when his firm won the competition to build the Jewish Museum in Berlin. Since then his work, often associated with the Deconstructivist movement, has been widely commissioned and highly sought after worldwide. Libeskind is particularly conscious of the social context and purpose of his designs, an approach that often results in a disruption of the buildings' natural perspectives and spaces, and that is able to meld theatrical views with functional spaces. His designs are often characterized by the use of large intersecting beams, planes of solid materials, and fractured glass. He draws inspiration for his structures from the work of Russian Formalists and Cubists rather than Postmodernists. Libeskind has often described architecture as a language that should communicate with both its human and natural environment.

■ Studio Weil, Port d'Andratx, 2003, Majorca, Spain

Libeskind worked with sculptor Barbara Weil to design a studio composed of nonconcentric circles, impenetrable planes, and gigantic lateral sections that distort the perspective of the horizon and create a contrast to the romantic Mediterranean landscape.

■ Jewish Museum, 1998, Berlin, Germany

The imposing zinc-clad facade is comprised of solid planes ntersected by zigzagged windows, which allow a creative use of natural light that also provides historical symbolism. Libeskind uses irregular angles and beam heights to create unpredictable interior spaces, including narrow axes and cavernous voids that aim to evoke a visceral experience.

Other Important Works by Libeskind

Felix Nussbaum Haus, 1998, Osnabrück, Germany

Imperial War Museum North, 2001, Manchester, UK

Danish Jewish Museum, 2003, Copenhagen

London Metropolitan University Graduate Center, 2004, London

The Wohl Center, 2005, Ramat-Gan, Israel

Memoria e Luce, 9/11 Memorial, 2005, Padua

Tangent, 2005, Seoul

Denver Art Museum Residences, 2006, Denver

Extension to the Denver Art Museum, 2006, Denver

Royal Ontario Museum, 2007, Toronto

Glass Courtyard, 2007, Berlin

The Ascent at Roebling's Bridge, 2007, Covington, Kentucky

Contemporary Jewish Museum, projected completion 2008, San Francisco

Daniel Libeskind

Rem Koolhaas

1944, Rotterdam

■ Philosopher, writer, and architect ■ Analytical, intellectual approach to design and urban experience ■ Dramatic, innovative use of trajectory
■ Interested in the link between urbanity and social practice ■ His work gives radical new forms to existing materials

■ **1944** Born in Rotterdam, the Netherlands
1966 Works as a reporter for the *Haagse Post*
1968 Begins studying at Architectural Association School of Architecture in London
1972 Studies at Cornell University in New York
1975 Cofounds the Office for Metropolitan Architecture (OMA) in London
1978 Publishes *Delirious New York*
1995 Publishes *S, M, L, XL* with Bruce Mau
1997 Cofounds architectural think tank AMO
2000 Awarded the Pritzker Prize

■ **Seattle Public Library**, 2004

A structural steel and glass skin unifies eight horizontal platforms that are connected by a series of elevators and escalators. These levels, all of different opacities, densities, sizes, and shapes, allow for versatile uses of space. The sloping glass ceilings and walls create unusual lighting and views of the urban surroundings.

Architecture after 1945

Born in Rotterdam, the Netherlands, Rem Koolhaas spent four years of his youth in Indonesia, where his father served as a cultural director. He first gained international recognition when he published *Delirious New York*, a book on architectural theory. Koolhaas's work searches for a link between technology and humanity. He uses an intelligent, analytic approach, and is renowned for his innovative and radical use of trajectory in his designs. He utilizes materials in a sculptural way, often elongating or flattening shapes and making rigid materials appear malleable. His designs draw from an eclectic mix of sources, including elements of Classicism and Modernism, Formalism and Deconstructivism, and transforms these ideas into inventive and new forms. Today he is one of the world's most sought-after architects, known for both his risk taking and his interest in the social and philosophical elements of the urban experience.

CCTV Headquarters, design, Beijing

A truly three-dimensional experience, the two gigantic towers of Koolhaas's design for the CCTV Headquarters rise from a common platform and join at the top in a cantilevered penthouse. A new icon of the Beijing skyline, the structure is a single interconnected loop, symbolically containing all the departments that make broadcasting possible.

Educatorium, 1997, Utrecht University, the Netherlands

Two dramatic planes fold and interlock to create a single trajectory that makes the concrete curves appear malleable. Sloped ceilings and densely packed I-beams generate a series of smaller spaces within large rooms. Cement and glass walls are used side by side to allow for both privacy and views.

Other Works by Koolhaas	
Netherlands Dance Theater, 1988, The Hague, the Netherlands	Casa da Música, 2001–05, Porto
	Royal Dutch Embassy, 2003, Berlin
Second Stage Theater, 1999, New York	Seoul National University Museum of Art, 2005

Rem Koolhaas

Herzog & de Meuron

1950, Basel

■ Engage in open dialogues and collaborations with contemporary artists ■ Push the boundaries of public expectation ■ Reference art and architectural history ■ Display an innovative use of color and materials ■ Employ original and unique treatment techniques

1950 Jacques Herzog and Pierre de Meuron are born in Basel, Switzerland

1975 They both graduate with a degree in architecture from the Swiss Federal Institute of Technology, Zurich

1978 Open Herzog & de Meuron in Basel

1983 Jacques Herzog teaches at Cornell in Ithaca, New York

1989–98 Both are professors at Harvard in Cambridge, Massachusetts

2000 Inauguration of the Tate Modern gallery in London

2001 Awarded the Pritzker Prize

Other Important Works

Schwitter residential and office building, 1988, Basel

Pilotengasse Residential Complex, 1991, Vienna-Aspern

Goetz Art Gallery, 1992, Munich

Tate Modern, 2000, London

Prada Store (Epicenter), 2003, Tokyo

Beijing National Stadium, projected completion 2008

Herzog & de Meuron is an architectural firm located in Basel, Switzerland. The creators, Jacques Herzog and Pierre de Meuron, are famous for their close collaboration with contemporary artists such as Gerhard Richter and Rémy Zaugg. Both architects share a desire to engage in dialogues that nurture, develop, and further artistic ideas. Perhaps best known for their transformation of a disused power station into the Tate Modern, Herzog & de Meuron are particularly innovative in their use of exterior materials, their practice of implementing new and innovative treatments on traditional materials, and the addition of pictorial or allegorical elements in their pursuit of new styles.

■ **Allianz Arena**, 2005, Munich

A colossal lozenge-shaped structure, the Allianz Arena is a spectacle of color and form. The white exterior hides the colorful and dramatic atmosphere of the interior. Its exterior is composed of inflatable ETFE (ethylene tetrafluoroethylene)-foil air panels that can be lit different colors.

■ **Forum Building**, 2004, Barcelona

An eccentric and perplexing structure, the Forum Building accentuates its mass through the use of bulging forms and cantilevered corners. Special attention is paid to the soffit, or underside, which is clad with stippled and smooth plates of stainless steel that refract light and give the building texture. These, used alongside mirrors, and an overall iconic ink-blue facade create a powerful and unique effect.

■ **Cottbus Technical University Library**, 2004, Germany

A sculptural, round, curtainlike facade encloses the library and cylindrical corner towers, and an impressive scale create a castlelike structure that contrasts with its largely industrial surroundings.

■ **Walker Art Center Expansion**, 2005, Minneapolis

Aimed at attracting audiences from the highway, the museum features broad, obliquely cut entrances and a creative use of brickwork that references Edward L. Barnes's neighboring design.

Herzog & de Meuron

Blobs

1992–Present

■ Digital modeling software creates infinite design possibilities ■ Architects are able to fast-track the design process ■ Designs respond with greater sensitivity to organic shapes in nature ■ A new expressive language for movement and motion that responds to human interaction and scale

■ **1992** Zappi research project pioneers glass as a structural element

1995 First use of the term *Blobitecture* by architect Greg Lynn

1997 Construction of Gehry's Guggenheim Museum Bilbao and the rise of sculptural architecture

2001 Karel Vollers publishes *Twist & Build*

2002 Development of Liquid Designed Buildings and complex 3-D design programs

First coined in 1995, the term *Blobs*, or *Blobitecture*, is used to refer to amoeboid, fluid designs that are created using digital modeling software. By manipulating the algorithms of the modeling program, architects are able to create new, previously unthinkable shapes and forms and streamline the design-to-production process. The innovations in technology such as computer programs, industrial adhesives, and connectors can produce infinite free-form and sculptural designs that can be made by spraying mortar over malleable reinforcing mesh. Corners and angular beams give way to curvaceous shapes that draw their inspiration from nature. Blobs are sculptural, protoplasmic structures that completely redefine the language and possibilities of architectural design.

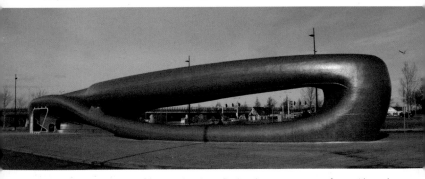

■ **NIO Architecten: Bus Station at Spaarne Hospital**, 2003, Hoofddorp, the Netherlands

The bus station at Spaarne Hospital is a long, fluid, and graceful design that makes innovative use of negative space. Composed of factory-cut polystyrene foam with a polyester skin, the design forms a sculptural roundabout that allows a free flow of activity.

■ Lars Spuybroek: Fresh H2O Expo Water Pavilion, 1997, Neeltje Jans, the Netherlands

A sensual and interactive structure, the Fresh H2O Expo Water Pavilion is regarded as the first "full" Blob building. No horizontals or verticals exist within the fluid, curvaceous form, and the sculptural geometry is in constant variation and flux. The interior is equipped with multiple motion sensors that detect visitor movement and respond with light, sound, and visual projections that ripple throughout the building. This creates a truly interactive environment that encourages the audience to realize their scale and relationship to the design.

Other Works

Experience Music Project, by Frank Gehry, 2000, Seattle

The Sage Gateshead, 2004, by Foster + Partners, Gateshead

Philological Library, Free University, by Foster + Partners, 2005, Berlin

Złote Tarasy, by Jerde Partnership, 2007, Warsaw

■ Foreign Office Architects Ltd.: Yokohama Port Terminal, 2002, Yokohama

A dynamic wavelike structure, the Yokohama Port Terminal creates a branch between urban and aquatic space. The design challenges previous linear structures by using looped and continuous throughways, sculptural forms, and a reduced color palate that encourages fluidity and movement while maintaining multifunctional and differentiated spaces.

Blobs

Index

Bold-faced page numbers indicate the main pages of the entry. *Italicized* entries indicate where the definitions for key terms are located.

503

Staff at Peter Delius Verlag

Authors: Daniel Borden (pp. 10–75), Jerzy Elżanowski (pp. 76–157, 368–387, 390–423, 434–437), Cornelia Lawrenz (pp. 158–217), Daniel Miller (pp. 438–441, 444–447, 450–459, 470–481), Adele Smith (pp. 424–433, 442–443, 482–485, 490–501), and Joni Taylor (pp. 218–367)
Contributing Authors: Stephanie Tuerk (pp. 448–449, 464–469, 486–488), Elizabeth Corso (pp. 388–389, 460–463)
Editors: Elizabeth Corso (Editor in Chief) and Gigi Adair
Translators: Charles Booth and Shannon Williams
Design: Burga Fillery
Layout Assistant: Angela Aumann

The publishers would like to express their gratitude to Agostino64, AJP79, akg-images Berlin/Paris/London, Alamy, Arcaid, Jamie Barras, Guus Basman, Jean-Christophe Benoist, Benutzer:Jcr, Thierry Bézecourt, Bibliothea Hertziana Fotothek, Bildarchiv Foto Marburg, Marco Bonavoglia, Justin Clements, Daderot, d_dodero, Eisenman Architects, Eusebius, FG + SG Fotografia de Arquitectura, Getty Images, Michael Graves & Associates, Greg Fairbrother, firzgene, Foreign Office Architects, Morie, Fernando González del Cueto, Zaha Hadid Architects, Hardnfast, Jim Harper, Paul Keleher, Nathan Kendall, Kries, Les Sulgrove, Studio Daniel Libeskind, Marcok, Muad'dib, NIO architecten, nivandrade2006, NOX/Lars Spuybroek, The Office for Metropolitan Architecture, Ishmael Orendain, Oscar, Janine Pohl, Jacopo Prisco, Karl Ernst Roehl, Matthias Rosenkranz, Sailko, Sbratte, Simon Fieldhouse, Georg Slickers, Christian Spanring, Structurae Image Licensing, Yosemite, Liao Yusheng, Venturi, Scott-Brown and Associates for the permission of image reproductions in this book. For detailed picture and credit information, please visit our Web site www.TheKnowledgePage.com

Cataloging-in-Publication Data has been applied for and may be obtained from the Library of Congress.

ISBN: 978-0-8109-9512-3

Printed and bound in China
10 9 8 7 6 5 4 3 2 1

HNA

harry n. abrams, inc.
a subsidiary of La Martinière Groupe
115 West 18th Street
New York, NY 10011
www.hnabooks.com

512